South-East Asian Social Science Monographs

The Bajau Laut

The Bajau Laut

Adaptation, History, and Fate in a Maritime Fishing Society of South-eastern Sabah

Clifford Sather

KUALA LUMPUR
OXFORD UNIVERSITY PRESS
OXFORD SINGAPORE NEW YORK
1997

Oxford University Press
Oxford New York
Athens Auckland Bangkok Bombay
Calcutta Cape Town Dar es Salaam Delhi
Florence Hong Kong Istanbul Karachi
Madras Madrid Melbourne Mexico City
Nairobi Paris Shah Alam Singapore
Taipei Tokyo Toronto
and associated companies in
Berlin Ibadan

Oxford is a trade mark of Oxford University Press

Published in the United States
by Oxford University Press, New York

British Library Cataloguing in Publication Data
Data available

Library of Congress Cataloging-in-Publication Data
Sather, Clifford.
The Bajau Laut: adaptation, history, and fate in a maritime
fishing society of south-eastern Sabah/Clifford Sather.
p. cm.—(South-East Asian social science monographs)
Includes bibliographical references and index.
ISBN 983 56 0015 5
1. Bajau (Southeast Asian people)—Malaysia—Sabah.
2. Sabah—Social life and customs.
I. Title. II. Series.
DS597.335.B35S27 1997
959.5'300495—dc20
96–25624
CIP

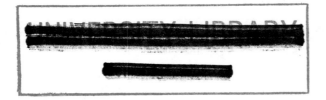

Typeset by Indah Photosetting Centre Sdn. Bhd., Malaysia
Printed by KHL Printing Co. (S) Pte. Ltd., Singapore
Published by Penerbit Fajar Bakti Sdn. Bhd. (008974-T),
under licence from Oxford University Press,
4 Jalan U1/15, Seksyen U1, 40000 Shah Alam,
Selangor Darul Ehsan, Malaysia

Preface

MUCH of the way of life described in this book has disappeared or been radically altered. The village in which it is set is today a semi-urban community, its former boundaries very largely effaced and its population increasingly merged and all but indistinguishable from that of the larger port town of Semporna which now almost wholly envelops it.

The research on which this book is based began just over thirty years ago. I first arrived in Semporna at the beginning of October 1964 as a young graduate student in social anthropology. My original plan had been to study the social organization of a sea-nomadic community. However, by the time I arrived in Semporna, the once nomadic Bajau Laut had settled in two permanent pile-house villages located at opposite sides of the narrow straits that separate the Semporna Peninsula from Bumbum Island. The larger of these two villages was Bangau-Bangau and here I began my research.

In 1964, Bangau-Bangau was still a newly founded village. The first houses had been built only nine years earlier, and although the intervening years had been a time of rapid transformation, many elements of the community's sea-nomadic past were still evident. A small section of the village population, somewhat less than one-fifth, remained boat-living; fishing was still the economic mainstay of the community, and most house-living families continued to return to their boats for extended intervals of sea fishing. The result was a pattern of social disjunction in which families moved between aggregation in a settled village community and dispersal at sea in ephemeral, variously organized fishing fleets. Both at sea and in the village, corporate groups were absent. Individuals largely organized their social relationships around collective activities rather than in terms of enduring groups with membership salient across all social and economic contexts. These distinctive features of Bajau Laut social relationships are examined at length in Chapters 5 and 6.

In the 1960s, when I began my research, conventional anthropological models of society were still poorly equipped to deal with communities in rapid transformation (Cohn, 1981). In my original dissertation (Sather, 1971b), I focused chiefly on the internal constitution of the Semporna community as it was at the time of my initial fieldwork, particularly on domestic relations, kinship, and leadership (see also Sather, 1976, 1978). From the outset, however, it was clear that Bajau Laut society also needed

to be understood contextually, as the product of a long-continuing interaction of sea and shore people, and historically, as shaped by events over
a longer time period than that encompassed by a single field study. In
the Semporna district, the Bajau Laut had been part of a traditional
maritime state in the past, the Sulu Sultanate, and the nature of their
identity as a community presupposed an encompassing structure of ethnic
stratification, trade, and patronage. In writing this book, one of my chief
purposes has been to locate this account within such a perspective so as
to allow Bajau Laut society to be seen, not only in its own terms, but
also both regionally and historically over time and against a changing
background of shore and sea relations.

From the beginning, the village of Bangau-Bangau formed the principal site of my fieldwork. For eleven months (October 1964 to mid-
September 1965) I lived in the house of the village headman, Panglima
Tiring bin Hawani, sharing meals and contributing to the household
budget as a member of the headman's large and active house group. I
also accompanied the headman, his wife Amjatul, and their younger
children on frequent fishing voyages. This arrangement proved to be an
especially happy one, both personally, owing to the kindness and con-
viviality of my hosts, and also in terms of my research. Panglima
Tiring's house group occupied the social and physical centre of the
Bangau-Bangau community and all matters of general concern were
brought, or eventually found their way, to the headman's house for discussion, debate, and, occasionally, for litigation, so that, from this well-
favoured vantage point, few occurrences in the village went unnoticed.
In August 1965, I paid a series of brief visits to additional sea-nomadic
and formerly nomadic communities in Sulu province of the Philippines,
spending two weeks in Sitangkai and visiting more briefly Sama Dilaut
communities in the Siasi and Tawitawi island groups, travelling also to
Jolo and Zamboanga. Some of this travel was done in the company of
Bajau Laut families; at other times, I made use of the small inter-island
passenger vessels that then plied the Sulu region. Returning by way of
Sitangkai, I left Semporna in mid-September 1965.

While a faculty member at the Universiti Sains Malaysia, Penang, I
had the good fortune to be able to return to Semporna for three weeks
in May 1974 and for a further two months (July and August) in 1979
for additional fieldwork. On the latter occasion, I was accompanied by
my wife and children, for whom this visit was their first introduction to
the Bajau Laut. My son, then nine years old, spent his days in the company of village boys of the same age, and proved himself, like the friends
he made, a remarkably adept fisherman and sailor, a natural-born *a'a
dilaut*. Altogether, the present book is based on fourteen months of fieldwork. The ethnographic present, except where otherwise indicated,
refers chiefly to the fifteen-year interval over which this fieldwork was
spread, from October 1964 to August 1979. In July 1994, I paid a further brief visit to Bangau-Bangau.

On a number of occasions in the chapters that follow, I make extended
use of individual case histories or record personal commentaries. In

doing so, I have generally used pseudonyms in place of personal names to protect the anonymity of those referred to. Otherwise places and events are, or were, as they appear.

Kuching   CLIFFORD SATHER
October 1995

Acknowledgements

MANY people and institutions assisted in making this study possible. I am
indebted in particular to Professor Douglas Oliver, who supervised my
graduate studies at Harvard University and provided guidance and practical advice during my initial fieldwork. My interest in maritime boat
people was given practical shape by Dr Ivan Polunin, formerly of the
School of Social Medicine, the National University of Singapore. It was
Dr Polunin who first suggested research among the Semporna Bajau
Laut, people with whom he had gained an acquaintance through earlier
epidemiological research. Dr George Appell read through the materials
presented here in various stages of completion, beginning with early drafts
of my original doctoral dissertation; the present study has benefited substantially from his many comments, suggestions, and continuing encouragement. The late Stephen Morris and Professor James J. Fox also read
through earlier drafts of this study. Professor Fox was, in addition, a
member of my original dissertation committee and his comments and
insights have been a continuing source of stimulation, without which this
book might never have been completed.

Over the years I have also profited greatly from correspondence
with a number of Sulu and Sama scholars; here I would like to acknowledge especially H. Arlo Nimmo, Eric Casiño, Thomas Kiefer, William
Geoghegan, Harald Beyer Broch, Inger Wulff, Bruno Bottignolo, and
Carol and James Warren. Professors James Collins and Sander Adelaar
provided helpful advice regarding the spelling of Sama terms and I have
also benefited greatly from the comments of Mohamad Said Hinayat,
Secretary, Persatuan Seni Budaya Bajau Sabah (PSBB), on questions of
Sama spelling and usage.

The initial fieldwork on which this book is based was made possible by
a pre-doctoral fellowship and grant (MH-10159-01) from the (US)
National Institute of Mental Health. Subsequent fieldwork in 1974 and
1979 was made possible through the sponsorship of Universiti Sains
Malaysia and the Sabah Museum, and in this connection I wish to
acknowledge the assistance of the former Museum Curator, the late
David McCredie and his staff, particularly Anthea Phillipps of the museum's botanical section. The preparation of this study for publication
was aided by a grant from the (US) National Science Foundation,
administered through the University of Oregon. Here I wish to thank my

colleagues Professors Vernon Dorjahn and Melvin Aikens of the University of Oregon for their support. The final completion of this manuscript was made possible by a senior research fellowship, awarded through the Comparative Austronesian Project in the Department of Anthropology, Research School of Pacific and Asian Studies, The Australian National University. It is impossible to conceive of a more congenial and intellectually engaging setting in which to write than that provided by the Research School and its staff. Finally, I wish to thank the government of Malaysia and the state government of Sabah for enabling me to pursue my research.

In Semporna I am especially grateful to Adilun Samaluddin of Kampung Rancangan Baru for his help in gathering materials relating to the history of the Semporna district; to the former Pegawai Daerah, Sadi Haji Hashah; and to the Penghulung Pegawai Daerah, and a valued acquaintance of long-standing, Ispal Haji Adok.

My greatest debt is due, of course, to the people of Bangau-Bangau. It is, perhaps, unjust to single out individuals as so many gave of their time and knowledge to help me gain some understanding of their way of life, yet I wish to thank in particular Laiti bin Dessal, who became, in Semporna and over the years between visits, a close personal friend. Both Laiti and his cousin, Koltis bin Salbangan, assisted me in gathering the numerical data presented in Chapters 5, 6, and 7. Panglima Haji Tiring bin Hawani, until his recent retirement the headman of Kampung Bangau-Bangau, and his wife Amjatul welcomed me into their household, which became my village home throughout my stay in Semporna. Without the generosity of Panglima Tiring's family and his own good-humour and patient instruction, the chapters that follow could never have been written. I only hope that this book, in some small way, repays his efforts.

Finally, I would like to acknowledge *Contributions to Southeast Asian Ethnography*, in which small sections of Chapters 2, 3, and 4, previously appeared (No. 4 (1984) and 5 (1985)), together with a number of photographs which are republished here with the editor's permission. Lastly, I owe an inestimable debt to my wife Georgeann for her forbearance throughout the writing of this book. A graphic designer, she also prepared the line-drawings and all but one of the maps that appear here. To all, *magsukul to'ongan*.

Contents

Tables

Figures

Maps

Plates

Note on Orthography

THE Bajau Laut of Semporna describe their speech as a variety of *ling Sama*, literally Sama speech. More specifically, they refer to themselves and to the particular dialect of Sama they speak as Sama Dilaut (or Sama Mandelaut). Throughout this book, I present this speech in italic.

In representing Sama Dilaut, I use the following orthography, adopted with minor modification from Allison (1979) and Pallesen and Pallesen (1965).

Vowels		International Phonetic Alphabet (IPA)
i	high, front, unrounded	i
u	high, back, rounded	u
é	mid, front, unrounded	e
o	mid, back, rounded	o
a	low, central, unrounded	a
e	mid, central, unrounded	ə

Consonants		
p	voiceless bilabial stop	p
t	voiceless alveolar stop	t
k	voiceless velar stop	k
b	voiced bilabial stop	b
d , -r-	voiced alveolar stop; intervocalically often rendered as a voiced flap	d/r
g	voiced velar stop	g
'	glottal stop	ʔ
j	voiced alveopalatal grooved affricate	j
h	voiceless glottal spirant	h
s	voiceless grooved alveolar fricative	s
l	alveolar lateral	l
m	bilabial nasal	m
n	alveolar nasal	n

ny	alveopalatal nasal	ɲ
ng	velar nasal	ŋ
w	bilabial semivowel	w
y	alveopalatal semivowel	y

I represent the glottal stop, here spelled ', only when it occurs in word medial or final positions. It should be noted that it also regularly occurs in initial position, preceding a vowel. Here, however, it is not phonemic. The phoneme /d/ is an alveolar stop with a voiced flap [r] allophone.

Allison (1979: 79) argues that, unlike most other Sama dialects, Sibutu Sama, which is phonologically similar to Semporna Sama Dilaut, lacks a schwa phoneme. In contrast, Pallesen (1979: 130) maintains that all dialects of Southern and Central Sama possess a phonemic schwa or pepet. With regard to Sama Dilaut, I leave it to linguists, who are better qualified than I, to resolve this question. Here, however, I follow Pallesen and Pallesen (1965) and represent Semporna Sama Dilaut with a six-vowel system, including the schwa /ə/, here spelled as e.

Exceptions to this orthography have been made in the case of geographical and personal names where accepted spellings are established (for example, Lahad Datu). Words in Malay (Bahasa Malaysia) are represented in italics within single quotes to distinguish them from Sama Dilaut, except for those that have been borrowed and are now fully assimilated in local Sama Dilaut (like *balanja'*).

In terms of pronunciation, stress, as a general feature of Sama languages, does not appear to be phonemic. Primary stress falls normally on the penultimate syllable of a word, often with lengthening of the stressed vowel, unless the word is monosyllabic, in which case, except for particles, it falls on the only syllable. Particles have zero stress. Words of four or more syllables generally carry a secondary stress on the first syllable. Long or geminate consonants may recur in initial or medial position, for example, *mma* 'father' and *matto'a* 'elder'. These geminate consonants are phonemic and, as noted by Pallesen (1985), contrast with short consonants. Hence, for example, *mato'a* 'parent-in-law'; *matto'a* 'elder'; *haka* 'news'; *hakka* a measure of length.

It needs, finally, to be noted that south-eastern Sabah is a region of extreme dialectical complexity. Thus, the dialect of Sama Dilaut spoken in Semporna district differs in notable ways from neighbouring Sama dialects and from other varieties of Sama Dilaut spoken elsewhere in the Sulu Archipelago of the Philippines (see Chapter 1). At present, further research is needed before the extent of these differences can be described with any certainty.

1
Introduction

They are of this nature, that they know no other home than their boats . . .
[and] are such enemies of the land, that it does not get from them the
slightest labor or industry, nor the profit of any fruit. All their work is in
fishing and by this they barter for what they need. (Francisco Combés,
1904.)

UNTIL the middle of the present century, the people described in this
book lived entirely afloat, as a boat-dwelling fishing and foraging
community. In 1955, a small number of families erected the first pile-
houses over a shallow bay which had previously served them as a
permanent boat anchorage. By 1964 this community had grown into a
burgeoning village of 510 people, 440 of whom lived in what was by
then a densely aggregated settlement of thirty-six pile-houses. The
remainder continued to live in boats.

This book describes the social organization and cultural premises that
structured daily life in this community, primarily over the fifteen-year
period from 1964 to 1979. During this time, the villagers abandoned
boat nomadism for a sedentary way of life, altering in the process their
identity as a group and their relationships with others in the larger, polyethnic society that historically enmeshed them.

A central theme of this book is the historical interpenetration of sea
and shore people in a south-eastern coastal district of Sabah. Although
forming only a small part of the population, maritime nomads have long
been a feature of local society and Chapter 1 examines the ties between
them and their principal shore- and land-dwelling neighbours. Chapter 2
describes the status of the sea nomads in the Sulu Sultanate, which was
the dominant polity of the region until the end of the nineteenth century.
It also traces the subsequent history of the community through the colonial
period to the present, focusing in particular on the factors that contributed to an abandonment of boat nomadism and on the social and
political consequences that have followed from the process of settling
down.

Chapter 3 explores the community's adaptation to the sea. Traditionally, the Bajau Laut lived poised between the shoreline and the open
sea, in a world of islands and inshore waters and the chapter considers
the ways in which this world was historically represented and utilized,
and how its nature has tended to shape interpersonal relations within the

Bajau Laut community itself. Chapter 4 describes the community's changing fishing economy, market trade, and intra-village sharing and exchange. Chapters 5 and 6 examine the basic units of village society, notably house groups and neighbourhood clusters, while Chapters 7 and 8 look at kinship and marriage as these define interpersonal relations both within and across these units. Chapter 7 also explores cultural notions relating to kinship and marriage, most notably those of debt, vow-taking, and the authenticity of personal feelings. Chapters 9 and 10 pursue ritual expressions of these notions relating in particular to God and the ancestors. Chapter 9 concerns prayer, rites of transformation, and the individual life cycle, while Chapter 10 covers village ritual specialists, curing, and concepts of the soul, and ends by examining underlying notions of fate, luck, and the ancestors. The concluding chapter looks at the Bajau Laut more generally in relation to other South-East Asian sea nomads, returning to the opening theme of adaptation and history in the ongoing interaction of sea and shore people.

The Sama

Both culturally and linguistically, the Bajau Laut belong to a much larger ambit of Sama–Bajau-speaking peoples. Included within this ambit are not only sea-nomadic and formerly nomadic communities, such as the one described here, but also shore- and even land-based peoples. Taken together, Sama–Bajau speakers comprise what is arguably the most widely dispersed ethnolinguistic group indigenous to insular South-East Asia (Geoghegan, 1984: 654; Sather, 1985: 166–7, 1993a: 30) (Map 1.1). Sea-nomadic and much more numerous strand and settled Sama speakers live scattered, and in most areas interspersed with one another, over a vast maritime zone 3.25 million square kilometres in extent, stretching from eastern Palawan, Samar, and coastal Mindanao in the north, through the Sulu Archipelago of the Philippines, to the northern and eastern coasts of Borneo, southward through the Straits of Makassar to Sulawesi, and from there over widely dispersed areas of eastern Indonesia, south and eastward to Flores, Roti, Timor, and the southern Moluccas (Sopher, 1965; Pelras, 1972; Sather, 1975a, 1993a, 1993b; Fox, 1977, 1984; Geoghegan, 1984).

Pallesen (1985) has proposed the general term 'Sama–Bajau' to cover the various dialects and languages spoken by members of this widely scattered population. In the whole of South-East Asia, Sama–Bajau speakers probably number 750,000 to 900,000.[1] Those referred to in the southern Philippines as 'Samal' form the largest single group, estimated at 243,000 in 1975 (Sather, 1993b: 218). A second Sama–Bajau group, the Yakan, number over 115,000, also in the southern Philippines, and a third, the Jama Mapun, about 25,000, including an estimated 5,000 in Sabah. A fourth group, the Abaknun of Capul Island, Samar, number 10,000 (Barbosa, 1995: 3). The total Sama–Bajau-speaking population of Sabah was over 72,000 in 1970, exclusive of recent Philippine immigrants, conservatively estimated at 30,000 to 40,000. In 1991, Sama–

MAP 1.1
Location of Sama–Bajau-speaking Peoples (as reported between
1830 and the present)

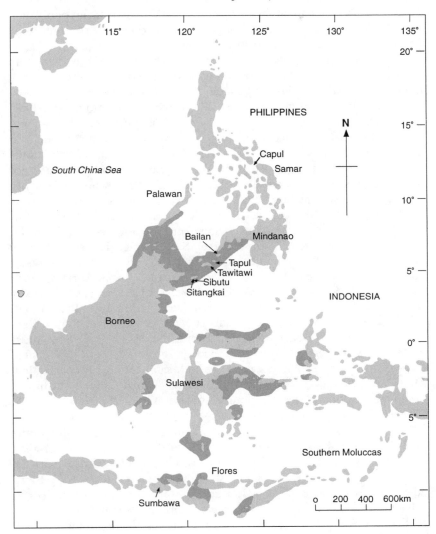

Bajau speakers numbered 212,000 in Sabah, excluding non-citizens. No
reliable population figures exist for eastern Indonesia, but recent
estimates place their numbers at between 150,000 and 230,000.

Boat-nomadic and formerly nomadic communities form only a tiny
minority of the total Sama–Bajau-speaking population. The number of
those who remain permanently boat-dwelling is rapidly declining and is
probably fewer than 5,000 in Malaysia, the Philippines, and Indonesia.
Settled groups of former nomads are much more numerous. In the
Semporna district, fewer than 200 Bajau Laut continue to live in boats,

most of them newcomers from the Tawitawi island group of southern Sulu, while the population of settled Bajau Laut now exceeds 3,500. The Bajau Laut population in Semporna increased from 660 in 1965 to over 2,100 in 1979, growing at the same rate as the Sama-speaking population as a whole, and represented, throughout this period, 4–5 per cent of all Sama–Bajau speakers in the district.

In Sabah, Sama speakers are generally known as 'Bajau' and are present along both the east and west coasts and in the foothills bordering the western coastal plains. In general, the west coast Bajau are less sea-oriented than those of the east coast. Many live inland from the coastline, traditionally practising, particularly in the heavily populated Tuaran and Kota Belud districts, mixed farming based on wet-rice cultivation and cattle-rearing. Those in the Kota Belud district are also well-known horsemen. On both coasts, large numbers are being drawn to the major urban centres of the state—Kota Kinabalu, Sandakan, and Tawau. In eastern Indonesia, the largest numbers of Sama–Bajau are found in the smaller islands and coastal districts of Sulawesi. Widely scattered communities, most of them pile-house settlements, are reported near Menado, Ambogaya, and Kendari; in the Banggai, Sula, and Togian island groups; along the Straits of Tioro; in the Gulf of Bone; and along the Makassar coast (Vosmaer, 1839; Matthes, 1872; Verschuer, 1883; Adriani, 1900; Kennedy, 1953; Zacot, 1978). Elsewhere, settlements are reportedly present near Balikpapan in East Kalimantan, on Maratua, Pulau Laut, and Kakaban, and in the Balabalangan islands off the eastern Kalimantan coast (Darmansjah and Basran Noor, 1979: 7–10; Sather, 1993a: 30). Others are reported widely dispersed from Halmahera through the southern Moluccas, along both sides of Sape Strait dividing Flores and Sumbawa; on Lombok, Lembata, Pantar, Adonara, Sumba, Ndao, and Roti; and near Sulamu in western Timor (Barnes, 1974: 19; Fox, 1977: 459; Verheijen, 1986: 24–6, v; Sather, 1993a: 30). Collins (1995: 1–2) reports two villages, with a total population of 2,000, in the Obi Straits off the island of Bacan, two further villages in the Kayoa islands north of Bacan, and two others in the Gane district, near the south-eastern tip of Halmahera. All these areas, together with Bajau communities in the Banggai island group, were once part of the Bacan sultanate. They were also, as was Bacan itself, in the sphere of influence of Ternate (Andaya, 1993). This latter sphere also included the southern coast of Gorontalo, the bays of Tomori and Kendari, and the islands of Butung and Muna, all areas frequented by small Sama–Bajau-speaking populations. In the Philippines, Sama–Bajau speakers are concentrated primarily in the islands of the Sulu Archipelago, particularly in the smaller coralline groups in the northern, southern, and western portions of the island chain where they generally predominate (Sather, 1993b: 218). There are also small enclaves in Zambales and northern Mindanao, and more numerous settlements in eastern Palawan, Balabac, and along the south-western coast of Mindanao.

In Sabah, boat nomads and former nomads are present in the Semporna district, at the extreme south-eastern corner of the state. In the

Philippines, they are found in small numbers from Zamboanga through the Tapul, western Tawitawi, and Sibutu island groups, with principal concentrations in the Bilatan islands, near Bongao, at Sanga-Sanga, and Sitangkai (Nimmo, 1972: 12–13; Sather, 1993a: 30).

Ethnic Labels: Sama and Sama Dilaut

In Malaysia and Indonesia, variants of the terms 'Bajau' and 'Bajo' (for example Badjaw, Badjao, Bajao, Bajo) are applied by outsiders to both nomadic and sedentary Sama speakers, including land-based agricultural communities, some of them, such as those of western Sabah, without an apparent history of past seafaring (Sather, 1993a: 30). In the southern Philippines, the term 'Bajau' (and its variants) is reserved exclusively for boat-nomadic and formerly nomadic groups, while more sedentary Sama speakers, particularly those living in the Sulu Archipelago, are generally known to outsiders as 'Samal', an ethnonym applied to them by the neighbouring Tausug, but also used widely by Christian Filipinos and others (Kiefer, 1972b: 22; Sather, 1993b: 217). In eastern Indonesia, Sama-speakers are called 'Bajo' by the Bugis, a term also widely used by others, and both 'Bayo' and 'Turije'ne' ('people of the water') by the Makassarese (Matthes, 1872: 17; Pelras, pers. comm.). In Borneo, they are termed 'Bajau' by the Brunei Malays and by other coastal Malay-speaking groups (Evans, 1952: 48). At present, the name Bajau has gained wide currency among all groups in Sabah including Sama speakers themselves.

Most Sama–Bajau speakers, with the principal exception of the Yakan and Jama Mapun, refer to themselves as 'Sama' or, particularly in central Sulu, as 'Sinama'. The term 'Sama' (or *a'a Sama*, 'Sama people') appears to be the most widely used autonym, employed in self-reference through-out the entire area of Sama–Bajau distribution. According to Pallesen (1985: 134), the term is also reconstructable as the proto-form of the autonym by which Sama–Bajau speakers have referred to themselves since early in the present millennium.

When used as an ethnic label, in self-reference, the term 'Sama' is normally coupled with a toponymic modifier, generally referring to a particular island, island cluster, or stretch of coastline. Use of these modifiers indicates the speaker's geographical and/or dialect affiliation (Sather, 1993b: 217). For example, 'Sama Sibaut' refers to the settled Sama speakers who inhabit or trace their origin to Sibaut Island, near Siasi, in the Tapul island group of Sulu. Toponymic names may also be used by themselves, with the term *a'a*, meaning 'people'. Hence, an individual may also identify himself, or the local group to which he belongs as, for example, the *a'a Sibaut*, 'the Sibaut people', particularly if he is addressing other Sama speakers. Toponymic referents generally signify a group's presumed homeland, its place of origin, or principal area of settlement. The Sama are a highly fragmented people, without overall political integration. Primary social identities tend to be strongly focused locally within these named and regionally recognized subgroups.

In Sabah and southern Sulu, boat-dwelling groups and those with a recent history of boat-nomadism commonly identify themselves as 'Sama Dilaut' or 'Sama Mandelaut', names that mean literally, the 'sea' (*laut*) or 'maritime Bajau', or as the *Sama to'ongan*, the 'real' or 'true Bajau' (Sather, 1971b: 16, 1984: 12–13, 1993a: 30; Frake, 1980: 324). They also call themselves *a'a dilaut*, 'sea people', in contrast to *a'a déa*, 'land people', by which they refer to all shore- and land-dwelling groups living around them. In Sulu and eastern Sabah, sea-nomadic and formerly nomadic groups are generally known to other Sama speakers as *Sama pala'au* (or *pala'u*) or *luwa'an*, and to the neighbouring Tausug as *Samal luwa'an* (Kiefer, 1972b: 22). Both names have pejorative connotations, reflecting the pariah status generally ascribed to the Bajau Laut by those living ashore.

Origin of the Term 'Bajau'

The cognate terms 'Bajau' and 'Bajo', with variations in spelling—Bajou, Badjo, Badjaw, Bajao, and others—appear with regularity, in both the English and the Dutch ethnographic literature, from the early eighteenth century onward (Sopher, 1965: 158–62). Fox (1977: 459–61), for example, cites use of the terms in Dutch historical sources of the 1720s. Other early Western references include the reports of Montanus and Padbrugge, written in the 1670s and 1680s, describing 'Bajo' settlements in north Sulawesi (Spreevwenberg, 1846: 35–41; Sopher, 1965: 300–2). According to Christian Pelras (pers. comm.), the earliest use of the term Bajau in a Western source is found in *The Suma Oriental of Tomé Pires; An Account of the East, from the Red Sea to Japan, written in Malacca and India in 1512–1515* (Pires, 1944). In the original Portuguese text, Pires writes the name, in the plural form, as 'Bajuus'. Until now, this reference has remained largely unnoticed because in the English translation, the translator, Armando Cortesão, replaced 'Bajuus' with 'Bugis' (Pires, 1944: Vol. 1, 147n), a confusion probably linked to the fact that Pires himself, in writing about native navigation in Sulawesi, had difficulty distinguishing between these two groups of people, very likely due to their frequent intermingling, down through the early twentieth century, in common fishing and *tripang*-collecting ventures (Pelras, 1972).

The name 'Bajau' is not, however, a Sama autonym. The term in the form of 'Bajau' is probably of Malay or Brunei Malay origin (Evans, 1952: 48; Pallesen, 1985: 134), while the cognate form, 'Bajo', is associated with Bugis and other maritime peoples of eastern Indonesia. In Borneo, early use of 'Bajau' appears in English in the writing of Captain Thomas Forrest, who, in 1774, sailed along the eastern Borneo coast, from Balambangan at the northern tip of present-day Sabah, to the islands east of Sulawesi. At points along the east coast of Borneo, Forrest met with groups of maritime nomads whom he called 'Badjoo' and described as 'a kind of itinerant fishermen' who 'live chiefly in small covered boats' (Forrest, 1780: 372). Later, he encountered additional 'Badjoo' in Sulawesi, and again in Sulu on a subsequent voyage from

New Guinea to Mindanao. He rightly noted the far-flung distribution of Sama–Bajau speakers. He also observed that many of these people were 'fixt and stationary', including the majority of those who lived along the west coast of what is now Sabah, 'where they not only fish, but make salt, and trade in small boats along the coast' (Forrest, 1779: 373). Forrest thus established for Borneo and eastern Indonesia a usage later followed by most subsequent English-language observers.

The earliest recorded use of the term 'Bajau' in an indigenous text from Borneo is probably that in a Brunei Malay royal genealogy published by Sweeney (1968: 54) from an original text attributed to Dato Imam Ya'akup, believed to have been written in 1735. This text is said to have been compiled from information provided by Sultans Muihidden and Kamaluddin, and by others (Sweeney, 1968: 2). The genealogy records what is purportedly a sixteenth-century marriage between Sultan Abdul Kahar, the father of Bendahara Seri Maharaja Sakam, and a 'Bajau Princess', through whom Bendahara Sakam is said to have inherited territorial possessions in what the text describes as 'Bajau lands' ('*tanah Bajau*'), extending from northern Borneo to Luzon. This inheritance was of special importance for it served to legitimize Brunei's political claims over the Sama-speaking peoples then inhabiting what is now Sabah and the southern Philippines. According to Spanish and Portuguese sources of the time, the sultanate effectively exercised these claims from the late sixteenth through the seventeenth centuries, after which time much of this region passed to the control of the Sulu Sultanate and Brunei's suzerainty over the Bajau came to be restricted to small populations living along the west coast districts of Sabah adjacent to its modern political frontier with Brunei. An almost identical reference can be found in Low (1880: 25). The genealogy recorded by Low identifies Bendahara Sakam as one of two brothers of Sultan Saif-ul-Rejal, who succeeded to the Brunei throne in 1578. Although other references to the Bajau occur in the Brunei royal genealogies, contrary to Harrisson and Harrisson (1971: 208), all early connections between Brunei and the Bajau mentioned in these sources relate to this same marriage.[2]

In Sulawesi, the earliest use of the term 'Bajo' occurs in Bugis narrative literature of the *La Galigo* cycle of which the earliest extant manuscripts date to the seventeenth century (Kern, 1939; Pelras, forthcoming). These manuscripts, however, appear to be based on earlier palm-leaf documents. According to Pelras, this monumental work was probably put into definite form between the fourteenth and fifteenth centuries. In these texts, 'Bajo' is usually qualified as 'Bajo Sereng', meaning the 'Bajo' of the Moluccas.[3] In Makassarese texts, the earliest use of the name 'Bajo' is found in the royal chronicle of Goa, where the first ruler, a woman, is said to have married 'Karaeng Bajo' or a Bajo lord (Wolhoff and Abdurrahim, 1960: 10, 80n).

In Malaysia and Indonesia the terms 'Bajau' and 'Bajo' are regularly used in the national vernaculars, Bahasa Malaysia and Bahasa Indonesia, as a general ethnic term for all Sama–Bajau speakers. Nomadic and formerly nomadic groups are commonly referred to as 'Bajau Laut', a usage followed here (Sather, 1993a: 30). Some ambiguity, however, attaches to these terms. 'Bajau Laut' may also be applied, not simply to boat nomads and former nomads, but to all coastal-dwelling 'Bajau', as opposed to those who live inland from the sea for whom the Malay label 'Bajau Darat', literally 'inland Bajau', is sometimes used (Asmah, 1980). In this book, the name 'Bajau Laut' is used in the prior sense, to refer exclusively to Sama-speaking sea nomads and former nomads, those who identify themselves in south-eastern Sabah as Sama Dilaut or *a'a dilaut*.

Language

Until recently, Sama–Bajau was thought to belong to the Philippine phyllum of Austronesian languages (Conklin, 1955; Sather, 1978: 172). However, it is now recognized by linguists as comprising a separate Sama–Bajau subgroup within the Western Malayo-Polynesian language family. Its wider affiliations have yet to be determined (Moody, 1984: 334; Pallesen, 1985: 117; Ross, 1994: 74–6).

The Sama–Bajau subgroup comprises an estimated ten languages, most strongly dialectalized (Pallesen, 1985). The most divergent of these languages are thought to be Abaknun, Yakan, and Sibuguey. Abaknun (or Abak) is spoken by the Abaknun, Christianized Sama–Bajau speakers who live on Capul Island in northern Samar, in the central Philippines (McFarland, 1980: 106; Barbosa, 1995). The Abaknun are believed to be the descendants of an early northward migration of Sama speakers from northern Sulu. The Yakan live chiefly on Basilan Island and the adjacent Zamboanga coast of Mindanao and are also thought to have originated from an early offshoot community. However, in contrast to the Abaknun, the Yakan appear to have become differentiated from other Sama speakers, not as a result of maritime migration and consequent geographical isolation but by remaining in place, close to what seems to have been the original proto-Sama–Bajau homeland (Pallesen, 1985: 117). In the more recent past, the Yakan, while acknowledging the suzerainty of the Sulu Sultanate, have traditionally resisted outside domination and so have preserved a larger degree of political and cultural independence than most other Sama groups. They now form an inland, largely swidden-agricultural population, ethnically distinct from other Sama–Bajau speakers, identifying themselves as Yakan rather than Sama, and living, in contrast to the latter, in dispersed inland settlements with no close ties to the sea (Wulff, 1964, 1971, 1984; Frake, 1969, 1980). The Sibuguey comprise a number of smaller, relatively isolated Sama-speaking groups, living mainly around Sibuguey Bay, along Olutanga Island and in the adjacent Mindanao coastal districts of Zamboanga del Sur Province (McFarland, 1980: 106).

Relationships between the remaining Sama–Bajau languages are still poorly understood. A relatively divergent dialect grouping, sometimes called Western Sama, is spoken in the North Ubian and Pangutaran island groups west of the main Sulu island chain (McFarland, 1980:

106). Another, Jama Mapun, is spoken by a distinct Sama subgroup living mainly on Cagayan de Sulu Island, southern Palawan, and on the smaller neighbouring islands (Balabac, Bakungan, and others) of the southern Philippines near the north-eastern tip of Sabah (Casiño, 1976: 8). Additional communities are present along the north-eastern coast of Sabah, from Sandakan Bay to Kudat and Banggi Island. Pallesen (1985: 171) has suggested that the migration route taken by the Jama Mapun in settling Cagayan de Sulu was by way of coastal Sabah, indicating that these latter communities may have been present in Sabah for a very long time, perhaps eight centuries (Walton and Moody, 1984: 114). In Sabah, the Jama Mapun are also known locally as the Kagayan or Sama Kagayan.

Northern Sama, like Western Sama, forms a relatively heterogeneous group of dialects. These are spoken chiefly in the islands of Basilan Strait, generally northward from Jolo to the Zamboanga Peninsula of Mindanao. Included in this group is Balangingi' (or Bāngingi) spoken in the Tongkil island group south of Basilan, on the islands and coastal areas bordering Basilan Island, and on the southern Zamboanga Peninsula (Diment, 1994: 375). A small community of Balangingi' speakers is also present at Telisai, in the Lahad Datu district of eastern Sabah (Walton and Moody, 1984: 114). Central Sama is spoken chiefly in the Tapul and eastern Tawitawi groups and in the smaller islands between Tawitawi and Jolo, including Siasi and Lapac. Dialects of Central Sama are also reportedly spoken in small, scattered enclaves around Basilan Island to the north. Closely related to Central Sulu, but internally much more homogeneous, Southern Sama is spoken from Tandubas Island in the western Tawitawi group, through the Sibutu island group, to the eastern coast of Sabah, where dialects of Southern Sama are spoken extensively from Sandakan Bay through the Semporna, Lahad Datu, and Tawau districts to the south (Allison, 1979: 63; Sather, 1984: 10; Walton and Moody, 1984: 116). Among Southern Sama speakers, the Sama Ubian, whose principal centre of settlement is on South Ubian Island in the Tawitawi island group, are also found in small, widely scattered enclaves further north along the east coast of Sabah, from Semporna to Kudat; on Banggi Island; at Kuala Abai in the Kota Belud district; at Gaya, Kota Kinabalu, and further southward along the west coast as far as Kuala Penyu. This distribution makes the Ubian probably the most widely distributed of all Sama dialects spoken in Sabah.

Varieties of Southern Sama, nearly all with close historical links in the Sulu Archipelago, are spoken along the whole east and south-eastern coast of Sabah, from Sandakan Bay to the Tawau district. These varieties have recently been found by Smith (1984: 12), on the basis of lexicostatistical analysis, to constitute a single chain-related group which he has tentatively called East Coast Bajau. Within this group Smith found 'a strongly interlocking central network of dialects linked by relationships of 85 PSC [per cent of shared cognates] or higher' (Smith, 1984: 15). Adding Philippine data, Walton and Moody (1984: 115–16) have shown that this central network of dialects, which includes that spoken by the Semporna Sama Dilaut, correlates with the larger dialect group usually

identified in the Philippines as Southern Sama. They therefore extend
the name Southern Sama to this chain-related east coast group (Walton
and Moody, 1984: 122). Although not recorded by Smith, or by Walton
and Moody, in the last decade a number of Central Sama speakers have
also begun to migrate to south-eastern Sabah, especially to the Semporna
district, coming chiefly from Siasi and the eastern Tawitawi region.

Dialects of a separate chain-related group, called West Coast Bajau,
are spoken in the western and northern coastal districts of Sabah, from
Kuala Penyu and Labuan in the south-west to Terusan in the Labuk-
Sugut district in the east (Banker, 1984: 102–3). Some overlap exists
with Jama Mapun and Southern Sama (notably Ubian) around the
northern coast of Sabah, particularly in the Kudat and Pitas districts. In
addition, a number of west coast Bajau have been recently resettled on
government schemes in the Kunak area of Lahad Datu and in the
Sandakan district (Walton and Moody, 1984: 114). Despite this partial
overlap, dialects of West Coast Bajau spoken in western and northern
Sabah, and of Southern Sama spoken on the south-eastern coast, are
mutually unintelligible (Banker, 1984: 109–10), although some Sama
speakers would disagree, having presumably learned enough through
contacts to have become multilingual. On the basis of lexico-statistical
comparison, each of these two major Bajau dialect groups has been
shown to form 'an independent dialect chain without an interconnecting
link' within the level of 75 per cent shared cognates, indicating a relatively long period of historical separation (Smith, 1984: 12).

Another group of dialects, known generally as Indonesian Bajau, is
spoken from Sulawesi and the eastern coast of Kalimantan to Timor and
Roti in eastern Indonesia (Darmansjah and Basran Noor, 1979; Verheijen,
1986). This group's closest links appear to be with Southern Sama.
Local dialects of Indonesian Bajau are said to be notably homogeneous
(Cense and Uhlenbeck, 1958: 27; Verheijen, 1986: 26–8), forming, according to Noorduyn (1991: 6), 'only one language', suggesting a relatively recent dispersion, very likely from the eastern coast of Borneo or from
south-western Sulu.

In the Semporna district of Sabah, during the period of my main
fieldwork, all forms of Bajau spoken locally were mutually intelligible,
including that spoken by the Bajau Laut. No speech barriers therefore
separated any of these groups, although dialect differences between
them were, in many cases, strongly marked. Within the district, all Sama
speakers, including the Sama Dilaut, described their speech as *ling* Sama,
literally, 'Sama' or 'Bajau speech'.[4] In this sense, they all describe themselves as speaking the same language. On the basis of lexico-statistical
analysis, all local Sama dialects have been shown to be dialects of
Southern Sama including Semporna Sama Dilaut (Walton and Moody,
1984: 116).

Contrary to Arong (1962: 135), boat-nomadic and formerly nomadic
communities do not appear to constitute a single linguistically homogeneous population. The Semporna Sama Dilaut maintain their closest links
with Sama Dilaut living in the southernmost Sibutu island group of

Sulu, particularly with those of Sitangkai, a community from which most Semporna Sama Dilaut trace their origins. Within the Semporna–Sibutu area, all Sama Dilaut speak the same dialect, which Walton and Moody (1984: 119) identify as a variety of Southern Sama. This dialect is readily intelligible to the members of neighbouring shore groups, all of whom similarly speak dialects and subdialects of Southern Sama. In contrast, boat-nomadic and formerly nomadic groups in Siasi and further north in the central and northern Sulu island groups, although they also identify themselves as Sama Dilaut, speak, according to Pallesen (1985: 46), dialects of Central Sama. It appears therefore that there are at least two major dialect groupings of Sama Dilaut in the Sulu-south-eastern Sabah region, both of them more closely related to neighbouring strand groups within the same area than to one another across these areas. This pattern of local speech differentiation suggests the overriding significance of local trade relations in determining inter-community contacts, and hence patterns of speech intelligibility.

Within the Semporna–southern Sulu region, local dialect communities, like the toponymically named subgroups they mirror, are not immutable, but alter over time, largely through intermarriage and the regional movement of people. Within this larger area, many local dialect communities have experienced considerable dispersion over the last century and a half as their speakers have scattered from original home islands to others. In the Semporna district, no fewer than fifteen named Sama subgroups were present in 1979, nearly all identified with places of origin in the southern Sulu Archipelago. Only one major group, the Sama Sikubang (or Kubang), is identified exclusively with the local Semporna region and nowhere else. It is also recognized that new dialects may emerge in time. Some of these names distinguish localized communities that have become differentiated through migration and the establishment of new areas of settlement. For example, in the course of the last two generations settled Sama Buna-Buna'an from Kampung Bait in the Semporna district have established a daughter village at Limau-Limau, less than 2 miles away by sea. Already, sufficient differences have developed to make it possible for Sama speakers to identify by speech individuals from one or the other of these two villages. Hence, locally they are sometimes described by village name, as forming different dialect subgroups. In the Semporna district, intermarriage is not infrequent between the members of different speech communities, particularly among shore groups. The in-marrying husband or wife is expected to adopt the dialect spoken by the community into which he or she marries. As a consequence of intermarriage, many Sama speakers can trace connections through their parents, grandparents, or more remote ancestors to a number of different dialect groups. Because of their outcaste status, intermarriage between shore groups and the Sama Dilaut has historically been less frequent, although it has and still occurs.

Most Bajau Laut men in Semporna are multidialectal, being able to converse in at least one or two local Sama dialects in addition to their own. This makes it difficult to judge levels of mutual intelligibility. The headman of Bangau-Bangau, whose house I shared, occasionally received Bajau visitors from nearby strand villages and from Semporna town. Even after I was able to converse in the Sama Dilaut dialect with some proficiency, I often found it difficult to follow these visitors' conversations, much to the chagrin of the headman and others, who were fond of introducing me, quite unjustifiably, as a *milikan* (American) who spoke *ling Sama* 'like us' (*buat kami*). The Bajau Laut villagers seemed to have no such difficulty although they were aware of, and regularly commented on, differences of speech between themselves and other local Sama speakers. In Semporna, these differences are frequently associated in folk notions with differences in collective personality. For example, the people of Tabak-Tabak, who have a history of former slave-raiding, are said to speak 'fiercely', while those of Selakan are said to speak 'softly'. Of the various local dialects of Bajau, Sama Sikubang is by far the most commonly spoken in the Semporna district and is the most frequent second dialect or language used between other Sama groups and by Chinese shopkeepers and other non-Sama speakers.

Among Sama speakers, the dialect of Sama spoken by the Bajau Laut, while easily intelligible, is immediately recognizable and is described as having a distinctive intonation pattern, often characterized as 'rhythmic' or 'sing-song', as well as by unique lexical features. Its use thus effectively announces the Sama Dilaut identity of those who speak it.

In addition to the language of everyday speech, Sama Dilaut includes a poetic register employed particularly in curative spells (*nawal*), songs, epics, and other traditional forms of story-telling (*kata-kata*). There is also a separate 'language' of the spirits (*saitan*) called *ling saitan*; this is the language in which Bajau Laut spirit-mediums 'converse' when they are in trance. Each medium employs an assistant whose chief task is to translate *ling saitan* into everyday *ling Sama* for the benefit of the medium's patients and lay audiences. Mastering 'spirit language' is part of a spirit-medium's apprenticeship; in the village of Bangau-Bangau, several mediums additionally 'write' *ling saitan* in pictographic characters on cloth banners (*panji*).

Many older Sama Dilaut in Semporna have some knowledge of Tausug (*ling Suk*), which served in the past as a regional lingua franca. Reflecting ethnic stereotypes, Tausug is sometimes interjected into humorous stories to indicate that the character speaking is being deceitful, falsely pious, or boastful. Malay is rapidly replacing Tausug as a lingua franca in situations involving non-Bajau speakers. Through schooling, newspapers, the radio, and now television, Malay has become a widely used second language in Semporna, especially among the younger generation.

The People: Sama Origins

The earliest historical reference to sea-nomadic peoples who can be identified with some certainty as Sama, perhaps even Sama Dilaut, comes from the northern Sulu–Mindanao region of the Philippines. Pigafetta, Magellan's chronicler, mentioned a brief encounter in 1521 with a boat-dwelling band near Saccol Island, close to the south-eastern tip of the Zamboanga Peninsula of Mindanao, an area still frequented by maritime Sama speakers (Pigafetta, 1906: Vol. II, 53). Over a century later, Francisco Combés, writing in 1667 in his history of the islands beyond the southern frontiers of Spanish rule in the Philippines, provided the first brief descriptive account of the maritime nomads of the Sulu region and of the complex social and political world they inhabited. Of these sea people, Combés (1904: 104–5) wrote:

They are of this nature, that they know no other home than their boats ... [and] are such enemies of the land, that it does not get from them the slightest labour or industry, nor the profit of any fruit. All of their work is in fishing and by this they barter for what they need.... And as they put down very few roots, they move easily to other parts, having no fixed dwelling but the sea; and this notwithstanding the fact that they acknowledge certain settlements where they are gathered, with a few families in them, dispersed along the coves and low beaches, convenient for their fishing.

Combés's knowledge of the sea nomads derived largely from southern Mindanao, Basilan, and the northern edge of the Sulu Archipelago, regions into which Spanish military forces had begun a protracted and largely unsuccessful campaign of colonial conquest. It seems likely that the sea people he described are ancestral to the Bajau Laut, although we cannot be certain of this. Neither the term 'Bajau' nor 'Sama' appears in Combés's description. Instead, Combés referred to the sea people as 'Lutaos', a name of uncertain etymology (Sopher, 1965: 308). He also suggested that most of the strand population of the Sulu Archipelago was also of 'Lutayan' origin, except for the nobles and major chiefs who, he wrote, appeared to be of a different stock. It is probable that Combés was making a distinction between Sama-speaking commoners and their Tausug and Magindanao rulers. In any event, his account has the special virtue of emphasizing the significance of trade and of pointing out the clear connections that existed at that time between trade, ethnicity, and political power. It was these connections that later ethnographic accounts often ignored, treating Sama speakers as constituting self-contained 'cultures'. Combés noted that the power of land-based rulers depended upon their ability to mobilize populations of sea people for the purposes of commerce and navigation. Fishing was engaged in for trade as well as for subsistence, and the products supplied by local sea nomadic communities were in demand in markets well beyond Mindanao and the Sulu Archipelago. By the seventeenth century, these products represented the major trading commodities of the region; they included shark fin, dried fish, pearls, turtle eggs, mother-of-pearl, and 'tripang' (sea cucumbers, holothurians, or bêche-de-mer). Consequently, Combés noted that local political leaders, 'the kings of Mindanao and Sulu and [their] chief lientenants', vied for the economic allegiance of the sea people. 'For this reason', he wrote, 'whoever has the most allies of this nation considers himself the most powerful ... becoming the master of the straits and of the places necessary for the commerce of these islands' (Combés, 1904: 108).

Until the nineteenth century observers continued to affirm the significance of the sea nomads as regional suppliers of maritime trading commodities, not only in Sulu, but also in the Bugis and Makassarese states of eastern Indonesia (Crawfurd, 1856: 283; Sopher, 1965: 241–9; Hunt, 1967). Outside the Sulu Archipelago, the southward spread of Sama speakers appears to have preceded, but been closely linked to, the rise of commercial polities. The emergence of maritime states seems to have been marked, as it was in the Sulu Archipelago, by the political subordination of Sama-speaking mariners by more powerful coastal populations. The related development of maritime trading networks, in particular the '*tripang*' collecting industries organized under Makassar and Bugis patronage, closely followed patterns of Sama–Bajau dispersion and voyaging (Pelras, 1972; Fox, 1977; Reid, 1983: 124–9). By the early seventeenth century, Dutch accounts of Sulawesi recorded the presence of large numbers of Bajau around Makassar. Following Makassar's defeat in 1669, many of these communities are said to have dispersed to other islands, spreading the distribution of Sama speakers further south and eastward. By the early eighteenth century, when the ethnographic record becomes fuller, fleets of Bajau were reportedly voyaging on fishing and '*tripang*' collecting expeditions as far south as Roti and Timor (Fox, 1977: 459). Most were described as being the sea-going dependants of either Bugis or Makassarese patrons. Under this patronage, Bajau mariners, including boat-nomadic groups, acted as the principal gatherers of '*tripang*' throughout the eastern Indonesian world for almost 200 years.

Nothing is known directly of the Sama before these early sixteenth and seventeenth century accounts. However, the linguist Kemp Pallesen (1985) has produced a linguistic reconstruction extending to the first millennium AD that adds not only to our understanding of the dispersion of Sama–Bajau speakers, but also of the internal relations that existed within this population, links to maritime movements, trade relations, interethnic politics, and state formation, all processes whose consequences we can continue to follow into the much fuller historical records of the nineteenth and early twentieth centuries.

As a language grouping, Sama–Bajau is reconstructable only to the first millennium AD (Pallesen, 1985: 117). Around AD 800, speakers of proto-Sama–Bajau can be placed with some confidence in the northern islands of the Sulu Archipelago, on Basilan, and along the adjacent Mindanao coastline bordering the Basilan Straits (Pallesen, 1985: 117). Lexical reconstruction suggests that these people were predominantly sea-oriented, but not exclusively so. The reconstructed lexicon also points to a long familiarity with farming, iron-forging, pottery-making and weaving, as well as with fishing and seafaring. Although their knowledge of the sea may have been intimate, these early proto-Sama–Bajau speakers were by no means wholly sea people. Instead, a marine orientation appears to have co-existed with 'a significant and coherent tradition of land-oriented activity' (Pallesen, 1985: 255), indicating the presence, 'already at this predispersion time [of] a divergence of orientation between the land and the coastal strand' (Pallesen, 1985: 117). Reflecting this divergence, proto-Sama groups appear to have focused their attentions, much as they continue to do today, on various permutations of this 'dual orientation', some concentrating their economic activities on the land, others on the sea or immediate littoral (Pallesen, 1985: 118). While some may have adopted sea-nomadism, it was not the sole, or probably even the principal, mode of early proto-Sama adaptation (Sather, 1995: 243).

Pallesen (1985: 118), in his reconstruction, sees the tenth century as the beginning of a major period of Sama–Bajau dispersion. A number of sea-oriented groups probed northward, establishing ports of call around the eastern coast of Mindanao and beyond. Others settled the broad zone of mangrove swamps at the head of Sibuguey Bay. At the same time, a third group, the Yakan, became linguistically distinct, not by sea-going migration, but by staying put, intensifying their land orientation, shunning the sea, and becoming settled, inland swidden cultivators (Pallesen, 1985: 118; see also Frake, 1980: 325–6). In the eleventh century, additional sea-oriented groups spread southward down the Sulu Archipelago. One branch, the probable ancestors of the west coast Bajau, settled the northern and western coasts of Sabah, while another established itself along the eastern coast, expanding southward into coastal Kalimantan. From here, or directly from southern Sulu, Sama entered the Straits of Makassar, spreading to Sulawesi and other parts of eastern Indonesia, these final movements occurring some centuries before the first European penetration of the region.

The turn of the millennium marked, in Pallesen's view, the beginning of a long period of Sama movement. In addition, 700 years ago, the Sama appear to have come into first contact with the Tausug. Pallesen (1985: 246–7) argues that these two events were related and that changing economic and political relations were the catalyst of both. Underlying these changes was the development of long-distance trade with China, India, and the Middle East. Pallesen (1985: 247) suggests that the Sama, in probing northward, established a network of trading colonies along the river-mouths and coastlines of the larger islands they encountered. This development was commercial in motive but, as he argues, it did not necessarily entail elaborate enterprise. Instead, Pallesen (1985: 248) suggests, 'a major early element of . . . trade may well have been the protein-starch exchange which underlies much economic activity in Sulu [to the present]'.

Dried fish is the major source of protein for inland peoples over virtually the whole of insular South-East Asia and it has been, throughout historical times, a principal item of trade for Sama–Bajau speakers and a major export commodity of Sulu.[5] Pallesen argues that this protein-starch exchange was probably a major factor in the early dispersion of the Sama. But once they had established a network of scattered bases, they were then well positioned to take advantage of further developments in trade. Pallesen (1985: 249) writes: 'The maritime skills of [the Sama] and the wide distribution of their settlements or ports of call would have given them an advantage in exploiting the growing trade opportunities in the centuries around 1000 A.D.' By the eleventh century, Jolo

Island, located at the centre of the Sulu Archipelago, emerged as the hub of this network and, lying across important sea lanes, began its ascent as the primary entrepôt for the whole of the archipelago.

Pallesen argues that this spread of Sama colonies brought Sama-speaking traders into contact with the ancestors of the Tausug. Linguistically, Tausug is a southern central Philippine language. Its nearest sister language is Butuanon, spoken today in a limited area at the mouth of the Agusan River in eastern Mindanao (Pallesen, 1985: 125 ff.). Lexico-statistical evidence suggests that the two languages separated 700 years ago. Pallesen considers it probable that Sama traders established a colony at the mouth of the Agusan River in order to command the local riverine trade into the interior and that, through intermarriage, some of these traders returned to central Sulu, bringing with them Tausug-speaking women and children. According to Pallesen (1985: 265), the present Tausug population had its genesis in a bilingual trading community established chiefly at Jolo by Sama traders and their Tausug-speaking wives and children.

By the time this trading community took form, Jolo was already a major commercial centre with links to China, the central and northern Philippines, Borneo, and to other parts of the eastern and western Malay world.[6] Taking advantage of its strategic location, a Jolo-based trading élite gained power and numerical strength, using its power not only to maintain Tausug as a distinct language, but also to absorb the more settled land-based Sama then present on the larger central islands of the Sulu Archipelago, assimilating them linguistically and culturally into a growing Tausug-speaking population. This process is still continuing. Economic differences were thus accentuated and the remaining Sama came to be increasingly associated with the peripheral islands of the archipelago and with the more maritime sectors of the islands' economy.

With the coming of Islam, and the emergence of the Sulu Sultanate, the Tausug assumed formal dominance over the Sama and others of the region, including the sea-nomadic Sama Dilaut. In the process, the Tausug evolved a distinctive ethnic identity to seal their political and economic domination so that, with the rise of the Sulu Sultanate, differences of rank, religion, and power came to assume the characteristics of a complex, well-defined system of ethnic stratification (Frake, 1980; Sather, 1984, 1993d).

Within the ethnic hierarchy that was created, the sea nomads came to occupy the lowest rung, beneath the dominant Tausug and the multitude of Sama-speaking shore and strand people. Without a territorial base of their own, they were perceived by their neighbours as living outside, and so only tangentially connected to, the system of personal coalitions that came to define political and economic relations in Sulu. Reflecting this status of social and political exclusion, sea-nomadic communities were identified by outsiders by pejorative terms, such as *pala'au* or *luwa'an*, meaning, literally, 'that which is spat or vomited out' (Kiefer, 1972a: 22; Sather, 1984: 12–13, 1993a: 30).

Origin Myths

This wider system of hierarchical relations found ideological underpinning in local origin myths and in political genealogies. In the Tausug genealogical histories of Sulu, the *tarsila*, Sama speakers are represented not as an early population, but as 'newcomers' who arrive from outside the islands and in settling the various island groups making up the Sulu Archipelago are allotted as dependent 'guests' among various lines of local Tausug aristocrats and their kin (Saleeby, 1908). Until recently, this portrayal was accepted as historically valid (Saleeby, 1905, 1908). However, new evidence indicates that the Sama predate the Tausug in the Sulu Archipelago. Yet the Tausug *tarsila* reflect a common folk tradition widely shared by both the Tausug and the Sama that the Sama arrived in the islands of the archipelago by sea, coming according to most traditions from Johore, in the western Malay world (Sopher, 1965: 141–2). Similar folk traditions have been recorded not only in Sulu (Follett, 1945: 129–30), but also in Sabah (Forrest, 1780: 372; Rutter, 1922: 73; Yap, 1978: 9), Kalimantan (Dewall, 1885: 446–7), and eastern Indonesia (Collins, 1995: 10–12; Verschuer, 1883: 4). For example, Dewall (1885: 446) recorded the following tradition at Tanjung Batu, on the eastern Kalimantan coast, in 1849:

The Bajau came originally from Johore. Once a Johore princess disappeared during a storm at sea. The Sultan of Johore organized a group of people to search for her. However, the lost princess could not be found, and the people who were looking for her found themselves far away from Johore, and were unable to find their way back again, and so they settled down along the coastal areas of Borneo, Sulawesi, and in the Sulu Archipelago.

According to a version of this tradition recorded in Sabah by Rutter (1922: 73), the Sultan of Johore had a beautiful daughter. The rulers of both Brunei and Sulu wished to marry her. Although the daughter favoured the Brunei prince, her father arranged for her marriage to Sulu, sending her to her husband-to-be under escort. At sea, however, the Brunei prince attacked the Johore fleet and took the princess away. The Johore people, unable to return to Johore for fear of punishment, remained at sea, wandering the islands, their descendants becoming the present-day Bajau.

The association of the Bajau with Johore, asserted in these myth, linked them to the most prestigious of all Malay kingdoms having historical connection with the region. By tradition, Sulu was a successor to Johore, having acquired its court rituals, courtly language, and principles of statecraft from this earlier kingdom. Johore in turn was the heir to Malacca, the latter claiming, through Palembang, an uninterrupted chain of succession from Srivijaya. Similarly, the Bajau in Sulawesi linked their mythic origins first to Luwu', then to Goa, and finally to Bone, reflecting, in the eastern Indonesian world, a parallel succession of political legitimacy (Sopher, 1965: 160–1). Taken together, these myths have more to do with political ideologies and the subordination of maritime peoples in a succession of sea-oriented trading states than they do with actual migrations or literal origins.

In Semporna, the Bajau Laut say that in the beginning there existed only eternal beings, the supreme being, *Tuhan* (God), and the *saitan*. *Tuhan* then created the first *mbo'* (human ancestors). According to the Semporna Bajau Laut, the first ancestors lived in Arabia and all Sama, whether sea or shore people, are descended from the same original ancestor created at this time by *Tuhan*.

After creating the *mbo'*, *Tuhan* informed the first ancestors that they would have to die, but that they could choose the form their death would take. They could die like the moon (*bulan*), and be reborn each month or, alternatively, they could die like the banana plant (*saging*), whose main stalk dies while its rootstock sends out new shoots to take its place. The ancestors chose this latter death, and so people today, the descendants of the ancestors, die, never to be reborn again. However, they bear children who, like the banana shoots, take their place and so continue life in the physical world as their 'descendants' (*turunan*).[7]

The ancestors, although not eternal beings like *Tuhan* and the spirits, exist for the Bajau Laut, both in and out of time. In choosing not to die like the moon, the *mbo'* thereby rendered human existence non-cyclical (Bottignolo, 1995: 25–8). At death, for each individual, mundane existence ends forever. The individual departs from the earthly world, never to return again, and in this world his or her place is taken by others who are similarly fated to die in time. However, in death each individual is thought to be transformed. He or she becomes *mbo'*, and so as an ancestor escapes the historical present—the contingent time of birth and death—and enters a dimension shared with the first ancestor. Although invisible, the ancestors become transcendent beings and so remain immediately present and forever accessible to their living descendants.

Most believe that from the time of the first ancestors, down through that of the Prophet Muhammad, the *mbo'* lived in Arabia. Here, like later ancestors, they made their homes in boats and subsisted by fishing. According to Panglima Tiring bin Hawani, one evening, in making a nightly anchorage, the leader of a group of boat-living families who were then anchoring together thrust his mooring pole not into the sandy sea floor, as he supposed, but into the gills of a giant ray asleep on the bottom of the sea. During the night, as the families slept, the ray awoke and swam off, carrying their boats, which were strung together in tandem, further and further across the sea. At dawn, when they awoke, they found themselves in a strange sea, surrounded by islands they had never seen before. Not knowing how to return, they remained, scattering and dividing over time into many different anchorage groups. According to the headman, the first landfall was made near the small, uninhabited islands in Darvel Bay north of Timbun Mata, less than a day's sail from Bangau-Bangau. Other villagers dispute this, saying that the first landfall was made further west, in the Sulu Archipelago. Still others say that the ancestors were dispersed from Arabia and scattered to Sulu and Sabah as a result of storms and strong winds that blew them into unfamiliar waters.

All agree, however, that their original place of settlement was at Sitangkai, in the southern Sibutu island group of Sulu. Indeed, the Semporna Bajau Laut generally perceive themselves to be part of a larger regional society which has Sitangkai as its centre. A great deal of intermarriage and movement of people occur between Semporna and Sitangkai, and while this movement has been strongly in the direction of Semporna over most of the present century, some reverse movement back to Sitangkai also occurs as a result of marriage or the relocation of families, some of it permanent, some for varying lengths of time, with persons, in the latter case, eventually returning to Semporna, often bringing with them spouses and children.

The surrounding land-based Bajau generally say that the ancestors of the Bajau Laut were brought to Semporna at different times in the past by their own ancestors, who migrated with them as their dependent clients as they moved westward from different island groups in Sulu, particularly from Bilatan and Tawitawi.

Throughout the Sulu–Semporna region there exists a common folk tradition that attributes to the ancestors of the Bajau Laut a separate origin as sea nomads. This tradition tells how the Bajau Laut became differentiated from more sedentary Sama. In these myths, which are shared by both the Tausug and more shore-dwelling Sama, the ancestors of the sea nomads are represented as a people cursed (*ka sukna*) by *Tuhan*, ejected from the Islamic faith, and so forced to live afloat (*makatandan*), 'like flotsam' (*buat kampal*), without a landed region or island homeland of their own with which they might, like more sedentary Sama, identify themselves (Sather, 1984: 13).

The following is the full version of a common Semporna variant of this tradition. Here the ancestors of the Sama Dilaut, or the Pala'au as they are called by the land Sama, are said to have lived in Arabia as fishermen.

The Prophet once fell ill and so asked his wife, Siti Aisah, to get a particular kind of fish for him so that he might recover. Siti Aisah went down to the beach and there she came to some people, the Pala'au. She asked them to sell her the fish. But a fisherman among them answered that he did not wish to sell it. She pleaded. So he said, 'If you really want this fish, then you must submit yourself to me. Then I will sell it. What is your answer?'

'Never mind', Siti Aisah answered. 'If the Prophet, my husband, cannot have the fish, then I will trust in God.' As the fisherman was about to force himself on her, the cat (*kuting mulia*) she was holding leapt onto him and clawed the end of his penis. He jumped up and ran away. Siti Aisah said, 'You had better take your fish'. But the fisherman said, 'Never mind'.

After this happened, the fisherman came to the Prophet Muhammad and asked for his forgiveness. The Prophet agreed to forgive him, but said, 'I have already cursed you. You and your descendants will suffer for seven generations; but after that, you will be forgiven. You cannot be forgiven earlier. You must also ask for God's forgiveness (*taubat ni Tuhan*).' But the fisherman kept asking for forgiveness. So, in the end, the Prophet advised the fisherman to prepare a feast (*kanduri*). 'This coming Friday, I will come to your house.' So early in the morning, all the Pala'au went out in search of animals to slaughter. But they could not find any except for one goat that was very thin and close to death. They killed the goat. But after removing the bones and organs, only a fistful of meat remained. 'This will never be enough. The Prophet will come with his followers: Prophet Ibrahim, Syedina Ali, Syedina Osman, Syedina Omar, Syedina Abu Bakar, and the Prophet's father, Abdul Mattali. There are seven and there is very little meat.'

So the Pala'au went out to look for meat again. But all they could find this time was a dog—only one dog. So the Pala'au killed the dog and cooked its meat. They then set places ready to serve the guests. The Prophet and his followers soon arrived. The Pala'au served the Prophet first. As soon as the Prophet pronounced the *bismillah*, the dog meat began to bark. The Prophet wondered where the barking was coming from. He intoned '*I haja ratun nabi*' and as he said this, the food on the plates barked. As he repeated the incantation each serving barked. Syedina Ali, hearing the barking, drew his *padang* sword to kill the Pala'au. But the Prophet commanded him to stop. 'God has already cursed the Pala'au. They will be punished by Him.'

So the Prophet and his followers left. As soon as they were away, Prophet Ibrahim uttered special verses. Immediately the land of the Pala'au sank into the sea. The Pala'au clung to logs to save themselves. All sank except the grand-father of the Pala'au who was holding on to a log. This time the curse of the Prophet will be forgiven only when the verses uttered by Prophet Ibrahim have vanished from this world. These verses are the words of God from the Koran. So while the Koran still exists in this world, the Pala'au must remain forever cursed, drifting like debris on the sea.

Many local variants of this tradition exist.[8] All are essentially aetiological myths (*usulan*) that 'explain', from the vantage point of those living ashore, how the sea nomads came into existence. In virtually all versions, their separate origin is attributed to an act of sacrilege, the commission of which places them outside the religiously constituted social world inhabited by their neighbours. Thus, the sea nomads are condemned to be, and in some versions must forever remain, a 'people without religion' (*a'a halam ania' ugama* or *a'a halam magugama*). Religion and political status are inseparably linked. Without a territorial base ashore, the sea nomads live afloat, despised by others as non-Muslims and so are denied a status, except as subject people, in a hierarchically ordered political realm other-wise composed of co-religionists with the sultan as their symbolic head.

In contradistinction, the boat people in Semporna have traditionally rejected this mythic exclusion, although they are well aware of it. They stress, instead, their common cultural and linguistic ties as Sama who share with the majority of other Sama–Bajau speakers a common maritime orientation. As Sama they have traditionally rejected pejorative terms like Pala'au and have called themselves, in addition to Sama Dilaut ('sea Sama'), the Sama *to'ongan*, meaning literally, the 'true', 'genuine', or 'real' Sama.

The Setting: Sabah and the Semporna District

Sabah lies at the northern apex of Borneo. A state in the Malaysian Federation, Sabah is divided for administrative purposes into four residencies: the West Coast, Interior, Sandakan, and Tawau. The Semporna district is one of four in the Tawau residency, bordered on the north by the Lahad Datu and Kunak districts and on the west by the Tawau district (Map 1.2).

The population of Sabah, which in 1991 stood at nearly 2 million, is highly diverse, but may be divided in very general terms between three major categories, each comprising roughly one-third of the total: a) indigenous agricultural groups, chiefly Kadazan–Dusun, occupying principally

MAP 1.2
Semporna District, Showing Location of Bajau Laut Settlements on
Bangau-Bangau and Labuan Haji

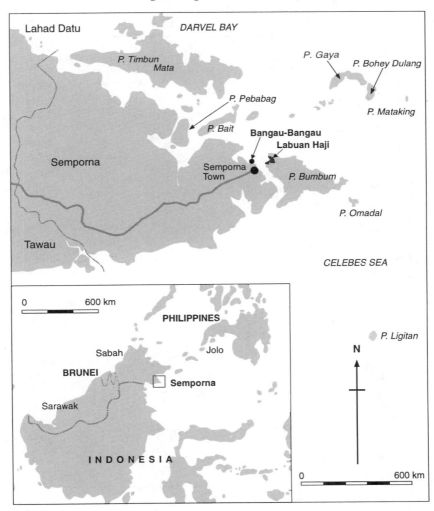

the coastal plains, intermontane valleys, and interior uplands; b) Chinese and other less numerous immigrant groups, settled mainly in and around the principal port and bazaar towns; and c) coastal peoples, all of them Muslim, occupying the coastal plains below the tidal reaches of the main rivers, the immediate coastal littoral, and offshore islands. The Bajau comprise the single most populous coastal group. In 1970, the Bajau numbered 72,323, or 11 per cent of the state's total population (Malaysia, Department of Statistics, 1972) (Tables 1.1 and 1.2). According to the most recent census, in 1991, their numbers have increased to 211,970 and their percentage of the total population to 15.2 per cent (Table 1.3). The largest increase has occurred on the east coast where a high rate of natural increase has been augmented by substantial immigration from the southern Philippines. Internally, there is also con-

TABLE 1.1
Population of Sabah, 1970

Group	Population
Indigenous	
Kadazan (Dusun)	184,512
Dusun (Dusun)	10,881
Murut	31,299
Bajau	72,323
Illanun	4,948
Orang Sungai	17,687
Tausug (Suluk)	10,864
Malay	18,365
Brunei Malay	27,452
Kadayan	10,490
Bisaya	13,998
Tidong	7,720
Sino-Native	10,345
Other Indigenous	16,194
Total	437,078
Others	
Chinese	139,509
Indonesians	39,526
Philippine Natives	20,367
Indians	7,103
Sarawak Natives	3,234
Cocos Islanders	2,731
Eurasians	872
Europeans	862
Others	1,982
Total	216,186
Sabah Total	653,264

Source: Malaysia, Department of Statistics (1972).

TABLE 1.2
Distribution of Bajau Population by District, 1970

District	Population	Population Change[a]
Semporna[b]	18,305	4,260
Kota Belud[c]	11,842	−1,422
Tuaran	10,638	2,642
Kota Kinabalu	7,669	1,320
Kudat	6,347	347
Papar	4,664	768
Sandakan	2,882	1,216
Lahad Datu	2,807	275
Penampang	2,607	2,607
Labuk	1,443	−487
Tawau	1,252	765
Kuala Penyu	914	396
Total	72,323	12,613

Source: Jones (1962); Malaysia, Department of Statistics (1972).
Notes: Data include only those districts with a Bajau population of more than 500 in 1970.
   Total figures are for all districts, including those not shown, hence the larger numbers.
[a]Increase/decrease in population from 1960 to 1970.
[b]These figures underenumerate the Bajau population of the district because they exclude many Philippine-born Bajau. As indicated in the text, a more accurate figure would be around 21,000.
[c]Penampang first appears as a separate enumeration district in the 1970 census. It incorporates part of the former Kota Belud district, thus the apparent decline indicated here in the Kota Belud population.

siderable movement from rural areas of both coasts to urban areas, mainly to Kota Kinabalu, Sandakan, and Tawau (Table 1.4).

The Bajau population of Sabah in 1970 was divided almost equally between the east and west coasts. By 1991, the largest numbers were found on the east coast particularly in the Semporna district, with smaller numbers in the Sandakan, Lahad Datu, Tawau, and Kudat districts (see Table 1.4). On the west coast, major areas of Bajau settlement are in the Kota Kinabalu, Kota Belud, and Tuaran districts, with smaller numbers in the Papar and Penampang districts. Semporna is the only district in Sabah in which the Bajau form an absolute majority of the population. In 1970, the population of Semporna stood at 24,682 (Malaysia, Department of Statistics, 1972: 87–91), of which Bajau speakers, both Sabah-born and immigrant, comprised approximately 21,000 or 80 per cent of the district's population.[9] By 1980, the population of Semporna district had increased to 52,215 and by 1990 to 91,989 (Malaysia, Department of Statistics, 1993: 11), much of this increase coming from immigration, mainly from the southern Philippines and, to a lesser degree, from eastern Indonesia. Of those arriving from the southern Philippines, the overwhelming majority are Sama–Bajau speakers. In 1991, the Bajau population of Semporna was 42,156. This figure, however, included only Malaysian

TABLE 1.3
Population of Sabah, 1991

Group	Population	Percentage
Indigenous		
Kadazan	114,459	8.2
Dusun	228,948	16.4
Murut	53,880	3.9
Bajau	211,970	15.2
Malay	123,810	8.9
Other Bumiputera	270,473	19.3
Total	1,003,540	71.9
Others		
Chinese	218,233	15.6
Indonesians	142,272	10.2
Indians	9,310	0.7
Others	25,518	1.8
Total	395,333	28.3
Total		
Malaysian Citizens	1,398,ᴫ,ᴶ	100.0
Non-Malaysian Citizens	464,486	
Sabah Total	1,863,359	

Source: Malaysia, Department of Statistics (1995: Vol. 2, 15–17).

Note: The figures and percentages included here are from the adjusted population census
figures for 1991 and, for 'Indigenous' and 'Others', include only Malaysian citizens.

citizens. By this year, the district also had a small Chinese population of
1,149 and 3,587 Indonesians, mainly eastern Indonesian labour migrants.
Over 40 per cent of the district population consisted in 1991 of non-citizens
(Malaysia, Department of Statistics, 1995: Vol. 2, 29), a large proportion of them Bajau speakers. If these latter are added, the total Bajau
population of the district, both citizens and non-citizens, was probably
close to 70,000. In view of its comparatively small area, 1200 square
kilometres, Semporna is one of the most heavily populated districts in
Sabah. In 1970, its population density was 20 persons per square kilometre,
nearly five times that of the state as a whole. In 1990, it was almost 76.

The Physical Setting

Physically, the Semporna district consists of a narrow, mountainous
peninsula, bordered by islands, many of them heavily dotted around
their shoreline with beach- and pile-house villages. The central spine of
the peninsula is formed of high volcanic peaks (455 to 575 metres),
representing, geologically, a continuation of the Sulu tectonic arc that
extends eastward through the Sulu Archipelago of the Philippines (Kirk,
1962: 3). These peaks fall away steeply to the sea on the north and
south and, moving eastward, gradually decrease in height, ending near
the tip of the peninsula in a series of steep volcanic hills. Once separate

TABLE 1.4
Distribution of Bajau Population by District, 1991

District	Population	Population Change[a]
Semporna[b]	42,156	23,851
Kota Kinabalu	23,742	16,073
Sandakan	20,201	17,319
Kota Belud	19,912	8,070
Tuaran	18,478	7,840
Lahad Datu	17,351	14,544
Tawau	17,094	15,842
Papar	9,542	4,878
Penampang	7,552	4,945
Kunak	5,975	5,975
Kota Marudu	5,335	5,335
Beluran	2,727	2,727
Pitas	2,289	2,289
Kudat[c]	4,919	−1,428
Kuala Penyu	1,335	421
Total	211,970	139,647

Source: Data from Malaysia, Department of Statistics, 1972 and 1995.
Notes: The table lists only districts with a Bajau population of more than 1,000 in 1991.
   Total figures are for all districts, hence the larger numbers.
[a]Increase/decrease in population from 1970 to 1991.
[b]These figures underenumerate the Bajau population of the district because they exclude
   non-Malaysian citizens. In 1991, over 40 per cent of the district population consisted of
   non-Malaysian citizens, the majority of them Sama–Bajau speakers. The district total, in
   1995, including both Malaysian citizens and non-citizens, was probably close to 70,000.
[c]The apparent decline in the Kudat population since 1970 is due to the redrawing of
   district boundaries and the creation of the Pitas and Kota Marudu districts from parts of
   the former Kudat district. Similarly, Kunak and Beluran became separate districts only
   after 1970.

islands, these hills are now joined together by narrow, irregular lowlands formed, as a result of a late Pliocene-Quaternary recession of the sea, largely of stranded coral limestone (Kirk, 1962: 30–2).

The district is a region of great scenic beauty, with the bold topography of the interior continuing offshore, through a series of high volcanic islands. Cliff-fringed Gaya Island, with peaks that rise in places almost vertically from the sea to over 300 metres, and neighbouring Bohey Dulang and Tetagan islands, comprise part of the rim of an ancient volcanic crater, now inundated and encircled by coral reefs. Immediately to the west of the Gaya group are several smaller high islands, and beyond them, the larger islands of Silawa, Bait, Pebabag, Puno-Puno, and the largest of all, mountainous Timbun Mata Island which extends offshore along nearly the entire northern coast of the Semporna Peninsula. Mount Sirongal (486 metres), near the eastern tip of Timbun Mata, is the highest offshore point in the district and serves as an important navigational landmark.

An anonymous European observer, writing in 1902, described the district's scenery in the following terms (Anon., 1902: 125):

Many a time ere now have the charms of this lovely stretch of coast been eulogized, but we cannot refrain from passing reference to the subject fresh in our mind's eye. From Lahad Datu onward a most picturesque coast-line is presented to view not the least beautiful portion of which being the verdant green of the south-east corner of Timba Mata [Timbun Mata]. But the distant view of Pulo Gaia [Pulau Gaya] far out to sea is alone well worth the trip itself. This island gives one the impression of having been split by some great revulsion of nature and its dizzy crags upon which even luxurious tropical vegetation is unable to obtain a foothold presents a very bold appearance.

At the time of this observer's visit, the Semporna Bajau Laut were still boat-living, and he goes on to describe their presence as one of the additional 'attractions' of the district.

The fact that this and the many other beautiful islands around Trusan Treacher are the haunts of those peculiar people, the sea-Bajaus or sea-Gypsies who lead a nomadic life in their quaint boats and who only go ashore to get wood, water and turtles' eggs adds to one's desire to visit and explore these savage wilds for a season. One shudders to think of 'the things as goes on' in these little colonies of boats which are now anchored behind one island and next day somewhere else, over reefs where no *kapal prang* [warship] can get at them. These seas simply teem with fish and the Bajau spends most of his time in collecting large stocks of sea produce, *bêche-de-mer* and *tripang* which he exchanges in Semporna for rice and other attractive commodities.

Along the southern edge of the peninsula is a chain of several small high islands, Menampilik, Nusa Tengah, and Si Amil. Interspersed with these, and with the Gaya group to the east, are more numerous low islands of stranded coral limestone. The largest and most important are Bumbum Island, the largest and most densely populated in the district, lying just off the eastern shore of the Semporna Peninsula; smaller Omadal Island to the south; and Larapan Island to the north. Surrounding these low coralline islands and parts of the peninsula coastline are fringing reefs and extensive formations of coral shoals and terraces.

By Borneo standards, Semporna has a relatively dry climate, with little seasonality. Annual rainfall at Semporna town averages 2150 millimetres (Kirk, 1962: 15; Paton, 1963: 5). Rainfall is generally erratic, varying in any given month from 0 to 380 millimetres. The coastal lowlands and lower offshore islands are significantly drier than the peninsula interior and periodically experience severe droughts lasting for up to three or four months. At such times, fresh water becomes scarce as island wells, springs, and other sources dry up.

Most rain falls in brief but heavy downpours. At the sign of an impending shower, or when winds begin to rise, the Bajau Laut normally suspend fishing and drive their boats close inshore, taking down sails and putting up palm-frond roofing (*sapau*) for shelter. During heavy rains, boats must be bailed repeatedly to prevent them from swamping and so from losing decking planks, oars, poles, and other gear. Downpours are particularly frequent in the evening and at night, leaving the days generally sunny and hot (Paton, 1963: 5). Daily temperatures are uniformly high, with the daily mean ranging from 24 to 33 °C (Kirk, 1962: 15). Although the climate is not monsoonal, the monsoons mark a significant shift in the direction of prevailing winds. The south-west monsoon usually blows from May to November, the north-east monsoon from January to March. While there is no well-defined wet or dry season, slightly more rain tends to fall during the south-west monsoon, while January and February are usually the driest months.

The population of the Semporna district is heavily concentrated along the coastal lowlands, immediate strand, and offshore islands. Unlike other parts of Sabah, the district had no agricultural hinterland in the past and, until road construction began in the mid-1960s, the interior of the district was entirely uninhabited. The natural climax vegetation over most of the interior is tropical hill and lowland dipterocarp forest (Paton, 1963: 17). However, logging has now denuded the district of its original forest cover. The British Borneo Timber Company began logging operations in the Semporna district in the late 1920s (North Borneo, 1929: 3), but large-scale felling began only in the early 1960s, culminating in a ten-year post-independence timber boom (1963–73), during which time virtually all marketable timber was removed. In addition to the dipterocarp forests, there are narrow bands of nipa (*pagung*) and mangrove (*bangkau*) forest along embayed sections of the coastline, and in the Sipit, Pegagau, and smaller river estuaries.

In earlier times, before the coastal forests were entirely cleared, the Bajau Laut made use of the many small tidal streams that lace the peninsula lowlands to fell trees, using the high tide to float out logs which, towed back to the village anchorage, they worked into boat-building timbers, keel sections, and planks. They also cut bamboo for poles, spear shafts, and mast spars. Beginning in the mid-1960s, the Sabah state government opened a series of agricultural schemes on the Semporna Peninsula which were intended to draw people from the outer islands of the district and resettle them inland on lands newly cleared of forest, thereby continuing a policy begun, more than half a century earlier, by the British North Borneo Chartered Company. Around Tagasan, Kubang Baru, and Rancangan Perempatan, land was planted with oil palm, near Sinallang with rubber, and at Tanjung Kapur with coconuts. Later, with government assistance, cocoa was also planted. Where the state government built housing, settlement was generally dispersed on individual landholdings, a pattern in sharp contrast to the strongly aggregated nature of traditional Bajau settlement. Large numbers of island people, mainly from Bumbum, Dinawan, Silawa, Larapan, and Menampilik, were resettled on these schemes, marking a significant shift of district population toward the peninsula and away from the outer islands. Roads were built joining these schemes to Semporna town, and in 1966 the first overland trunk road was completed, connecting Semporna to Lahad Datu to the north and to the administrative centre of the residency, Tawau, to the south-east. Previously, all travel in and out of the district was by sea (Rutter, 1922: 42). In the 1960s, a small-craft air service was also introduced and in 1979 there were three weekly flights connecting Semporna

with Tawau, Lahad Datu, and Sandakan. Until these developments, virtually all local travel in the district was by sea. The principal means of
communication for many villagers is still the sea and at most times of the
day the surrounding waters are dotted with small boats, some powered,
others under sail, plying between the coastline and offshore islands or,
further out to sea, sailing from island to island.

In 1979, the Bajau population of the district was divided between a
sizeable urban community of over 4,000, living in Semporna town and
its outskirts, and a highly diverse coastal population divided between
nearly sixty villages, most of them compact pile-house settlements built
over the sea or along the immediate strand. Large, aggregated settlements
have traditionally been favoured locally for reasons of security and because
political leadership is based chiefly on localized kindred support. In a
region of endemic piracy, larger settlements have historically been easier
to defend than smaller, dispersed ones, while localized, preferentially
endogamous kin groups have comprised, and continue to form, the primary units of local political support. On the coastal lowlands and more
heavily settled islands, coconuts (*seloka*) formed the principal cash crop
during the 1964–79 period, while cassava (*panggi kayu*; *Manihot* spp.),
grown in smaller plots, was the chief dietary staple. A small amount of
rice (*pai*) was grown chiefly by *Sama Buna-Buna'an* cultivators on
southern Timbun Mata Island and near Lihak-Lihak on the Semporna
Peninsula. Fruit trees, including papaya, bananas, rambutan, *langsat*, jack-
fruit, limes, and other citrus fruits, were planted surrounding most shore
villages. Fishing was a major economic activity; in 1964, according to a
State Fisheries Department survey (Goh, 1964), Semporna had a greater
proportion of fishermen per capita than any other district in Sabah.

In 1965, the Bajau Laut population of the district was 660. It was
divided between two pile-house villages. Bangau-Bangau, the larger, with
a population of 510, was located near the northern tip of the Semporna
Peninsula, while the second, Labuan Haji, was situated directly across
the Tandu Bulong Channel, on the north-western tip of Bumbum Island
(see Map 1.2). Each settlement contained, in addition to its house-living
families, a small boat-dwelling population, totalling, between the two
settlements, twenty-five to thirty families. The present study deals
primarily with Bangau-Bangau, which by 1979 had a population of 1,982.
The settlement has since been divided into two villages, Kampung
Bangau-Bangau and Kampung Sri Kanangan. There is also a new (fourth)
village, Kampung Halo, connected by a stilt-bridge to Kampung Sri
Kanangan, comprising Bajau Laut refugees from the Philippines.

An Ethnic Mosaic: Sea and Shore People in Semporna

South-eastern Sabah lies strategically at the juncture of the Sulu Archipelago of the Philippines and the eastern coast of Borneo. Within the
region, the Semporna district, with its bridging peninsula, offshore
islands, and rich 'coral gardens', has long been a focus of marine
settlement and a channel of sea-going trade between the island world of
Sulu and the eastern coastal districts of Borneo (Sather, 1984: 8–11).

During the early decades of the nineteenth century, the district served as an important conduit of regional commerce. From Idahan settlements to the north came forest products, beeswax, camphor, and birds' nests, and from the Tidong districts to the south came rice and sago. Transhipped through the district, these goods moved on to markets in central Sulu. In the opposite direction flowed slaves and imported goods, the former coming mainly from slaving communities in central and northern Sulu and destined chiefly for Bulungan and the smaller Bugis markets of eastern Kalimantan to the south. From Semporna itself came sea products, notably *bêche-de-mer*, dried fish, and turtle eggs, destined chiefly for Sulu.

The earliest published source to mention sea nomads in reference to what is almost certainly the Semporna region is a report written by Hermann von Dewall, a German ethnographer who was the first European officer to be posted to East Kalimantan by the Dutch East Indies government. In his report, Dewall mentioned the arrival in May 1849 of eighteen Bajau boats at Pulau Panjang, on the north-eastern Kalimantan coast, from what he called 'the Sulu island of Dinawan' (*solokhsche eiland Dinawan*) (Dewall, 1855: 447). The reference is probably to Dinawan (or Danawan) Island, which, at the time, was an important centre of Sulu authority in the Semporna district. The island lies near the edge of the main Bajau Laut fishing grounds in the Semporna region, the Ligitan reefs, near the district's southern frontier, directly north along the coast from Pulau Panjang. In the early nineteenth century, leaders of the Dinawan community are said to have held a concession grant from the Sultan of Sulu giving them exclusive rights to collect and trade in sea-turtle eggs from nearby Sipadan Island. Dinawan was thus a place of some significance. In addition to Sulu, its leadership maintained political connections with Bulungan.[10] In this light, it is worth recounting Dewall's report in full (Dewall, 1855: 445-7).[11]

The Bajaus. This curious wandering tribe (*volkstam*), who might be called the 'gitanos', the gypsies or pagans of the archipelago, are described in Part XVII of *Verhandelingen van het Bataviaasch Genootschap* by J. N. Vosmaer [1839]. His comments, however, apply only to the south-eastern peninsula of Sulawesi. Our comments here relate to that part of this tribe who live, or were living in 1849, along the north-eastern coast of Borneo.

On the first of January of that year [1849] about 20 boats or families lived on the south-west side of Pulau Panjang Island. They were under the authority of two chiefs, who assumed the titles of *penggawa* and *panglima muda*. Of all these people, only two families lived on land in two houses; the rest lived in boats. Every family provided the Sultan of Gunong Tebur with an annual tribute of 12 *katis* of *tripang* and 100 dried fish, for which they received in return cloth and agricultural produce. They bartered for rice in Berau. The Bajau also trade with the people of Berau and Kutai, and with the inhabitants of the west coast of Sulawesi, who come to Pulau Panjang to collect sea products from the area. In earlier times, boats from Sulu came to Pulau Panjang to fight over these products. Also pirates from Balangingi (*zeeschuimers van Blahnjiehnjeh*) who harried the Bajaus, so that they moved away to Tondoni and Toli-Toli on the coast of Sulawesi up until last year, when they returned again to Pulau Panjang. Here they have not been disturbed since then. They fly a Dutch flag to show that they have surrendered to the 'Company' and the *panggawa* [*penggawa*] has an open letter from the king of Gowa, which is used as a kind of passport or recommendation. About twenty Bajau families also live in the islands to the south of the Kuran River (under Tanjung); their leaders are Sri-Bangsawan and Pakassah.

The Bajau came originally from Johore ... they settled down along the coastal areas of Borneo, Sulawesi, and in the Sulu Archipelago. Most of them live on the Sulu island of Dinawan. In general they inhabit the islands along the northeastern coast of Borneo. In May of 1849, 18 Bajau boats came from Dinawan and established themselves at Pulau Panjang, while others, 50 boats, settled in the islands of Berau.

The Bajau are probably related to the Orang Laut of the Malay Archipelago. They are Mohammedans and born seafarers. In the Malay Archipelago they are called the Orang Raja; on Billiton they are called the Orang Seka; and in other places the Orang Johore; in Makassar they are called Tau-ri-djene, while the Javanese call them Orang Kambang, floating-people. A full description of their customs and practices is given by Vosmaer.... There are no Bajau in Bulungan, but there are in Berau.

Bulungan and Berau were petty kingdoms on the east coast of Kalimantan south of the present Sabah border. In the third paragraph, it is not clear from Dewall's account whether the additional fifty boats he mentions also arrived from Dinawan, although this is suggested. The reference is interesting in that the Semporna Bajau Laut, according to oral tradition, claim to have made regular voyages until the 1920s to the areas of eastern Kalimantan referred to by Dewall. Some of this voyaging is said to have occurred on an annual basis, exploiting the monsoon winds. From eastern Kalimantan, Bajau Laut fleets regularly crossed the Straits of Makassar to southern Sulawesi where they visited Sama Dilaut communities; here they were received with hospitality, often by kinsmen. If the identification of Dinawan is correct, Dewall's account suggests that during the early nineteenth century, Semporna may well have served as a rendezvous and staging point from which Bajau Laut fleets sailed southward into Indonesian waters. This would corroborate local Bajau Laut oral tradition which points to regular contacts in the past between Semporna and Bajau Laut settlements in the Straits of Makassar.[12] Sometime prior to the Japanese Occupation, older villagers say, this pattern of long-distance voyaging ceased.

The Bajau population of Semporna, as of the Sulu Archipelago beyond, is fragmented into a number of named subgroups, each associated with a particular island homeland, place of origin, or area of local settlement. In the past, none of these subgroups was large enough to function as an independent political entity. At the same time, each was, and remains to some degree, interlinked with others by a pattern of exchange-related economic specialization. Some groups focus their economic life primarily ashore, as agriculturalists; others specialize in boat-building, pottery-making, pandanus mat-weaving, metal-working, and other artisan crafts; or operate chiefly at sea, as fishermen or inter-island traders. As sea nomads, the Bajau Laut were in some respects the most specialized and exchange-dependent of all these subgroups. Living in small boat-

dwelling bands, local Bajau Laut communities were identified with permanent anchorage sites through which they maintained long-term
exchange relations with neighbouring communities ashore. While these
exchange relations were extensive, and involved a number of different
shore groups, they were none the less mediated, in the case of each individual anchorage site, by a principal patron who guaranteed his clients'
physical security in return for a privileged trading relationship. In the
past, patrons were also channels of tribute and formed the principal
links between the Bajau Laut and the Sulu State which, until the end of
the nineteenth century, exercised loose political control over the district.
Essential to this system of inter-group specialization was the existence of
a regional network of exchange relations based on barter called *magsam-
bi* (Sather, 1985: 168–72).

Within the Semporna district, the Sama (or *a'a*) Sikubang was and
remains the largest subgroup within this exchange-related mosaic. Sikubang
villages are found chiefly on Omadal Island, Larapan, and around the
southern, northern, and eastern coasts of Bumbum Island.[13] The group
takes its name from the region in which the oldest of these settlements
are concentrated, Omadal Island and along the closely facing southern
shore of Bumbum Island (see Map 1.2). Because of the numerical
dominance of the Sikubang group, and its long association with the
region, the whole Semporna district was formerly known to other Sama
speakers as Kubang, and the Sama Sikubang were regarded, and continue to be seen by others, as the original Sama inhabitants of the district.
Older Bajau Laut still use the name Kubang, as a geographical term,
to refer to the Semporna region. According to Sikubang oral tradition,
the island of Omadal was granted to the Kubang people ten to eleven
generations ago by the Sultan of Sulu. Most other Bajau communities in
the district go back five or six generations at most, and many are considerably more recent. In general, the Sikubang people have favoured
island settlement for reasons of economic self-sufficiency, living in most
cases on the immediate foreshore, where they are able to exploit the
resources of both the land and the sea. In 1964–5, most Sikubang communities consisted of mixed fishing and agricultural villages. With the
development of a copra industry in the early twentieth century, coconut
palms were extensively planted and today cover most Sikubang land in
the district.

However, the Kubang group has also a long connection with trade.
Until the mid-nineteenth century, the Kubang settlement at Omadal was
an important staging port, easily defended because of its surrounding
reef, that served as a transhipment point for goods from the adjacent
Borneo coast, notably birds' nests and forest and sea products. Regular
trading voyages were also made from Omadal northward along the
eastern Sabah coast and southward to east Kalimantan and Makassar.
Following the establishment of Chartered Company rule, Sikubang
traders became active in the local inter-island carrier trade, dealing, in
the early days of Company rule, primarily in copra and dried fish.
Because of their numbers, they also later gained political control of the

district after first resisting the Company government. To a large extent, leaders of the community continue to hold this control.

Despite the predominantly mixed nature of the Kubang economy, there was also a marked element of economic specialization within the group linked to the community's role in regional trade. The most highly specialized communities were artisan settlements located around the north-eastern shore of Bumbum Island. In stranded coral inlets behind Sisipan Island were pile-house and strand villages whose population, lacking other resources, traditionally gained a major share of its live-lihood as smiths, woodcarvers, and boatwrights. Kubang woodcarvers in these villages traditionally supplied others in the district, including the Bajau Laut, with grave markers and finely made boats. They also pro-duced tortoiseshell pendants and combs, and were the principal black-smiths regionally, making fish-spears, hooks, tridents, knife blades, adzes, and other tools for virtually all other Sama subgroups in the district. In 1964–5, the Bajau Laut population of Bangau-Bangau still obtained their fish-spears, knives, and metal household implements from Sikubang smiths operating village forges on Bumbum Island. In addition, Sama Dilaut boat-dwellers from as far away as Tongkallong and Tongbangkau in the Tawitawi island group visited Sikubang boat-wrights on Bumbum Island to purchase boats. In 1965, at any given time, usually two or three boat-dwelling families could be seen anchored along the nearby reefs waiting to take delivery of a completed boat.[14]

Several Kubang villages notably Tongkalloh, and to a lesser degree, Hampalan and Sulabayan also specialized in fishing. Tongkalloh village is located at the extreme south-western corner of Bumbum Island, at the edge of Creagh Reef. At low tide, a vast area of reef terrace is uncovered, extending nearly 3 kilometres from Tongkalloh headlands to Karindingan Island. A shallow, branching channel runs across this area, connecting the main reef to the open sea. The Tongkalloh and Hampalan villagers set nets across the channel during falling tides, when fish attracted to the reefs seek to return to the open sea. Netting yields large, reliable landings and in the past the villagers exchanged their surplus with other commu-nities within the region.

A number of Sama subgroups from southern Sulu maintained trading enclaves in Semporna in the past, usually operating from boats. How-ever, permanent migration to the district appears to have begun only during the early nineteenth century, when the Sultan of Sulu, under siege by the Spanish, issued a series of title grants to Bajau leaders, most from the Tawitawi island group of Sulu, giving them rights to settle with their followers on specific islands or areas of coastline. One major group to arrive at this time was the Sama Buna-Buna'an, from the Buna-Buna'an region of Bilatan Island. They settled on Silawa, Bait, Pebabak, and Selangan islands, and along the adjoining northern coast of the Semporna Peninsula. Unlike other Bajau groups in the district, the Buna-Buna'an people were chiefly agriculturalists and so became the major local suppliers of agricultural produce, including rice. In addition, the Buna-Buna'an village of Limau-Limau was, until the mid-1960s, the chief centre of local thatch-making in Semporna. The Limau-Limau people gathered nipah fronds from the swamps at Gading-Gading, Sungai Sega-rong, and along the lower reaches of the Pegagau River; they stitched the fronds into thatching which they traded as roofing material throughout the Semporna region and northward into the Lahad Datu district.

Further west, the people of Tampé Kapur, on the Semporna Penin-sula facing Pebabag Island, specialized in the production of earthenware pottery. In 1979, they were still producing this pottery, although on a much reduced scale. Their products traditionally included water jars, cooking pots, and, most importantly, portable hearths (lappohan). The latter, carried by the Bajau Laut aboard their boats, were used for cooking at sea. The Sama Banaran community at Labusai, tracing its origin to Banaran Island in the Tawitawi group, formerly specialized in the manufacture of sapau roofing mats made from the fronds of the coastal tigul palm (unidentified) and in the jungle collection of rattan (buai) and resin (butik). In 1964–5, sapau mats were used by the Bajau Laut to roof the living quarters of their boats, while resin was traded locally as a boat-caulking material. The Sama Banaran formed two communities in Semporna, one at Labusai, the other at Tabak-Tabak, on the south-eastern shore of Bumbum Island. In the pre-Company period, the Sama Banaran were also active slave raiders. Another early community in Semporna was Dinawan (or Danawan). As noted earlier, leaders of the Dinawan settlement, some of whom traced Tausug ancestry, were responsible in the past for overseeing the collection and trade in sea-turtle eggs from Sipadan Island, now part of a recently established marine park.

Just before the turn of the century with the establishment of Semporna town as a regional port of trade, a second wave of Bajau migration began. Among these migrants were several specialized trading communities. The Sama Sikubung, from Sikubung Island in Sulu, established their principal settlement, together with a smaller community of Sama Ubian, at Trusan Baru, on Bumbum Island, immediately across the Tandu Bulong Straits from Semporna town. The Sikubung were early copra traders who operate today chiefly as inter-island traders. Another com-mercial group, the Sama Simunul, settled chiefly in and around Semporna town. Simunul migration is said to have been initially prompted by the introduction of compulsory public education by American colonial authorities in the southern Philippines. As a religiously conservative group, many Simunul trading families migrated from Sulu to Semporna and other east coast towns, including Lahad Datu and Sandakan, in order to avoid secular schooling, particularly for girls. Smuggling has also long been a major economic activity in south-eastern Sabah, and since the beginning of this century, the Sama Simunul have played a major role in this trade on both sides of the Malaysian–Philippine border. Sama Sibutu, coming from nearby Sibutu Island, settled chiefly in the Kampung Air section of Semporna town.

Historically, these separate Bajau subgroups were joined locally in an inter-ethnic division of labour. Chapter 2 situates these relations histor-ically, showing how, within this division of labour, patron–client rela-tions linked the Bajau Laut not only to other communities within the district, but also to a wider field of political and economic relations that extended well beyond Semporna. Patronage was also central to the social identity of the Bajau Laut, for it was largely through specific patron–client relations that sea and shore people were brought into sustained contact in ways that tended to define their mutual status.

1. I have substantially revised these estimates from my dissertation and earlier publications (Sather, 1971b; 1975a; 1978) in the light of more recent population figures, particularly for the Philippines and Indonesia.

2. I am grateful to Robert Nicholl (pers. comm.) for pointing out the significance of this genealogy and confirming the dates cited here. Brunei genealogies not only establish an early Malay use of the term 'Bajau' but also suggest that Bajau settlements were present in Sabah by at least the early sixteenth century and probably earlier. This early date is supported by current linguistic evidence (see 'The People: Sama Origins').

3. I wish to thank Christian Pelras for drawing my attention to this important source and others relating to eastern Indonesia.

4. *Ling*, speech, language; *aheling* (verb form), to speak.

5. In a parallel way, Pallesen (1985: 249) suggests that dried fish, supplied by Orang Laut fishermen, was similarly an important export item to the early Malay states, contributing to their initial growth as commercial powers.

6. Independently, Harrisson (1973–4: 39–40) has proposed that Bajau mariners, dealing in Chinese import goods, were engaged in early trade in the Sarawak river delta and possibly other parts of coastal Borneo prior to the rise of the Sulu Sultanate.

7. Nimmo (1990: 12) records an almost identical version of this myth from Tawitawi (see also Bottignolo, 1995: 25). Versions of the giant ray and storm myths appear to be told throughout the whole Sulu–Semporna region (Nimmo, 1990: 12–13).

8. The source for the version presented here is Panglima Haji Jammal bin Panglima Bandal of Kampung Bait, Semporna. Elsewhere (Sather, 1984: 13) I have published a summarized form of this myth. The opening episode of this tradition, the attempted assault on the Prophet's wife, appears to be remarkably widely distributed. Sandbukt (1982: 4–5) records a similar myth for the Duano, which, apparently, the Duano themselves share (see Chapter 10). Evans (1953: 490–1) records a Dusun version from the Kota Belud district of Sabah told in apparent explanation of the Bajau practice of circumcision (that is, clawing the penis).

9. Officially, the Bajau numbered 18,305 in Semporna according to the 1970 census; however, included in the district population was also a separate category of 'Philippine Natives', the great majority of whom were also 'Bajau', hence the higher estimate. Since 1970, immigration into Semporna has accelerated, as reflected in the 1991 census figures.

10. These connections are the source of a current diplomatic dispute between Malaysia and Indonesia regarding the sovereignty status of Sipadan Island.

11. For this English translation, from the original Dutch, I wish to thank Ria van der Zandt, Research School of Pacific and Asian Studies, Australian National University, and Dr K. A. Adelaar, Department of Language Studies, Melbourne University.

12. My original fieldwork took place during the Kronfrontasi period when it was not possible to travel into Indonesian waters from Malaysia or to visit border areas where there was military action. I did, however, sail several times with Bajau Laut families into the Celebes Sea on fishing voyages; at night we sometimes watched the flashes of naval batteries firing around Sebatik Island on the Kalimantan border.

13. It is worth noting that possible cognate terms appear elsewhere; thus Bajau living in the vicinity of Manado are known locally as 'Bajo Kobang' (Pelras, pers. comm.).

14. Sikubang boatwrights may have developed the *lepa*, which was in 1964–5, the distinctive vessel of the Semporna Bajau Laut (see Chapter 4).

2

History of the Semporna
Bajau Laut: From Sea Nomads
to Settled Villagers

The most industrious and useful race of men about Sulo and the circum-adjacent islands, are the Bajows or orang laut; to these men Sulo is principally indebted for her submarine wealth. (J. Hunt, 1967.)

MARITIME cultural traditions have deep historical roots in south-eastern Sabah. Recent archaeological findings reveal the presence of coastal-adapted people in the Semporna district, already engaged in long-distance voyaging and exploiting both the sea and immediate shoreline 3,000 years ago (Bellwood, 1989; Bellwood and Koon, 1989). With the later intensification of trade, particularly with China during the Sung (960–1279) and Yuan (1280–1368) periods, the eastern coastal waters of Borneo became increasingly linked to a growing network of commercial traffic then connecting insular South-East Asia, China, and the south and south-east Asian mainland. Sometime between the tenth and thirteenth centuries, the central islands of the Sulu Archipelago, most notably Jolo, emerged as a major focus of regional trade. The presence of early Ming and Sawankhalok porcelains in archaeological sites in the Lahad Datu district, immediately north of Semporna, suggests that by the early fifteenth century, the eastern coast of Sabah was part of this emergent sphere of maritime trade and sea-going contact (Harrisson and Harrisson, 1971: 221–3).

Sama–Bajau speakers almost certainly played a role in these developments. Linguistic evidence suggests that 800 years ago, Sama–Bajau speakers had spread down through the Sulu Archipelago and had begun to settle the far northern and eastern coasts of Borneo. These movements appear to have been related to a growth in maritime trade. This trade may have initially involved only a relatively simple protein-starch exchange, with Sama speakers contributing chiefly fish. However, once dispersal began and the Sama succeeded in establishing a network of maritime settlements and ports of call, they were well positioned, as Pallesen (1985: 245) has argued, to take advantage of subsequent developments in trade. Harrisson (1973–4) believes that Bajau mariners in coastal Borneo pioneered the early distribution of Chinese trade goods, which he speculates may have been carried initially, not by Chinese traders directly, but by Bajau seafarers and middlemen. While the evidence for this remains inconclusive, it is clear that by the time of the first European penetration of insular South-East Asia, Bajau speakers were an already widely dispersed population, internally diverse and heavily engaged in sea-going commerce. Early European observers frequently remarked on their notable trade dependence, describing many local communities as relying on trade even for subsistence goods (Pryer, 1887; Hunt, 1967).

Bajau society, in addition to being geographically dispersed, appears from the earliest European accounts of the sixteenth and seventeenth centuries to have also been highly fissiparous. Linguistically heterogeneous, Sama–Bajau populations were historically, and still are, highly fragmented, being divided into a multitude of distinct subgroups, all locally named and most geographically interspersed with one another and with non-Sama-speaking peoples as well. Many of these smaller communities are heavily trade-dependent and, taken together, have adapted themselves to an array of diverse coastal and island environments. By accommodating this heterogeneity, Sama–Bajau society has taken on a form particularly suited to a dispersed population, one spread over a vast maritime landscape of islands and shoreline, much of it possessing only very limited natural resources. Through sea travel, members of different groups maintain trading links with one another while, at the same time, differentiating themselves into smaller groups through their identification with more narrowly defined home islands, places of origin, or within these areas, adaptive, trade-related specializations. These smaller groups, while the primary focus of social and political loyalties, are, by their nature, easily re-defined as populations disperse, become separated over time, or establish themselves in new centres of settlement. The chief internal dynamic appears to be one of social and geographic proliferation.

Finally, among all these groups, the most mobile, the sea nomads, distinguish themselves not by the name of a particular island or island group, but by identification with the sea itself, as 'sea people' (a'a dilaut). As a consequence, the nomadic Sama possessed the most readily transportable identity of all, one capable of being carried in the past virtually anywhere within the entire vast archipelagic world inhabited by Sama–Bajau speakers.

While well adapted to dispersion, this pattern of overall community organization characterizing the Bajau appears to have been eminently ill suited to large-scale political integration. Political loyalties are locally focused and none of the subgroups in which they are centred were large enough in the past to have functioned as independent political entities, nor did there exist within the Sama–Bajau population internal relations of authority capable of welding these different groups together into a wider political unity. Political integration, when it occurred, was historically imposed from the outside, by members of other ethnic groups.

Sea Nomads in the Pre-colonial Sulu Sultanate

By the early fourteenth century, several of the petty states then dominating local trade in the southern Philippine–Borneo region appear to have grown increasingly centralized. In the process, scattered Sama-speaking groups came to be subordinated locally within a number of emerging maritime polities, all dominated by other ethnic groups—Tausug, Magindanao, Brunei, Bugis, and others. In the Sulu Archipelago, the dominant group to emerge in this process was the Tausug, a populous, largely agrarian people occupying mainly the larger central islands of the Sulu Archipelago, in particular Jolo.

These developments appear to have coincided, as in many other parts of insular South-East Asia, with the spread of Islam. The date of the earliest Islamic penetration of the Sulu region is uncertain, but initial contact possibly began in late Sung times, when Arab merchants opened direct trading links with southern China by way of the Sulu Archipelago (Sather, 1993c: 262). There is also evidence of early proselytizing by Chinese Muslims who came to dominate China's maritime commerce with the southern Philippines after the thirteenth century (Majul, 1966a, 1966b). Tausug genealogical histories (*tarsila*) also suggest proselytizing connections with Brunei and the Malay Peninsula, especially with Johore (Saleeby, 1905). The Sulu Sultanate was formally founded in the mid-fifteenth century, putatively by the legendary Salip (Sharif) Abu Bakkar or Sultan Shariful Hashim. With the establishment of the sultanate the Tausug consolidated their ascendancy and furthered their social and economic differentiation from the Sama-speaking 'Samal'. Through its control of trade, the sultanate gained power and extended its authority not only among the numerically dominant Tausug, but also over peripheral ethnic groups living primarily at the geographical and political fringes of the state, including the nomadic Bajau Laut.

Following Spain's colonization of the Philippines in the sixteenth century, the Spanish and the Tausug began 300 years of almost continuous warfare. Despite occasional setbacks, Sulu preserved its independence and, indeed, reached the peak of its power in the eighteenth and early nineteenth centuries, at a time when most other indigenous states in the region were in decline or in the process of European subjugation. In 1876, Spanish troops succeeded in occupying Jolo town, where they established a permanent garrison for the first time. However, Spanish authority scarcely extended beyond the town's walls. After Spain's defeat in the Spanish–American War, American troops occupied Jolo town in 1899, but stiff resistance prevented them from gaining control of the interior of the island until 1913. During this time, Sulu Province was ruled by an American military administration. In 1915, Sultan Jamal ul-Kiram II relinquished all secular power, although retaining a religious role, which still survives, thereby bringing to an end the Sulu Sultanate as a formal political power.

Politically, until the end of the nineteenth century, when the surrounding region was partitioned between American and European colonial powers, the south-eastern coast of Sabah was part of a larger political sphere centred in the adjoining Sulu Archipelago of the Philippines, but which, at various times, extended beyond Sulu to eastern Palawan, the south-western foreshore of Mindanao, and the north-eastern coast of Borneo. This sphere formed what the historian James Warren (1981: xxi) has called the 'Sulu Zone', a complex maritime region dominated by the Sulu Sultanate, as its prime redistributive centre, through which 'a loosely integrated political system ... embraced island and coastal populace, maritime, nomadic fishermen, and slash and burn agriculturalists ... provid[ing] a sociocultural context for intersocietal relations and commerce within the [Sulu] state and beyond....' (Warren, 1981: xxi.) Until the beginning of the twentieth century, the Semporna district came within the southern margins of this zone.

Power, Rank, and Ethnicity in Sulu

Thomas Kiefer (1972a, 1972b) has described the traditional Sulu Sultanate as a 'segmentary state', that is, a state composed of sub-units which are structurally and functionally equivalent at every level of the political system (Southall, n.d.). At each level, leaders exercise the same powers and responsibilities. Centralized government exists, but peripheral sub-units, although acknowledging its presence, are largely independent of the centre. Territorial sovereignty is recognized, but is strong only at the centre of the state, fading to a largely ritual hegemony in its outlying districts (Kiefer, 1972a; 1972b: 109).

Throughout the Sulu region, corporate institutions appear to have been weakly developed in the past. The traditional political system was founded on dyadic bonds and operated chiefly through networks of person-to-person alliances, rather than through a formal administrative hierarchy (Kiefer, 1972b: 105–6). An individual's primary loyalties were to his immediate leader. Power was correspondingly diffuse and authority in the sultanate 'was predicated on factional politics and revolved around highly variable leader-centred groups' (Warren, 1981: xxii). The position of an individual leader within this factional hierarchy was based primarily on the size of the following he could mobilize at any given moment. Friendship and patronage linked smaller groups to larger ones in an ever ramifying, pyramidal series of alliances that encompassed the entire sultanate, running from village headmen and local chiefs at its base to the sultan and his kindred at the apex of the system.

Reflecting the 'segmentary' nature of the sultanate,

there [were] no political powers available to the sultan which [were] not available to a lesser extent to each of the regional and community headmen. While the sultan possesse[d] a religious role and prestige which [was] denied to lower headmen ... this prestige [while] quite useful ... [did] not give him any formal political authority which [did] not have its counterpart on the local level (Kiefer, 1972b: 109).

Indeed, particularly powerful local leaders occasionally appropriated a degree of authority theoretically belonging only to the sultan. This was particularly so in the frontier regions of the Sulu zone such as coastal Borneo.

Kiefer (1972b: 109) notes that the sultan and the village headman were 'mirror images of each other; both hav[ing essentially] the same rights and obligations vis-à-vis the political system'. He identifies eight of these rights and obligations as primary:

1. Right to perform legal functions;
2. Right to appoint and regulate religious officials;
3. Right to control territory;
4. Right to control subject people;
5. Right to wage external warfare;
6. Right to tribute and legal fees;
7. Right to control markets; and
8. Right to mediate private feuds (Kiefer, 1972b: 110–11).

In exercising these rights, the sultan, like lesser leaders, had

to depend on the extent and range of his own alliance network.... [W]hile all headmen [gave] at least some nominal loyalty to the sultan..., some [were] clearly more active in their support than others. In the traditional Tausug state, power was more fully concentrated at the bottom of the system—at the community level—and then diffused upward in an ever more precarious system of alliances (Kiefer, 1972b: 109).

The sultan, as a bestower of titles and in his symbolic role as head of an Islamic state, nevertheless exercised certain unique functions not performed by lesser leaders. Thus, while power moved upward

and ultimately cumulate[d] in the sultan, the symbols of authority [titles and the power they symbolize] diffuse[d] downward. The sultanate provide[d] the prestige for political authority and delegate[d] this prestige to various local officials, while the local officials in turn [gave] up some of their *de facto* power through [their] support of the sultan (Kiefer, 1972b: 109).

Historically, Sama speakers formed a subordinate population in Sulu. However, the Semporna district, lying at the periphery of the Sulu zone, differed from the central islands of the Sulu Archipelago in that the sultan's commission, as ultimate 'owner' of the region's inhabitants, was exercised through Bajau, rather than Tausug leaders. In the past, no significant numbers of Tausug were present in Semporna, the district's population being almost entirely Sama–Bajau speakers. In Semporna, the power of the sultanate was represented primarily by local Bajau leaders, village headmen, and regional chiefs. The most powerful of these were invested by the sultan with titles (for example, *panglima, olang kaya, marahajja, settia,* and others) which legitimized their exercise of political rights over local populations living within a particular area of coastline, an island, or group of islands, including rights over subject peoples, among them local communities of Sama Dilaut (Sather, 1984: 10–11). Investitures were often accompanied by a letter of entitlement (*surat*) and carried with them the expectation that the recipient would collect tribute (*sukai*), maintain order among his followers, hold court (*maghukum*), and provide favourable conditions for trade. There was also an expectation that the title-bearer would make periodic visits to the court seat of Jolo.

Although strongly centralized as a state, the Sulu Sultanate was throughout its history a loosely structured polity. Not only were individual Sama admitted to positions of power, but there was also considerable vertical mobility. Titles were generally conferred by the sultan in acknowledgement of the power which a leader had previously achieved by his own efforts. As a result, the ranking of titles gave a rough indication of the power of individual leaders and their relative position *vis-à-vis* others within the alliance pyramid. In legitimizing delegations of authority, titles also helped to secure the loyalty of peripheral leaders to the sultan, as the former gained authority from the prestige which a title conferred. Peripheral leaders thus had an interest in preserving this prestige and so the authority of the sultan.

Supporting the position of the sultan, and this hierarchical network of leader-centred alliances, was a system of ranking. Prestige, which attached primarily to titles and those who bestowed them, was perpetuated by a formal ranking system. In theory, the sultan was the supreme sovereign and the source of all political rights within the sultanate. Some of these rights he delegated to subordinate leaders by investing them with titles; others he reserved for himself or his kindred. The sultan, his kindred, and other hereditary title-bearers constituted what Kiefer (1972b: 30) has called an 'aristocratic estate'. Aristocrats dominated the political system, particularly at its geographical centre where the Tausug were numerically dominant. Beneath the aristocrats were the commoners, people without ascribed status who lacked the necessary wealth and prestige to attract an independent following. Historically, both estates had formal legal definition. Commoners depended on aristocrats for security and, in return, owed their leaders political allegiance, labour service, and other forms of economic tribute. Beneath the commoners were communities of subject peoples, including the nomadic Bajau Laut who, being highly mobile, were scattered over much of the Sulu zone and beyond. Finally, at the bottom of the system, were slaves (*ata*, in Sama) (Sather, 1984: 4). Slaves consisted overwhelmingly of captives taken from outside the Sulu region, although they also included small numbers of debt-slaves and people taken from within the area, including Sama Dilaut whose patrons failed to protect them from capture. Slavery was a major social institution in eighteenth- and nineteenth-century Sulu and was maintained, through the political patronage of Tausug aristocrats, by a system of active marauding; some of it carried out by Sama–Bajau subjects, notably Balangingi' Samal, and by non-Sama speaking Illanun and others. From the second half of the eighteenth century until the mid-nineteenth century, slaves and their descendants are believed to have comprised almost half of the total population of the Sulu Archipelago, and over half the population of Jolo, the principal seat of Tausug power (Warren, 1981: 209–11). Nearly all slaves were owned by aristocrats or wealthy commoners (Warren, 1981: 220–1).

Kiefer has characterized the ranking system as one of 'status-conscious egalitarianism'. High ascribed status gave social prestige, but not power.

The latter required, in addition, wealth and leadership. Those who combined all three attracted followers and so established themselves as recognized leaders within the alliance hierarchy and, by virtue of their position, controlled markets and procurement trade. To some degree, wealth and power were achieved independently of inherited titles, so that men of humble origin—including Sama commoners and even, on occasion, slaves—often gained great influence and, in acknowledgement, received appointive titles and secured for themselves positions of prominence within the coalitional pyramid.

Trade, Religion, and Ethnic Hierarchy

The Sulu Archipelago, extending from Mindanao to the eastern coast of Borneo, is bisected by historical sea routes connecting the Philippines, eastern Indonesia, mainland Asia, and the western Malay world (Warren, 1981: xix). Within the archipelago, maritime trade has long been an important unifying principle, welding together people in what is otherwise a zone of great cultural and linguistic diversity (Sather, 1985: 168–75). From the time of its founding, tributary trade was a central feature of the Sulu Sultanate, its primary integrative element and economic life-blood. Power within the sultanate derived chiefly from control over trading commodities and the people who procured them. The authority of the sultan and of the aristocratic estate was sustained by a procurement economy, articulated by coalitional politics, in which labour and locally produced trade commodities were supplied by a variety of differently adapted groups, including sea nomads and other maritime Sama communities. In very general terms, the Sama–Bajau provided their services as skilled seamen, boat-builders, artisans, pilots, fishermen, and inter-island traders (Warren, 1981: 65–70; Sather, 1984: 7–8). The most prestigious and politically independent Sama-speaking groups acted as maritime raiders, procuring slaves for the Tausug markets of Jolo (Warren, 1978, 1981; Sather, 1984, 1993b).[1] By contrast, the boat nomads, while supplying highly valued trade commodities, such as mother-of-pearl, *bêche-de-mer*, shark fin, and dried fish, formed, together with swidden cultivators living at the northern and southern margins of the Sulu zone, the least esteemed and lowest ranking group within the state.[2]

Countervailing the centrifugal tendencies inherent in the segmentary structure of the sultanate, Islam acted as the prime legitimizer of the sultan's authority. The sultan was looked upon as God's representative on earth. His position was expressed through rituals of office which validated his authority and made it possible for him to bestow prestige on those who served his interests. His person was to some degree sacrosanct. As the highest ecclesiastical authority in the sultanate, he was expected to exemplify ideal qualities of character, such as wisdom, religiosity, and charity (Majul, 1971: 9–10), and, as a force emanating from his person, was believed to possess *barakat*, a state of religious grace or blessing (Kiefer, 1972b: 107). The sultan was also the highest religious official and, in his person, 'symbolized the community of the faithful on earth and their communal membership and participation in Dar-al-Islam' (Warren, 1981: xxv). At the heart of the Sulu Sultanate, religion and politics were conjoined. The institutions of the sultanate served, in Kiefer's (1972b: 109) words, 'two major functions: ... ritual or religious, in which the sultanate ... [embodied] the community of the faithful ...; [and] legal, in which the sultanate serve[d] to channel and control conflict'.

Advising the sultan was the sultanate's *kadi* (*khatib*), who acted as his religious counsellor and the principal administrator of Islamic law within the sultanate. Beneath him, and serving the sultan, was an ecclesiastical hierarchy of local *kadi* and *imam*, acting as catechists and juridical advisers, who administered religious law (*sara*) on the sultan's behalf and so established his ecclesiastical authority throughout the realm.

At every level of the sultanate, religion played a critical role in maintaining its hierarchical structure of power and ranking. The sultan was the acknowledged head of an Islamic state. He was the symbolic representative of the community of co-religionists on earth, while his official genealogies traced his descent from the Prophet. His position was therefore invested with religious authority. In addition, corresponding to his position at the apex of the political pyramid, the sultan was also the highest religious authority in the sultanate. Paralleling the political hierarchy was a religious one, united at the top in the person of the sultan, and consisting, from state to local levels, of local and regional *kadi* and *imam*.

Political and religious hierarchies were the defining characteristics of the Sulu Sultanate. But more importantly, the sultanate was also ethnically segmented. In Barth's terms (1969: 16–17), Sulu constituted a 'polyethnic society', within which political alliance, rank, and religion were all united in a single, encompassing system of ethnic stratification.

At the top of the ethnic hierarchy were the Tausug. Controlling the network of redistributive trade and monopolizing the aristocratic estate at the apex of the political order, the Tausug thoroughly dominated the Sulu Sultanate from its founding until its final dissolution. Although non-Tausug were admitted to positions of rank and leadership, the Tausug monopolized the hereditary titles of aristocratic status. They also formed the principal trading class and composed the main population of agricultural commoners. In addition, the Tausug viewed themselves as culturally superior to subordinate groups, most notably the Sama, and presented themselves as warlike and domineering. They also laid claim to greater Islamic purity and, as a group, controlled most religious offices, as well as most secular ones with religious functions, most notably that of the sultan.

Unlike the Bajau, the Tausug form a notably homogeneous population and speak a single Meso-Philippine (East Mindanao) language, with only minor dialectal differences from one end of the Sulu Archipelago to the other (Pallesen, 1985: 125–7).[3] Reflecting this homogeneity, the Tausug identify themselves by a single autonym, as *tau sug*, meaning, literally, 'people (*tau*) of the current', or more precisely, 'people of Jolo (*sug*)', in Tausug, the term *sug* referring at once to the principal port, seat of state power, and central 'high' island of the Sulu Archipelago as well as to the sea current (Frake, 1980: 327; Sather, 1993c: 261). Significantly, the Tausug identify themselves, not, like the Sama, with a multitude of peripheral islands and island groups, but with what was, and remains, the political and economic centre of the Sulu region, Jolo Island. For the Tausug, Jolo represents their exclusive place of origin from which they believe themselves to derive, having no other homeland. Indeed, so powerfully centralizing is this identity that the main internal distinction drawn by Tausug speakers is between Tau Sug proper, those who live on Jolo Island, and Tau Pu, 'people of the [other] islands (pu)', referring to all others (Sather, 1993c: 261).[4]

The Tausug are comparatively recent arrivals in Sulu, not appearing in the islands before the eleventh century (Spoehr, 1973: 22). Their genesis as an ethnic group appears to be related to an early northward spread of Sama speakers and the resulting creation of a bilingual trading community composed of Sama-speaking men and Tausug-speaking women and children (Pallesen, 1985: 265). Subsequently, as this Jolo-based trading élite gained power and numerical strength, it appears to have used its power not only to maintain Tausug as a distinct language, but to assimilate the more settled, land-based Sama then living on the larger central islands, including Jolo itself. Between the twelfth and fifteenth centuries, a marked change appears to have occurred in the linguistic make-up of central Sulu. From being the language of a small trading élite, Tausug became the dominant language of the archipelago, as Tausug speakers came to control and expand a growing procurement economy with Jolo Island as its principal redistributive centre. With the coming of Islam and the founding of the Sulu Sultanate, the Tausug assumed formal dominance over the other ethnic groups of the Sulu Archipelago, most notably the heterogeneous Sama–Bajau speakers, and in the process they evolved a separate ethnic identity by way of sealing their political and economic domination. Ethnogenesis appears to have been related, therefore, to the process of state formation (Frake, 1980; Bentley, 1981; Pallesen, 1985). Emerging differences of rank and political status were invested with cultural significance and ascribed to differences of language, culture, and origin. As a result, ethnicity became the dominant medium through which the social order was interpreted and acted upon, and increasingly it came to determine, as it still does, the ways in which inequalities of power and status are subjectively experienced from within.

Beneath the Tausug in this polyethnic hierarchy came diverse Sama–Bajau-speaking populations. In the formal constitution of the sultanate, these populations were allocated locally as dependant 'guests' between different lines of Tausug leaders and hereditary title-holding aristocrats (Saleeby, 1908). Thus, 'in the nineteenth century, Samal islands in the south were said to be "owned" by Tausug aristocrats associated with the sultan, and this was true in the sense that if the Samal group did not provide at least a token amount of loyalty and tribute to its Tausug lord, they might be subject to raids and depredations at the hand of Tausug pirates' (Kiefer, 1972b: 23). 'Ownership' in this connection implied rights of jurisdiction, expressed above all in terms of protection. As Kiefer (1972b: 23) notes, when a Tausug claims to 'own' something, he thereby asserts that, 'he will use his personal power to protect it against transgression; one owns something if one is ultimately responsible for its protection.... Hence, when a Tausug headman says that he owns a group of Samal, he is not referring to them as slaves, but rather stressing a certain form of authority over them.' Physical coercion, or its threat, was an inherent aspect of leadership in Sulu, underlying such relations of protection. Indeed, violence was, and continues to be, a systemic feature of political relations, and at every level of the political pyramid, from the sultan to village headmen, leaders in the past maintained armed retinues (Kiefer 1969, 1972b; Sather, 1971a). The authority that individual leaders commanded depended largely on their willingness to use physical coercion and to 'protect' those subject to their authority from the will of others, by force if necessary.

In contrast to the Tausug, the Sama are associated historically with the geographical margins of the Sulu Sultanate, the peripheries of power and trade, political clientage, the sea and shoreline rather than the land, lesser degrees of religious orthodoxy, and in the case of the boat nomads, exclusion from the community of co-religionists altogether, as a people 'without religion'. This fundamental Sama–Tausug cleavage defined the principal terms by which ethnic stratification was culturally constituted and apprehended in the Sulu zone, including south-eastern Sabah. Inequalities were represented in cultural terms and perpetuated by means of ethnic group affiliations. Inequalities were thereby 'naturalized' and 'ascribed' to the intrinsic nature of the principal groups concerned—Tausug, Sama, and Bajau Laut. Their ascriptive character became the core element in each group's identity (Sather, 1993d). Hence the Tausug were identified with the political and religious centre of the Sulu Sultanate; the diverse Sama–Bajau with its peripheries, and so with political and religious marginality. The Tausug were essentially landbased; the Sama basically maritime. The Tausug presented themselves as assertive and warlike; the Sama, retiring and tractable. In each case, the Tausug end of the scale was the prestigious end. 'At the other extreme, the further one [went] to sea, the more one wanders from the central places, the meeker one presents oneself, the lower becomes one's position in the scheme of things' (Frake, 1980: 329). At the bottom of the ethnic hierarchy were the nomadic Bajau Laut, perceived by those ashore as a despised people, without rank or political status, who depended for their survival on the protection of their settled neighbours.

Company Rule

In 1877, most of present-day Sabah, including the whole east coast, was ceded by the sultans of Brunei and Sulu to what, in 1881, was constituted as the British North Borneo Chartered Company (Black, 1983: 1–5). The first government station was established on the east coast by William Pryer, later a Company resident, at Sandakan in February 1878. However, aside from occasional forays into the area to curb piracy and slave trading, the Company's presence was little felt in the Semporna region for another two decades.

Prior to the establishment of a Company station at Sandakan, within the Semporna district, Omadal Island served as a staging port and maritime link in the network of regional trade that extended from central Sulu to the eastern Borneo coast. Slaves were a major trading commodity and moved from Sulu through Omadal to Bulungan in eastern Kalimantan, then an important regional slave market. Later, Illanun and Balangingi' pirates founded a staging base at Tungku, on the north-eastern coast of Sabah, under an Illanun chief known as Datu Kurunding (Black, 1983: 23). From this base, slaving fleets carried out raids along the northern Borneo coast (Warren, 1971: 43). In 1879, the British gunboat HMS *Kestrel* destroyed the Tungku settlement and many of the Bajau followers of Datu Kurunding fled to Omadal Island, where they established themselves beyond Company control (Warren, 1971: 44).

Against this background, in December 1879, William Pryer, after a brief visit to Darvel Bay, dispatched a native agent to the region to confer with Bajau, Tausug, and Idahan headmen on ways to put an end to piracy. Out of these talks came a plan to establish Silam, in what is now the Lahad Datu district, as a centre of trade and administration for the eventual pacification of the south-eastern coast of Sabah. A station was established at Silam in 1882; for a time it was manned by a European assistant resident. Later, an experimental garden was established for testing potential plantation crops (Black, 1971: 102). These developments succeeded in attracting to the region small numbers of Chinese and Bajau traders.

Outside Sandakan and Silam, the Company's power on the east coast was virtually non-existent. In 1882, the government's total European staff was twenty-three officers in the whole of Sabah; in 1887, after retrenchments, it was only eighteen. With such meagre resources, the notion of Company 'rule' was, as Black (1971: 128) has observed, largely an illusion. The Company made no effort to administer the local population. Its authority was largely confined to a small number of coastal stations where, given its financial impoverishment, the principal concern of its officers was to encourage trade and collect customs revenue. By necessity, the Company exerted such influence as it could through existing local leaders. Acting as go-betweens, the latter frequently manipulated the relationship to enhance their own power and commercial interests (Black, 1971: 131–3). In the eastern coastal districts, most held power by virtue of their connection with the Sulu Sultanate. As a consequence, despite the formal cession of the region, the traditional political structure remained very largely intact throughout the first decades of Company government.

In 1884, Governor Treacher instructed Pryer to subsidize local chiefs who agreed to act as Company agents. Nakoda Gumah, a Tausug trader, was appointed the first native magistrate at Silam. In theory his authority extended over the entire Darvel Bay region, including Semporna. In 1891, a formal system of native administration was established and the first native chief for Semporna was appointed in 1898. By then, however, a trading station had been established. Economic change came much more quickly, so that by the time of this appointment Semporna town had already emerged as a flourishing centre of regional trade.

Silam, on the other hand, proved a disappointment. The settlement failed to grow, and when a tobacco estate was opened at Lahad Datu in 1888 the government station was moved there. In subsequent years, Lahad Datu became for a time the seat of the East Coast Residency. Despite the growth of trade and settlement, Semporna remained a centre of anti-government activity. As the Company, from its base in Sandakan, increasingly pacified the north-eastern coast, recalcitrant leaders and their followers found refuge in the Semporna region, with its islands and close connections to Sulu. Company efforts to assert its authority in the district met with local opposition, particularly from the long-established and numerically dominant Kubang community on Omadal, Larapan, and surrounding islands. In 1891, the people of Dinawan were implicated in a raid against Tambak village, near Tungku, and the Dinawan settlement was razed by constabulary from the cruiser *Petrel*. The next year, a major punitive expedition was mounted against Omadal Island. Seven Bajau were killed in an engagement with the *Petrel*, including the son of the Sama Kubang chief, Panglima Abdul Rahman (Warren, 1971: 72). In 1895, a gunboat was sent to Gusong Melanta; in 1899, the *Petrel* returned to Dinawan, and in later years repeated expeditions were sent to Omadal and Bumbum islands (Warren, 1971: 72–8). In order to strengthen its control of the coast, in 1892 the Company sent Chinese traders to found a trading station at Tawau. A Tidong chief, Puado, was given responsibility for overseeing the political affairs of the district on the Company's behalf.[5] The majority of the population consisted of escaped slaves, many of them from Semporna and southern Sulu. In six years, the population of the settlement increased tenfold, as Tidong in particular were drawn to the district by the development of trade and political security. Tawau soon became the principal south-eastern port, quickly surpassing Semporna, and in time replaced Lahad Datu as the administrative centre of the East Coast Residency.

Following the appointment of the first native chief, a system of indirect rule slowly evolved in Semporna. In time, a hierarchy of native leaders was established with salaried district and native chiefs acting as paramount local authorities in matters involving the Bajau population. Initial appointments were made from the ranks of recognized local leaders. In this way, the Company very largely incorporated the traditional pyramidal networks of patron–client relations. Following the establishment of permanent administrative stations at Tawau and Lahad Datu, Semporna was visited by a Company officer on a fortnightly schedule. During these visits, the officer conferred with the salaried chiefs and unpaid village headmen, heard complaints, and reviewed the actions taken by leaders in the district. Although the government made appointments and reserved the power to remove chiefs and countermand their decisions, the influence of the visiting officer was otherwise limited. He depended largely on the chiefs, who were men of considerable political acumen and local influence. Except for these fortnightly visits, he maintained little direct oversight of district affairs.

Between 1901 and 1910, the Company introduced a number of policies meant to restrict the mobility of the Bajau and bring them more fully under its control. Governor Birch was particularly concerned with what he saw as the situation in Semporna. He observed: 'I was told ... there are some 400 boats belonging to about 700 Bajaus in the neighboring islands. They are the terror of everyone—Piracy, robbing on the high seas and on land and murder are of common occurrence and these lawless people own no authority and pay no taxes' (quoted in Black, 1971: 384). One positive measure taken by the government meant to promote greater permanency of Bajau settlement was to encourage coconut planting (Warren, 1971: 79). This policy was a considerable success. By 1910, most of the inhabited low islands and coastline of the district were cleared of jungle and planted with coconut palms. Copra became the major cash crop in Semporna and the main source for the monetization of the local economy. The development of plantations at Lahad Datu and Tawau provided additional opportunities for earning money. With money income, Semporna town became an increasingly important centre of shopping and trade, with far-reaching consequences for the Bajau Laut.

As a more restrictive measure, the Company introduced in 1901 a system of boat licensing directed primarily against the Bajau. For the next decade virtually all of the government's involvement in the district was occupied with enforcing boat registration (Molyneux, 1902: 32–3; Warren, 1971). The system had three main purposes. The first and most important was to register native vessels, making it possible for the government to maintain control over the sea-going movement of the Bajau. The second was revenue collection. In licensing his vessel, each boat-owner was required to pay a licence fee amounting in most cases to one dollar per annum. This fee was treated as a substitute for a head- or house-tax imposed elsewhere in British North Borneo on more settled people. Finally, payment of this fee was looked upon as an acknowledgement of Company sovereignty.

Initially, boat registration provoked widespread resistance in the district. Many strand communities refused to co-operate. The governor was forced to assign two full-time officers, a launch, and a detachment of Iban police to the Residency to enforce the tax. The houses of those who refused registration were razed, their trees cut down, and their crops destroyed (Black, 1971: 384). Given these Draconian measures, open resistance eventually ended and the boat tax, although disliked, was accepted. Its imposition had two major consequences. One was to draw the Bajau still further into the developing cash economy by requiring that each boat-owner pay the annual licence fee in cash. It also brought the villagers into direct contact with the government and in turn gave local authorities a degree of control over their coming and goings. Upon payment of the boat tax, the boat-owner was assigned a licence number which he was required to display on the prow of his vessel. This made it possible for the police to keep close tabs on the movement of boats and to restrict unauthorized travel between Sabah and the southern Philippines. A short time later, a similar system of boat licensing was imposed by American colonial authorities in the Philippines. These moves, and the political partition of the surrounding region between the Dutch East Indies, British North Borneo, and the Philippines, hindered the previously free movement of people by sea. It was during this time that the Semporna Bajau Laut abandoned their previous practice of periodic long-distance voyaging into Indonesian waters.

Finally, the acceptance of boat licensing was largely due to a further innovation. This was a reorganization of native leadership and the elevation to positions of authority of men who owed their first loyalty to the Company government. As a result, traditional claims to rank became less important than willingness to carry out government decisions. In 1903, a critical appointment was made. The previous native chief, Maharajah Alani, a brother of the Kubang leader Panglima Abdul Rahman of Omadal, was removed from office for dealing in Sulu titles as an agent of the sultan, and was replaced by Panglima Udang. Unlike his predecessor, Panglima Udang was not a Sulu title-holder, but a man of relatively humble origin (Cook, 1924: 58). Moreover, his rank was not a Sulu title, but was conferred by the Company governor, Ernest Birch, in a formal investiture ceremony held in Semporna town in 1903 (Birch, 1903: 272). Through this ceremony, the Company formally appropriated Sulu's role in granting titles. Backed by its growing coercive power, the legitimacy of Company titles was gradually accepted, and in this way, the Chartered Company government transferred much of the symbolic legitimacy and prestige of Sulu state to itself. In later years, the title of Panglima was reduced in rank and bestowed by the Company government on trusted village headmen, while native chiefs were given the title of Orang Kaya and district chiefs, Orang Kaya Kaya. Udang also came from the numerically dominant Sama Kubang community. This, too, was significant, for unique among local shore groups, the Sama Sikubang are associated exclusively with the Semporna region. Finally, Panglima Udang was a man of considerable political genius, whose followers credited him with supernatural powers, particularly that of invulnerability (*kobol*) (Cook, 1924: 58). He succeeded in founding a family dynasty whose members continue to dominate the political life of the Semporna district. Through his political skill, and with the backing of the government, Udang was able to transform a precarious system of indirect rule into an effective and truly hierarchical native administrative system, with himself as paramount leader. For the first time, separate communities were brought under the authority of a single set of village and regional leaders between whom there existed, despite the personal nature of their influence, a formal chain of command. The power of Udang's kin and descendants also ensured that even during the period of later British colonial rule when, in 1961, Semporna was elevated to the status of a separate administrative district with, for a brief time, its own European district officer, native leaders retained their dominant influence.

As a further element of policy, the Company government attempted to bring the Bajau in Semporna under more direct supervision by encouraging their relocation to the mainland and resettlement in areas closer to Semporna town. From Pryer's time onward, the official *British North Borneo Herald* contained repeated pronouncements regarding the desirability of resettling the Semporna Bajau ashore. For example, in 1902, the Tawau District Officer, J. H. Molyneux (1902: 32–3), in describing a punitive campaign in which the launch *Normanhurst* with a force of twenty-nine Dayak police arrested local Bajau leaders, conducted searches of island villages for weapons, and razed those whose inhabitants resisted search, ended:

In conclusion I would suggest that all Bajaus be first expelled as soon as possible from the island of Bum Bum, and removed to one settlement approachable by boat, and from which there are less means of escape than from an island surrounded by extensive coral-reefs. If that was done, they could be made to pay their boat-taxes, could be induced to take out passes for hunting jungle produce like other natives, and would be forced to desist from indulging in slave-dealing, which I discovered is a pretty well-organized trade among them. There are 7 villages on Bum Bum, each with a considerable population, and by settling them effectively, and making them a law-abiding people, they would benefit Government, benefit themselves, and prove an inducement to other Bajaus in their neighbourhood to follow their example. There is no reason why Bajaus should not cease their roving, piratical habits and become a steady, settled people (Molyneux, 1902: 33).

From the turn of the century, newly arrived Sama from the southern Philippines were required to settle in the vicinity of Semporna town or along the adjacent Tandu Bulong Straits. At the same time, Company policy sought to draw the Bajau from outlying islands where they were difficult to police, and where they were suspected by authorities of slave-trading and of harbouring lawless elements, and encourage them to settle ashore where it was hoped they would take up a more sedentary, agricultural way of life. Since independence, the same policy has been pursued by subsequent state governments.

At the time of Semporna's founding as a Company station, the interior of the district was uninhabited. This was due not only to the maritime orientation of its Bajau population, but also, in the view of older Bajau residents, to the presence of travelling Segai-i (or Segai) warriors who, during the nineteenth century, passed through the area on their way to the Madai and Baturong caves and to the headwaters of the Kinabatangan River where they reportedly carried out head-hunting expeditions against Idahan and other Dusunic peoples (Valera, 1962: 40–1). These Segai-i war parties are believed to have originated in the headwaters of the Segah and Kelai rivers in eastern Kalimantan and remained a menace in eastern Sabah during the final decades of the nineteenth century (Pryer, 1887: 229; Warren, 1981: 92). Occasionally, they directed forays against coastal settlements and were said to have been a constant danger to jungle collecting parties ashore. In Semporna, Bajau oral tradition tells of numerous encounters with Segai-i warriors. Yap (1978: 18) records an Omadal tradition of Segai-i harassment and the defeat of a Segai-i war party by a local Bajau force on Karindingan Island in precolonial times. These attacks generally ceased around 1900, following the founding of Tawau and the pacification of East Kalimantan. Semporna Bajau Laut tradition tells, however, of a final attack, which took place at the beginning of the Japanese Occupation, after the collapse of local colonial authority. The attack occurred at night and was made against the Bajau Laut boat-living community then anchored at Balimbang, near Bumbum Island. The attack was successfully repulsed by the Bajau Laut, who defended themselves with fish-spears and knives. However, after this attack a number of families left the anchorage and moved across the Philippine border to Sitangkai, where they remained until after the Japanese surrender.

Founding of Semporna as a Market Centre

The Chartered Company had originally hoped that royalties from trade, and particularly from the collection of edible birds' nests, might provide sufficient revenue to subsidize the costs of administration, at least until the anticipated plantation sector of the economy became established (Warren, 1981: 139). Birds' nests were the most important commercial resource on the east coast of Sabah at the beginning of Company rule. The main nesting caves were located at Madai and Segalung, north of Semporna in the present Lahad Datu district. Traditionally, nests were gathered by Idahan collectors and disposed of through coastal traders. In the pre-Company period, the majority appear to have been tran-shipped by way of Omadal Island to Maimbung and Jolo, the chief market ports of Sulu, and to Bulungan and Berau in East Kalimantan. Being beyond the sphere of Company control, the Semporna district became, following the establishment of Sandakan, a refuge for those who continued to profit from this traditional procurement economy, including the birds' nest trade.

The Company attempted to check this southward flow of trade in 1884 by posting to Omadal Island a native customs clerk empowered to require trade declarations and collect duties. He was quickly forced to flee as the Company was unable to impose its presence by force (Warren, 1981: 140). A year earlier, D. D. Daly, a Company officer visited Semporna together with William Pryer. Daly's account gives some sense of the unsettled conditions of the time.

We left Silam at 7 a.m. the 20th [October] and at 1 p.m. arrived at the mouth of the *trusan* leading from near Timba Mata [Timbun Mata] to Sepangau—since named Trusan Treacher. We here saw perfect crowds of boats, and I do not think I overstate, if I say that we saw over three hundred boats in the *trusan*. We never had less than 8 fathoms of water the whole way. We saw numerous villages, but could not approach them as the tide was out. A great part of the country appears to have been cultivated a long time, but all the Bajaus we meet were *trepang* fishing. We anchored in Port Elphinstone [Semporna] within thirty yards of the shore, in six fathoms, and Mr Pryer and I landed where some fifty or sixty Bajaus were fishing. On landing these men all crowded around us, armed, but when they found that we were not 'Orang Blanda' (Dutchmen), all the men took off their arms and put them into their boats. (One man said that he would kill any Orang Blanda he met). The women and children shortly after this came out of the jungle where they had been living. All these people complained bitterly of the ravages of the elephants and pigs in their plantations, saying that they had to depend on their fishing, as their plantations were ruined.... The men also complained of being hunted down by the Dutch vessels of war, as pirates, although they say that they never have been guilty of piracy. The chief of these people who was present, is Ahtang, a son of Panglima Ahdulraman [Abdul Rahman] ... Mr Pryer considers it very necessary to have a block house here, with some half a dozen constables, so as to concentrate the trade in one place, as this would at once induce Chinese to open shops here (Daly, 1883: 13).

These suggestions would soon be put into effect.

In 1885, William Pryer took the first effective measures to impose Company control over the birds' nest traffic. In doing so, he, knowingly or not, set the stage for the eventual subjugation of Semporna. The Company assumed formal leasing rights to Madai and Segalung caves and arranged for the collection and sale of the nests through the recently established agricultural station at Silam (Warren, 1981: 140). Conflict was inevitable. Cut out of this traffic, Bajau from Omadal attacked Silam and several Idahan villages. Reprisal came swiftly and for the first time the government intervened decisively in the district. A gunboat, the HMS *Zephyr*, was dispatched from Labuan and destroyed villages and native boats on Omadal and Bumbum islands. A second warship, the HMS *Satellite*, was also sent to reinforce the Company's naval presence in Semporna (Treacher, 1890: 100; Warren, 1981: 140).

In the months that followed the visit of the *Zephyr*, Semporna was relatively peaceful. On 10 May 1887, Governor Treacher visited Omadal. Here he learned that the local chiefs, following the Company's retaliation for their raid on Silam, had gone to Sulu to offer their allegiance to the young sultan. Realizing the need for a permanent administrative base in the district to bring about its lasting pacification—and taking advantage of the absence of the more independent of the local Bajau leaders—the Governor sailed to the narrow straits separating the mainland from Bumbum Island. Here he chose the site for a new government trading station. The site he chose was a stretch of coastal lowlands along the extreme northern tip of the straits near its deepwater mouth. This area was known to the Bajau as Tong Talun ('jungle cape'). Governor Treacher renamed it Semporna, a Malay name signifying a 'place of peace' or 'rest' (Warren, 1971: 62–4). The new station was inaugurated the following month by the acting Governor, William Crocker.

The first settlers were Chinese who had fled to Sandakan following the destruction of the main Sulu port of Maimbung by Spanish forces in 1886. They were led by a merchant named Toonah (Warren, 1971: 63). Governor Treacher encouraged them to settle, and the Sandakan administration placed Toonah at Semporna to found the Company's trading station there. It was hoped that Toonah's influence among the Tausug and his fellow Chinese traders would assure the settlement's success (Warren, 1971: 63–4). These hopes were not disappointed. Toonah was made the first *kapitan china* of Semporna town. He was authorized to fly the Company flag, and was employed to collect trade duties, as the Company's first customs officer. Toonah, as Warren (1981: 141n) observes,

was no ordinary trader. He had two Tausug wives and had resided first in Jolo and later Maimbung for 23 years before coming to ... Borneo. As a consequence of his intermarriage with Tausug, his command of the language and his wealth, Toonah had considerable influence among the Tausug of Maimbung, especially with the mother and family of the deceased Sultan, Jamal ul-Azam. The Company could not have had better fortune. Toonah's godown would always be filled with rattans and tripang exchanged for his stock in trade: gaudy silk and cotton sarongs and piece goods of English manufacture, Chinese tobacco, fish hooks and lines, brass vessels and boxes.

At the time of Semporna's founding, the Spanish were making a determined effort to subjugate Sulu and bring the archipelago under the control of Manila. Realizing that sea-going trade formed the basis of the sultanate's power, the Spanish imposed a naval blockade on the southern islands, destroyed native shipping, and razed coastal villages engaged in navigation and boat-building (Warren, 1981: 118–25). While this blockade was not entirely successful, Sulu's position as a centre of redistributive trade rapidly collapsed. Sandakan drew the trade of north-eastern Borneo and within a short time, that of southern Palawan and Cagayan de Sulu as well. In later decades, trade patterns reversed and Sabah became the destination of trade for much of southern Sulu. The final Spanish conquest of 1886 set off a major exodus of traders, both Bajau and Chinese, to the newly founded coastal ports of eastern Sabah.

Toonah erected a warehouse and wharf, and Semporna quickly became a magnet of local trade (Warren, 1971: 65). The Bajau Laut played a significant part in the station's prosperity, supplying maritime products—dried fish, shark fin, and most importantly 'tripang'—which, from the beginning, represented the station's chief trade commodity. In June 1887, a month after the station was founded, the Governor visited Semporna aboard a trading ship, the *Paknam*. He noted the enthusiasm with which the Bajau engaged in trade, and remarked on the rapid progress of the settlement. Besides Toonah's godown and wharf, his Excellency counted twenty-three houses making up the nucleus of what would eventually become Semporna town. He wrote:

Already signs of vitality and progress are evident. Toonah has put in hand a most substantial building of solid and durable timber.... He is also constructing a wharf at a long distance from the shore, at which, when completed, steamers can anchor in 3 fathoms at low water.

At present the nucleus of what is certain to prove a most prosperous settlement consists of some twenty-three houses. The 'Paknam' having unloaded, took on board one hundred piculs or over six tons of produce, which is a splendid beginning when it is taken into consideration that Toonah is not yet one month settled in the place is a highly encouraging augury as to the future.... From all points of view the new station appears to have a great future before it and the benefit of a thriving township in this locality ... cannot be over estimated. We must congratulate the Acting Governor for his foresight in selecting such an eligible site in a locality where the influence of a peaceable trading station cannot fail to have a most successful influence over the Bajows of the neighbourhood (Crocker, 1887: 162).

Although Toonah's business failed following his death in 1895, Semporna town continued to flourish and his initial success quickly attracted others. In 1903, the Company government required that all Chinese shops in the district be relocated in Semporna town to facilitate police protection and customs collection. A government wharf was built and streets were laid out; from then on, the town emerged as the regional market centre and trading port.

In 1887, L. B. von Donop (1887: 186–7) described the newly founded station at Semporna in optimistic terms. He also escorted Toonah, on the Company's behalf, to southern Sulu in order to promote further trade.

The wharf is 1/4 mile long and ships can come alongside. Toonah the Captain China is building a substantial house with iron roof and two others which he intends to rent out. He seems pleased with the prospects before him. I noticed he had a good quantity of pearl shell, tortoise shell, *trepang*, rattans, etc. Having arranged to take him to Maimbun and Tiangi and some of the Tawi Tawi islands at which places he had many debts due to him we left the same day at 9 a.m. Toonah informed me that he wished to obtain Sulus who are experienced pearl divers and intends to try and induce some to come and settle at Simporna.... Three Chinese traders have accompanied him from different islands to spy the land and possibly settle with him at Simporna. He is confident that a great deal of the sea produce which now goes to Sulu will instead be brought to Simporna.

Von Donop (1887: 187) went on to note that fresh water was a 'difficulty' in Semporna, a problem that would persist, and reported spending two days in search of a water source. At the end of the year, another government visitor to the district, F. G. Callaghan (1887: 263) noted that, 'nearly all the Bajows now trade their produce for sale to Simporna, evidently preferring the better prices paid them by Toonah to the Silam traders'. According to local tradition, during this time the original Bajau settlement at Semporna town was founded under the leadership of Settia Amarin, who had the first well (*ahinang bohé'*) dug at Kampung Perigi.

The development of trade outside the traditional procurement economy brought about profound changes in the nature of indigenous society in Semporna. The Sulu Sultanate's role as a focus of economic redistribution ended in the final decades of the nineteenth century. The establishment of thriving regional trading ports like Semporna town effectively ended Sulu's control over local commerce in south-eastern Sabah. At the same time, these ports provided security, backed by police and occasional naval presence. Control over external trade passed out of local hands and become increasingly concentrated, at the local level, in those of immigrant Chinese traders such as Toonah. While Warren (1981: 142–3) has read into this development a decline of native trade, for Semporna at least this was far from the case. In general, Warren's analysis, focusing as it does on wider political developments, necessarily highlights the role of tributary trade. However, from the point of view of the local Bajau Laut and their neighbours, such trade was always secondary to, and largely an adjunct of, what might be called local 'symbiotic trade'. The coming of the Company increased rather than decreased the volume of such trade. A major economic innovation of Company rule was the introduction of cash, the use of which effectively linked this indigenous sphere of trade to a wider global economy. Money transactions quickly replaced barter, becoming the basis on which inter-community trade was conducted. Its use greatly expanded the value and volume of local trade, in some cases intensified economic specialization, and effectively linked local trade to global markets well beyond the district.

Reflecting this expansion of indigenous trade, the period between 1886 and 1910 was marked by a massive immigration of Bajau-speaking peoples into the Semporna district from the islands of southern Sulu. By 1910, the population of the region had assumed much of its present mosaic character. Traders formed a significant proportion of these migrants and their arrival coincided with an increase in local trading activity. At the same time, these trading groups tended to be strongly religious and introduced into Semporna a reformist strain of Islam which in time, would also, have far-reaching consequences for the Bajau Laut and others.

Life in the district underwent a significant transformation during these years. Initially, the greatest source of change for the Bajau Laut was the emergence of a commercial market, notably for fish and other marine products (Sather, 1985: 173). As soon as Semporna town was founded, the Bajau Laut disposed of the greater part of their catch directly through the town market. At the same time, the Semporna market diverted the flow of export commodities, including *bêche-de-mer* and dried fish, from Sulu, re-orienting it instead through Sandakan, Singapore, and other developing colonial ports. The related development of copra smallholdings similarly drew neighbouring island- and shore-based Bajau into a cash economy, thereby making it easier for the Bajau Laut to meet their subsistence needs by trade within the Semporna market-place, as these other groups, too, turned to market trading for cash income (Sather, 1984: 17–18; 1985: 173). As a consequence, the traditional network of barter relations was rapidly supplanted by market transactions mediated through Semporna town (Sather, 1985: 173–4). This development not only affected relations between local sea and shore groups, but profoundly altered the former pattern of band deployment among the Bajau Laut themselves. Nomadic bands coalesced into larger groups and these gravitated closer and closer to Semporna town which, in addition to its role as the focal point of local trade, offered security and a source of agricultural foodstuffs and other essential goods.

From Nomads to Settled Villagers

In eastern Sabah, historical sources of the nineteenth century describe the presence of boat-dwelling bands near Labuk and in Sandakan Bay, as well as in the Semporna region to the south. Prior to the establishment of Company rule, the pearl fisheries at Lingkabu, near the mouth of the Labuk River, were claimed by the Sultan of Sulu and were worked annually by what were almost certainly Sama Dilaut clients supervised by Tausug agents loyal to the sultan. Bajau Laut divers were paid each year in trade goods before the beginning of the pearl collecting season. In 1858, Spenser St John (1863: Vol. II, 231–2), while sailing in Sabah waters, met a Bajau Laut pearling fleet in Labuk Bay and has left us a vivid account of this encounter.

Shortly before St John's arrival at the entrance to the Bay, Sherif Yasin [Yassin], the principal Sulu chief at Labuk, seized a European-owned schooner, the *Dolphin*, which had been brought into Labuk Bay by Illanun pirates operating out of Tungku. After the pirates were driven off, the schooner was brought up the Labuk River and placed under guard to prevent the Illanun from recapturing it.[6] With the arrival of St John's party by steamer, it was decided to tow the schooner back out to sea. But as the party departed from the bay, they met with a fleet of boats.

All rushed on deck, thinking they might be the Lanuns about to attack Benggaya [Sherif Yasin's settlement].... We steamed towards them; they drew up on the beach and presently we saw the crews hurrying with their goods on shore; as we neared, they gradually appeared smaller and smaller; we had, in fact, been completely deceived by their looming over the water. When abreast of them we anchored, and I went off in the gig to see who they were, intending to hail them and speak; but as we drew near our guides declared they were Baju boats, and this we soon found to be the case. They were small, neatly constructed, and fitted up for the residence of a family.

As we closed with the beach we waved a white handkerchief to them, and hailed; presently three men showed themselves, and came to us. One was a Sulu, two others were Bajus. The latter were rather big men, featured much like Dayaks. They came from Banguey, and were bringing new boats to sell to Sherif Yasin. I invited them to come on board; they said they were in a great state of alarm, and men, women, and children rushed into the jungle, hiding their goods, as the Sulu thought we might be Spaniards. They afterwards came on board, and we found that these men had never lived in houses, but made their boats the dwelling-places for their wives and families (St John, 1863: Vol. II, 222–3).

The group, under the charge of a Tausug [Sulu] overlord, had brought a consignment of boats from Sulu for trade locally and was on its way to Lingkabu, off the mouth of the Labuk River, to collect pearls for the sultan.

Further south along the coast, the Bajau Laut appear to have been employed mainly in 'tripang' collection (Hunt, 1967: 54–5; Warren, 1981: 69–71) which together with birds' nests was an important element in the local procurement economy. The expansion of Western commercial activity in China in the late eighteenth century greatly stimulated the demand for 'tripang' throughout South-East Asia, including eastern Sabah and the southern Philippines. Hunt (1967: 50, 53–8) mentions boat-dwelling bands engaged in the collection of 'tripang' in the area of Sitangkai and along the adjoining south-eastern coast of Sabah. Some of these bands were almost certainly ancestors of the present Semporna Bajau Laut. Here, in contrast to Lingkabu, Bajau Laut bands were part of a permanent regional population, rather than seasonal visitors. Further south, along the Kalimantan coast, Dalrymple (1808: Vol. II, 530) mentions that Tausug traders dug freshwater wells in order to encourage boat-dwelling bands to anchor and exploit the rich 'tripang' collecting grounds near Maratua Island, in the Tirun district (see also Warren, 1981: 69).

At the time of his first arrival, William Pryer (1883: 91) mentions the presence of a small number of boat-dwelling Bajau in Sandakan Bay. Living along the bay were also settled Bajau and initially both, by his account, 'are in a great measure oppressed by the Sulus [Tausug] whose chiefs "requisition" them for anything they want that the Bajaus can make or collect, while Sulu traders establish themselves near every community and carry on barter business at extraordinary rates of profit.' Later, with the pacification of the bay, former boat-dwellers disappeared, apparently absorbed into the growing strand population.

Band Organization

Until the middle of this century, the Bajau Laut of Semporna lived permanently in boats. Each boat (lepa) typically housed a single family comprising a married couple plus their dependent children and occasionally one or more additional members, usually an aged or widowed parent or an unmarried sibling. Family size averaged five to six persons. Each family identified itself with a 'band' or local moorage community. Bands varied greatly in size, ranging from two or three to as many as forty families, with smaller bands generally made up of closely related families. Band size increased in the district following the founding of Semporna town.

Traditionally, each band was identified with a permanent anchorage, situated in a protected area of inshore water, to which member families regularly returned between fishing voyages.[7] Bands were essentially groups of families that regularly moored together at the same sheltered anchorage site. Within an anchorage, closely related families tended to moor together in a tightly aggregated group, often tying their boats in tandem, securing them to one or possibly several common moorage posts (soan). Such groups were called pagmunda' and generally comprised a 'family alliance' group (Nimmo, 1972: 25). Most were organized around a set of married siblings of either sex, or, less often, a parental couple and several married sons and daughters. Larger pagmunda' were typically formed of two or more sibling sets related by marriage. In some instances, these larger groups formed separate anchorage communities; larger bands, by contrast, tended to be more heterogeneous in composition.

Bands within the same region—for example, those living within the Semporna district—generally fished the same fishing grounds, with families from neighbouring bands sometimes fishing together. There was a natural tendency, however, for families to fish most intensively those areas closest to their home anchorage. Thus the anchorage site tended to give a partial sense of territorial definition to the dispersal and voyaging of band members. It is crucial to note, however, that fishing grounds were traditionally viewed by the Sama Dilaut as an 'unowned resource' and no band restricted access to other groups. In this sense, there were no exclusive band territories, and the areas exploited by different groups overlapped extensively. In the course of fishing voyages, families from different bands frequently encountered one another at sea. When meetings occurred at a fishing site, these families often combined their nets and fished together in short-term fleets.[8] As a result, families living in the same region were never total strangers to one other, and wider ties of acquaintance and co-operation were maintained across band boundaries. These contacts were an important factor later on in the consolidation of bands that followed the establishment of Semporna town as a regional trading station.

Band membership was notably fluid. There was frequent movement of families between bands, not only in the Semporna district, but also between Semporna and the Sibutu island group. At any given time, some bands lost members or dissolved, while others grew in size as families moved from anchorage to anchorage, or shifted from one island area to another. This pattern of mobility is still apparent, even after the establishment of pile-house settlements.

Above the level of individual bands, the Bajau Laut population of the Semporna–Sibutu area was divided into three regional subgroups, each identified with a common cemetery site (*kubul*). The Semporna Bajau Laut formed the westernmost of these subgroups. From the beginning of this century, they buried their dead on two of three tiny islets known as Pu' Bangau-Bangau near the northern tip of the Semporna Peninsula. The Ligitan reefs formed, as they still do, the group's principal fishing grounds. The second subgroup, with a common burial place on Sitangkai Island, lived in the western portion of the Sibutu island group, around the edge of the vast Tumindao reef complex, its primary fishing area (Map 2.1). In 1965, the largest Bajau Laut settlement was Sitangkai itself, by then almost entirely sedentary with a population of over 3,300 (Plate 1). West of Tumindao, a Bajau Laut anchorage was formerly found near Andulingan Island. North of Tumindao are several smaller islands, including Sipangkot, which, in 1965, was the site of a substantial Bajau Laut pile-house village of 300 people, composed of two hamlets. Beyond Sipangkot is a somewhat larger island, known as Mapui or Omapuy. Like Andulingan, this island was once the site of an important boat anchorage, now abandoned. A third group, with a burial place ashore near the southern tip of Sibutu Island, was present in the eastern Sibutu island group. In 1965, the group comprised five settlements. One was located at Tanduowak Island, off the south-eastern tip of Sibutu. In the past, Tanduowak was a major boat anchorage, but by 1965 many of its families had moved to Tongihat, a second settlement, largely sedentary, located to the north along the eastern coast of Sibutu Island. In 1965, when I visited the region, Tanduowak's population barely exceeded 100. Tongihat is situated just north of the shore villages of Ligayan and Ungas-Ungas. By 1965, it had become the principal centre of Bajau Laut population in the eastern half of the Sibutu group and contained more than 300 people. Further north, midway along the eastern shore of

58

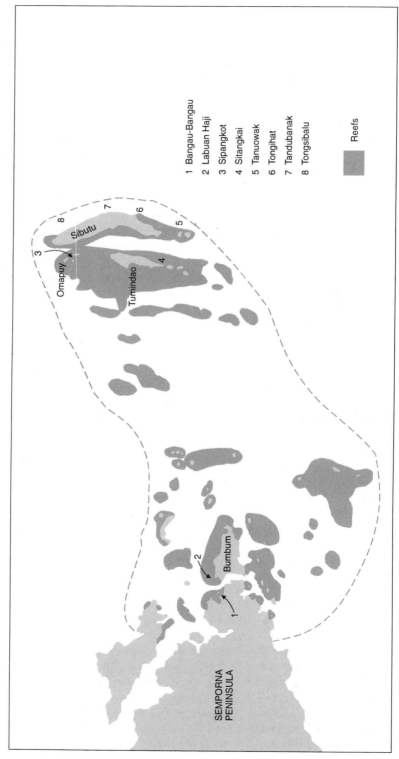

MAP 2.1
Bajau Laut Villages in the Semporna–Sibutu Region

1 Bangau-Bangau
2 Labuan Haji
3 Sipangkot
4 Sitangkai
5 Tanuowak
6 Tongihat
7 Tandubanak
8 Tongsibalu

Reefs

Sibutu

Omapuy

Tumindao

Bumbum

SEMPORNA
PENINSULA

Sibutu Island, was a much smaller Bajau Laut village, Tandubanak, located near a much larger shore community of the same name. In 1965, it comprised only five households. Beyond Tandubanak, close to the north-eastern tip of Sibutu Island, was an even smaller settlement, Tongsibalu, containing only three house groups in that same year. In the past, the Semporna Bajau Laut maintained their closest ties with those of Sitangkai and nearby islands of the western Sibutu group. Until recent large-scale migration to Semporna, Sitangkai Island, which is located less than 64 kilometres by sea from Semporna town, represented the principal centre of Bajau Laut population for the whole Sibutu–Semporna area.

In the past marriage tended to be largely endogamous within this major regional grouping of bands and burial groups. Most marriages were contracted between kin, often as a way of consolidating or extending *pagmunda'* relations. Within the band, closely related families tended to group together; in the case of smaller bands, the entire anchorage group might comprise one or two closely allied *pagmunda'*. However, given the mobility of families and the highly fluid composition of local anchorage and burial groups, the addition of newcomers was always possible and, indeed, frequent. Normally, families preferred to join an anchorage in which they already had close kindred. This was not always possible, however, so that newcomers were sometimes unrelated or only very distantly connected to those already present. Over time, however, such families tended to be incorporated through intermarriage.

Formerly, each of these three subgroups was defined by the use of a shared burial place (Sather, 1978: 173). These sites were generally located away from band anchorages with the exception of Sitangkai and were typically reached by boat. Within each subgroup, band affiliation was loose, with individuals as well as families moving freely between anchorage groups in response to quarrels, the pressures and pulls of kinship, marriage, economic opportunities, physical security, and other factors (Sather, 1976: 43–4). Intermarriage and exchange of visits were frequent. Fishing was largely confined to subgroup areas and tended to centre on locally familiar fishing grounds surrounding burial and anchorage sites as fixed points of orientation.

Outside the Semporna–Sibutu region, contacts with other Sama Dilaut were much more sporadic. Because of the relatively fixed nature of band anchorages, most Bajau Laut movement occurred within well-circumscribed territorial limits. However, the Bajau Laut also engaged in more extended voyaging. Until the 1920s, the Semporna Sama Dilaut, who were then still boat-living, regularly sailed southward through the Straits of Makassar to visit related Sama Dilaut communities along the eastern coast of Kalimantan. From here, a few sailed on to southern Sulawesi. Extended voyages were usually undertaken by parties of men, but families also occasionally took part. Although such voyages have ceased, the Semporna Bajau Laut continue to regard those living in East Kalimantan as, belonging like themselves, to a larger Sama Dilaut population. Voyages were also made north-eastward, through Sibutu islands, to the Tawitawi and Tampul island groups of Sulu. These voyages

combined occasional fishing and trade with visits to local Bajau Laut
bands. Visitors could expect to be received with hospitality by other
Sama Dilaut along the routes they sailed; these visits sometimes resulted
in marriage and the creation of kin ties. In addition, those visited travelled occasionally to Semporna to pay return visits. Through this pattern
of voyaging, a larger sense of awareness was maintained of membership
in a more inclusive community of 'sea people', the outer extent of which
no single individual, no matter how well-travelled, could fully comprehend.

Clientage Relations and Their Breakdown

Within the traditional political structure of the Sulu zone, the Bajau Laut
occupied a distinctive place. The sultan claimed proprietary rights over
all non-sedentary Sama, as a subject people. More specifically, through a
delegation of these rights, the members of each band were considered
the political clients of one or possibly several leaders ashore who claimed
effective authority over the area in which the band's anchorage site was
located. Use of this site was itself one of the 'privileges' accorded by the
patron to his Sama Dilaut clients. The band was said to be 'owned'
(taga) by its patron, and in theory the Bajau Laut lacked an independent
political existence separate from the individual patrons ashore who accorded them protection. In the central islands of Sulu patrons were
generally Tausug, including the sultan and his kindred, but in the Semporna district, they were local Bajau leaders (Sather, 1971a: 58–9;
Kiefer, 1972b).

Ownership in the context of Bajau Laut clientage meant that a patron
was prepared to defend his clients, and to protect his interests in them
against any rival leader who might seek to encroach upon this relationship. The patron and his followers guaranteed to protect his clients
against raids and harassment by other land-based groups, including
slave-raiding communities. Historically, violence was an integral part of
political relations in the Sulu zone. To some degree their client status
insulated the Bajau Laut from the internecine feuding that took place
among neighbouring shore groups, as land-based leaders competed with
one another for power and followers. Forrest (1780: 329), writing of
the sea nomads in the late eighteenth century, reported that, as a result
of the value placed upon their trade, 'their superiors are more tender of
oppressing them than [they are] their immediate vassals' on land. However,
as scattered boat people, the Bajau Laut were relatively defenceless
against attack and without the protection of a patron no band could
expect to exist for long unharassed. While a band might sever its ties
with one patron, its member families had always to re-establish them
with another. Though it seems clear from oral tradition that the Bajau Laut
were sometimes harassed and raided, and occasionally taken captive or
even killed, the clientage system seems to have worked reasonably well.
It assured band members of some degree of safety as they moved
between their anchorage sites and scattered fishing grounds by generally
creating a precarious stand-off in which regional leaders typically vied
among themselves to act as their protectors and partners in trade. At the

same time, violence served as the ultimate sanction that maintained continuing patronage relations. While raids and harassment proved a constant threat to the equilibrium of existing ties, the possibility of raids was a major force binding Bajau Laut bands to their individual patrons. In this sense, violence, rather than being a sign of disorder, was an inherent feature of relations between sea and shore people (Sather, 1971a).

The patron, in return for guaranteeing his clients' physical security, enjoyed a privileged trading relationship with his clients. Historically, trading relations included both symbiotic and procurement trade. Symbiotic exchange centred mainly on the exchange of subsistence and locally produced artisan goods and was related to a pattern of economic specialization between local communities in regular contact with one another. For the Bajau Laut, much of this trade occurred within the context of patron–client relations. As in other contexts, exchange was conducted by barter through long-term person-to-person partnerships. Trading partners described each other, reciprocally, as 'friends' (*bagai*). In addition to providing an anchorage site where his clients were free to moor their boats in relative safety, patrons allowed their clients to draw fresh water and cut firewood from lands they or their followers owned ashore. Typically, when a Bajau Laut family landed at the village of its patron, the family head was expected to take part of his catch to the house of his trading partner, usually the patron himself and not to engage in barter with 'strangers'. In return for fish, the Bajau Laut partner received cassava, young coconuts, fruit, areca nuts, '*sireh*', and other agricultural produce, as well as cloth and other manufactured goods. Often patrons made requests to client families for the delivery of fish on specific occasions, such as a wedding or other village gathering. In order to fill these requests, a Bajau Laut partner might enlist the aid of his kinsmen, so that trade often involved the efforts of more than immediate 'friends'. Alternatively, in return for foodstuffs and trade goods, a patron might engage a fleet of families on a fishing expedition, particularly to gather trade commodities such as dried fish, '*tripang*', and mother-of-pearl. Similarly, if the patron was unable to fill his client's requests for particular goods, such as rice or fruit, he might call upon his followers to supply them on his behalf. Apart from trade and security, patrons and clients had no formal responsibilities toward one another.

In the case of symbiotic exchange, the Bajau Laut did not restrict their trade entirely to patronage relations. All bands appear to have also engaged in occasional trade with other groups, particularly with artisan communities from whom they obtained forged iron goods, plaited roofing, pandanus sleeping mats, tortoiseshell combs, earthenware hearths, water jars, and other craft products, even at times, fishing boats. Shore communities went to some length to retain this trade, showing their Bajau Laut *bagai* special hospitality on their visits ashore—for example, by addressing them as 'friends' and presenting them with small gifts and other favours.

In addition to symbiotic trade, and closely linked, Bajau Laut clients provided their patrons with occasional labour service and supplied goods, such as dried fish and *bêche-de-mer*, not for local consumption, but for external markets beyond the Semporna region. The relationship therefore involved an element of appropriation, representing a diversion of Bajau Laut labour from subsistence production for the benefit of the patron and his followers. In this sense, trade was not only an economic activity but also expressed relations of status and political subordination. For the patron, his Bajau Laut clients represented an important source of trading wealth in addition to supplying fish for food. The sea products supplied by the Sama Dilaut were used by shore-based leaders to further their own political interests—cementing relations not only with their own followers ashore, but forging trade links with more powerful leaders further up the alliance hierarchy. In this sense, although the details are difficult to reconstruct, it seems clear that through the institution of patronage Bajau Laut production was partially channelled into a wider redistributive economy.

Apart from trade, patrons and others ashore interfered very little in the internal affairs of their Bajau Laut clients. Bajau Laut bands were defined by their member families' links to a common anchorage site. Here each family enjoyed notable autonomy. All were loosely organized in a series of leader-centred groupings, ranging from the individual families, through *pagmunda'* groups, to the band as a whole. Each moorage group was typically identified with a small set of elders (*matto'a*), mature and experienced men representing the heads of its constituent families and *pagmunda'*. Often these were the eldest men in the band to whom younger family heads were related, particularly in smaller bands, as sons, sons-in-law, or grandchildren. Being marginal to sources of formal power, the Bajau Laut were largely free to organize their own internal political relations along lines that were quite different from those that applied outside their own community (Sather, 1971a: 60). Within each band, interpersonal relations were notably egalitarian. There was no ascriptive ranking and the *matto'a*, as band leaders, owed their influence primarily to their ability to conciliate and contain contention among those who looked to them for guidance. In daily life, threats and direct physical confrontation were carefully avoided, and, in contrast to surrounding shore communities, the Bajau Laut identified themselves, and still do, as a peaceful, non-violent people, who 'fight only with their mouths'.

Being boat-dwellers, Bajau Laut families could readily detach themselves from any particular anchorage site and scatter or reassemble at others. Living afloat prevented their close surveillance by outsiders, and it was impossible for land people to enforce clientage relations with individual bands without some degree of compliance on the part of the Bajau Laut. If patrons interfered in the internal affairs of their client families, acting arbitrarily, or placed burdensome demands on them, the latter might simply move, taking their trade with them, and join another group, or establish themselves at a new site under the protection of a rival leader.[9] Generally there was little difficulty to find others willing to 'befriend' them. Although shore groups were the dominant party, having armed retinues at their command, and regarded their Bajau Laut clients as 'inferiors', patrons, in practice, exercised little real power over the Bajau

Laut. As Panglima Haji Jammal observed, in describing the patron–client relations that existed between local Bajau Laut bands and the Sama Buna-Buna'an community in his father's generation, 'We did not control our boat followers—"our people" (*mundusia kami*). They came to us because they needed someone to look after them and required produce from the land. When they came, they brought fish to barter. At most they were our *bagai*. Otherwise, we had little contact with them.' In consequence, sea nomads were treated with some degree of care. In turn, they were expected to display a degree of outward deference towards their patron and his followers. Clientage relations, although couched in a cultural idiom of long-term 'friendship', were generally fragile; for the Bajau Laut, they always reflected an uneasy balance between a local group's need for protection in an endemic violent world and a desire for community autonomy and freedom of movement. Adapted to the political and economic realities of pre-colonial Sulu, patron–client ties allowed the Bajau Laut to maintain, by choice, a semi-nomadic way of life which assured them a sizeable measure of independence.

In the past, patron–client ties were central to perceptions of Bajau Laut identity and to interethnic relations between sea and shore people, in that it was chiefly through these ties that the Bajau Laut and their neighbours interacted and maintained regular contacts with one another. In addition, patronage linked the Bajau Laut to the wider procurement economy. Within the Semporna district, sea and shore communities were also joined by ecological interdependence and it was largely through such trade-related specialization that the identity of the Sama Dilaut, as 'sea people', was defined.

With the establishment of a trading station at Semporna, the Bajau Laut were quick to transfer their trade to the town market-place. Although they continued to engage in barter exchange with surrounding shore communities into the early 1920s, this exchange rapidly lost its connections with tribute and patronage. Critically, it was trade in export commodities, such as '*tripang*', that was first conducted on a cash basis, which broke down traditional redistributive ties. To the extent that monetization depersonalized economic transactions, its effects can be described as socially and politically liberating from the Bajau Laut viewpoint, as monetization effectively stripped trade of its former connotations of clientage and political subordination (Sather, 1984: 18).

History of the Bangau-Bangau Community

The earliest reference to Bajau-speaking sea nomads identifiable with the Semporna district was from Dewall (1885), the first European resident posted to East Kalimantan. Earlier references made only general mention of the eastern Borneo coast. Later, following the establishment of Company stations at Sandakan and Silam, government correspondence makes repeated mention of boat nomads in the Semporna district. For example, in 1902 J. H. Molyneux (1902: 219–20), reported the presence of a large 'floating village' near Bumbum Island. From this community,

he registered forty to fifty 'house boats', suggesting a boat-living population of some 200–300 people. Whether these comprised a single anchorage group or not is unclear, as is the precise location of this 'village'.

According to Bajau Laut elders, a number of scattered anchorage
groups were present in the district at the time of the founding of the
Semporna station. The number of these quickly declined, however, as
bands combined. By 1930, only three anchorage groups are said to have
remained, all of them based at moorage sites within 3 kilometres of
Semporna town. Two groups were located to the south of Semporna along
the narrow straits that separate the Semporna Peninsula from Bumbum
Island, one on the Bumbum side of the straits, near the present shore
village of Balimbang. The other was due west, on the peninsula side, at a
site called Samar-Samar. The third anchorage was located at the north-
eastern entrance to the straits, near the site of present-day Labuan Haji.
Over the years, families from Samar-Samar gradually moved to the
Balimbang anchorage, so that by the outbreak of the Second World War,
only two anchorage groups are said to have remained in the district. The
Balimbang community was by far the larger of the two.

During the Japanese Occupation, the Bajau Laut population dispersed
once more. Some families established temporary anchorages around the
outer islands, in some cases at moorage sites frequented by bands at the
beginning of the century. Many others moved into the Sibutu island
group where, unlike Semporna, there was no permanent Japanese garrison. Most joined the large Bajau Laut community at Sitangkai, already
the major focal point of the Bajau Laut population. After the Japanese
surrender, families from the former Balimbang and Samar-Samar communities, together with newcomers, most coming directly from Sitangkai,
established their main anchorage at Pasar Laut, in the Semporna harbour,
directly offshore from the town market-place (pasar). To the Bajau Laut,
this anchorage was known as Marilaut Kedai. The Balimbang community
gradually dissolved as families shifted to this new site.

In the immediate post-war years, weapons were plentiful in the southern Philippines, and piracy experienced a resurgence. In 1952, Semporna
town was attacked by pirates, and in 1954, pirates briefly seized and
looted the town, surprising and killing its block-house defenders
(Tregonning, 1960: 205–10). In the aftermath of these attacks, native
boats were not allowed by the marine police to enter or leave the town
harbour after nightfall. Those wishing to call at the town wharf were
permitted to do so only during daylight hours under police surveillance.
These measures were still in effect when I began fieldwork in 1964 and
on a number of occasions I had to remain outside the harbour, anchored
with returning fishing parties, waiting for dawn in order to accompany
families wishing to land their fish at the town market. In line with these
measures, the Bajau Laut were required to quit the town harbour and to
find a new anchorage site elsewhere.

The main Bajau Laut community therefore relocated its anchorage in
a large, shallow bay, part of a stranded, reef-fringed inlet located north
of Semporna town, along the north-western entrance to the Tandu

Bulong Straits (see Map 3.1). The bay has a long association with the Bajau Laut. It is said to have served at various times in the past as an anchorage site. Near its centre is a row of three tiny coralline islets (*pu'*), which the Bajau Laut call Pu' Bangau-Bangau. These take their name from white herons (*kalau bangau*) that seasonally gather in large flocks around them and over the nearby shallows. Within living memory, the middle and easternmost islets have served as a common burial place used by the members of local bands from throughout the Semporna region to inter their dead. The community established here following this relocation took its name from these islets and came to be known officially as Kampung Bangau-Bangau.

In 1955, a year after the relocation of the band, the first two pile-houses were built over the Bangau-Bangau anchorage site, midway between Pu' Bangau-Bangau and the south-eastern shore of the bay. These first houses were built by the husbands of two sisters (Hajal and Amjatul), friends named Salimbara and Tiring. Both couples were members of a large family alliance group headed by the government-appointed leader of the Semporna Bajau Laut community at the time, Panglima Atani, who was also the older brother of Hajal's husband. He headed what was then the largest family alliance group in the region, and it was from the families comprising this group that the first cluster of permanent pile-houses was formed. Following Panglima Atani's death, which occurred shortly after the move to Bangau-Bangau, the group was headed by Amjatul's husband, Panglima Tiring who, as the village took form, became its first headman, a position he retained through 1979.[10] Within a short time, these two house-dwelling families were joined by the families of a married son of Panglima Atani, a brother of Hajal and Amjatul, and a third sister, whose husband Gilang was a brother of Panglima Tiring. All these families, it is important to note, belonged originally to Panglima Atani's alliance group; thus the original nucleus of the village developed directly from a single boat-dwelling family alliance group. These families also formed the initial house group cluster which remained, during the succeeding years, the largest and politically most influential in the community. In establishing a settled village, family alliance groups thus served as the basis around which multifamily house groups and clusters developed as the principal units of a newly emergent village society (see Chapters 5 and 6).

In the years that followed, additional families belonging to various family alliance groups built houses over the anchorage site, forming new house-group clusters both to the north and south of the original group headed by Panglima Tiring. At the same time, four new families joined the original cluster, which later split in two as a result of quarrels between two of its founders. In 1963, the newly established District Council financed the erection of an elevated walkway from the nearest point of land, at the south-eastern tip of the bay, to Panglima Tiring's house platform at the centre of the village. From here, individually constructed plank-walks extended to most of the other houses in the village. The walkway later fell into disrepair, but was subsequently rebuilt and repaired a number of times, and its upkeep, since 1976, has been managed by a village committee. By October 1964, when I began my first fieldwork, the great majority of families had become house-living. By the time I left the village, a year later, Bangau-Bangau consisted of thirty-six pile-houses, formed into nine house-group clusters, with a total population of some 510, 440 of whom were house-living (Plate 2). Figure 2.1 shows the breakdown of this house-living population by age and sex. Only twelve families remained boat-dwelling; and two of these were then in the process of erecting houses.

Directly across the straits, facing Bangau-Bangau, was, and remains, a second, much smaller Bajau Laut settlement known officially as Kampung Labuan Haji. This settlement is located in an irregular cove near the north-west corner of Bumbum Island, and is said to have a longer continuous history as an anchorage than Bangau-Bangau. However, the process of house construction began later here, and although it was well advanced in 1964, it was not so complete. In 1965, Labuan Haji consisted of a row of nine pile-houses, joined to one another and to the land by a continuous catwalk, and twelve to fifteen boat-living families. Altogether, its population at the time was approximately 140.

While the construction of permanent pile-houses marked a radical

FIGURE 2.1

Population of Bangau-Bangau by Age and Sex, 1965

Age[a]	Male			Female	Total
0– 5	50			65	115
6–10	35			28	63
11–15	28			22	50
16–20	22			24	46
21–25	20			18	38
26–30	17			19	36
31–35	12			9	21
36–40	9			9	18
41–45	7			6	13
46–50	8			7	15
51–55	5			5	10
56–60	3			6	9
61 and over	1			5	6
Total	217			223	440

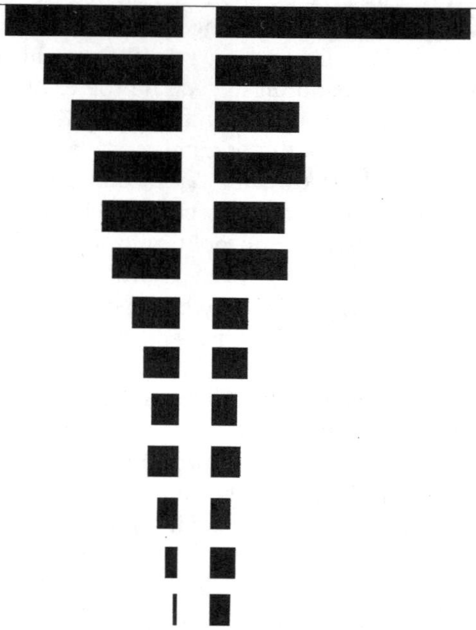

departure from the past, there was, however, some precedent. Tradition-ally in the Semporna–Sibutu region, Bajau Laut families, even though boat-living, occasionally erected temporary stilted shelters over their moorage site whenever unusual circumstances, such as a serious illness or the construction of a new boat, required that a family remain at the site for an extended period of time. These shelters were called *kubu'-kubu'* and typically consisted of a small stilted platform, covered with a roofed shelter made normally of '*kajang*' matting. Like the living quar-ters aboard a houseboat, the roofed ceiling, at its highest, stood usually little more than a metre above the platform floor, so that those inside could only sit or lay down. Families sometimes re-occupied these shelters from time to time over a period of a year or so.

The movement from boat- to house-living represents the culmination of a long, gradual process that began with the founding of Semporna town. Traditionally trade-dependent, Bajau Laut families rapidly grav-itated toward the town as they became increasingly enmeshed in a cash economy. The last major anchorage site before the community's move to Bangau-Bangau was located in the Semporna town harbour directly in front of the public fish market. By the time the first houses were built, the Bajau Laut were already fishing primarily for the town market and for urban middlemen supplying more distant markets outside the district. Until the surrounding region was opened by road, beginning in the late 1960s, the villagers marketed most of their catch as dried fish (*daing toho'*). Processing was done by the fishermen themselves and their families and when houses were constructed, they were built with an open platform for use by family members for drying fish and nets. From the founding of Semporna until 1965, most dried fish was sold to Chinese shophouse owners in Semporna town. Although a small amount was retailed locally, the main Semporna buyers acted essentially as trading agents, handling the onward shipment of dried fish to larger wholesalers in Sandakan, Tawau, and Kota Kinabalu. Since then, as the Bajau Laut have become increasingly sedentary, they have entered directly into this urban market as buyers and licensed market-traders.

In 1965, a path led from the end of the Bangau-Bangau walkway to Semporna town through a coconut estate and around a steep knoll, covered at the time by a small stand of secondary forest. Most traffic between the town and village was by sea. In subsequent years, the knoll was levelled, most of the coconut palms were felled, and a road was built from the town centre to the edge of the bay, close to the end of the village walk-way. Houses and government staff quarters have since been built in the area opened by this road. Hence part of the urban growth of Semporna town has been in the direction of Bangau-Bangau, so that the village is no longer physically separated from the town area, but is now a peri-urban settlement. Near the shore of the bay, a branch road now ends in a newly developed area of urban housing, while the main road from the town centre turns westward to the district hospital, completed in 1970, which is partially visible from the village through the mangrove trees that fringe the bay. Unless they are bringing a landing of fish to market, most villagers now make the journey to town on foot or by taxi. In the morning and late afternoon, there is a heavy stream of villagers, walking along the roadway or travelling by taxis, returning or on their way to town, to work or do their daily shopping.

In 1965, five shops regularly purchased dried fish from village fishermen and supplied them with cotton twine for net-making. Located at the town harbour was the public fish market where Bajau Laut fishermen sold roughly one-third of their marketed catch. By 1979, the district council had built a much larger fresh-fish market, and beside it a smaller dried-fish market. Licensed trade in dried fish was no longer handled by Chinese shopkeepers. In 1979, Bajau Laut traders held all the district dried-fish trading licences and the market was under the supervision of Amjatul, Panglima Tiring's wife.

Social ties between Bangau-Bangau and Labuan Haji were close in 1965. The two villages are within sight of one another and there was constant traffic between them. Intermarriage was, and continues to be, frequent, and during important house group celebrations, such as weddings, funerals, or death memorial rites, invited guests typically include families from the opposite community. Respected curers have patients in both settlements, and when receiving treatment, the latter sometimes stay overnight with the curer's family or with relatives living in the other settlement. When families from Labuan Haji come to Semporna to sell fish or shop, they often visit friends and relatives in Bangau-Bangau before returning home. Reflecting these close relationships, the people of Bangau-Bangau generally refer to those of Labuan Haji, not by village name, but as 'the other half' (*dambila*). Despite the outward appearance of tight-knit aggregation, both villages remain open communities, like earlier moorage groups, and families may freely move from one village to the other.

Post-colonial Semporna

The British North Borneo Chartered Company governed Sabah until the Japanese Occupation in 1942. Following a brief post-war period of British colonial rule which saw rapid economic development in the Semporna district, Sabah gained its independence in 1963, as a state within the Malaysian Federation.

In 1961, Semporna was made, for the first time, a separate administrative district. Semporna town, with a population of 3,371 in 1970, was, and remains, the only urban centre and is today the seat of local government in the district. Here are located the district office, the district police station, court rooms, a post office, the district council building, public markets, and the district council civic centre. Several state government departments also maintain offices in Semporna. The state Customs and Marine Departments have offices at the government wharf. The Marine Department is responsible for licensing all commercial vessels that operate out of the district, principally tugs and small cargo and passenger boats. In the past, all local boat-owners, including Bajau

Laut fishermen, were required to license their vessels with the Marine Department, a requirement that was still in effect in 1964–5. Licensing was introduced by the Chartered Company, and was the source of considerable unrest during the early decades of Company government. After Independence, the requirement was relaxed and finally waived altogether for local fishermen, although in 1979 some villagers in Bangau-Bangau continued to register their fishing boats voluntarily with the Marine Department, as a safeguard against their theft by pirates. The main Marine Police installation in the district is also at the wharf; there is also a smaller station at Si Amil Island, near the Philippine border. Here trading vessels entering Malaysian waters are required to call and surrender any firearms they may be carrying. The two stations are in radio contact with one another and with the Marine Police launches that, operating out of Semporna, regularly patrol the surrounding waters. Prior to 1979, a pirate watch, in radio contact with the Marine Police station in Semporna, was maintained at the summit of Gaya Island (Budgaya), which, in clear weather, commands a view of most of the district coastline and all the islands eastward to Sitangkai in the Philippines.

Semporna town is also the centre of commercial activity in the district. It is a port of call for coastal shipping and was, in 1964–5, the sole shopping and market centre for the surrounding rural population. The main commercial centre of the town consisted in 1965 of six blocks of two- and three-storey shophouses containing hardware and general goods stores, textile dealers, coffee-shops, goldsmiths, a medicine hall, a photographic studio, an automotive parts shop and garage, a stationery and school-supply shop, and a small hotel. Just behind the main shop blocks was an open produce market and food-stalls and, beside them, a small wooden movie theatre. The main blocks were laid out parallel to the harbour. Directly fronting the harbour is the district council market building, a large two-storey concrete structure completed in 1978. Here local farm produce is marketed; from early morning until late afternoon the market is crowded with shoppers, rural people bringing goods to market, market traders, and wholesale buyers. Adjoining the main market are open stalls selling snacks, drinks, locally made ironwork, mats, pottery, and minor sundry goods, cloth, and religious texts and prayer mats. Extending from one side of the market is the council jetty and boat-landing. Here is situated the town fish market, containing separate stalls for fresh and dried fish and an open area for receiving landings.

In 1979, there was, according to the district council, no gazetted town plan for Semporna, with the result that the council had little legal authority to evict people or to control house-building. The result was a great deal of unauthorized construction. The arrival of large numbers of refugees and migrants added not only to the district population, but to the urban character of Semporna town, whose population mushroomed during the 1970s and 1980s. Many recent refugees from the Philippines arrived as traders and engaged in unlicensed hawking and even shop-keeping in Semporna town. By 1990, a number had become wealthy.

A government wharf and commercial warehouses are located to the south of the main business district, from which they are separated by a central *padang* (sports field) and the district office and district council buildings. Beyond the wharf is a relatively recent, heavily populated area known as Kampung Simunul. The area, besides being the home of a large, commercially active Philippine immigrant community, is the site of a small ice factory and a factory jetty. Ice is used to preserve fish and the factory jetty serves as a second major fish market. Here, however, the buyers are chiefly wholesale dealers, the majority of whom purchase fish from local fishermen to ice and transport overland by the main trunk road to Tawau. Whereas the council fish market is active during morning hours, the factory market is most active in the late afternoons and evenings, when trucks carrying loads of iced fish leave for Tawau in order to arrive in time for the early morning opening of the Tawau fish market.

A state Agricultural Department office and farm station is located on the outskirts of Semporna town. A small Fisheries Department office occupies the same compound and was staffed by its first permanent officer in 1979. The present fisheries officer is responsible for providing technical assistance to local fishermen, collecting statistics on local fish prices and landings, and accepting applications for engine grants and subsidies. The latter, in 1979, were forwarded to an independent agency, Ko-Nalayan in Kota Kinabalu, which managed the state's fisheries assistance programme. Three Bangau-Bangau fishermen, including the village headman, obtained inboard engine grants under this programme during the 1970s.

The principal administrative officer locally is the district officer (Pegawai Daerah), who is also the district magistrate and presides over the district court in Semporna. Directly linked to the district administration is also a hierarchy of native offices. Since independence, these have been reorganized and the district is now represented by one district chief, responsible directly to the Pegawai Daerah and bearing the title of Ketua Daerah. Under his charge are three native chiefs, or Ketua Anak Negeri, each having under his jurisdiction roughly one-third of the local villages in the district. In 1979, Bangau-Bangau came under the jurisdiction of Penghulu Hindi bin Bassarani, who lives in Semporna town. The district chief, assisted by the native chiefs, presides over the native court which rules on cases, usually referred to it by village headmen, involving local customary law, mostly in matters of marriage, inheritance, and the division of native estates. Criminal cases and civil suits are brought before the district court and are dealt with directly by the Pegawai Daerah. Serious matters, such as homicide and piracy, are referred directly to the residency court in Tawau. The district *imam* (Imam Daerah) also sits on the native court and assists the chiefs in cases involving religious law. The district *imam* is also in charge of the district mosque located near the main commercial area of Semporna town and for the registration of Muslim marriages and divorces. Both the district and native chiefs are selected by appointment and receive a monthly salary determined by their experience and seniority. All in Semporna, in 1979, were considered to be men of means.

At the bottom of the native hierarchy, mediating between the villagers and the district administration, are the local village headmen or Ketua Kampung. During the colonial period, village headmen, then called Orang Tua, were unpaid. Although not technically salaried, headmen in 1979 received a monthly stipend of RM100, paid quarterly. Each headman is responsible for maintaining village order, settling minor disputes among his followers, and referring more serious matters to the native chief with jurisdiction over his community, or to the police. In larger villages, the Ketua Kampung is aided by one, or possibly several unpaid assistant headmen, or Wakil Ketua Kampung.

Kampong development committees were established in each village in the district after the change in government that followed the 1976 state elections in Sabah. Committee members are elected every two years and are guided by an elected executive board made up of prominent village members. Committees are advised by a district development officer and are eligible for small grants of money for community improvement projects initiated and managed by the committee executive board. Development committees are independent of the district administration. In Semporna, they are overseen by the political secretary of the governing political party and are perceived locally as a channel for the distribution of political favours. In some communities, the executive board is chaired by the village headman, or someone close to him; in others the committee represents a rival focus of leadership, often reinforcing the already fissiparous nature of local-level Bajau politics.

In addition to the district administration, native hierarchy, and village development committees, there are three levels of elective government represented in Semporna: federal, state, and district. In 1979, the Semporna district, together with the Lahad Datu district and Kunak subdistrict, made up a federal parliamentary constituency called Kuasan Silam. The Member of Parliament for Kuasan Silam at the time was Datuk (later Tan Sri Datuk) Sakaran Dandai, who had also been a state cabinet minister in the previous government (1967–76). Datuk Sakaran had a following among some, though not all elements of the Bajau Laut community. In 1964–5, when I began my research, he had not yet entered politics and was then the Semporna district chief (Orang Kaya Kaya), succeeding his father-in-law and uncle, Panglima Datuk Abdullah, who was the son and successor of Panglima Udang, the major political figure in the early Chartered Company administration of Semporna. At the state level, Semporna comprises a separate assembly district, and Tan Sri Sakaran was also in 1979 the State Assemblyman for Semporna. He is now Governor of Sabah.

At the local level, most public services in Semporna town and its surroundings, such as lighting, water, garbage collection, and street repairs, are provided by the District Council or Majlis Daerah. The council also oversees and maintains the town jetty and wharf, the public fish market, a newly constructed two-storey produce market, a district civic centre and council offices. The council is the chief taxing authority locally and licenses shops and traders and collects licence fees, water rates, and titled land assessments. Prior to the 1976 elections, the council was chaired by Panglima Datuk Abdullah. After the election, its chairman was the Pegawai Daerah. Since 1970, the council has provided water and electricity to Bangau-Bangau. The villagers do not pay land rates, as the community is built over the water, but households receiving electricity are issued monthly bills by the district clerk.

During the years of the United Sabah National Organization (USNO) government that preceded the 1976 elections, the Chief Minister of Sabah created a system of highly personal rule in Semporna and other north and east coast districts. Picking Bajau leaders loyal to him directly, he gave them almost complete power locally. In Semporna, Datuk Abdullah, acting as chairman of the district council, controlled revenue collection, business licences, and hundreds of patronage jobs. More importantly, he served as executive in charge of the Native Trust (Syarikat Anak Negeri), a position that gave him control over local timber concessions. However, by amassing considerable personal wealth and commercial property in Semporna town, he eventually alienated rival leaders, causing him to be removed from control of the Native Trust, and in 1979 he had left the Semporna district and was living in political retirement in Tawau.

Education

In 1979, there were twenty-one government schools in the Semporna district. Five, including one Chinese school, a large urban primary school, and the only secondary school were located on the Semporna peninsula. The remaining sixteen schools, all rural primary schools, were located on the smaller outlying islands. The district secondary school was located near Kampung Bubul, 6 kilometres inland from Semporna town. Most of its students, who came from throughout the district, were boarders. There was also a separate religious school, supported by the state religious council attached to the district mosque near the commercial centre of Semporna. It was attended by both full-time students and by part-time students who received Koranic instruction after regular school hours.

Most local schools are relatively recent. The first school in Semporna opened in 1919 with an enrolment of seventeen pupils, thirteen boys and four girls (Anon., 1919). The Chartered Company government paid the teacher's salary, but the building in which classes were held was erected and maintained by the local Chinese and Bajau communities. Later, the Chinese community founded its own school. It was only during the British colonial period and after Malaysian independence that educational opportunities were expanded and an effort was made to make primary education universally available. Nearly every village is now within easy walking distance of a government primary school offering at least a lower elementary education.

Children from Bangau-Bangau attend either the main primary school in Semporna town, which was built during the British colonial period, or the district religious school. Bajau Laut children only began to attend school in the early 1960s, after the first village pile-houses were con-structed. The first group of schoolchildren met with considerable hostility from youngsters from other Bajau groups. Between 1965 and 1979, school attendance greatly increased, but was still low compared to other communities, with only one-third of those eligible regularly attending lower primary school. Girls attended in much smaller numbers than boys, and enrolments for both declined rapidly in the upper grades, so that few completed the full elementary course. Fewer than twenty Bajau Laut youngsters went on to secondary school between the founding of the Bubul school in 1965 and 1979. In 1979, fifteen village adults attended adult literacy classes, which were held in Bangau-Bangau three times a week under a programme funded by the Malaysian federal government. In 1965, Bajau Laut youngsters from Labuan Haji attended the rural primary school at Tanjung Baru.

In 1982, a primary school was built on the easternmost of the three Bangau-Bangau islets. The old Bajau Laut burial grounds (*kubul*) became the school garden, while a new burial ground was established ashore on the Semporna Peninsula. Through funds from an international grant, two rows of classrooms, a small library, offices, and teachers' quarters were constructed. An extended walkway was erected between the islet and Bangau-Bangau village. The school proved immensely pop-ular with the villagers. It opened with a single primary one class, but expanded quickly, so that by 1992, it offered all primary classes, one to six. Enrolment outgrew the school buildings, so that classes had to be given in double sessions, morning and afternoon, with, in 1992, four classes of primary one, three of primary two, two of primary three and four, and one of primary five and six. In 1991, the Ministry of Educa-tion decided that the previous headmaster was inadequately trained to oversee such a large school, and it was announced that he would be re-placed by someone more qualified. In 1993, just before the headmaster's retirement, during the night, the school offices were mysteriously set on fire with petrol. The fire not only burned the offices to the ground, but also destroyed the school library and badly damaged most of the class-rooms before being put out. Although formal charges were never brought against him, many villagers suspected that the headmaster was respons-ible and had hired professional arsonists, who were, at the time, a familiar fixture in the district, to destroy the school's financial records in order to cover up an alleged misappropriation of school funds set aside for the purchase of school books and shoes for needy village students. During the 1993–4 school year, the Bangau-Bangau school remained in ruins and children had to return to the main urban school in Semporna town.

Instruction at both the primary and secondary level is in Bahasa Malaysia and follows a national curriculum set by the Malaysian Ministry of Education.

Health

In 1965, there was only a small government dispensary and clinic in Semporna town, staffed by a senior dresser, two assistants, three attend-ants, and three rural health nurses. A medical officer from Tawau, then a British doctor, visited Semporna once a month by launch; he usually also called at the main offshore islands: Bumbum, Menampilik, Larapan, and Omadal.

In 1979, Semporna town had a small 85-bed district hospital, with a resident doctor, a dispensary and a paranatal clinic. The hospital is located only a few minutes' walk from Bangau-Bangau. There were also eight village group subcentres located outside Semporna town, at Bait, Tanjung Kapur, Sungai Buaya, Tagasan Baru, Kabogan, Bubul, Egang-Egang, and Hampalan. These serve largely rural and island populations, each with a permanent rural health nurse providing primarily maternal and child health care. The Semporna hospital, which was first opened in 1970, has a staff, in addition to its resident doctor, of eight staff nurses, three hospital assistants, and fourteen assistant nurses. Most planned surgery is referred to the residency hospital in Tawau, but the Semporna hospital is equipped for most types of emergency surgery. It also has a small tuberculosis treatment unit and an environmental health unit. The latter has on its staff a public health inspector responsible for inspecting eating places, hawkers, and for port health, water supply, and rural sanitation. The hospital does not keep full statistics on its patients, but the staff estimates that they attend, on average, seventy patients per day, including twenty to thirty per week from Bangau-Bangau. The most common complaints are respiratory infections, fevers, diarrhoea, and gastro-enteritis.

In addition to the government health facilities, in 1979 a former army medical officer from Peninsular Malaysia had started a private practice in Semporna town and the former government dresser, who was then retired, operated a small medical hall where he treated local patients on a private basis.

Water is a serious problem everywhere in the Semporna district. The founding of Semporna town was linked to the digging of freshwater wells, and in the neighbouring islands of the Sulu Archipelago control over springs and other freshwater sources was, and remains, an important source of local political power, with access to water being one of the 'privileges' patrons provided their boat-living clients. During the drought months of August and September 1979, even in Semporna town, the piped water supply was intermittent, operating at best for only several hours a day. At the time, Bangau-Bangau was linked to the Semporna piped water supply, but for much of the time was without drinking water. Water was then a marketed commodity, and families with large storage tanks made considerable profit from selling water. On the low-lying and coralline outer islands of the district, the supply of drinking water is even more precarious, particularly during dry spells and droughts. In 1979, the environmental health unit was investigating the possibility of supplying island villages with rain-catchment equipment. Most of the well water in Semporna district is highly saline, to the extent that outsiders, unaccustomed to it, often find it impossible to drink. In 1965, a commonly told joke was that when Bajau from Semporna visited other parts of Sabah, they had to mix the local drinking water half-and-half with sea water in order to make it 'palatable'. In the past, outbreaks of cholera frequently occurred in the outer island settlements during prolonged droughts, sometimes causing a number of deaths (Cook, 1924: 82–90). Even in the 1960s cholera remained a danger.

Despite the greatly improved health care facilities available by the early 1990s, the general level of health in Bangau-Bangau still compared unfavourably with many other rural communities in Malaysia. The most serious health problems relate to malaria, tuberculosis, and typhoid. Malaria was endemic in the district during the 1960s and 1970s, particularly on the Semporna Peninsula, though it was fairly unusual in the outer islands. In 1979, the district hospital treated between thirty and forty cases of malaria each week, while additional patients sought private treatment. In 1965, most adult villagers in Bangau-Bangau, including virtually all of those who had worked recently on agricultural estates or in timber camps, showed chronic malaria symptoms. Throughout the 1970s there was an active malaria eradication programme in the district, with two cycles of spraying a year. At the time, the programme appeared largely ineffective, possibly because of the frequent coming and going of peoples from malaria-endemic regions of Indonesia and the Philippines. Dengue fever, although less prevalent, was also present.[11] Tuberculosis was also widespread, and a number of villagers received treatment in the Semporna hospital tuberculosis unit. According to hospital staff, less serious, internal parasites including hookworms were common, while tinea, skin lesions, open leg sores, and skin infections, particularly impetigo, were especially prevalent among village youngsters. Because of the abundance of fish in the villagers' diet, protein malnutrition, not infrequent in interior districts of Sabah, is unknown. Fish, however, are a poor source of iron, and dietary anaemia is common in Bangau-Bangau. Because of the high birth-rate, it is particularly prevalent among women of childbearing age.

From the maternal history data I recorded, beginning in 1965, I calculated the rate of paranatal and infant mortality in the community to be approximately 10.4 per 100 births. Because of the high birth-rate, however, nearly 44 per cent of all women experienced the loss of at least one child during their reproductive years. The principal causes of infant death appear to have been severe diarrhoea and gastro-enteritis, pneumonia, respiratory infections, and in the case of preadolescent children, chiefly malaria and typhoid. A few children also died by accidental drowning, although no instance occurred in my sample of maternal histories. Maternal mortality is infrequent; only one instance occurred in Bangau-Bangau during the fifteen-year period of 1964–79. In 1965, sterility was almost unknown; there were no cases in my maternal history sample.

Until the early 1950s, leprosy was not uncommon in the district. A note in the official *British North Borneo Herald* of 5 April 1902, in reference to the region, observed 'that a large percentage of the Bajau population is suffering from leprosy; these cases are seldom noticed as so few of the Bajau settlements can be visited by Europeans' (Anon., 1902b: 110). The Bajau Laut refer to leprosy as *ipul*. They generally look upon the disease with revulsion and greatly fear contact with those suffering from it. During the colonial period, the government sent lepers to a leprosarium on Berhala Island in Sandakan Bay. The villagers in Bangau-Bangau say that in the past, out of compassion, strand Bajau hid members of their family suffering from the disease so that they would not be taken away. There were communities of lepers, according to elderly Bajau Laut, hidden from sight in the scrub forest near Tongkalloh and Hampalan villages on Bumbum Island. The people of these and neighbouring communities are said to have supplied them with food and otherwise looked after their material needs. For this reason, elderly Bajau Laut say that in the past, they and other boat people carefully avoided putting into shore at these two villages. Today, leprosy appears to have been eradicated locally, although in 1965 it could still be seen occasionally in refugees from the southern Philippines.

Religion and Redefining an Ethnic Identity

Although speaking the same language, the Sama Dilaut were sharply differentiated from their more settled Sama-speaking neighbours. Differences of identity, origin myths, economic specialization, and inequalities of power and social status formed elements of a larger system of ethnic stratification. This system acted not merely to maintain ethnic boundaries, but also, in the case of sea and shore people, to uphold distinctively different ways of life, making it difficult for individuals or communities to cross these boundaries.

Colonialism and an expanding world system transformed this traditional pattern of stratification, breaking down former relations of patronage and tributary trade, reconstituting politics and the economy along new lines. None the less, ethnic consciousness remains a central feature of society. Rather than trying to remove the entire structure of inequality, the Bajau Laut have sought instead to negate those particular cultural differences that served in the past to situate them at the bottom of the ethnic hierarchy—patronage, boat nomadism, and religious exclusion. Of these, religion proved to be the most fundamental, although it was clearly linked to the others, so that religious change was possible only after the community had abandoned boat nomadism and freed itself from former patronage relations.

In the past, shore-living Bajau in the Semporna district contrasted themselves with the Sama Dilaut as being 'Sama Islam' or 'Muslim Bajau'. In contrast, the Bajau Laut were said to be 'without religion' (*halam ania' ugama* or *halam ugamaan*). As in other contexts, religion and status were equated. The outcaste status of the Sama Dilaut was thus conceptualized in religious terms, and hence their separate origin as an ethnic group was represented as an act of divine exclusion.

Following Malaysian independence, the Semporna Bajau Laut, in challenging the terms of their traditional status, obtained support from Islamic reformist elements in the district, both local Muslim leaders and the state Religious Affairs Department (Sather, 1984: 22). Until then, local Bajau had debarred them from actively participating in the formal religious life of the district on the grounds that they were non-Muslim.[12] Religious exclusion was physically enforced in the past. The Bajau Laut had not been permitted to bury their dead in the local Muslim cemeteries or to enter the district mosque or village prayer-houses ashore (Sather, 1971a). These prohibitions, linked to myths of divine expulsion, were believed by many to have scriptural authority, and so failure to observe them was believed to provoke supernatural punishment (*busung*) in the form of droughts and other natural disasters.

In undermining these notions, the Bajau Laut found support, in particular, from the first *ustaz* (district religious teacher) in Semporna and from the former district *khatib*. At the time of Sabah's independence, a Koranic school was established adjacent to the district mosque. State religious authorities appointed as the first *ustaz*, a peninsular Malay, Ustaz Mohamed Said. At the time of his arrival in Semporna, Ustaz Said was already an elderly man. Although respected for his piety and learning, he made himself a controversial figure by arguing that there was no scriptural basis to the generally held view that the Bajau Laut were cursed by God. In the 1960s, many local Bajau in the district believed that versions of the mythic tradition related in Chapter 1 derived directly from the Koran or, some said, from sacred traditions relating to the Prophet's life. Ustaz Said taught that, on the contrary, sea nomads are nowhere mentioned in the Koran or in any of the other scriptures. Moreover, he argued that those who acted to exclude from the faith persons who wished to embrace it and practise its tenets were themselves behaving contrary to Islamic principles. Over local objections, he not only opened the Koranic school to Bajau Laut children, but spoke with the headman of Bangau-Bangau and other parents, encouraging them to send their children to his school.

Also important was the district *khatib*, Khatib Andau and his son Haji Abdul Majid, who in 1979 was the senior government hospital assistant in Semporna. Until his death, Khatib Andau was responsible for delivering the Friday sermons in the Semporna district mosque. He frequently lectured on the Bajau Laut and the theme that all Muslims are duty-bound to welcome into the faith anyone who wishes to embrace it. Khatib Andau and his son were Simunul Bajau and related to the native chief, Haji Mohamed Dara. Khatib Andau also gave religious instruction at his house, at Mile Two, outside Semporna town. Many from Bangau-Bangau were instructed by him, including Panglima Tiring and his eldest son, Imam Wayijal. Those going for instruction walked overland by a footpath from Bangau-Bangau, and until the construction of a village mosque, the *khatib*'s house served the principal place of religious teaching and assembly for village men.

With Khatib Andau's instruction, a founding cadre of village *imam* and future mosque officials was created, opening the way for the establishment of the first community mosque in Bangau-Bangau. The first mosque (*maskid*) was built in 1967, and rebuilt and enlarged in 1969 with village labour and materials supplied by the state government

(Sather, 1984: 22). In a strict sense, it is not a true mosque ('*masjid*' in Bahasa Malaysia), a term that applies in Semporna only to the imposing concrete district mosque in Semporna town, but rather a village prayer-house ('*surau*'). In Sama, however, no such distinction is drawn. Both village prayer-houses and the district mosque are referred to by the same term, *maskid*. Responsibility for maintaining the mosque rests with a mosque committee whose duty is not only to look after the physical structure but to arrange for Friday prayers and other gatherings. The committee includes three appointed village officials, the *imam*, village *kadi* (*khatib*), and *bilal* (muezzin). The term *imam* is also used by the Bajau Laut in a more general sense to refer to any villager, including all three mosque officials, who is capable of reading the scriptures and leading other men in prayer.

The construction of a village prayer-house was an event of major symbolic importance for the Bajau Laut community. Throughout the Sulu–Semporna region, the prayer-house has served historically, not only as the centre of local religious life, but as the meeting place and minimal focus of all leader-centred political coalitions (Sather, 1993b: 219). Locally, religion and secular authority were, and remain, inseparably related. A mosque congregation thus constitutes a primary political constituency. Local prayer-houses are typically under the care of a local political leader, who generally acts as their primary financial patron; at the same time, the *maskid* serves as the chief gathering place of his principal supporters. Leaders are accorded respect to the extent that they are seen as upholding the faith and supporting its institutions, including its mosques and prayer-houses. In the past, the Bajau Laut, as boat-dwellers, were without *maskid*. This was because, as a basic requirement, a *maskid* must be a fixed, permanent structure. To outsiders, this absence of a prayer-house not only symbolized the religious exclusion of the Bajau Laut, as being 'without religion', but also demonstrated their 'leaderless' status. Being without a *maskid* meant that they could only be a subject people, without the outwardly tangible attributes of a political constituency, standing outside and apart from an otherwise enveloping network of leader-centred coalitions.

As religion traditionally expressed political status, so the exclusion of the Bajau Laut symbolized their 'outcaste' status and debarred them from assuming a formal place in the dominant political order of the region, except as clients. In erecting a prayer-house, the Bajau Laut overtly reconstituted their community as a congregation of co-religionists. In doing so, they presented themselves not only as Muslims (Sama Islam) but as active participants in a wider political order, forming an acknowledged political constituency as well within a religiously ordered and politically centralized society. Ironically, their action, while challenging the ascriptive terms by which they were formerly stigmatized, at the same time reinforced the continuing primacy of ethnicity as the principal basis of social differentiation and status.

To many in Semporna, the Bajau Laut, as a consequence of building a prayer-house and organizing themselves as a congregation, have gained gradual acceptance as Muslims. Since the early 1970s, they have been able to attend the district mosque and a number of villagers have since been buried in the main Muslim cemetery in Semporna town.[13] Panglima Jammal, from whom I collected the mythic account of sea nomad origins related in Chapter 1, concedes that many of the Bangau-Bangau people are now Sama Islam. 'Before we did not mix with them. Now many have become Muslims. We people control them more and have more contacts. Before they had no religion; now they mix with us.'

A Changing Village Economy

From the time of the station's founding by the Chartered Company government, the Bajau Laut were drawn to Semporna town as a regional market-place. They disposed of the greater part of their *bêche-de-mer*, dried fish, and other maritime produce through its town traders who were largely divorced from the earlier political order. At the same time, cash from market trading became an essential part of the villager's existence. Not only rice, cassava, and other staples were obtained through the town market, but also goods such as manufactured cordage, sail-cloth, netting twine, fish hooks, and kerosene lanterns, all becoming economic necessities to the Sama Dilaut by the early twentieth century.

Bangau-Bangau is a socially heterogeneous community as a result of two major changes since it became a sedentary village. The first is increased occupational and economic differentiation; the second, closely linked to the first, is growing urbanization. In 1965, fishing was still the mainstay of the village economy, though even then a sizeable number of village men were taking up wage work. By 1974, less than half of those gainfully employed engaged in full-time fishing. The proportion has continued to decline, although not as dramatically as during the late 1960s and early 1970s. In 1979, fishing was the main source of income for only a quarter (24 per cent) of all village house groups. For the remainder, the primary source was wage employment, salaries, and petty trade.

Ironically, the movement to wage work was fostered in part by changes in the nature of fishing itself. In the late 1950s and early 1960s, jobs became available outside the village, chiefly as a result of road-building and the opening of agricultural estates in the Lahad Datu and Tawau districts. At the same time, small $1\frac{1}{2}$ hp outboard engines were introduced. By 1965, most village house groups owned at least one engine. A number of village men took up wage work in order to obtain the cash necessary to buy an engine or to pay for its replacement or repairs. In 1965, outboard engines were still used sparingly because of the high cost and scarcity of petrol. Even so, their use had already introduced a number of important changes in village fishing. The villagers fished the same areas as before, but the time they spent in travelling to these areas was reduced. Less time was spent at sea, even among those who continued to fish full-time. The opening of timber camps in the interior and later the main Tawau trunk road greatly increased the local demand for fresh fish, which the villagers were able to respond to by using outboard engines, allowing them to bring landings to market more quickly. At the same time, as less and less fish was being dried at sea, fishermen became less dependent upon the labour of their wives and children. One result was a major shift in the nature of boat crews, away from family units toward short-term, all-male crews (Sather, 1984). This shift was also made possible by the move to house-living, which allowed wives and younger children to remain in the village while the men fished. Similarly, while greater demand for fish increased cash earnings, the use of engines increased cash expenses.

Wage work, often of a temporary, casual nature, offered a means by which to meet these increased cash needs. In the early 1960s, a Japanese company opened a tuna trolling operation near Si Amil Island, employing a number of Bajau Laut men, many of whom took their families to live with them in boats near the island. The company ceased operations at the end of 1962. During the 1960s and early 1970s, the Public Works Department was the chief employer of village labour, although many villagers also worked for short periods as temporary contract labourers on agricultural estates. Public Works Department crews were assembled daily in Semporna town for road construction and maintenance work, and such employment was easily combined with part-time fishing or could be undertaken for a limited time with a specific cash need in mind. In time, however, the villagers became increasingly committed to permanent wage employment. In 1979, the Public Works Department was still the largest employer of village labour, but many more villagers worked for other employers. Even within the Public Works Department, by 1980 village employment had become much more diverse and included villagers in permanent skilled labour, clerical, and supervisory positions, as well as daily-paid manual labourers. The villagers had also entered a wide variety of other occupations, only a few of which, such as fish-marketing and boat-building, remained closely connected with traditional fishing activities.

Another consequence of the villagers' increased involvement in a money economy was the breakdown of former relations of subsistence sharing between village kin. To be effective, food-sharing requires that all, or the great majority, participate. As families withdrew from fishing, the reciprocal basis of food sharing was destroyed as many families were no longer able to reciprocate with return gifts of fish. At the same time, those who continued to fish found it more profitable to market their catch. After the opening of the main trunk road in 1967, and the construction of a local ice plant soon afterwards, the demand for fish soared as scores of outside buyers entered the Semporna market. Between 1965 and 1974, market prices more than doubled and by 1979, tripled, even though they remained low by Malaysian standards.

At the same time, cash expenses increased. In addition to the cost of petrol and engine repairs, nylon nets were introduced in the early 1970s and outboard engines were replaced by more powerful and reliable inboard engines in the mid-1970s. Traditional fishing boats were replaced during the 1980s by plank-constructed vessels (*pombot* and *kumpit*). The latter are cheaper to build and better suited to the use of inboard engines. By 1994, none of the traditional boats in use in 1965 were still in service. These investments have drawn village fishermen even more thoroughly into the cash economy and opened new opportunities for village boat-builders and mechanics.

As a consequence of these changes, outside the immediate house group, fish are almost entirely a market commodity. In marked contrast to the past, fish are regularly bought and sold within the village. As a consequence, all fishermen are engaged in some marketing. A number of them now regularly trade in fish, buying and marketing the landings made by other fishermen as well as their own catch. In 1979, there were six Bajau Laut and eight non-Bajau Laut fish buyers resident in Bangau-Bangau, and another twenty to thirty, both Bajau Laut and non-Bajau Laut, who engaged in occasional trading, mainly to supply interior vendors or transporters. In addition, a number of village families have entered the town market, some as informal hawkers, others as licensed traders. In 1979, the headman's wife, Amjatul, supervised the dried fish market, for which she collected a 10 per cent commission (*sukai*) from fishermen who brought her their dried fish for sale. Four villagers held licences for fresh-fish stalls in the main public market, including the headman, the headman's younger brother, and the former chairman of the kampong development committee. However, none of these men actually trade in the market but, like most other licence-holders in Semporna, farm out their stalls, either for a fixed monthly sum or for a share of the daily take, to those who actually trade, mostly 'refugees' from the Philippines who are legally debarred from holding stall licences, but who include many experienced market-traders.

In addition, a substantial informal market has grown up on the shore at the foot of the village walkway. Here produce such as fruit, vegetables, and cassava, also dried goods, drinks, cooked food, and snacks are sold. In the village itself, a good deal of marketing is done directly to other villagers, or to professional buyers. It is common in Semporna for hawkers to deal in more commodities than are specified in their licences, and those who handle produce generally also trade in small stocks of fish whenever these are available. Reflecting the complex economy of the present village, there were, in 1979, twelve shops ('*kedai*') operating in Bangau-Bangau. Two of these, which were unlicensed, sold only snacks and cakes. One occasionally offered produce, fresh vegetables, and local fruit. The remainder were general goods stores selling sweets, cooking oil, school supplies such as pencils and exercise books, inexpensive canned goods, cigarettes, batteries, rubber-soled slippers, bottled drinks, and other small items. The largest shop in the village, which was operated by one of two Iban businessmen married to Bajau Laut women, also contained in 1979 a small coffee shop-canteen, selling coffee and refrigerated soft drinks.[14] The other two large shops occupy the same premises and are operated by owners, one Iban, the other Visayan, who have married into the same Bajau Laut house group. All three shops were well stocked and sold goods at prices competitive with those offered in Semporna town. The other shops in the village were all small, most consisting of little more than a single row of open shelves, and dealt mainly in sweets, fresh fruit, and cigarettes. While a few were profitable, most were short-lived. Operators bought their stocks on a cash basis from town retailers at prices only slightly below village selling prices.

Legally, shop owners as well as others engaging in buying and selling, are required to obtain an annual trading licence issued by the revenue clerk at the district office. In taking out a licence, the holder is asked to specify the kind of trade he or she intends to engage in. In August 1979, eleven villagers held valid trading licences in Bangau-Bangau. Three of these were not actively trading at the time, at least on a regular basis; two were licensed fish dealers; and the remaining six were licensed as shopkeepers. Of the latter, three were licence-holders acting on behalf of others who conducted the actual business. Except for the largest traders, there was a reluctance to take out licences, the main reason being, it is said, fear of tax auditing.

In addition to the village shops, a good deal of more informal trading now takes place in Bangau-Bangau. In the mornings and evenings, members of fishing families generally sell fish informally all along the main village walkway. There are also village women who prepare cakes and other snacks for sale throughout the day, but particularly to youngsters and schoolchildren in the early mornings. Also in the mornings, a small informal food and produce market operates in the open area at the end of the village walkway, beside the sheds where village owners garage their taxis. In the evenings, water is sold here from metal storage tanks. Water-selling is one of the most lucrative of all village businesses. In 1979, the villagers generally purchased water in 4-gallon (18-litre) containers at 40 cents. Water-selling was at the time dominated by two Bajau Laut house groups, both of whom obtained their water from the district council at the rate of $2 per 1,000 gallons (4540 litres or roughly one-fifth of cent per gallon). The trade was thus highly profitable. It required constant attention, however, as the flow of piped water was intermittent. A number of other families had roof-catchment tanks for rain-water, which they sold whenever they had more than they could use.

With the construction of the main trunk road, a number of village men invested in private taxis. Until the early 1980s, much of the road remained unsurfaced and many of these initial investors failed to anticipate the heavy repairs and maintenance expenses involved, and so were forced to sell out. In 1979, seven villagers owned taxis. Five drove their taxis; the two other owners hired drivers. Another villager worked as a driver for a non-Bajau Laut car owner. Most taxi owners are relatively well-off by village standards and operate locally, chiefly carrying other villagers within the vicinity of Semporna town.

A small number of villagers hold salaried jobs, mainly clerical, skilled labour, or supervisory positions. All are regarded as well-to-do and several are in a position to find work for others. Two have additional business interests, one as an occasional fish dealer and carrier, the other as a licensed market stall operator. A number of others are self-employed including a Sikubang Bajau from Omadal Island, who lives in the village with his Bajau Laut wife and her family. During the timber boom, he amassed a considerable personal fortune as a Forestry Department officer. In 1979, he owned a tyre dealership and an automotive parts shop in Semporna town and a fleet of three trucks and a taxi. He employed three of his wife's relatives as shop mechanics and drivers.

Population Change

Between 1965 and 1979, the nature of Bangau-Bangau changed dramatically from that of a small fishing village inhabited entirely by Bajau Laut to a large, semi-urban community containing members of other ethnic groups as well. The village's total population increased nearly fourfold during these years, from 510 in 1965 to 1,982 in 1979 (Table 2.1). This rapid growth came about largely through immigration. While the Bajau Laut remained the clear majority, forming 135 of the 189 house groups making up the village, nearly half of the population growth since 1965 was due to the arrival of non-Bajau Laut newcomers, most of them Bajau-speaking migrants from the southern Philippines. During the

TABLE 2.1
Population of Bangau-Bangau, 1979

| Ethnic Group | Number of House Groups | Population | | Total |
		Male	Female	
Bajau Laut	135	725	747	1,472
Other Bajau				
Sibutu	19	91	80	171
Sibaut	14	95	92	187
Simunul	2	7	4	11
Ubian	2	5	7	12
Others	10	27	27	54
Non-Bajau				
Bugis	4	12	13	25
Button	2	12	7	19
Bulungan	–	–	1	1
Dusun	–	2	–	2
Iban	–	2	–	2
Javanese	–	1	–	1
Timorese	–	4	–	4
Tidong	–	1	–	1
Tausug	1	7	8	15
Visayan	–	3	1	4
Chinese	–	1	–	1
Total	189	995	987	1,982

same period, Labuan Haji experienced similar growth; by 1979, the village comprised 63 pile-houses with a population of roughly 700.

Not only did outsiders take up residence in the village, but the Bajau Laut population itself became increasingly heterogeneous, as large numbers of Bajau Laut migrants settled in Bangau-Bangau. While most were close kin of families already present, and so were readily incorporated into the existing network of house groups and clusters, others came without prior kin connections, as 'refugees', many from the Tawitawi island group. These have been incorporated on a very different basis, as the clients of long-established village members. Since 1979, the population of Bangau-Bangau has continued to grow rapidly, although the entry of further non-Bajau Laut has now largely ceased, except through intermarriage. By the early 1990s, the village was formally divided into two, each with its own headman and kampong development committee. The name Kampung Bangau-Bangau was retained by that part of the settlement located closest to the shore, while the half located further into the bay, including the house of the former village headman, Panglima Tiring, who has since been succeeded by his son, Haji Arka, has been named Kampung Sri Kanangan. In addition, since 1980, a third village, Kampung Halo, comprised of Bajau Laut refugees from Tawitawi, has been founded. The village is situated along the seaward shore of the middle Bangau-Bangau islet and its members pay nominal rent to established Bajau Laut patrons as the islet's owners.

In the mid-1960s, employment opportunities in the Semporna district grew rapidly, mainly as a consequence of the flourishing timber industry, which reached its peak in the early 1970s. Logging operations, together with the construction of roads and the opening of the interior to agricultural settlement and estates, produced an unprecedented economic boom. The Bajau Laut responded by entering the labour market in large numbers, bringing about the transformation of the economic make-up of the community. By the early 1970s, more than half the men of working age in Bangau-Bangau held regular jobs outside the community. A number also engaged in circular labour migration. Already by 1965, a small transient population of Bajau Laut labourers from Semporna were living in the Sim-Sim section of Sandakan. Since then, their numbers have greatly increased, with others going also to Tawau and Kota Kinabalu in search of work.

The growth of job opportunities, together with sectarian violence, population pressure, and deteriorating economic conditions in the southern Philippines, brought a massive inflow of migrants into the district and resulted in a rapid increase in the population of Semporna town. With timber wealth and roads, the town increased its importance as a centre of marketing and service activity, and part of the resulting expansion of the town occurred in the direction of Bangau-Bangau. Roads were laid out, and in 1970 the district hospital opened on a site just south of the village. With these developments, piped water and electricity were extended to the village.

In the early 1960s, the main area of Bajau settlement in Semporna town was in the Kampung Air area, along the edge of the town harbour. By 1970, this area had become highly congested and with the construction of the district hospital, urban growth spread northward from Kampung Air toward Bangau-Bangau, both over the water and along the shoreline. However, with the development of a government rest house and administrative and hospital staff quarters in the area immediately ashore from Bangau-Bangau, the village was spared from being totally enveloped in this growth, as the district government banned further house-building in the area adjoining Bangau-Bangau.

Though spared, the village is located close enough to the town area to make it possible for those living in the village to commute daily to jobs in Semporna town. As a result, most of those drawn to wage work during the district timber boom continue to hold jobs outside the village and almost none of their children, born since the early 1960s, continue to fish. Because of its proximity to the town, the village became an attractive residence and during the early 1970s, a number of villagers made a business of building houses to sell to non-Bajau Laut buyers. It was in this way, and through intermarriage, that a significant number of non-Bajau Laut came to enter the village. Of 189 house groups in 1979, 54 were headed by non-Bajau Laut house owners (see Table 2.1). Eight of these are married to Bajau Laut women. Nearly all the others are located at the landward edge of the settlement, in present-day Kampung Bangau-Bangau.

Although the Bajau Laut comprise the great majority of the village population, the presence of others is strongly felt. The greatest tension exists between the Bajau Laut and the Bugis and Buttonese. Most of the latter are fish traders and petty hawkers and are accused by the Bajau Laut of engaging in sharp business practices, even within the village. Especially disliked is an elderly Buttonese trader, whom the villagers have nicknamed 'Haji Bohé' because he initially established himself in the community as its principal water (*bohé*) seller. Later, in the early 1970s, Bajau Laut employees of the Public Works Department laid down what were initially unauthorized water pipes to the village and in this way broke the Haji's monopoly. Using these pipes as their main source, two Bajau Laut families displaced Haji Bohé as the village's main water seller. Both have carefully cultivated the goodwill of their customers by observing traditional rules of generosity. In contrast, the Bajau Laut point out numerous examples of Haji Bohé's meanness. In 1979, for example, he was the only house owner in Bangau-Bangau to rent out a portion of his house (the front porch) to a refugee widow and her children. The Bugis, in particular, are accused of keeping aloof, and it is said that, even after ten years of living in Bangau-Bangau, Bugis women are unable to speak Sama and so never mix with the other villagers.

There was in 1979 one Tausug household in the village, surrounded by Bajau Laut neighbours in what is now Kampung Sri Kanangan. Its members were well liked. The head of the household was a barber, while his married son tended a small farm on the outskirts of Semporna town. Although the family generally kept to itself, its members were looked upon by the Bajau Laut as exemplary villagers, hard-working, honest, and peaceable. There were also two other Tausug, a man and a woman, married into Bajau Laut families. A second Tausug woman was the first wife of one of the village *imam*, a Simunul Bajau. The *imam*'s second wife was a Bajau Laut refugee from the Philippines and the two co-wives and their children lived in the same house beside the village mosque.

Relations with other Bajau are generally more intimate. Included in the 'Other Bajau' category are five households composed of local strand Bajau from other parts of the Semporna district. The remainder are mostly recent migrants from the southern Philippines. The largest group is the Sama Sibaut. As a whole, the Sibaut people are less well-off than the others, and there is said to be a small criminal element within the community. In 1979, Sama Sibaut were blamed for most snatch thefts and village house burglaries. The two Sama Simunul households were both well-off, had intermarried, and so maintained close ties with their Bajau Laut neighbours.

Nearly all long-time Bajau Laut families in the village express strong misgivings about the entry of non-Bajau Laut residents. The most frequent complaint is that the latter look down on the Bajau Laut or hold themselves up as superior. Some also complain that they are treated as if they are not genuine Muslims. One elderly medium complained that, while he and his family had always led upright lives, there were newcomers in the village stirring up ill-feelings by preaching that they are heretical. These same people, he added, 'only came to Bangau-Bangau to conduct business, cheat people, and make money'. The most commonly expressed fear in 1979 was that non-Bajau Laut might take over leadership of the community. At the moment, there appears to be little chance of this occurring. This fear, however, was clearly reflected in events that followed the founding of the first kampong development committee in 1976.

The committee was founded with four elected executive members: a chairman, treasurer, secretary, and assistant secretary. All were elected from the original Bajau Laut population and were men I knew well from 1965. In 1979, the man who served as first chairman had become the committee treasurer. The new chairman in 1979, elected the previous year, was a son of Panglima Tiring, the village headman. The committee secretary is a cousin of the chairman and, like the latter, a government employee with secondary education. The assistant secretary was a private timber-boat operator, the husband of Panglima Atani's daughter, and the secretary's father-in-law. All four men have important ties outside the village. The committee has become an effective vehicle of majority opinion in the village and has dealt with two of its main concerns, the maintenance of the main village walkway and control over the entry of outsiders. The committee undertook a complete rebuilding of the walkway and has since looked after its routine maintenance and arranged from time to time for emergency repairs. In this the committee has been highly successful. Of equal importance, the committee now regulates house-building and transfers of house ownership in the village. The committee has been able to stop the practice of selling houses to outsiders as the committee's approval is required before village house sales can take place. In addition, as building space has become increasingly scarce, the committee is now an important arbitrating body, dealing with disputes between potential house-builders.

Refugees and the Return of Clientage

In 1979, almost half the population of Bangau-Bangau consisted of people known as 'refugees' (*pelarian*, from the root word *lari*, to run). Included were nearly 40 per cent of all Bajau Laut and 77 per cent of all other residents in the village. The term *pelarian* refers essentially to an alien, an individual without Malaysian citizenship. The category came into existence only with the formation of Malaysia and the careful enforcement of national boundaries in the years since Independence.

In the past, the Bajau Laut moved easily between Sabah, the southern Philippines, eastern Kalimantan, and Sulawesi. Following independence, citizenship became a matter of considerable importance and created for the first time a major social division within the Sama Dilaut community in Semporna. Anyone living in Sabah at the time of independence was legally eligible to apply for citizenship. However, not all who were eligible applied, and in some cases those who did were unable to provide proof of residence when their applications came up for review. Before 1963, all births took place in the village and very few were officially registered. Moreover, the full importance of citizenship was not immediately apparent to many villagers who were accustomed to travel and often pay extended visits across national boundaries. Later on, establishing eligibility became more difficult.[15] As a consequence, the definition of alien status is to some degree arbitrary. In the years following independence, large numbers of Bajau Laut and other Sama speakers, both newcomers and, in some instances, long-established residents, found themselves classified as aliens and subject to a number of legal disadvantages.

But more significantly, since independence large numbers of refugees have migrated to Semporna, chiefly from the southern Philippines. A conservative estimation of the refugees residing in the Semporna district in 1979 was said to be 30,000. The welfare of these people came under the federal Ministry of Home Affairs and was dealt with independently of the ordinary district government. In addition, the Sabah government received assistance in 1979 from the United Nations and the Saudi Arabian government for refugee relief. In Semporna, refugees have been settled in a number of places. One of these areas is north of the town wharf, in the Kampung Air area, mainly of strand Bajau from the Sibutu island group. A second area is south of the town wharf, at Kampung Simunul. Settled here are mainly Simunul and Sibutu Bajau and, in smaller numbers, Tausug. A third area is Sibangkat Island. Uninhabited in 1965, this small island was in 1979 the site of a very large refugee settlement visible from Semporna town. Finally, the fourth is

Bangau-Bangau. The refugees here are chiefly Bajau Laut from Sitangkai, although a variety of others have also established themselves in the village. The majority are settled with kin. More recent refugees from Tawitawi, however, have established a separate community, Kampung Halo, adjacent to Bangau-Bangau and Sri Kanangan. Many other refugees have settled in other existing villages where they have relatives, making an accurate estimate of their numbers impossible.

In order to remain in the Semporna district legally, an alien must be sponsored by a local citizen. The sponsor is known as a *jalmin* and the individual he sponsors is known as his *jalminan*. Sponsors are usually local fish traders, village and house group leaders, shopkeepers, and local kin. In return for sponsorship, the client is expected to offer unpaid services or to make payments in cash or kind to his sponsor. Technically, sponsorship is arranged through a work permit system. The sponsor is required by the Immigration Department to give written assurance that he is prepared to offer his client gainful employment. However, sponsorship operates, in most cases, as a form of indenture in which the sponsor assumes no legal obligation to provide employment or guarantee the livelihood of his clients. According to the villagers, individual sponsors are limited to a maximum of five client families.

The presence of large numbers of 'refugees' in Bangau-Bangau is closely related to the continuing importance of fishing in the village economy. Fishing remained, even in 1979, the most important source of village livelihood. However, while its importance has rapidly declined among locally born Bajau Laut residents, refugees are disproportionately involved in fishing. In effect, as the original villagers have given up fishing, their place has been taken by 'refugees'. While making up 40 per cent of the Bajau Laut population in 1979, more than half of the house groups dependent on fishing as their principal income source were headed by *pelarian*. There are a number of reasons for this. First, little capital is required beyond that which most refugees brought with them, namely a boat, nets, and fishing skills. Second, there are fewer restrictions on fishing by aliens than there are on trade and wage employment. Fishing grounds are unowned and anyone may work them. But most importantly, a number of village fish buyers, both full-time and occasional, are willing to extend sponsorship to *jalminan* who agree to supply them with regular market landings. In Bangau-Bangau, in 1979, there were at least eight Bajau Laut fish buyers and occasional village assemblers who acted as major sponsors and at least an equal number of non-Bajau Laut *jalmin*.

The organization of fleets and individual fishing teams has been altered by the large numbers of client fishermen. A small number of Bajau Laut sponsors in Bangau-Bangau have emerged as fleet organizers. The most innovative and successful is a man named Tangelad (pseudonym), a senior house group elder who was already a prominent village leader in 1965. Unlike many others, he remained a fisherman, and as market prices have improved, he and his son-in-law have prospered. In 1973, Tangelad acquired through the state fisheries assistance programme a 16-hp inboard engine, which he installed in a fishing *kumpit*. Noting that many refugees were without engines, he arranged to tow their boats to fishing grounds offshore. In 1979, Tangelad fished regularly with a group of fifteen *jalminan*, both Bajau Laut and Sibaut refugees, whom he and others in his family have sponsored. Using his *kumpit*, he tows their small boats to the reefs near Omadal Island where he anchors while his *jalminan* scatter in their boats, mainly trolling for cuttlefish and octopus. Tangelad, who has a reputation for fairness, acts as the marketing agent for the group. After deducting expenses, which include petrol and the cost of feeding his followers, he reportedly divides the proceeds equally between each trolling crew.

Another villager, Samelang (pseudonym) operates a somewhat similar system, except that his followers work in more conventional netting fleets. In return for having their boats towed, the fishermen offer their catch to Samelang at a prearranged price, roughly a quarter of Semporna market prices. In 1979, for example, Samelang was buying all types of white fish (*daing poté*') at eight fish per RM1. The Semporna market rate at the time was roughly two per RM1. Samelang charges nothing for towing, the cost being deducted from profits. Samelang, who owns both a *kumpit* and a *pombot*, makes at least four trips a month, with usually two to four days in the village between trips, and on each trip is usually accompanied by one to three crews of *jalminan*. These arrangements are somewhat atypical, however. Most fishing is done by individual fishing teams. In the case of *jalminan*, marketing is usually arranged by the sponsoring village dealer or assembler on the basis of what the villagers describe as a *magpajak* system. Literally, *pajak* means to 'guess' or estimate the value of something. In this instance, it means that a dealer agrees beforehand to purchase the fisherman's catch at a predetermined price. The dealer assumes all market risks. For the dealer, the advantage is that the price he sets is generally well below the current market price. In addition, he is assured of his client's catch. In return, he is generally expected to advance his *jalminan* cash in order to tide their families over during the periods when they are away at sea.

The legal disabilities of *jalminan* status have created for the first time a sharp social cleavage within the Bajau Laut community. In the past, Bajau Laut bands were internally egalitarian communities. Today, however, the values of the larger society increasingly permeate relations within the community. As the Bajau Laut have succeeded in freeing themselves from the patronage of surrounding shore groups, very similar relations are being created within the community itself, as well as outside it, as long-established, locally born families become the patrons of newly arrived refugees. As a form of indenture, these ties have produced a system of clientage very similar to that which existed between sea and shore peoples in the past. While many house group leaders see sponsorship as a fulfilment of traditional obligations of hospitality, particularly when those being sponsored are kin, others, however, have clearly gained socially and economically through the relationship, using their wealth and client-followers to advance their status and political influence in the community.

1. Early sources relating to the history of Sulu suggest an original dual pattern of governance, with complementary land and sea authorities. The Balangingi and other Sama groups provided the naval forces of the sultanate. Later Tausug historiography has tended to obscure the importance of Sama mariners in the formation of the state, but there is evidence to suggest that they played a critical role, much like that of the Orang Laut in the rise of the first Malay states in the Straits of Malacca (see Chapter 11).

2. It is significant to note that this pattern of ethnic hierarchy, with the sea nomads occupying a pariah-like status at the bottom, reflects distinctive conditions of political life in Sulu. In South Sulawesi, the Bajau appear to have enjoyed a greater degree of autonomy, and while they entered into economic partnerships with Bugis and Makassarese mariners, they generally preserved their own internal leadership, with Bajau leaders often accorded special titles. Elsewhere (Sather, 1995b), I have suggested that the status of the Bajau Laut in the traditional Sulu Sultanate reflected the relatively 'open' nature of political ranking, which allowed greater mobility at the upper levels of the political order, but which, ironically, imposed exclusion at the bottom.

3. The Tausug are also present in eastern Sabah (Sather, 1993c: 261–2). Here they are generally known in the ethnographic literature as Suluk and to local Bajau as *a'a Su'uk* or Suk. In 1970, they numbered 10,900 in Sabah. Their numbers are rapidly increasing, due chiefly to immigration from the southern Philippines, and current estimates place them anywhere from 20,000 to as many as 100,000 (Sather, 1993c: 262).

4. As indicated here, regional differentiation is minimal, although on Jolo Island a minor distinction is drawn between inland (*gimba*) and coastal (*higad*) peoples, for example, between Tau Gimba and Tau Higad (Sather, 1993c: 261). This distinction, however, has little social salience.

5. There is some inconsistency in the literature regarding Puado's ethnic identity; he has also been identified as a Bugis leader (Black, 1971: 383). Such confusion is not surprising given the prevalence of slavery and the relative open ranking system. At the time of Pryer's arrival in Sandakan, the head of the Sandakan Bajau community, 'Tuan Imam', was of Bugis origin. Captured by Tausug pirates as a child, he had found favour at the Sulu court and so was sent to Sandakan, where he consolidated his position of leadership by marrying a well-born Bajau woman (Black, 1983: 12).

6. Two Europeans aboard the *Dolphin* were killed in this attack, one of them the Borneo explorer and ethnologist Robert Burns.

7. In areas exposed to monsoon winds, groups sometimes moved between two, or possibly three, seasonal anchorage sites.

8. See Chapter 4.

9. Even after the Bajau Laut community in Semporna had become largely sedentary, movement was still looked upon as a way of dealing with what was perceived as undue interference. In early 1965, during Konfrontasi with Indonesia, soon after I had begun fieldwork in Bangau-Bangau, notices were sent through the district office requiring a number of young men in the village to present themselves in Sandakan for physical examinations with the possibility of their conscription into the armed forces. The notices caused great alarm, particularly as the ages listed on most of the men's identity cards were highly inaccurate; a few were already middle-aged with large families to support. Until the notices were finally rescinded, there was serious talk in the village of abandoning Bangau-Bangau and moving as a group to Sitangkai in the Philippines.

10. I lived throughout the initial fieldwork period as part of Panglima Tiring's house group. Consequently, I lived in what was one of the first two houses to make up the village. As the Panglima's house group had grown in size, the house had been enlarged, chiefly to accommodate the families of two of the headman's married daughters. Salimbara died two years before I arrived in Bangau-Bangau. He was succeeded by his widow, Hajal, who, owing to her personality and extensive family ties, remained an influential house group leader. Gilang, who headed for a time the largest house group in the village, died in 1976.

11. In 1965 I was evacuated from Semporna with dengue fever and spent a week recovering in the residency hospital in Tawau.

12. This overt exclusion was still in effect when I began fieldwork in 1964.

13. One of the principal centres of opposition to allowing the Bajau Laut to enter the district mosque came from the Sama Sibutu community of Kampung Air. This community was also a centre of support for the previous government. Following the political changes of the late 1970s, a large part of Kampung Air was condemned, some say in political retaliation, and was torn down to make way for the district council market, public jetty, and fish stalls, prompting one villager in Bangau-Bangau to observe in 1979 that it now appeared to be Kampung Air, not Bangau-Bangau, that God was 'punishing'.

14. The two Iban were friends and had been employed as security guards in the Japanese cultured pearl fisheries at Gaya Island.

15. In 1963, the Malaysian constitution provided for a ten-year period in which applications could be made by those present in the country at the time of independence.

3

A World of Sea and Islands

Magtangunggu' mandelaut,
angigal mandéa —
goyak maka seloka.

Music from the sea, dancing ashore
— waves and coconut palms. (Traditional Bajau Laut riddle)

Orientation

THE Bajau Laut inhabit a physical world dominated by sea and islands. Here the conjunction of land and sea creates an ever-present opposition that informs their collective representations of orientation and direction. Islands, in a sense, define Bajau Laut geography and by their existence provide its primary points of reference. The Bajau Laut perceptually order the universe they inhabit in terms of an ever-present interface of sea and land, by reference to 'landward' (*kaléa*) or 'seaward' (*kaut*) co-ordinates, or by means of an object's or person's location 'at sea' (*dilaut*) or 'inland or ashore' (*déa*). Even their identity reflects this opposition. Hence, in contrast to their neighbours, the *a'a déa* or 'people ashore', they call themselves the *a'a dilaut*, or 'sea people'.

The terms 'landward' and 'seaward' may also be used to give directions, even within a built environment, such as the village or the interior of a pile-house. For example, a person may describe the location of his house as 'seaward' from that of his neighbour, or, in answer to the customary greeting, 'where are you going?' (*pingga ka*), is likely to answer either 'landward' or 'seaward'. In the latter case, 'seaward' signifies the direction that a family travels when they fish. 'Landward', on the other hand, signifies the direction of their return, when they sail home again at the end of a fishing voyage. Hence the terms 'landward' and 'seaward' also chart the orientational pulse of village life, the constant aggregation and dispersal of its members, as they move between the settlement, with its land-defined setting, and dispersal at sea.

In contrast to the terms *kaut* and *kaléa*, the Bajau Laut employ cardinal directions only in reference to winds (*baliu*) and sea currents (*sollog*), not as general co-ordinates that apply to the physical landscape itself. Winds in the Semporna district are identified by the villagers with seven cardinal directions: (a) 'north' (*uttala'*), (b) 'north-east' (*uttala' lo'ok*),

(c) 'east' (*timul*), (d) south-east (*tungala'*), (e) 'south' (*satan*), (f) 'west' (*hilaga'*), and (g) 'north-west' (*habagat*) (Figure 3.1). The strongest winds are said to blow from the north-west. Winds from the north-east, south-east, and west are generally the weakest and, in the case of the first two (*uttala' lo'ok'* and *tungala'*), blow only sporadically.

The five seasonally prevailing winds are said to rotate direction annually in fixed succession, blowing at the beginning of the year from the north-west, then moving to the north, north-east, east, and south, until, finally, at the start of a new year, they rotate back to the north-west again (Figure 3.2). This rotation produces an annual succession of four major wind seasons (*musim baliu*), corresponding roughly to the north-east and south-west monsoons, the major seasonal wind regime of the Sulu–Borneo region. The first of these seasons is *musim habagat*, a brief period of approximately one month in January in which the prevailing wind blows from the north–north-west, corresponding to the onset of the north-east monsoon. Winds during this period are said to be the strongest, and at times, most dangerous of the annual cycle. This is followed by *musim uttala'*, in February and March, during which period winds blow predominantly from the north; and then by *musim timul*, in March and April, in which they blow predominantly from the east. Next follows a period of calm and no wind (*teddo'*), and finally *musim*

FIGURE 3.1
Baliu, Wind Directions

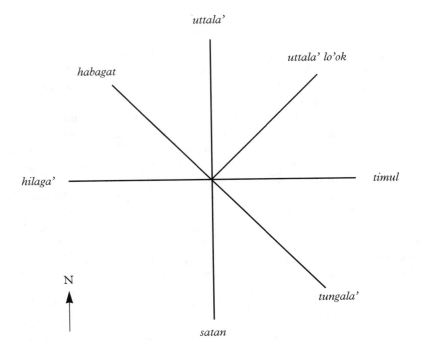

FIGURE 3.2

Seasonal Shifts in Prevailing Winds in the Semporna District

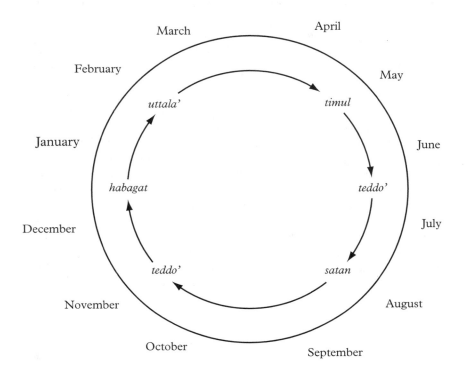

satan, lasting approximately three months, from late May to September or early October, corresponding to the south-west monsoon, when winds blow predominantly from the south–south-west. This is followed by a second, longer period of calm. After this, in January, the cycle of wind seasons begins again with *musim habagat.*

During this annual cycle, first one prevailing wind and then another dominates, some for longer, others for shorter periods, while the inter-monsoon intervals which separate some, but not all, of these seasons mark periods of calm or uncertain wind. The strongest winds are said to blow during the brief *habagat* season; the second strongest during the much longer *satan* season; the third during the *timul* season; and the weakest winds during the *uttala'* season.

This annual succession of prevailing winds imposes a major period-icity on the lives of the Bajau Laut. It is visualized spatially with winds named and their succession defined in terms of the directions from which they blow. The succession itself ascribes an annual temporal cycle influencing navigation and fishing and, in the past, the timing and direc-tion of more extended voyages. Despite irregularities, the cycle is pre-dictable. Older Bajau Laut can readily specify the approximate duration and timing of each successive wind season and can calculate, at any given time of year, the probable strength and direction of the prevailing wind, describing this annual seasonality in directional terms (see Figure 3.2).

Finally, in addition to landward and seaward oppositions—and to the cardinal directions of the seasonally prevailing winds—the daily movement of the sun from east to west, as it appears to cross the sky from one horizon to another, defines a further set of orientational co-ordinates. The direction of the rising sun in the east (*kaluwa'an*) and the direction of the setting sun in the west (*kasoddopan*) are used in ritual contexts to determine, for example, the direction in which prayers are addressed, or to fix the orientation of life-cycle rites, including those relating to birth and death. The movement of the sun across the sky also corresponds to an important temporal cycle. However, unlike wind directions, this is a daily, rather than an annual, cycle and has, as will be seen in later chapters, special significance in relation to the timing and internal ordering of village ritual events.

The Open Sea and Intertidal Zones

The Bajau Laut are predominantly reef and inshore fishermen. They exploit chiefly the coral reefs and shoals of the Semporna region and the associated intertidal shallows that lie between tidemark (*tampé*) and the open sea (*sellang* or *alalom*).

The sea in Semporna, particularly the district's extensive coral reef formations, shelters an exceptionally rich and varied marine life (Wood, 1979). The largest of these formations, the Ligitan reef complex, represents a major fishing area that has supported Bajau Laut communities for as long as the villagers can remember.

The Bajau Laut distinguish by name over 200 varieties of fish (*daing*), all of which are caught and eaten, if only rarely. In addition to fish, *daing* includes a small number of marine reptiles and mammals, including sea snakes, dolphins, and porpoises. As Sahalibulan, an elderly fisherman, said 'We eat all *daing*, except for *soa* (sea snakes).' Some *daing*, however, are consumed only rarely, or in times of extreme scarcity.[1] Around forty varieties of fish, representing as many species, or possibly more, form part of the villagers' regular diet. Among them, reef fish predominate. These include wrasse (Labridae and Scaridae), cardinalfish, damselfish, angelfish, and fusiliers. In deeper reefs, including areas of outer reef-face, catches also include butterfly perch, bass, parrotfish, bream, snapper, rock cod, surgeonfish, and mullet.

The Bajau Laut also eat over forty varieties of shellfish, including spider-conches (*kohanga*), giant clams (*kima*, *Tridacna* sp.), and cowries (*kuba*). They also collect by hand, traps, and snares a number of crustaceans, including spiny lobsters (*ka'ulang*), several varieties of crabs (*kagong* and *kéyot*), and mantis prawns (*kamun*). Crustaceans, however, are eaten much less frequently than fish. In combining *daing* with other food, some proscriptions apply. Thus fish and crabs, for example, may not be eaten together at the same meal; their 'mixing' is said to cause 'intoxication' (*makalangoh*).

The villagers also catch squid and octopus (*kanu'us*, *kohita'*, and *kula-butan*), mostly using nets, wooden prawn-lures (*udang kayu*), and jigs (*sabit*), and hunt dolphins (*ebbung*) and several varieties of giant rays (*sanga* and *pasa*) with harpoons. Now most villagers, in keeping with their greater Islamic orthodoxy, regard dolphin flesh as '*haram*' ('forbidden'), but in 1964–5 it was still widely eaten. Besides fish, shellfish, and crustaceans, the villagers' diet also includes sea urchins (*tayum*), algae (*unas*), and sea grapes (*lato'*). Sea-turtles (*bokko'*) are hunted for their eggs (*entello*) and egg-sacs (*bulinga*); but their flesh is never eaten.[2] Also never eaten are sea snakes. *Holothuria*, *bêche de mer*, or sea cucumbers (*bat*) are collected and dried for market sale, often smoked over a small fire, but are never eaten by the Bajau Laut themselves, serving only as a trade commodity. With the exception of shore-birds, which were taken in the past using snares and small nets, the Bajau Laut have traditionally avoided consuming any kind of land animal. Even in 1979, most families continued to observe this avoidance.

Fishing Zones by Depth

The Bajau Laut divide the stretch of water that extends from the tide-mark to the open sea into four major zones, each distinguished by water depth and coloration, and by its distinctive populations of fish and other marine life. Each zone is the focus of different kinds of fishing and collecting activities.

The shallowest of these zones, immediately fringing the tidemark, is called the *tebba*. Here, at low tide, the villagers gather shellfish, sea cucumbers, crustaceans, and edible algae. Within this zone, the water is normally transparent and the sea floor consists mostly of coral sand or stranded-coral limestone. Where the sea floor is relatively sandy, the *tebba* zone is also used for beach-netting and for erecting stationary traps called *bungsud* constructed of nets and upright poles.

Somewhat deeper than *tebba* is the *halo* zone. Here the water is characteristically green, rather than transparent. The sea floor, however, is still visible. As tides rise and fall, the dividing line between the *tebba* and *halo* zones moves first shoreward, then seaward. Most beach-netting is done along this dividing line on falling tides, as the *tebba* zone moves seaward with the retreating tide. Water in the *halo* zone is too deep for drift-nets to be anchored directly to the sea floor except along its *tebba* fringe, but as tides fall, floating nets gradually become anchored, trapping fish behind them, and so prevent their return to deeper water.

Often the *halo* zone is enclosed by a second, outer zone of *tebba*. Here the sea floor rises again to approach within a fathom or two of the surface or even, in some areas, to emerge above the surface at ebb tides. In Semporna, much of this outer *tebba* zone consists of coral-terraces and back- and fringing-reefs. Hence its contours are often complex. Often the *halo* zone is discontinuous, consisting of a series of deep hollows or pools, with rims of *tebba* extending from the shoreline to the outer edge of the reefs. The second, outer band of *tebba* is the single most important netting zone for the Bajau Laut. Here village fishermen catch a large variety of coral fish, using mainly drift-nets and spears. Outer *tebba* areas, where the sea floor is relatively sandy, are also important sites for spear-fishing, especially for skates and rays. The Bajau Laut also fish the outer *tebba* zone for shellfish which they collect by hand or by diving. Larger areas of coral-terrace are typically transected by underwater channels (*soang*), or are penetrated by deep holes or fissures (*kéhé* or *bua papak*). Both channels and fissures are important sites for specialized net-fishing, as is the outer reef-face called *angan*. Like the *halo* zone, water in the *angan* is characteristically green and is too deep to anchor drift-nets except along its inner edge. In addition to drift-netting, the water over the reef-face is also fished with handlines (*amissi*) and by divers using spearguns (*pana'*). The use of drift-nets and other gear within these different zones is described at length in Chapter 4.

The open sea (*sellang*) beyond the *angan* zone is much less frequently exploited. Here the water is deep blue and the sea floor cannot be seen. For brief seasonal periods, especially during the north-east monsoon, some fishermen troll (*nonda'*) the offshore waters for *panit* and *sobad* (tuna and varieties of mackerel) using lures or baited hooks. Less often, they hunt dolphins, giant rays, and sea-turtles, using harpoons (*sangkil* and *bujak*). The latter have a detachable iron head secured by heavy cables. Dolphins are hunted mainly in the open sea beyond the continental shelf south-east of the Ligitan reefs, where they are frequently encountered in large herds (Plate 3) (Map 3.1). Occasionally, the villagers also fish the open waters closer inshore for smaller sharks and skates, using mainly anchored long-lines (*lawai*).

Tides and the Lunar Cycle

The daily pattern of fishing activity within the reefs and intertidal shallows is determined primarily by tides, wind conditions, currents and, to a lesser degree, by the seasonal migration of pelagic fish. Tides and local current patterns are too complex to deal with here except in basic outline. Bajau Laut knowledge of both is intimate and detailed. Tides in Semporna are semidiurnal, with the average tidal range, which appears relatively constant throughout the district, of approximately 1.3 metres.

The monthly lunar cycle, upon which the timing and strength of the tides depends, is carefully observed by Bajau Laut fishermen, who have a complex vocabulary with which to describe both major lunar phases as well as minor nightly changes in the moon's rising and appearance. The Bajau Laut distinguish by numerical terms twenty-nine or thirty nightly changes (*hali*) in a single waxing and waning moon, beginning with the first appearance of the new moon (*anak bulan*). The first night's moon is called *sahali bulan*; the second, *dua hali bulan*; the third, *tellu hali bulan*, and so on until either *dua empu maka siam* (twenty-nine) *hali bulan* or *tellu empu* (thirty) *hali bulan*. On one night in each lunation, the setting

MAP 3.1
Location of Major Reefs off the Semporna Peninsula

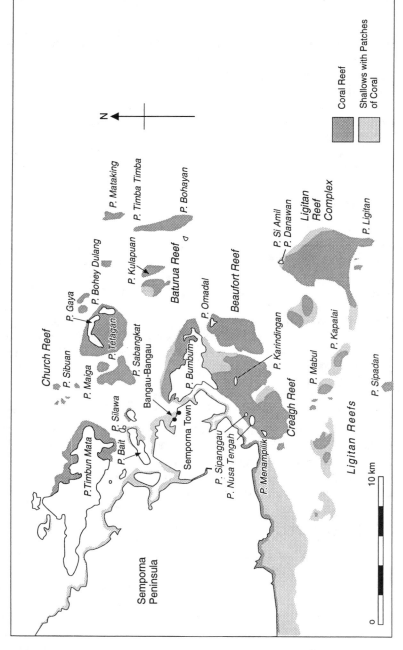

of the sun and moon coincide, so that there is no visible moon throughout the night. This is called *patai bulan* or *bulan amatai*. It marks, for the Bajau Laut, the end or 'death' (*patai*) of one lunation (or 'moon' (*bulan*)) and is followed the next night by the start of a new moon. The counting of nightly *hali* then begins again.

The reckoning of nightly moons is of great importance to the Bajau Laut. Indeed, it can be said that the lunar month and its nightly subdivisions constitute, for the villagers, the basic units of social and economic time.[3] It is common to ask, *Dangai hali?*, 'How many nightly moons?', when setting the times to fish at a particular fishing ground or in arranging for a netting-fleet rendezvous. Also when fishermen, as described presently, memorize the location of fishing grounds by use of sightings (*pandoga*), they also characteristically commit to memory the lunar interval, measured in numbers of *hali*, when tide and current conditions are especially favourable for fishing.

On the night following its first appearance, the new moon appears in the west at twilight; on subsequent nights, it rises above the western horizon, appearing gradually further and further eastward after sunset.[4] The moon also waxes during this period; on the open sea the nights grow noticeably lighter as the size of the visible moon increases. The Bajau Laut describe this time as the period of the 'young moon' (*anak bulan*). For the villagers, it is an important time for net fishing, when schools of carangids—notably yellow-tails and jackfish (*langohan* and *anduhau*)—invade the outer reefs of the Ligitan complex, where they are netted by Bajau Laut fleets, sometimes in large-scale drives. It is generally a time of calm water (*tahik selambat* or *selambat*), when currents slacken. According to villagers, during this time, which usually lasts for four or five nights during the *anak bulan* phase, fish invade the reefs and *angan* zone to feed and spawn. During the brief no moon period, currents become momentarily unpredictable, a situation sometimes called *tahik gila* (literally, 'mad sea').

The seventh nightly (*pitu hali*) moon coincides with the half moon. The tenth night (*sangpu hali*) following no moon marks the beginning of what the villagers call a 'bright moon' phase (*tellak bulan*). Nights at sea are now much lighter. This culminates in the appearance of the full moon on what the villagers say is usually the fifteenth night (*sangpu maka lima hali*). This is another important fishing period, particularly during daytime, for ebb tide gathering (*anebba*) and inshore netting. At night, cuttlefish are frequently caught during this period using jigs and prawn-lures.

After the twentieth night, the moon rises later and later each night as it heads into its last quarter. The period that follows is known as the phase of the '[late-]rising moon' (*bulan pinaluas*).[5] During the moonless hours of the night that precedes its appearance, deepwater fish invade the submerged reefs and shallows to feed. Here they are caught by village fishing parties using driftnets, or with spears and kerosene lanterns during night-time or early morning falling tides. The villagers also consider the moonless hours of *bulan pinaluas* to be a time of supernatural danger. Spirits (*saitan*) and ghosts of the dead (*panggua'*) are thought to be active, and in the village, house doors and windows are barred and lights are kept burning throughout the hours of darkness that precede the moon's rising. Hence, this period is also called *bulan panggua'*, 'ghost moon'.

As the moon wanes, the cycle enters a 'dark phase' called *lendoman*,[6] which continues until the appearance of the new moon. This is a time for night fishing using spears and lanterns. On the twenty-ninth or thirtieth night, moonset and sunset coincide, so that the old moon 'dies' and a new cycle of nightly moons begins again.

Currents are strongest during the 'bright moon' and 'dark moon' phases, around the nights of full moon and no moon. During the intermediate phases, currents generally weaken. Peak flood currents (*song umanso'*) coincide with moonset and moonrise, while peak ebb currents (*song luma'ang*) occur when the moon is at its zenith. Between these peaks, a change in current direction occurs, resulting, village fishermen say, in a period of slack water. Currents then increase in strength until they peak again. Maximum high tide is called *balosok*; maximum low tide, *agot*.

Within this monthly lunar cycle, the times of peak ebb and flood currents are also important periods of fishing activity. During maximum high tide larger fish, including schooling species, enter the inshore zones to feed. During such times, village fishermen engage, in particular, in drift-net fishing along the fringing reefs, back reefs, reef channels, and coves (*lo'ok*). It is at this time, during the *anak bulan* period, that large-scale netting drives take place (see Sather, 1985: 203–8). On the other hand, periods of maximum ebb tide (*agot* or *atoho'*), particularly daytime lows, are important times for tidal gathering, spear-fishing, and for some types of inshore and shoal netting.

Whatever the lunar phase, the Bajau Laut do nearly all their net-fishing during periods of falling tide. As the tide begins to fall, fishing parties at sea begin to scatter in smaller groups in order to set out their nets. Tides are the most important factor governing fishing activity, and while family crews are at sea they ordinarily fish both daily falling tides, whether these occur in daylight hours or at night. Nearly half of all fishing is done at night, with families using the intervals between tides to rest or sleep. The Bajau Laut rely heavily on visual sightings to locate fish (Plate 4), and at night the movement of fish characteristically produces a phosphorescent flashing, called *ma'as* or *ngama'as* which makes night-time sightings not only possible, particularly of schooling species, but in some cases easier and more reliable than daylight sightings.

Navigation and the Monsoon Cycle

In addition to this monthly tidal cycle, local currents are influenced by underwater topography, the presence of offshore islands and shoals, as well as by the longer-term cycle of prevailing winds. Each of these factors affects the dispersal and movement of fishing parties and the routes they travel in moving to and from fishing sites. According to village fishermen, winds exert a highly predictive influence on currents. The prevailing winds shift direction annually in a revolving movement (see Figure 3.2). The strongest (*kosog*) of these annual winds typically blows from the north-west and is frequently accompanied by brief squalls and occasional high seas. These rapidly lessen and, from late January until March, prevailing winds shift first from the north and then from the east. A second period of strong winds, blowing principally from the south, begins in late May or June. These diminish, ending in a season of calm, with occasional gentle winds blowing from the west. During the intervening months, winds tend to be variable, or calm. The direction of prevailing winds is significant for sailing (*maglamak*). In addition to the movement of fishing fleets, the season of prevailing east winds in March is favoured, for example, by Bajau Laut families as the time in which to sail from Sitangkai to Semporna.

Offshore and deep-water channel currents are strongly affected by the direction and strength of prevailing winds. In addition to rough seas, powerful currents along the outer fringing reefs make it hazardous at times to fish areas exposed to the prevailing north-east monsoon, particularly in January and February. Strong winds also hamper surface visibility, making it difficult to sight fish. Each year during this period, the Bajau Laut respond by shifting to more protected fishing grounds, mainly to the lee of the larger offshore islands. In general, however, Semporna is relatively sheltered, both by its high offshore islands and by the Borneo land mass. Consequently, sailing and fishing continue throughout both monsoon seasons, as well as during the generally calmer intermonsoon months, without serious interruption.[7]

Both winds and currents figure significantly in the selection of navigational destinations and travel routes. In 1965, Bajau Laut boats were propelled mainly by sail (*lamak*) and, in shallower water, by poling. The underwater topography of the region is complex, and along the numerous reef channels and deep-water passages, currents are strong at times. This is particularly so during the lunar periods of maximum current strength, corresponding to what the villagers describe as the 'bright' and 'dark' moon phases. When sailing, the villagers frequently set a course to take advantage of these currents, particularly channel and tidal currents. Sea currents are also important when sailing beyond the sight of familiar landmarks. Before setting a heading, the villagers take a reading by dropping small pieces of wood into the water. Noting the direction in which these are carried by the current, they then set a heading to compensate for the current's pull. Should the current later change direction, they readjust their heading accordingly. In this way, the villagers are able to maintain a rough course until they are able to fix their location by landmark sightings on islands. In Semporna, Bajau Laut boats are without a rudder; so that when changing course, the boat is steered by using an oar held usually at the stern and steadied with the foot or leg.

Sailing requires, in addition to a knowledge of winds, currents, and tides, an intricate understanding of sea-floor features, particularly the location of deep-water channels (*soang*), submerged shoals, and reefs. For navigation, a knowledge of channel locations is particularly important, but such knowledge is also needed for the location of fishing grounds. To locate features such as submerged coral-heads or isolated reefs, which present little, or no, visible indication above the surface, the villagers use a location-finding system based on a triangular alignment of landmarks, called *pandoga* (or *gindan*; verb form, *amandoga*). Alignments are usually made using three or four landmarks; occasionally two, and sometimes more than four are used. One landmark serves as a general sailing course while the others are brought into alignment to fix the viewer's precise position. For example, in the early 1970s Laiti discovered a small reef located over a mile out to sea from Maiga Island which proved to be an excellent fishing site. He fixed its position by setting a course toward Maiga Island, with the easternmost peak of Timbun Mata, Mount Sirongal, within a few degrees of conjunction with Larapan Island on the left, and with Tetagan and Bohey Dulang islands in line with one another on the right. In this case, the relative alignment of six landmarks was used to fix the reef's position. Most sightings involve fewer points of reference, but the same principles apply. Once fishing sites are fixed, changing currents and other varying conditions are typically related to nightly moons to identify ideal fishing times particular to the site.

Sightings are continually followed during sailing, or when moving between fishing sites, and the process of *pandoga* is an important part of Bajau Laut navigation. Traditional sailing songs (*kalangan tebba*) make frequent reference to landmarks. One song called 'Tellu Bud' (Three Mountains) locates the home of a distant sweetheart by a sighting in which three mountains (*bud*) are brought into alignment. Figuratively, to have one's bearings is to be aware or conscious. Conversely, to be without bearings is to be disoriented or confused. When I asked Garani, a village spirit-medium, what it felt like to be in trance (*patika'*), he answered that the feeling was 'like being without sightings' (*buat halam pandogan*).

While sailing, the Bajau Laut monitor their bearings by making sightings on passing landmarks. In this way, they are able to relate their travel course to features of the underwater terrain they are sailing over. Every experienced fisherman carries in his mind a knowledge of scores of such alignments; by following the movement of familiar landmarks, usually islands or features of island terrain such as hills or capes, he is able to maintain a constant fix on his location in relation to various underwater features such as reef channels and inter-island passages. When he finds a submerged channel or a reef that he wishes to remember, he takes sightings and, like Laiti, using landmarks, he fixes its location in his mind. In this way, he makes it part of his personal map and so is able to return to it in the future. As noted, Bajau Laut geography is defined by islands, and to find oneself without islands as sighting-points is to be, in a very real sense, in a world without orientation or direction.

Occasionally, however, the villagers must sail beyond the sight of islands. This is always an occasion for anxiety. In travelling from Mataking Island, for example, across Alice passage into the Sibutu island group of

Sulu, boats must cross an area of deep water nearly 16 kilometres wide in which there are no visible landmarks to use as headings. In clear weather, the return trip can easily be made from the Philippine side by setting a heading toward the peaks on Budgaya and Bohey Dulang islands in Sabah, although on most days these peaks are obscured by clouds for at least part of the time. The passage into the Philippines is more difficult as there are no landmarks visible from the Sabah side. Crossings are usually made at night, to lessen the likelihood of being sighted by pirates, using stars (*bitu'un*) to maintain course. Most villagers are highly confident of their knowledge of stars and insist that as long as there are stars visible, it is impossible to miss a landfall by any great distance. If islands orient the Bajau Laut world by daylight, stars orient it by night. Not surprisingly, the Bajau Laut refer to stars and islands in similar terms, describing constellations of stars (*paliama*) by the names of island groups (*pu'-pu'*). For older villagers, the appearance of constellations above the nightly horizon, and their ascent to the top of the sky, are also linked to the annual succession of changing winds, providing an interrelated calendar by which experienced fishermen are able to anticipate changes in wind directions and strength.

Before setting a heading, the direction of the current is determined, and the heading is adjusted correspondingly. The villagers say that this adjustment is one of the most difficult navigational judgements to make. Hence, there is always some apprehension until familiar islands come into view and one's bearings can be re-confirmed by sightings. To be off course is called *gumantung*. If the time passes in which a landfall should be made without a sighting, the villagers generally backtrack by setting a course against the current, until they are back on course and can fix their location by sightings once more. Even highly knowledgeable fishermen occasionally experience *gumantung*. Dessal's eldest son, Karim, for example, once missed his landfall when sailing from Bangau-Bangau to Sitangkai. He backtracked against the current until he made a landfall on Sikulan Island, about 11 kilometres east of his original destination. If a storm comes up at night, travel is usually broken off until daylight, or the sky clears sufficiently for the stars to become visible.

Except for brief squalls, the surrounding sea is comparatively calm, even well offshore. Only one boat from Semporna has been lost at sea in living memory, and that with all on board on a voyage to Sulawesi over fifty years ago, long before the founding of the present Bangau-Bangau village. A few villagers are believed to possess spells capable of causing storms to abate, but otherwise there is little magic associated with either navigation or fishing. However, boats may be treated with spells (*haligmun*) to render them invisible to pirates, or to make them impervious to bullets (*panglias*). Pirates are perceived to be the greatest danger that fishermen face at sea. In January 1979, Udin (pseudonym) was fishing at night with two other boat crews near Pulau Budgaya, when they were approached by pirates.

They called us to stop. Instead, we abandoned our nets—we had just set them out—and fled single-file across the reefs. Fortunately, the lead crew leader knew the underwater channels at night, and the pirates weren't able to follow us. As we drew out of range, we could hear them talking—debating whether to fire on us or not. We made our way to Maiga Island, where there are now lots of refugees living. We stayed there overnight. At daylight we went back to look for our nets. That was a bad time (the previous year, 1978). Almost every week, someone was attacked. Boats couldn't stay at sea without being robbed of their catch.

Shortly after this, a lone family from Bangau-Bangau was attacked near Bohey Dulang. While the wife hid beneath the deck of the boat, her husband shouted for help. As the pirates threw him overboard, a police boat appeared and gave chase. Two pirates were caught, while five others escaped by jumping into the sea. In July 1979, while I was living in Semporna, the husband and Selati (pseudonym), the head of the house group in which the couple lived, were called to Tawau, the residency centre, to testify in the High Court at the pirates' trial. When they returned to Bangau-Bangau later in the month, they reported that the two had been sentenced to hang. In the meantime, there were no further attacks, suggesting that this group had probably been responsible for a number of attacks. In May 1994, when I returned to the village, one pirate was killed in a gun battle with marine police near the Ligitan Reefs. At the time, the villagers complained that the law enforcement situation had deteriorated to such an extent that it was no longer possible to fish the outer reefs without being robbed, particularly of outboard engines. Some robbers wore masks, suggesting to the villagers that the marine police themselves might be involved. A few villagers held federal government authorities responsible for granting easy residence to Tausug refugees, some of whom, they claim, arrived in Malaysia as professional robbers.

The sea itself is associated with little sense of peril. Only two underwater features are regularly avoided by the villagers. One is underwater spots of light, called *gallap*, seen at night, singly, in pairs, or occasionally threes. The other is the unusually deep holes found in the outer *tebba* zone, the bottom of which cannot be seen. These holes are called *minipa* and appear to be subject to powerful undertows. Within the district there is one well-known *minipa* near the village of Labuan Haji, across the Tandu Bulong Straits from Bangau-Bangau (see Map 1.2). The villagers believe it is connected with the open sea by a deep underground tunnel that runs beneath the reefs. Although fish live in *minipa*, people are afraid to dive into them for fear that they will be sucked down and not be able to swim to the surface again. It is said that at low tide, powerful currents can be seen churning deep inside these holes. Many will not go near them.

Fishing Grounds

Bajau Laut boat crews are highly mobile, and in 1964–5 ranged alone or in fleets over much of the Semporna district. It was not uncommon at the time for families to sail 48 kilometres to the east and southeast of Bangau-Bangau, and some 24–32 kilometres to the north, south, and west. Map 3.1 shows the location of the main reef formations within this sailing range.[8] Longer voyages of 64–80 kilometres are occasionally made eastward into the Philippines and northward across Darvel Bay to the Lahad Datu district, although these trips are generally made for reasons other than fishing. Prior to the Second World War, fleets from the Semporna district also sailed even further southward, into the Straits of Makassar to the offshore islands of East Kalimantan. From here, some crossed to southern Sulawesi before returning again by the same route.

The nearest major fishing grounds to Bangau-Bangau are in the Sabangkat atoll.[9] Here drift-net fishing is carried out over a broad stretch of shallow coral flats and terraces, rimmed by an extensive fringing reef, and enclosing along its inner edge a narrow L-shaped lagoon lined with an inner reef (for a brief description of this atoll, see Wood, 1979: 108). The lagoon itself is also studded with coral heads, sandbanks and shoals. Here, in addition to net-fishing, shellfish, including cowries used as net-weights, are collected by the Bajau Laut. Separated from the northern tip of Sabangkat atoll by a narrow channel is Maiga Island. In 1965, this island, like Sabangkat, was uninhabited. Surrounding the island is an extensive fringing reef, forming another major fishing area. Like Sabangkat, Maiga is, or at least was in 1964–5, an important rendezvous point for Bajau Laut boat crews. Further north, crews also regularly fish Church Reef and the back reefs and sandy shoals that surround Sibuan Island (see Map 3.1).

Directly east of Sibuan lies another major fishing area, the Gaya complex. Towering above the sea, 455 metre-high Gaya Island, or Budgaya, along with adjacent Tetagan Island, form the northern rim of an extinct volcanic crater, while Bohey Dulang Island comprises part of its eastern rim. These three high islands form a set of prominent navigational landmarks that are visible throughout the district and well into the Sibutu island group of the Philippines. Between them lies a vast coral-fringed lagoon, 5 kilometres in diameter, bordered on the south by a long, broad arc of submerged reef. In 1965, fleets from Bangau-Bangau regularly fished these southern reefs. In periods of relatively calm weather, they also fished the northern fringing reefs around Budgaya and Tetagan islands.

Sailing further east and south, beyond Bohey Dulang, village boat crews occasionally visit Si Amil, Kulapuan, and Bohayan reefs. These areas are also fished by nearby strand Bajau.[10]

South of Si Amil, bordering the open sea along the south-eastern edge of the district, 15–20 kilometres offshore, lies the largest of all reef formations and the most important Bajau Laut fishing grounds in the district, the Ligitan reef complex. The tiny island of Ligitan (see Maps 2.1 and 3.1), standing only a metre or so above the tidemark, lies near the southern end of this complex. The island is uninhabited, but is the site of an unmanned beacon which is readily visible at night to Bajau Laut fleets at sea.[11] The island is also a breeding-ground for sea snakes. Surrounding it are submerged veins of igneous rock, areas of coral flats and sandbanks, all exposed, or partly exposed, at ebb tide (Plate 5). The whole area is, and has been for generations, a major rendezvous point for Bajau Laut fishing parties not only from Bangau-Bangau and Labuan Haji, but also from Sitangkai and other Bajau Laut communities in the Sibutu island group. Here fishing reaches its peak during the four or five days that coincide with the appearance of schools of *langohan* and *anduhau*.

Extending southward from the Ligitan complex are the Ligitan reefs, a continuous reef-chain dotted with small islands, running along the edge of the Borneo shelf and forming the only major barrier reef off the Sabah coast (Wood, 1979: 125). Bajau Laut netting parties regularly fish this chain, particularly sites around Mabul and Kapalai islands. To reach the Ligitan complex, including this southern reef-chain, fishing parties must either skirt the northern shore of Bumbum Island or cross Creagh Reef to the south. Either way, they pass through secondary fishing areas also fished by local strand Bajau from Omadal and Bumbum islands (see Map 3.1).

Occasionally, crews sail northward from Bangau-Bangau on shorter voyages, fishing the rim of the bay in which the village is located, or the reefs that border eastern Silawa and the south-eastern tip of Timbun Mata Island. Some daily fishing is also done in the Bangau-Bangau Bay itself.

Within the district, individual fishing sites are unowned. Neither the village nor its separate families limit access to these sites or exclude others from making use of them. However, rights of priority are recognized. Once a party has set its nets, crews arriving at the site later are expected to avoid fishing the same area and, if they fish close by, to take care to avoid hampering the first party's netting. These rights also extend to artificial fish-corrals and, more recently, to stationary fish-traps. Artificial corrals (*kubu' batu*) consist of coral mounds constructed on the sea floor. Most are built close to Bangau-Bangau. To take the fish, the corral is usually surrounded with nets. The coral mound is then pulled apart and the fish are caught with poison, spears, spear-guns, or nets. Afterwards, the owner frequently rebuilds the corral. As long as he continues to fish it, no one may remove fish from the structure without his permission. When fence-traps (*kelong*) were first introduced to the Semporna district in the mid-1970s, similar rights were created by their construction. In addition, fence-traps are licensed with the Fisheries Department, further sanctioning the owner's rights of tenure. In 1979, four *kelong*, all located near Bohey Dulang Island,[12] were operated by owners from Bangau-Bangau, all four of whom were also licenced market-traders.

As with many terrestrial foragers in insular South-East Asia (Sellato, 1989: 200–1), very little ritual is associated with traditional Bajau Laut fishing. There is a belief held by many older villagers that localized spirits (*saitan*) claim the fish that live within the reef areas in which they reside. For example, when families fish the Ligitan area, family heads often ask permission (*amuhun*) of the *saitan* that is thought to reside on the Ligitan islet. This request is frequently accompanied by a gift of a cloth banner or a small offering of food or firewood. While this spirit is usually ignored during brief visits, in 1964–5 its permission was regularly sought when fleets gathered at Ligitan reefs to engage in communal netting drives. *Amuhun* was performed by the drive leader (*nakura'*) before the drive commenced, as other families assembled. If ignored or irritated, it was said that the spirits might then cause illness (see Chapter 9).

1. An example is *buntal* (porcupine fish), of which the Bajau Laut distinguish four named varieties. Another is *kapok* (scorpion fish), which causes painful wounds if stepped on, and which is similarly not ordinarily sought, but which is occasionally eaten.

2. The term *bokko'* refers to soft- or leather-back sea-turtles. The Bajau Laut distinguish four varieties of *bokko'* locally (*bokko' bulan, b. lannus, b. pandiman,* and *b. lakit*). They also hunt one variety of sea-turtle having a hard carapace (*tohongan*). *Bokko'* and *tohongan* are distinguished from freshwater turtles (*labi-labi*) and land tortoises (*kola-kola*), neither of which are hunted. Eighteenth- and early nineteenth-century reports suggest that sea-turtle hunting was once a much more important economic activity among sea nomads than it is at present, having possibly lost some of its importance as Bajau Laut net technology has improved, making the Sama Dilaut more proficient reef fishermen.

3. It is interesting to note that the apparent Malay cognate of *hali* is '*hari*', the latter referring to the interval of daylight or, more simply, 'day'. Hence, while Malay speakers commonly reckon time in terms of '*berapa hari*', 'how many days'; the equivalent Sama Dilaut expression *dangai hali?*, refers, instead, to nightly intervals calculated, as noted here, by reference to the cyclic waxing and waning of the moon.

4. Technically, when the moon appears in its new phase just after dark, it has not just risen. Rather, this is when it first becomes visible after its passage through the sky during the day. The moon appears to move higher above the western horizon as the month progresses because it rises in the east later in the day and hence sets later. I am grateful to Dr Ian Walker of the Mount Stromlo Observatory, Australian National University, for reading and commenting on this section.

5. *Pinaluas* is the term for 'rising', when applied to the moon (*bulan*). 'Setting' is *pahagom*.

6. From the root *lendom,* 'dark'.

7. By contrast, on the west coast of Sabah monsoon seasonality is marked, and causes an annual suspension of fishing activities in many areas.

8. See P. G. Morris (1978) and Wood (1979) for a brief discussion of the major reef formations in the Semporna region.

9. Now a major refugee resettlement site (as noted in Chapter 2).

10. In the early 1960s, Si Amil was the processing base for a Japanese tuna trolling operation, which at its peak employed many Bajau Laut from Semporna as troll fishermen. It ceased operation, however, before I began fieldwork. Near Budgaya is a large Japanese-owned cultured pearl fishery, started around the same time, and still in operation in the 1980s. After the murder of one of its managers by pirates, it ceased operation in 1993 and the area in which it was located is now part of a national marine park.

11. There are also beacons on Si Amil and Mataking Islands. Bajau Laut crews normally take night-time sightings on these lights when they cross Alice Channel. According to

older villagers, Ligitan Island was larger in the past, with a small patch of stunted forest and extensive beaches; now the island is barely awash at high tide. Similarly, Kapalai Island, which in the early part of the century was a Bajau Laut anchorage site, is said to have then had a small interior forest and coconut palms; now the island is almost entirely barren.

12. In August 1979, there were, according to the local Fisheries Department officer, sixty-seven licenced *kelong* in the Semporna district. All are recent. In 1964–5, when I carried out my initial fieldwork, there were none.

4

The Fishing Economy

Daing-daing ai, dalua luana, magsaddi léssana?
— bohé' maka tahik.

What kind of fish looks the same but tastes different?
— freshwater and seawater. (Traditional Bajau Laut riddle)

As with fishing economies generally (Stirrat, 1975: 141), production among Bajau Laut fishermen in Semporna in 1964–5 was geared largely towards exchange rather than immediate use. While families typically consumed part of their catch, a more significant share was either sold to outsiders or distributed within the community as food gifts.

The nature of external trade has been radically transformed in the course of the last century. Until the end of the nineteenth century, trade outside the community combined local symbiotic exchange with tributary trade. The members of sea-nomadic bands supplied patrons and other partners ashore with maritime commodities as both food and trade goods. Following the founding of Semporna town, external trade came to be dominated by local Chinese middlemen. Since the mid-1960s, however, the Bajau Laut have entered directly into the fish marketing network and now control together with other Sama speakers most of the licensed trade in fish within the district. Growing numbers earn a living, or at least supplement their income, as fish-buyers, assemblers, and urban market-stall operators. As a consequence, the embeddedness of fishing, and the role of the Bajau Laut in the district economy have both become increasingly diversified, as has also the economic make-up of the Bajau Laut community itself. Further complicating these changes has been the arrival of large numbers of Sama Dilaut 'refugees'. While established villagers have moved into market trade, or non-fishing occupations, newcomers have largely taken over the productive side of fishing, since the mid-1970s becoming the principal village fishermen.

As a result of these changes, commercial relations now permeate economic transactions within the village. The clear distinction that once separated internal exchange from outside trade has now largely disappeared. Most transactions involving fish are conducted in cash. In 1964–5, these changes were much less pervasive. Most families still fished for their livelihood and the exchange of food between village kin, including gifts of fish, was still a central feature of village life.

Traditional food-exchange relations are discussed in Chapters 5 and 6 in relation to village social organization, in particular in connection with house group membership and ties of kinship. The principal concern of the present chapter is with the fishing economy; the social organization of fishing activities; control of income, labour, and fishing assets; and the basic features of market relations as they existed in the 1964–5 period.

Non-fishing Employment

In 1964–5 fishing was the principal source of village income. However, even then, it was not the sole source. Twenty-nine married men, most with families, including two of the thirty-six house group leaders in the village, regularly worked for wages outside the community. Included were nine non-Bajau Laut men married to village women.[1] Two were employed as marine policemen, two as boat operators, three as estate labourers, one as a shophouse labourer, and another as a barber in Lahad Datu. In addition, a number of Bajau Laut men worked outside Semporna, mainly in Tawau and Sandakan, principally as stevedores and construction labourers, or in Lahad Datu and Kunak as estate workers. Three men were employed as deck-hands on estate supply boats and one worked as a full-time driver for the district medical department. In 1965, others supplemented fishing with occasional wage work, mainly with the Public Works Department (Jabatan Kerja Raya or JKR), or signed on from time to time as short-term contract labourers with agricultural estates in the Lahad Datu district. Including dependants, over 30 per cent of the population of Bangau-Bangau in August 1965 derived its chief income from sources other than fishing, and even among full-time fishermen, some occasional wage labour was the norm.

Family Fishing Crews

In 1965, just over 60 per cent of the village population, including wives and children fished on a regular basis. A small number of people, including two elderly house group leaders were too old or infirm to fish. In early 1965, when I completed the first of two village censuses, there were fifty-two fishing boats (lepa) in use in Bangau-Bangau. Table 4.1 shows the distribution of boat ownership between the thirty-six house groups that made up the village. Most groups (21) contained only one resident boat owner, but a significant minority (14) contained either two (11) or three (3). The average number of boats per house group was 1.44. The largest and economically most successful house groups generally had the largest number of boat owners, while the members of only one house group were without a boat in 1965 (Table 4.1). The situation of this group, which was co-headed by two elderly women, is discussed at length in Chapter 5.

TABLE 4.1
Family Boat Crews per House Group, 1965

Number of Crews per House Group		Incidence	Percentage
0		1	2.8
1		21	58.3
2		11	30.6
3		3	8.3
Total	6	36	100.0

Those who fish together as a single boat crew are called *dabalutu* ('those of one living-quarters'), or *dalepa* ('those of one boat'). In 1965, most crews comprised a married couple or a conjugal family headed normally by the boat-owner, as husband and male family head. Occasionally additional persons were included in the crew. A small number of boats were owned by men who worked at other jobs and so these were used only irregularly. Some family members remained in the village when sick or faced with other pressing work, temporarily reducing crew size. On longer voyages, the presence of the boat-owner's wife became increasingly valuable, not only domestically, in preparing meals and looking after younger children, but also in assisting her husband in cleaning and preparing fish for drying. On shorter voyages, a family was less likely to dry its catch, and so there is less need for the wife's labour. Family fishing crews in 1965 averaged five persons and the largest contained ten.

Fishing boats are individually owned. Most boats were purchased or built by their owner. In families that subsist by fishing, providing a boat is considered the family head's responsibility. However, a newly married husband may occasionally fish as a crew member for his father, his wife's father, or, less often, of another kin. Such arrangements are regarded as only temporary—adopted until the husband is able to purchase or build a boat of his own. A man may also borrow a boat, but in 1965 none of the fishing boats in use in Bangau-Bangau was shared or jointly owned. Lending applies to a single voyage or for a stipulated time period and when boats are used for fishing, the owner expects to receive a share in the catch.

Boats and Boat Ownership

In 1964–5, the Semporna Sama Dilaut made use of two types of boat: the *lepa*, the primary fishing boat, and the much smaller, ancillary *boggo'* or dug-out.

The *lepa* and *boggo'* have essentially different functions. The *boggo'* is used exclusively inshore, while the larger *lepa* serves as both the main fishing vessel and is used for voyaging, providing living quarters for its crew.

Boggo'

The *boggo'* is an extremely beamy dug-out, 3–5 metres long, hollowed by means of an adze (*patuk*), and usually fire, from a single tree-trunk. In profile the bottom line and gunwale are slightly concave. Because of its extreme beaminess and lack of freeboard, considerable agility is required to keep the *boggo'* from tipping. In the vicinity of the village, the *boggo'* is frequently used by younger people, including adolescents and children, and is the principal means used to reach houses unconnected by catwalks to the main village bridge. It is most often propelled by poling or by the use of paddles (Plate 6). However, a few *boggo'* are made with a mast socket and can be used with sails. Unlike the *lepa*, it generally carries only one or two persons and is used close inshore, mainly for intertidal collecting and line-fishing. Occasionally, a *boggo'* may be towed behind the family's *lepa* and used at sea to set out or haul drift-nets in shallow water.

Lepa

The much larger *lepa* is 7–12 metres long (average 8.5 metres) and of 1.5–1.9 metres beam (Plate 7).[2] Its beam is relatively constant, while its length varies. It has an average draft of 0.6 metre. The *lepa* is constructed of a solid keel section (*teddas*), bow and raised poling-platform (*tuja'*), fitted bowsprit (*jungal*), stern section (*tuja' buli'*), frame ribs (*sengkol*), and tightly fitted side planks (*dinding*) (Figure 4.1). The sections are held together with wooden pegs (*pasok*).

The midsection of the *lepa* is floored with fitted but removable decking (*lantai*). Decking planks can be taken up for bailing and for stowing fish beneath the deck. Along the midsection, the freeboard extends upward on each side of the *lepa* to enclose relatively roomy living and sleeping quarters (*balutu* or *kubu*), comprising roughly half the overall length of the boat.[3] The bow (*munda'*) and stern (*buli'*), in contrast, are low in the water and open-sided. This is to facilitate the handling of nets and the use of poles and oars.

Separating the bow and stern sections from the living area of the *lepa*, both fore and aft, are large cross-beams called *sa'am*. These curve upward from the deck and extend a short distance above the top of the freeboard. The ends of the *sa'am* are fitted with rack-like branches called *panga'*. From these are hung fish-spears, bamboo poles, and masts. The upper ends of the *sa'am* are frequently ornamented with carved designs (*ukilan*), as is the lower edge of the bowsprit.

At the fore and aft ends of the living area, deep sockets are set in the keel. When the boat is under sail, the forward socket receives the base of the mast, which is stepped slightly forward. At other times, for example at night, or when family members wish to take shelter from the weather, the two sockets are fitted with shorter posts. These are forked at the top to receive a long pole-beam. Over this beam a '*kajang*' mat (*sapau*) is spread to form a pitched roof, covering the entire midsection living area. The eaves of the roof extend just beyond the top of the freeboard on

FIGURE 4.1
Bajau Laut *Lepa*

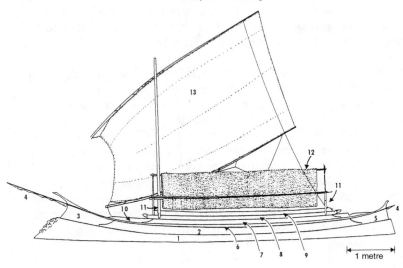

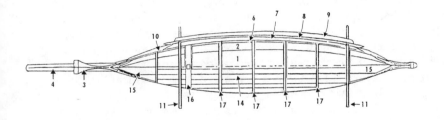

1 *Teddas* (keel)	9 *Dinding* (wall of living quarters)
2 *Pangahapit* (strake)	10 *Ajong ajong* (forward side-piece)
3 *Tuja'* (bow section with raised poling platform)	11 *Sa'am* (cross-beams enclosing living quarters fore and aft)
4 *Jungal* (side-pieces ending forward in a projecting bowsprit and aft in a small stern projection)	12 *Sapau* (roof)
	13 *Lamak* (sail)
5 *Tuja' buli'* (stern section)	14 *Lantai* (deck planks)
6 *Bengkol* (lower sideboard forming fitted gunwale)	15 *Panansa'an* (bow and stern deck)
7 *Kapi kapi* (middle sideboard)	16 *Patarukan* (forward cross-piece and mast support)
8 *Koyang koyang* (upper sideboard)	17 *Sengkol* (cross-pieces reinforcing hull and supporting deck planks)

each side of the *lepa* and are held in place by the poles and masts hung from the *panga'* at each end of the *sa'am*. When not in use, the *sapau* is removed, rolled up and stowed out of the way, together with the shorter posts, leaving the deck free to serve as a family work area.

While at sea, family members sleep and store extra clothing and other personal effects in the midsection living area. The stern of the boat is used mainly for cooking and for stowing water jars (*kibut*) and food stores (*lutu*), principally large cakes of cassava flour wrapped in sacking or banana leaves. The stern is associated with female tasks, such as preparing meals.[4] The bow is reserved chiefly for fishing, poling, and for manning the sails and storing nets, all principally male activities. In addition to the bow, stern, and midsection, every *lepa* has a lateral *kokan* ('headside'), where family members store their personal effects and lay their heads (*kok*) when sleeping, with their bodies crossways in the boat.[5]

All fishing boats, as already noted, are individually owned. Although the villagers say that a woman may inherit her husband's boat upon his death, in 1965 none of the fifty-two *lepa* then in use were owned by a woman. The great majority of boats were built or purchased by their owner, although a smaller number were inherited or received as gifts, usually from a parent, normally the owner's father. In the past, it was expected that at the time of marriage, a young man would be outfitted by his family with his own fishing boat and gear so that he and his new wife would be able to form a separate boat crew. The expectation was that they would begin their married life by enjoying a degree of immediate economic autonomy, as an independent fishing unit. As families were boat-living in the past, outfitting the son with a boat also assured the couple's immediate residential and domestic independence, separate from their parental families. Responsibility for providing the boat fell, and continues to fall, principally on the young man's father. Parents who fail to provide a son with a boat are said to 'throw their son away', meaning, force him into possible dependence upon his wife's kin. In 1965, most young men in Bangau-Bangau preferred wage work to fishing. As a result, it was no longer considered necessary to outfit a son with a boat at marriage, although a few families continued to do so, including those that were still boat-living. In taking up wage work, not all young men ceased to fish. Several used their cash income to purchase a boat, using it to fish occasionally while working in Semporna town. In the past, nearly all men remained boat-owners from the time that they first married onward, for as long as they remained physically active. In old age, a man generally passed his boat on to a son. If at a boat-owner's death, his sons already had boats, the vessel was usually disassembled and its pieces used to make a coffin. Most old people strive to remain economically independent for as long as they can, and in 1965 two active boat-owners were in their late sixties or early seventies. Both went to sea with their wives and fished as independent crews.

More than half of the *lepa* are said to have been purchased. They are bought, usually under a contract arrangement, either from a village boat-builder or from a Sama Kubang boatwright. The latter live chiefly in villages along the northern shore of Bumbum Island, where village men have long practised boat-building as a traditional craft specialization (Sather, 1984: 11). The average price of a *lepa* in 1965 was said to be RM800–900 (US$270–300), with the cost of the finest-made boats approaching RM2,000 (US$670).[6] A growing scarcity of lowland timber has meant that most wood now has to be purchased from local sawmills. In the past, it was possible to pole up estuarine streams along the peninsula mainland and fell trees for boat-making. The logs were floated out to the sea, where they were then towed to the anchorage and worked by the feller into boat sections and planks. By 1965, even if a man built his own boat, the purchased materials alone seldom cost less than RM400–500 (US$130–170). In terms of village incomes, boats therefore represent a very considerable investment.

Those who build their own boat generally do so in stages, thus spreading the cost of materials over a period of time. Between stages, savings may be accumulated, or fishing undertaken for the purpose of acquiring the cash needed for the next stage of construction. Much the same principle applies when boats are purchased. Agreements of purchase are made in the form of a promissory vow (*janji'*) concluded between the purchaser and boatwright. Vow-taking is a major feature of village social relationships. In this case the vow assumes a narrower commercial form. According to its terms, the purchaser ordinarily advances the builder part of the price of the boat for materials and expenses; he then makes additional payments from time to time while the boat is under construction, paying the balance upon its completion. In 1964–5, the village stock of boats was no longer being maintained. Only one new boat was added during the year, although another *lepa* was under construction when I left the village.

Once it is put into use, a *lepa* requires continuous care. During maximum ebb tides, *lepa* are regularly careened (see Plate 7). In 1965, this was done most often in exposed areas of the bay floor to the shoreward side of Bangau-Bangau village. As the tide falls, the boat is positioned with stones or with wooden mooring stakes and after the hull is exposed, it is fire-treated below the water-line with palm-frond torches (Plate 8). Careening is usually done by the boat-owner or a son. Every few years, older boats are partially disassembled, and worn pegs, decking planks, and sideboards are repaired or replaced if necessary. Occasionally, major sections of the boat are rebuilt. This work is normally done on the owner's house platform. When sideboards and other fitted sections are reassembled, the joints are caulked or filled with a soft inner bark called *gellom* from a small tree of the same name which grows along the coralline beach-line. The wood of the *gellom* tree is also used during boat construction to make the *sa'am* and *gellom* branches are typically used for the *panga'* racks.[7]

Most men begin to acquire a knowledge of boat construction in childhood when they help their father careen and care for the family *lepa*. Later in life, many apply this knowledge to build boats of their own (Plate 9). In the beginning, they are likely to seek the help of more experienced kinsmen. Later, having built one or possibly several boats, they are likely to be called on by younger kin for advice. The most durable parts of the *lepa* are the keel, bow, and stern sections. These are generally maintained for the life of the boat. Some other elements such as the roofing and the poles are replaced every few years.

In addition to a boat, the family head is also responsible for providing the nets, spears, and other fishing gear used by the crew at sea. Nets, like boats, are individually owned although most family members assist in making and repairing them. Damaged nets may be repaired at sea, but most major mending takes place between voyages. In the village, net-making and mending are major evening activities, absorbing, together with the drying of nets, a significant share of the villagers' time between voyages. In 1964–5, nets were made of manufactured cotton twine (*saban*). The cost of twine was deducted directly from current income. The five principal shops in Semporna town that purchased dried fish in 1965 also sold twine, generally discounting its price from fish deliveries. In addition to the cost of mending nets, every family head must set aside savings for their periodic replacement. In general, the villagers calculate the working life of a net to be around two or three years. In order to prolong its life, a newly made net is often treated with red dye made from the bark of the *kampang tuli* tree (*Sesbania grandiflora*).[8] This dye is also said to make nets less visible to fish. After use, nets are dried. The work of drying nets absorbs considerable labour. At sea, nets are often spread over the *sapau* of the boat, or are hung from the poles along the sides (Plate 10). Upon returning to the village, nets are given a thorough drying on the house platform before being mended and put away in preparation for the family's next voyage. Most family heads own, on average, three or four sets of nets. In 1965, the largest number of nets owned by a single family head was twelve. It is said that in the past young men began acquiring nets before marriage.

In 1964–5 village *lepa* were propelled chiefly by sail. However, twenty-one of the fifty-two boat-owners in Bangau-Bangau also owned small 4.5-hp outboard engines. These were used only sparingly, however, because of the high cost and scarcity of petrol. In 1964–5, the Semporna district was accessible only by sea. As a consequence, only small deliveries of petrol were made by ship to Semporna town, and between shipments supplies frequently ran out, making petrol periodically unavailable. None the less, the use of engines, even on a limited scale, considerably reduced the time spent in travelling. By 1965, this time-saving was already beginning to change patterns of fishing activity, reducing the duration of voyaging for many families. In early 1965, small outboard engines ('Seagull' and 'British Anzoni') cost RM450–500 (US$150–200).

Gear

Drift-nets

Most village fishing is done with drift-nets which, reflecting the diversity of fish caught by the Bajau Laut, are notably varied (Plate 11). In Semporna the Bajau Laut distinguish two major classes of drift-nets: *linggi'* and *selibut*. *Linggi'* are generally larger and heavier nets and are intended for a larger catch, including skates (*pahi*) and sea-turtles (*bokko'*). Each class of nets is subdivided into a number of individual varieties, distinguished mainly by mesh size and weight and named in each case for a specific variety of fish (for example, *linggi' owak*, *selibut tibuk*, *selibut togéng*, and others).

Mesh openings are called *mata* ('eyes') and are measured diagonally from corner to corner. For *linggi'*, the principal measures are the (a) *tunju'*, measured from the tip of the raised thumb to the tip of the first finger (approximately 15 centimetres); (b) *hakka*, from the tip of the thumb to the tip of the index finger (18 centimetres); (c) *kaki*, (22 centimetres); and (much less common) (d) *akiput*, slightly less than one *tunju'* (13 centimetres). The smaller *selibut* are measured mainly in terms of *tambu*, or finger-breadths. Both length and width are variable, being constrained mainly by weight. Long nets, particularly those made of heavy twine, are heavy and so cumbersome to shoot and haul, especially when wet. The villagers generally make their nets relatively short, not more than 14 or 15 fathoms long, providing for greater length by tying nets together to form a variety of compound structures. Length is measured in fathoms (*depa'*), the distance across the outstretched arms, from fingertip to fingertip, while width is measured in feet (*kaki*); *bila dakan*, the distance from the centre of the chest (*dakan*) to the fingertips of one outstretched . arm (1 metre); *siku*, the distance from the tip of the elbow (*siku*), across the chest, to the fingertips of the opposite outstretched arm (1.5 metre); and fathoms.

In 1965, the villagers made regular use of three types of *linggi'* and four types of *selibut*, although a number of additional types of nets were also used. The *linggi'* are employed mainly for larger, deep-water fish, including carangids and other pelagic species, skates, sharks, and larger wrasse; while the *selibut* represent the main day-to-day nets and are used chiefly for smaller coral and reef fish. Of the three main *linggi'*, the largest in common use is the *linggi' owak*, with a mesh opening measuring one *hakka*.[9] Somewhat smaller, and less frequently used, is the *linggi' kihampau*, with a mesh opening of one *tunju'*. The smallest and lightest of the *linggi'* is the *linggi' ulapai* or *linggi' bangallus*, with a mesh opening of four finger-breadths. The four *selibut* in common use are the *selibut tatik*, *selibut togéng*, *selibut tentong*, and *selibut ulapai*. The *selibut tatik*, with a mesh opening of three finger-breadths, and the *selibut tentong* (or *banak*), with a mesh opening of two finger-breadths, are the most frequently used of all nets. Most families carry at least one or two of each of these nets.

The use of cotton twine, which was replaced by nylon (*tansi*) in the 1970s, had superseded locally made bark-fibre twine. It is uncertain when cotton twine first became available in Semporna, but the villagers say that it was introduced not long after the first Chinese shops were opened in the district, probably during the first or second decade of the twentieth century. Both cotton twine and manufactured cordage were almost certainly available by the late 1920s. However, cotton twine probably replaced bark-fibre twine only gradually, for a visitor to Sitangkai in 1931 (Taylor, 1931), mentions that nets of locally made fibre were still in use at the time. In Semporna, nets were traditionally made of the bark of three local trees: *bagu* (unidentified), *nunuk (Ficus microcarpa)*, and *téyak* (unidentified). *Bagu* was the most favoured. Young trees with a trunk breadth roughly equal to that of the widest part of a man's forearm were felled and stripped of bark. This was dried and then pulled apart to yield a strong hair-like fibre which the villagers twisted by hand (*sisek*) to make not only netting twine but also various kinds of ropes and cordage. Some elderly villagers in Bangau-Bangau still collect bark and braid cordage as a pastime (Sather, 1985: 173n). The work is highly time-consuming, and before the introduction of manufactured twine, the Bajau Laut must have spent much of their time between voyages making and braiding netting (Sather, 1985: 173). Fibre nets, however, are said to have been longer-lasting than the cotton nets that replaced them.

Technically both *linggi'* and *selibut* are drift-nets. In the water, they form a curtain of netting, suspended between a floating headline and a weighted footline. Fish swimming against this curtain, unless they are sufficiently small to pass through it, are gilled or entangled in the mesh of the nets. The headline is buoyed by evenly spaced floats (*patau*) made from the light, pithy trunk of the *patau* tree (*Macaranga tanarius*), a small soft-wood which grows abundantly in the Semporna district along the strand. The size and spacing of floats varies with the width and weight of the net (Plate 12). The footline is weighted with cowrie-shell sinkers (*kuba*), and both headline and footline are made of heavy cordage (*kellat*).

Fish-spears

Besides nets, each family crew in 1965 also carried a number of fish-spears hung from the racks on each side of its *lepa*. In the Semporna region, two types of spears are employed by the Bajau Laut: (a) *pogol*, with from 2–4 tines, and (b) *selikit*, with from 5–12 tines. The most commonly used are barbed tridents called *pogol tellu*. Both *pogol* and *selikit* are mounted on long, flexible bamboo shafts 1.8 metres long. Spear shafts also double as poles. When spear-fishing, the fisherman typically stands on the bowsprit platform, while he or another crew member poles or rows the boat through the water. Spear-fishing is done mainly during periods of calm including night-time calms. At night, a kerosene pressure-lantern is often suspended beneath the bowsprit of the *lepa* for illumination.

Larger fish and sea mammals are hunted with harpoons (*sangkil* and *bujak*), particularly giant rays and dolphins. Spear guns (*pana'*) are used for underwater fishing, particularly in outer reef-face areas, while simple handline fishing (*amissi*) is often done where the water is too deep for netting. At high tides, youngsters also engage in handline fishing from the house platforms and village catwalks. Four families in the village own longline gear which they occasionally set out to take smaller sharks and skates. The gear consists of a mainline, approximately 18 metres long, to which are attached, at roughly 30-centimetre intervals, a series of short lines, each ending in a large barbed hook. The two ends of the mainline are weighted with anchor stones. While one end is attached to a floated buoy, the other is retained aboard the fisherman's boat. The gear is usually set out in the evening in 4–6 fathoms of water, left overnight, and then hauled in again in the morning.

Explosives

Economically, after drift-netting and spear-fishing, the next most important method of fishing is with the use of explosives (*timbak daing*). For a short time, from the early to mid-1970s, such fishing was practised on a wide scale in Semporna, not only by the Bajau Laut, but also by other fishermen in response to a greatly increased market demand for fish created by the opening of a trunk road to the larger urban market and timber town of Tawau to the south. It was heavily promoted by commercial traders who supplied local fishermen with fuses and other materials for making explosives. In 1964–5, explosives, although well known, were used only occasionally and by 1979 their use was again declining. Such fishing does serious damage to living coral and is outlawed by the state government. In 1979, those apprehended using explosives were reportedly fined up to RM200. However, market inspection and the punishment of traders dealing in bombed fish are the only effective means of controlling the use of explosives, as traders are the principal promoters. Fisheries officers lack the authority to conduct market inspections or to prosecute traders dealing in bombed fish. Police boat patrols are too infrequent to be effective and cannot begin to cover the widely scattered fishing grounds of the district. In addition, much of the bombing is done at night in waters too shallow for patrol boats to enter. In 1979, the most compelling deterrent, so far as the villagers were concerned, was the danger of injury involved in the handling of explosives. A number of village fishermen have suffered injuries, including one near fatality. One village boat was split open and sunk as a result of a bombing accident, when explosives detonated prematurely in the water immediately beneath the vessel.

Explosives are made by the villagers of a mixture of powdered dammar, sodium chlorate, and sulphur, and are usually packed inside a glass bottle, which is sealed with a waterproof stopper through which a locally made fuse is inserted. Stoppers are usually made of rubber slipper soles. The fuse is ignited by matches inserted in the stopper. The length of the fuse may be varied depending on the depth at which the bomb is meant to explode. Fish may be sighted from the surface or by diving, and at night schools of fish are usually detected by the phosphorescent flashes they produce. As soon as a sighting is made, the bomb is lit and thrown into the water, its fuse adjusted for depth. After it explodes, the fishing party begins collecting the catch. Since fish killed by concussion do not float to the surface, but sink, the catch must be recovered by diving. At night, a floating buoy is usually set out to mark the location, so that the crew can return at sunrise when there is enough light to begin diving. There is some variation in methods of collecting fish depending on the depth of the water in which they are taken. In deep water (6 fathoms or deeper) a diver is usually lowered by rope with lead or stone weights. A second weighted rope is used as a signal line. The diver carries a container around his waist to hold the fish which he collects from the sea floor. When he can no longer hold his breath, he jerks on the signal line, and is pulled to the surface by the rest of the crew. Using this method,

fish can be taken from as deep as 15–16 fathoms. However, most bombing is done in shallower water. A variety of fish are taken by bombing,
but fusiliers (*Caesio* spp.), large schools of which regularly appear in
shallower waters, appear to be a major target.

Fishing Expeditions

The amount of time that a family spends at sea varies. Based on estimates
made by a small sample of family heads in 1965, the average number of
days was said to be between 90 and 150. These estimates accord closely
with my own observations. The smallest number of days a family spent
at sea was thirty. Because of the scattered location of fishing sites, as well
as the distance of many of these sites from the village, most fishing trips
lasted from one or two days to several weeks. The intensity of fishing is
governed primarily by tides and the monthly lunar cycle, but social com-
mitments also influence fishing plans. For example, the death of an
elderly villager is likely to draw most families back to the settlement for a
period of at least several days, usually through the funeral and first
memorial rites (*bahangi*).[10] At the first sign of serious illness, boats are
frequently dispatched to call back kin from wherever they are fishing so
that they may attend the sick and be present in the village should he or
she die. At other times, families may intensify their fishing, staying at sea
for longer periods of time in order to increase their income to meet some
major social expense, such as a son's marriage or a boy's circumcision.
For most families, the time they spend at sea is divided each year
between twenty and fifty voyages, not counting briefer daily fishing
trips, separated by what are usually longer intervals spent in the village.

While most voyages are undertaken for purposes of fishing, not all the
time that a family spends at sea is taken up with fishing or in travelling
to and from fishing sites. On either the outward or return voyage, a
family may stop over, for example, in Labuan Haji, possibly remaining
overnight or for several days, to visit kin and exchange news. Trips are
also made explicitly to visit relatives, either in Labuan Haji or Sitangkai.
During such trips family members may attend a sick relative; await a
birth; or participate in marriage negotiations. While at sea, families often
put into islands or an area of beach in order to fell mangrove trees
(*bangkau*) for firewood, collect pandanus (*pandan*) to make sleeping
mats, or to cut down small *patau* trees to make net floats. Occasionally
in the course of a voyage, families visit areas of coastal forest, poling up
the estuarine creeks to collect bamboo for poles, fish-spear shafts and
masts, to gather rattan cables, or to fell trees for making house-timbers,
piling, and planks. On longer voyages, families sometimes call on strand
settlements to trade or purchase fresh supplies of drinking water. On
their homeward voyage, crews often stop in Semporna town to sell their
fish and to visit the market and town shops.

While at sea, family members work together as a fishing team. Few
crews are without children, whose presence, particularly that of sons, is
an important asset. Youngsters are taught to swim at an early age. By
the age of eleven or twelve, most boys are adept at handling spears,

hand-lines, spear guns, and other gear and regularly join their fathers and others in laying out and hauling in nets. By adolescence, their labour is usually an important economic resource to the family. Girls take an active part in intertidal gathering and later join the small, informal collecting groups formed by their older sisters and friends. At adolescence, girls also take over much of the care of their younger siblings and so free the women to help their husbands.

Most family crews reach the peak of their productivity as the couple's older children attain marriageable age. This is the period when men are most likely to divert a significant share of the family's earnings into the construction of a village pile-house. Peak productivity thus marks for most families the beginnings of house group independence. Most heads of family fishing crews also become house group leaders during this time, using family income from fishing to bring about this major change in their village status. Later, as their children marry and establish separate fishing crews of their own, older men are in a position, as house group leaders, to retain at least one of these crews within their house group. The most successful leaders are generally those who are able to retain more than one crew, in addition to their own or, today, a son or son-in-law holding a job outside the village.

Upon returning to the village at the conclusion of a fishing voyage, family members are subject to wider obligations of food sharing and gift exchange. Only after setting aside fish or market income sufficient to meet these obligations is a family ordinarily free to market the remainder of its catch. Marketing is exclusively a family matter; whatever income is received belongs to individual family members alone rather than to the (usually) larger house group to which they may belong. Despite food-sharing obligations, family crews preserve their economic autonomy within the village. This fact, as we shall see in the chapters that follow, is of utmost sociological importance.

Netting Fleets

Most family crews at least occasionally fish by themselves. However, when drift-netting, it is generally advantageous to fish together with at least one or two other families. In 1964–5, it was more common for families to fish in fleets, pooling their nets and labour with other crews. Often families set out from the village in small groups; on longer voyages, those who set out together sometimes remain fishing partners for the duration of their travels. Alternatively, they might split up at sea or join other crews to form still larger fleets. After a time, some families may decide to return to the village, while others continue to fish, possibly setting off for different fishing sites or linking up with new partners. Thus, fleet alignments are typically fluid and short-lived.

At sea, family crews regularly encounter others. Such encounters are sometimes pre-arranged before families depart from the village, but more often they occur by chance. Ligitan, Sabangkat, Maiga, and the reefs south of Gaya all serve as important rendezvous points where family crews regularly meet. But meetings also occur at other less frequented sites. Occasionally, such encounters take place as a result of news of successful landings being carried back to Bangau-Bangau by returning families, causing others to set out for the same destination. Whatever the case, family crews meeting at sea may decide to fish together. If conditions favour large-scale netting, a number of crews may come together in this way, including some that otherwise seldom fish together. Decisions to join in a fleet rest with the families involved and the resulting partnerships are entirely voluntary. As they are easily entered into, they may be just as readily broken off. Consequently, the fleets formed tend to be varied in composition, ephemeral, and capable of responding quickly to the changing opportunities that arise at sea.

Netting fleets range in size from as few as two, to as many as fifty or sixty crews. Larger fleets are typically short-lived, but smaller ones tend to be much more enduring. Smaller groups often set out from Bangau-Bangau together and remain partners throughout a voyage, both in order to fish together, and also for security and companionship. Such partnerships are generally formed between kin and village neighbours.

Each family crew carries its own complement of nets and other gear. Nets, both *linggi'* and *selibut,* are designed for catching different kinds of fish and for use in different types of netting operations. But the most important characteristic, shared by all Bajau Laut nets, is that their floating headline ends, on both sides, in lengths of free cord, 20–5 centimetres long. These lengths of cord are called *talinga* ('ears'). While a single net may be used alone, more often several nets are tied together by their 'ears' to form a larger composite structure. Using nets tied together in this manner, the Bajau Laut are able to construct net barriers, corrals, and other types of encirclement or engulfing structures which they either anchor to the sea floor, or manoeuvre in the water to engulf, surround, or trap fish. The largest of these structures may incorporate thirty or forty individual nets, or possibly more, belonging to as many different families. Generally, crews carry nets of at least two different types; most families carry enough nets to construct smaller encirclements. However, larger structures require co-operation and the combined nets of more than one family crew. To form such structures, at least two or three families are needed, not only to pool their nets, but also to supply the labour necessary to lay them out and manoeuvre them in the water. The sociological significance of Bajau Laut nets lies in the way their use encourages co-operation and allows for considerable variation, across family lines, in the creation and maintaining of fishing partnerships and in the deployment and combining of family labour (Sather, 1985). This variation can be better understood by looking at the different types of netting Bajau Laut fishermen engaged in during 1964–5.

Major Forms of Netting

The simplest form of drift-net fishing engaged in by the villagers in 1965 was called *anakop.* Often *anakop* is carried out by a single family crew. Frequently, however, several crews work together, combining their nets.

Typically, a submerged outcrop of coral or an isolated coral-head is encircled with a small net-surround set in place by diving. In order to prevent the escape of fish, a second circle of nets is often laid down around the first, particularly if more than one family join in the operation (Plate 13). Once the structure is in place, a diver with a pole (*soak*) or spear flushes the fish from the coral (Plate 14). As they emerge, the fish are speared or trapped in the nets. The return from *anakop* fishing is generally small. However, the technique is relatively dependable and in 1965, yielded a significant proportion of the fish that entered the village food-sharing network.

Occasionally, *anakop* netting is used to fish coral fissures or deep holes in the coral terraces or reefs. In this case, the surround is set out around the mouth of the opening, and fishermen sometimes use *tuba* poison (*Derris elliptica*) or spear guns, as well as spears and nets in taking fish trapped in this way. The poison is pounded on the gunwale or forward deck of the *lepa* and released into the water by diving. A submerged sail is sometimes used to cover the mouth of the hole after the poison has been released to prevent it from being dispersed by the current. Sails, buoyed by trapped air, are also used to gather in the drugged fish as they float to the surface. When the technique is used without poison, fish are again flushed with poles or fish-spears.

To fish underwater reef channels, the villagers employ a rather more complex form of net fishing, requiring the co-operation of at least two or three family crews. Called *amahan* or *anaga*, it involves the laying down of a compound structure of nets across the channel. This is done as the tide begins to ebb, at a point where the surrounding fringing reef makes it difficult for fish to escape around the sides of the net. While some members of the netting fleet are laying down the nets, others are stationed at the sides to prevent the premature escape of fish over the top of the reef. A long rattan cable (*bahan*) is frequently run from each end of the net structure into the inshore shallows. These cables, which are said to vibrate in the water, form a pair of long wings opening outward which, as the fish seek deeper water, guide them towards the channel in which the net barrier has been placed. Sometimes, parties of youngsters are stationed inshore, on either side of the ends of these cable wings, to drive the fish inward, towards the net barrier as well as to prevent them from escaping through the shallows at either side.

Most channel netting is done during periods of maximum flood tide. At such times, particularly when the moon is late in rising, night-time or early morning *anaga* fishing frequently yields large landings. But the risk of failure is considerable. As a rule, Bajau Laut fishing is conducted without ritual observance. Channel-netting is an exception, perhaps because of its unpredictability. While *anaga* fishing, the villagers observe a number of restrictions which are said to reduce the chances of failure. These include a taboo on joking, making loud noises, dragging feet in the water over the side of the boat, or using sea water to wash utensils in which food has been prepared or eaten. Fish are said to take affront at these acts.

Binankad, or beach-netting, is another form of fishing that often requires the co-operation of at least two or three family crews. Very often, more take part. As the tide ebbs, a net structure is laid out along a sandy beach, typically along the inshore edge of the *halo* zone. It is usually formed of medium- or small-meshed *selibut* nets. The two ends of the structure are drawn up towards the shore to form a flattened, semicircular enclosure, secured by bamboo poles which are either driven into the sea floor, or attached to boats anchored in the shallows or beached in the surf. As the structure is being secured in place, some members of the netting party are dispatched in each direction along the fringing reef. When they are some distance from the enclosure, they cross into the inner *tebba* zone dragging rattan cables, or striking the water with poles. In this way, fish are driven shoreward and along the shallows into the net enclosure. As the tide continues to ebb, the structure is manoeuvred shoreward; at the same time, the ends of the net encirclement are closed and drawn on to the beach. Once the ends of the encirclement are closed, the weighted footline of the nets is anchored to the sea floor, stranding the fish inside the encirclement. In order to keep the outer netting vertical, particularly where there are strong tows or beach currents, the nets are often supported by additional poles driven into the sand.

From time to time, single family crews engage in much more limited forms of beach-netting, using a small anchored encirclement, or sometimes a stationary trap (*bungsud*) made from nets secured with poles. The landings made by these latter methods are generally small.

Larger fleets are required for inlet- (*lo'ok*) or cove-netting, known as *amokot*. Cove-netting is done at night or during the early hours of the morning, shortly before dawn. It requires considerable co-ordination on the part of the participating crews. Most crews range their boats seaward of the cove and, at a signal from the netting leader, drive fish inward by striking the water with poles or oars. As the fish enter the cove, part of the fleet, moving from both sides of the cove entrance, either in boats or wading in the water, quickly lay down a wall of netting across the cove's mouth. Meeting at the centre, they tie their lengths of netting together, turning the cove into a trap. If the drive is successful, a second wall of netting is generally laid down as soon as the first is in position. With this second row of nets secured, the ends of the first are drawn into a circle and then progressively tightened. In this way, the fishermen make a sweep of the cove. Any fish that might have escaped can then be taken in a second sweep, made with the next row of nets. At the same time, fish attempting to escape to the open water are speared by crews stationed around the outer nets.

The most extensive and highly co-ordinated form of netting occurs in connection with large-scale fish drives called *ambit* or *magambit*.[11] In the Semporna district, these drives, lasting from three to five days, take place in the Ligitan reef complex during the 'new moon' phase (*anak bulan*) of the lunar cycle, when, according to the villagers, schools of *langohan* and *anduhau* migrate from the deep water, across the fringing reef, and into the surrounding coral shallows.[12]

As these migrations begin, boat crews arrive in the Ligitan reef complex, coming not only from Bangau-Bangau and Labuan Haji, but also from Sitangkai and other Bajau Laut settlements in the Sibutu island group. If conditions are ideal, as many as fifty or sixty crews may assemble. Because of the large numbers involved, *magambit* demands a higher degree of organization than any other netting method. As crews assemble, the more senior crew leaders gather and select a group of netting leaders, naming one as the principal *nakura'*, responsible for overseeing the drive. The *nakura'* acts through this group, each member of which represents a small number of crews.

Before the drive gets under way, the netting leaders collect nets from each of the crews under their charge. During the drive leaders are responsible for assigning and overseeing the specific tasks that each family crew undertakes during the drive. The *nakura'* are also responsible for policing the drive and maintaining general order. This is not always easy, as large drives may bring together families involved in long-lasting animosities.[13] When fishing the Ligitan area, the principal *nakura'* is also responsible for petitioning (*amuhun*) the resident spirit of the reefs, before netting begins.

After nets have been collected from each boat crew, they are assembled to make a large horseshoe-shaped structure. The main net assembly is carried, not in the boat of the *nakura'*, but usually in a second boat called the *anua' tebba* or lead boat. From the *anua' tebba*, the structure is laid out under the direction of the *nakura'*, with one of its long sides anchored by its footline along the edge of the fringing reef (Figure 4.2). The remainder of the structure floats free in the deeper water beyond. While some boat crews, including that of the *nakura'*, are busy laying out this structure, the majority move out into the open water. Here, under the direction of the netting leaders, the boats are ranged in a large arc—its size depending on the number of crews taking part in the drive—which extends from the reef rim, at the open end of the horseshoe, out to sea, and then curves back again toward the seaward edge of the structure. The more distant boats making up this arc are, in larger drives, often barely visible to those stationed along the edge of the reef. As with individual nets, the two ends of this arc are called *talinga* or 'ears'.

At least two boats, the *anua' tebba* and that of the *nakura'*, stay back, standing ready with additional nets tied to the seaward end of the structure. A number of additional crews are strung out in a line, seaward from the mouth of the structure, to prevent the escape of fish around the seaward edge of the nets. A small number of boats, often including individual fishermen in *boggo'*, are positioned along the top of the reef edge to watch for the approach of fish and prevent their escape over the top of the reef.

When all the crews are in place, the netting leaders give a signal which is passed along the arc of boats. The boats then move forward, their crews beating against the boat sides with pieces of firewood or oars and striking the water with bamboo poles as they advance. In this way, fish are driven inward, against the edge of the reef and along the reef rim towards the open mouth of the horseshoe structure (see Figure 4.2). At

FIGURE 4.2
Magambit Netting

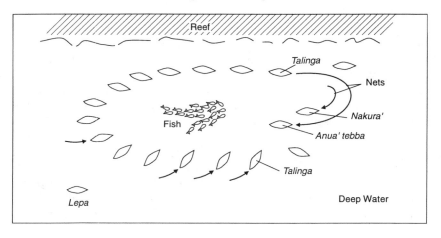

this stage, co-ordination is crucial. Each netting leader stationed within the arc has to maintain strict order among the boats under his charge, preventing gaps from developing in their lines and restraining individual crews from moving forward ahead of the others, or from falling behind.

As the fish begin to stream by, the crews stationed along the reef rim signal by shouting. The moment the dark mass of fish is seen to enter the horseshoe encirclement, those waiting by its mouth, led by the *nakura'*, quickly seal off the structure by laying down a curtain of nets across its entrance. As soon as this is done, a second and third circles of nets are laid down around the outside of the main encirclement.

The whole fleet soon gathers around the outside of the nets. Taking hold of the headline from the bow of their boats, crew members manoeuvre the structure of nets into shallower water (Plate 15). As they do so, the back-up nets prevent any escaping fish from reaching the open water. Divers now secure the footline of the main encirclement to the sea floor. After the back-up nets have been repositioned, one end of the original encirclement is untied and dragged around the inside of the nets, drawing the circle tighter (Plate 16). On instruction from the *naku-ra'*, one or two boats are sent to the centre of the circle and there begin hauling in the nets. Even though relatively large-meshed *linggi'* are used for the main encirclement, frequently many of the trapped fish are too large to be gilled. Instead, they are entangled in the nets and dragged from the water.

As the crews at the centre, particularly the crew aboard the *anua' tebba*, continue to haul in the entangled fish and nets (Plates 17 and 18), others spear any escaping fish, either while swimming in the water or from the bowsprit platforms of their boats (Plate 19). After the first haul is completed, and the spearing has been brought under control by the *nakura'* and other netting leaders, the fish are allowed to regroup within the second circle of nets. If the size of the landing seems to warrant it, additional circles of nets might be laid down, and a second haul made, usually followed by a third, and possibly more.

When the last haul is over, the fleet temporarily breaks up (Plate 20). The *nakura'* and other leaders take stock of the catch, disassemble the netting structure and collect together each crew's nets. Drives always take place on a falling tide. Afterwards, families often take advantage of the ebb tide to disperse in smaller groups to fish or gather shellfish. For many Bangau-Bangau families, the break is also an opportunity to meet with friends and kin from other villages.

As the tide rises again, the fleet gradually reassembles. The *nakura'* and netting leaders then go from boat to boat, returning the nets to their owners and dividing the catch based on their estimation of its size. Reflecting the basic autonomy of each family crew, the catch is divided into equal shares (*magbahagi*), regardless of crew size or the particular task its members performed. In addition to its main share of the catch, each family is also allowed to keep aside a small amount of fish for its own personal use. This is placed at the stern of the boat, near the family's cooking hearth. It is not unknown for families to attempt to conceal more than their legitimate share of fish from the *nakura'* and other leaders. For example, Layang (pseudonym, a man in his late thirties in 1974) told me in conversation one afternoon that the most vivid memory he retains of his childhood is of an occurrence that took place in the Ligitan complex during a *magambit* drive.

I was still very young then, maybe six or seven. After the drive was over, my father and a cousin moved their boats off a little from the others. I happened to see my father and this cousin hiding fish under a clump of fan-coral. I went up to where they were and watched. I asked father what he was doing, and he told me to be quiet and not mention what I had seen to anyone. The fish, he said, were to buy clothing for the family. A little later, when the leaders came to our boat—I don't know why I did it—but I told everything. Some men went out and came back with the fish. All this time, father said nothing, but I could see that his face had turned a deep red. After that, I ran away from our boat and lived for the next two days—I think it was—with Panglima Atani. (This incident took place shortly before the founding of Bangau-Bangau, when Panglima Atani was still headman of the Bajau Laut community in Semporna. At the time Atani, who was Layang's mother's brother, was *nakura'* of the drive).

To prevent such concealment, when the leaders arrive at each boat to divide the catch they generally carry out a quick inspection, looking under the decking-planks and in the rolled-up roofing for concealed fish.

As soon as the landing is divided, each of the participating crews is free to go its own way. If further drives are planned, families may elect to rejoin the fleet. But the decision is entirely their own, there being no compulsion to remain.

By 1974, *magambit* drives occurred only intermittently on a much reduced scale from 1965, and in 1979 they had ceased altogether. In the 1964–5 period, these drives were the major source of the best quality dried fish (*daing toho'*) produced by the Bajau Laut in Semporna and so were of major importance in the village economy. In 1994, *magambit* netting was still being practised at Sitangkai, in the waters immediately around the island itself, although on a much reduced scale and for lesser grades of fish than in the past (Nagatsu, 1995).

Netting-Fleet Organization

Fleet relations are highly responsive to the different methods of drift-netting. Although variable and short-lived, co-operative relations are considerably more patterned than they appear to be at first sight because the great majority of fleets are organized around a core of relatively enduring dyadic partnerships. Every active family head has a small circle of four to twelve regular partners or 'companions' (séhè') with whom he and the members of his family repeatedly fish. These men or their wives are almost exclusively close cognatic kin of approximately the same age and generation. Most commonly, they are siblings (denakan), brothers-in-law (ipal), or men whose wives are sisters (bilas). Collateral relations tend to be stressed. However, newly married men, just entering the active age group, and older men nearing retirement often enter alignments with older and younger crew leaders. Most often included are the established partners of their parents and, for older fishermen, the partners of their married children, both sons and daughters. Village house groups and residential clusters act as important reservoirs of regular fishing partners. The majority of most crew leaders' regular companions come from among the same or adjacent house group clusters within the village, although partnerships are also formed outside these groups.

While relationships between regular partners are relatively stable, the smaller fleets formed on the basis of these relationships tend to be short-lived and often vary in composition from one voyage to another or even in the course of the same voyage. At most, regular partners depart from the village and fish together for the duration of a single voyage, sailing home together at its conclusion. While it is not uncommon for the same families to team up again the next time they go to sea, fleets rarely have precisely the same composition for more than two or three consecutive voyages. They often vary even during a single voyage. Fleets are relatively ephemeral, and family boat crew is the sole enduring unit of Bajau Laut fishing organization.

From the vantage point of an individual fisherman, relations between his regular partners are best thought of as comprising what I have elsewhere called a 'personal roster' (Sather, 1976: 60–1; 1985)—a set of individuals linked by dyadic relations repeatedly drawn upon in recruiting fishing and sailing 'companions'. Each fisherman has his own unique roster. The personal rosters of an individual's regular partners are rarely, if ever, entirely identical, although there is usually considerable overlap. For example, the headman of Bangau-Bangau, Panglima Tiring, whose crew I regularly accompanied, included among his personal roster three brothers, Gilang, Rugo-Rugo, and Kubang; a son-in-law, Saharati; and the latter's brother and his family. Saharati and his brother, Umaldani, are also nephews of Amjatul, Panglima Tiring's wife. While all belonged at the time to the headman's roster, the three brothers were not regular partners of the two younger men, although as individuals all frequently joined fleets in which the headman was a member. It follows that not all of those who fish together, even in relatively small fleets, are necessarily frequent 'companions', although all, as a rule, have at least one roster member in any fleet they join, whatever its size.

In addition to his brothers, the headman fished with Tandoh, a friend and distant kin of his wife; with Amjatul's brother, Labu; and, less often, with Isalhani, the husband of his first cousin. Until the latter's death, he also fished with his elder sister and her husband. Of these men, only Tandoh and Labu are regular companions. They are linked to Isalhani only through their common tie with Panglima Tiring. Saharati is a member of the Panglima's house group, together with his wife and children, while Gilang and Umaldani lived in the same house group cluster, although in different houses. Tandoh, Rugo-Rugo, Labu, and Isalhani all live in different though neighbouring house group clusters. In 1965, Panglima Tiring's youngest brother, Kubang, was still boat-living and so did not belong to any house group. The headman's roster relations appear to be generally typical of other senior fishermen in the community.

Fleets disband at the conclusion of every voyage or, in the case of larger nettings, at the conclusion of each operation. Although they may regroup again at the next opportunity, individual families may also fish alone or with others, some or all of whom may be unrelated by roster ties. In practice, roster relations include a wider periphery of more casual and irregular alignments. As a result, the fleets that the villagers form remain potentially variable and capable of considerable expansion around, for each individual boat-crew leader, an inner core of relatively enduring, individual-focused roster partnerships.

Marketing and Food Sharing

At sea, the family crew is the primary unit of economic process. Whether its members fish alone or with others, it remains the principal unit of fishing production, its members making independent decisions about when and where to fish, working together as a single fishing team, and managing their own assets, earnings, and labour. Crew members also form an independent commensal unit at sea, sharing a common hearth, food stores, fresh water, and living quarters.

In returning to the village, each family is socially enmeshed in a wider network of political and economic relations. The chapters that follow explore these relations in detail. But here it is significant to note that they entail, among other things, obligations of food sharing with regard to fish (*binuanan daing*). On rejoining the village, each family crew is expected to reserve part of its catch for its house group's use and to meet wider gift-giving obligations to its village kin and cluster allies living outside the house group.[14] Once provisions have been made to meet these obligations, the remainder of the family's catch is generally marketed. Some of it may be sold directly in the town market or brought back to the village to dry on the family's house platform for later sale. In either case, family members are exclusively responsible for marketing and enjoy full control over whatever income they receive, independently of other village housemates, including, in the case of larger house groups, the house group leader (*nakura' luma'*). In the 1964–5 period, a sharp distinction was drawn between food-sharing obligations and market income, with control over the latter resting exclusively with the members of the family fishing crew. By 1979, food sharing of fish had all but ceased.

Most fresh fish is sold through the public fish market in Semporna town. The market is maintained by the Semporna district council which lets stall space to licensed traders in return for the payment of an annual licence fee. In most cases, licensees farm out their stall to others who engage in direct selling. In 1965, traders did not actually buy the fishermen's catch. Instead, for a small commission, usually 20 cents for a small catch, or 10 per cent of the price received for a larger catch, they allowed the fisherman to use their stall to display his fish and these were sold to customers on the fisherman's behalf. Usually, the fisherman also engaged in selling, and accounts were settled when the landing was sold, often with some concession to the fisherman to retain his trade. Market prices fluctuate, depending on daily supplies. Most fresh fish is tied up in small bundles with a loop of rattan, while larger fish are cut into sections which are sold individually. Fresh fish is rarely sold by measured weight, and prices vary considerably between different types of fish, making precise estimates of market prices difficult. However, during the 1964–5 period, average market prices for fish in Semporna were extremely low, even by Sabah standards, in a state where fish are comparatively abundant. The average price for most types of fresh fish was 20–30 cents (7–10 US cents) per '*kati*' (0.6 kilogram) with the range varying from 10 cents to a maximum of 80 cents (3–27 US cents).

In addition to selling through market traders, a small amount of fresh fish is sold directly to townspeople outside the market stalls. Strand villagers also occasionally visit Bajau Laut fleets at sea to buy fish directly from fishing crews. All such transactions are for cash. In addition, a number of food stalls in Semporna town also buy fish, particularly cuttlefish, octopus, and premium quality white fish, usually at a better price than market-stall rates. Also, in 1964–5 Teck Guan, then the largest Chinese trading company in Semporna, had a supply contract with the Malaysian army and also bought premium quality fresh fish, which the company iced in Semporna and reshipped to Tawau. At the time, many fishermen sold regularly through the company.

On longer voyages, most of a crew's catch is dried (or salted). In 1964–5 dried/salt fish was a major item of commercial trade in Semporna and was estimated to comprise 40 per cent of the total district's fish landings (Goh, 1964: 19). The Bajau Laut are the principal dried fish producers in Semporna. As already noted, five shops were the main buyers of dried fish, although several others also made occasional purchases. The main buyers were all general goods shops that acted as export agents, reshipping most of their dried fish purchases to larger urban markets, primarily Kota Kinabalu (then Jesselton), Sandakan, and Tawau. Dried fish marketing was, in 1965, the only area of Bajau Laut fishing in which there was some limited credit involvement on the part of outsiders. All five shops offered bags of salt on credit, deducting the price from the fisherman's catch. This involvement, however, was highly limited, both in terms of the numbers of fishermen involved and the value of the credit offered. Few fishermen used salt, preferring instead to use sea water and to dry their catch in the sun. In contrast to fresh fish, market prices for dried fish are relatively stable, averaging 35–50 cents (11–17 US cents) per 'kati', depending on the quality.[15] The largest part of most crews' cash income comes from the sale of dried fish; the proportion of income from this source generally increases the more active and experienced the fishing crew leader.

There is a large element of unpredictability in Bajau Laut fishing. There are times when netting ventures are a total failure, and even experienced fishermen return to the village from time to time empty-handed or with not enough fish to market. From time to time during the year, fishing may barely cover the immediate food needs of the family's house group. According to the estimates of village fishermen, the average earnings from a marketed landing ranged in 1964–5 from RM8 to RM15. Larger catches are generally dried. Cash earnings from fishing are consequently small, even for families that go to sea regularly. Earnings also tend to be highly variable, with families occasionally making a series of substantial market landings after which they may receive little or no cash income for several months, although they generally obtain sufficient catch to feed themselves and meet their village food-sharing obligations.

Although fishing was the principal source of village income in 1965, it was not the only source. In addition to wage employment, village curers and midwives earned a small income from their skills, being paid in both cash and more traditional forms of kind. Two elderly widows made a small income by selling shells and dried sea cucumbers (bat) to Chinese buyers in Semporna town, while several others occasionally sold cakes in the village, mainly to schoolchildren, and one woman marketed sea urchins and sea grapes at the town market-place. Others collected and dried sea cucumbers for sale, to augment family income. A few men earned money from boat-building as a part-time occupation, while two who are highly skilled wood-carvers were called upon to make carved designs for boats and grave markers.

Husbands have primary responsibility for family marketing, although wives also take part. By 1974, a number of village women, including the headman's wife, had become active market traders in Semporna town; women are as much involved in money transactions as men. Husbands and wives share equally in decisions regarding expenditure, and any cash savings that a family retains are normally entrusted to the wife for safe keeping. Aside from small daily purchases, monetary gifts, and contributions required from time to time to meet common household expenses, most families attempt to set aside a cash reserve to meet larger expenditures than can normally be met out of their immediate, day-to-day income. These include the purchase of durable goods. Once acquired, these goods become the separate property of the individual family members for whom they were purchased. In economic terms, the most significant of these purchases are, for the husband, fishing boats and house-construction materials, and, for the wife, gold jewellery (*dublun*). Because it is redeemable for cash in times of need, gold jewellery also constitutes a form of family savings. Again, the wife has primary say in its management.

Fishing income belongs exclusively to the family fishing crew. Out of this income, the family head must meet the recurrent costs of maintaining his boat, nets, and other gear. Most families seek to meet these and other recurrent expenses out of their immediate income. To some extent, fishing is well-suited to this, as some income is usually gained at the conclusion of every voyage, rather than coming, as with agriculture, in a large annual yield followed by long periods with little or no income. Also, the frequency of fishing can be increased to meet unusual expenses. Not all these expenses are necessarily related to fishing, or to family subsistence. Some, such as the expenses entailed by a son's marriage or by a long-term family illness may, in the short-run, be beyond the ability of a single family to meet from its own resources. At such times, village house group members and other kin are likely to be turned to. In this way, the family is again linked to a wider web of economic relationships. Receiving aid creates future obligations of return. The resulting transactions of debt and credit dominate the village economy and are closely bound up with the nature of fishing, in which income is received in relatively small, but variable amounts, at times surpassing family needs, at other times barely covering its subsistence requirements. The existence of this wider system of economic relations, linking village families to one another, complements the relative independence of the family in day-to-day fishing, and so forms a vital element in the larger social and economic life of the community.

1. In 1965, five of these men were Tidong; one a Bajau from the west coast of Sabah; and three were Indonesians, two from Timor and one from the Sangihe islands.

2. In 1964–5, the *lepa* was the distinctive fishing vessel of the Semporna–Sibutu Bajau Laut. Outside the area, types of boats differ from region to region. In the Sulu Archipelago, from Tawitawi eastward, Bajau Laut (that is, Sama Dilaut) boats are typically equipped with single or double outriggers (see Nimmo (1965) for Tawitawi, also Kurais (1975) and Spoehr (1971)). According to village informants, the *lepa* was first made for trade by Sama Kubang boatwrights. Its introduction may have been as recent as the beginning of the twentieth century, although this is uncertain. However, photographs of the 1910s and early 1920s show outrigger vessels in Semporna (see for example, Cook, 1924: 120). In 1965 the finest *lepa* were still produced by Sama Kubang builders at Kambimbangan, Nusalalung, and other villages along the northern shore of Bumbum Island. Apart from the Semporna community, *lepa* were traded to the Sitangkai Sama Dilaut and in smaller numbers to Bongao and Sanga-Sanga, as far east as the Siasi island group. For a detailed account of *lepa* design and construction, see Martenot (1981: 186–94) and Burningham (1992: 200–2). In 1979, although *lepa* were still occasionally

built, they were being rapidly replaced as the main fishing boat by the *pombot*, a plank-constructed vessel powered by a small inboard engine of 10–16 hp. Without the *lepa*'s solid keel, bow and stern sections, the *pombot* is much cheaper to build, particularly as timber has become increasingly scarce. In 1994, the villagers had completely ceased building *lepa*.

3. In Sitangkai and the Tawitawi island group, the term *balutu* is reportedly applied to a particular type of Sama vessel with roomy living quarters (Martenot, 1981: 198–202). In 1965, such boats were unknown in Semporna.

4. This association of the stern (*buli'*) with female tasks, the bow (*munda'*) with male tasks, is carried over into death. When the body of the dead (*bangkai*) is carried on its final voyage from the village to the community's burial place, a white flag is borne from the bow of the boat in the case of a man, and from the stern in the case of a woman (see Chapter 9).

5. The *kokan* is discussed later in connection with village houses, body symbolism, and the ritual use of space. What should be noted here is that only the corpse of the dead may lay lengthwise in a boat, with its head to the bow and feet to the stern. The living must lay crosswise, with their head at the *kokan* side. Being somewhat taller than most Bajau Laut, observing this latter rule was something of a trial when I lived with families at sea, although I eventually became accustomed to it. Early on, I was sometimes awakened at night by family members pointing out that, in my sleep, I had assumed a more comfortable 'corpse-like' position, lengthwise in the boat.

6. The rate of exchange in 1964–5 was approximately RM3 = US$1. The 1979 rate was roughly RM2.25 = US$1.

7. *Gellom* (*Osbornia octadonata*) grows particularly at the tidemark edge of stranded coralline flats, which the Bajau Laut call *lakit*. Contrary to Kurais (1975: 115), *gellom* is not associated with mangrove forests, at least not in the Semporna district. The villagers say that the tree avoids the estuarine areas favoured by mangrove (*bangkau*); instead, it is a common shoreline shrub or small tree on the low coralline islands of the district, such as Bumbum Island. The soft inner bark has an oily texture which, the villagers say, is impervious to water. Occasionally, the *gellom* grows to a medium-sized tree. Its wood is said to be particularly resistant to salt water and is used for house pilings as well as in boat construction. *Gellom* bark is also carried aboard the *lepa* and used by the Bajau Laut to patch leaks at sea.

8. A planted tree in the Semporna district.

9. After 1974, two new types of *linggi'* were introduced, both apparently from the Philippines. The first, the *linggi' bokko'*, is used exclusively to capture sea-turtles and is made of heavy nylon line, 13–16 fathoms long, 2 fathoms wide, with a 60-centimetre mesh opening. The second is the *linggi' pahi*, used exclusively for skates, made of medium nylon line, also with a 60-centimetre mesh opening.

10. See Chapter 9.

11. Literally, to move together, in co-ordination. The term may also be used to describe friends who walk together, arm-in-arm, or holding hands.

12. See Chapter 3.

13. In the two drives I took part in, fishermen had to be physically separated by their leaders to prevent fist-fights.

14. *Binuanan* means to give or share with others and applies also to rice (*pai*) and other foodstuffs.

15. Even though dried fish prices are relatively stable, the Bajau Laut are highly sensitive to price variations. At the conclusion of a particularly successful *ambit* drive, Panglima Tiring and his son-in-law Saharati sailed with their families all the way to Lahad Datu on a rumour, which proved to be unfounded, that fish buyers there were paying a higher price than in Semporna.

5
The House Group

Pasod ka ebéttong enggo'nu
— luma'.

Mother into whose womb you are delivered
— the house. (Traditional Bajau Laut riddle)

THE village community represents the principal focus of Bajau Laut
social and ritual life. Here married couples and families—both house-
and boat-living—make regular return between intervals of fishing. Upon
their return, house-living families are absorbed into generally larger
leader-centred groups—'house groups' (*luma'*) and 'clusters' (*ba'anan*),
which together comprise the organizational context for most village undertakings.

Mataan

A married couple, with or without dependant children, is distinguished
by the Bajau Laut by the term *mataan*. The term derives from the root
word *mata*, the usual meaning of which is 'eye', but which in this instance refers to the 'mesh' or individual openings of a fishing net.[1] The
notion of *mataan* refers therefore not to a free-standing entity that exists
independently of others, but to what is perceived as an interconnected
part of a larger whole made up of a plurality of similar parts. In other
words, each individual 'mesh', although distinguished, is seen as joined
to others. Like an 'eye' within the meshwork of a fishing net, it comprises
part of an outward-extending field made up of similar 'eyes', each consisting of closely related couples and families.

The metaphor is an appropriate one. Under ordinary circumstances, a
married couple or pair with children never exist alone, isolated from others.
Instead, each individual *mataan* is seen as part of a larger field comprised
of similar couples and families, each related to the others. The ties that
connect individuals within this meshwork act like the knotted strands
that bind one 'mesh' to another to form a fishing net. Minimally, to follow the metaphor further, each spouse or family member may be likened
to the knot in a net. His or her relationships with other family members
thus form the individual strands that define an opening or 'eye'. In this
sense, the Bajau Laut refer to a couple, or single family, as a *damataan*,

literally '(those of) one mesh', while the latter refer to themselves as *kami damataan*, 'we of one mesh'.

The term *mataan* is also used in a more general sense to refer to the larger meshwork itself. Hence, the semantic connotations of the term are essentially relational. Those of one 'eye' are joined to others both outwardly, in relational terms, and temporally from one generation to another. Not only does a parental couple count themselves as *mataan*, but so, too, may parents and the families of their married children, as well as the families of married brothers and sisters. In this wider sense, one's *mataan* include persons related not only within the same 'mesh', but through closely interlocked 'mesh' within a more extended family-centred meshwork made up of related couples and families, all of whom are linked to one another by strands of marriage and filiation.

At marriage, a husband and wife are said to initiate a new *mataan*. The birth of a child adds new strands to this 'eye', while death breaks previous strands, sometimes causing the loss of an 'eye' from the larger meshwork that previously enveloped it. The total field of *mataan* relationships that a married couple acknowledges thus changes over time as strands within this more extended field are added or lost. New knots, strands, and even 'eyes', are added, mainly through birth and marriage; while old connections may be lost, broken, or rent apart, mainly by death, enmity, and the increasing attenuation of relationships. It is important to stress that *mataan* ties are seen by the Bajau Laut as 'close' (*asékot*) both genealogically and in emotional terms. In order to prevent the disintegration of this meshwork, that is the loss of 'closeness', the Bajau Laut seek to renew these ties through endogamous marriage between close bilateral kin, chiefly cousins (*kaki*). In this way, families related by prior *mataan* ties are continually rewoven back into the meshwork, a social process closely analogous to the mending of a fishing net.

Finally, *mataan* ties form the relational basis of the two principal leader-centred groups within the village—the *luma'* ('house group') and the *ba'anan* ('cluster'). Yet the Bajau Laut remain faithful to their perception of the *mataan* as a relational meshwork. Rather than thinking in terms of ontologically prior 'groups', with leaders recruited from within who succeed one another in 'office', they conceive of houses and clusters as coming into existence through the concrete actions of leaders and followers, each drawing on *mataan* ties to cement their association. Both *luma'* and *ba'anan* are fluid groupings, constituted by the individual leaders and followers who comprise them and by the common activities that bring them together and sustain their association, from their founding to their eventual dissolution.

The House and House Group (*Luma'*)

The village consists, in a physical sense, of a compact group of rectangular, plank houses (*luma'*) (Map 5.1). Each house stands on 3- to 4-kilometre piles driven into the sea floor (Plate 21). Nearly all the houses are grouped into small, tightly crowded clusters (Plate 22). Most face

MAP 5.1
Map of Bangau-Bangau

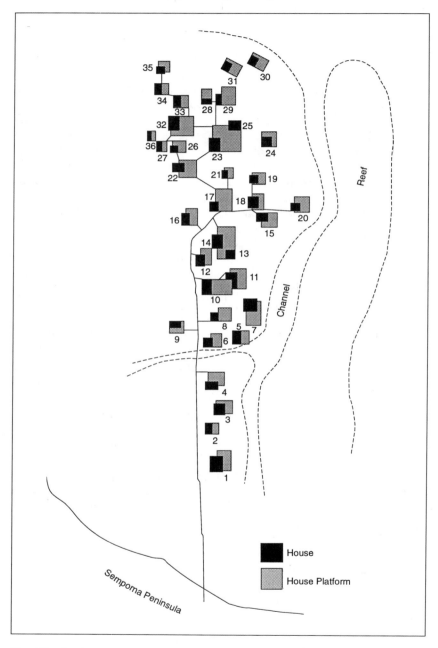

Note: The figures correspond to the house numbers in Table 5.1 and are used throughout the text as well.

'seaward' (*kaut*), toward the mouth of the bay in which the village
stands, and all open on to an uncovered platform or landing-stage,
called the *pantan*, made of wooden planks and raised, like the houses, on
piles. In 1965, four of the thirty-six houses in the village shared a common *pantan*, while others each maintained a separate platform. Most
pantan are accessible to one of a number of deeper channels that drain
the surrounding bay floor, linking it to the open water beyond. By using
these channels, and their knowledge of channel turnings and entrances,
family crews are able to enter and leave the community by fishing boat
(*lepa*) even during periods of ebb tide. From the *pantan*, a ladder (*haro-
nan*) descends to the sea floor beneath the house. Here or to the house
piles, families tie up their boats between voyages, using the ladder to
gain access to the platform floor above. At high tide, the sea generally
rises to within 30 centimetres of the house and platform floors, which
both stand at the same level, carrying away refuse and raising the tethered
boats to the level of the surrounding house platforms and catwalks.

A main walkway joins the village of Bangau-Bangau to the land (see
Map 5.1). Its seaward terminus is near the centre of the village, at the
edge of Panglima Tiring's *pantan* (no. 17) (Table 5.1). Its location
reflects the headman's position as community leader. From this terminus, a secondary network of planks and catwalks radiates outward,
linking together most of the remaining houses. A few, however, are
unconnected, either to the main walkway or to their nearest neighbours.
These are reached by wading, when the tide is out, or by the use of a
dug-out canoe (*boggo'*) or *lepa* during high tide.

The people who live together in one house under the authority of the
same house leader refer to themselves as *kami daluma'* ('we of one
house'), or simply, *daluma'*, ('[those of] one house'). Each house group
is known by the name of the man or woman who is recognized as its
nakura' luma', literally its 'house leader'. Thus the house group headed
by Lamarani is known as *luma' Lamarani*, 'Lamarani's house', and that
headed by Dessal, as *luma' Dessal*, 'Dessal's house'. Every villager,
except for those who are boat-living, is identified with a single house
group and its leader.

The house itself is considered to be the property of the *nakura' luma'*.
As house owner and acknowledged leader of a group of housemates, the
nakura' luma' is expected to offer advice, make decisions, and represent
the views of his followers in litigation and public discussions. As one
house leader, Salbangan, said 'We have *nakura'* because, in doing
things, there must always be someone who can think for (*pikilan*) others.'
Pikilan, in this instance, implies deliberating and making judgements on
behalf of others, in this case, the members of the household that bears
the leader's name. The *nakura' luma'* describes his housemates—those
who acknowledge themselves as members of his 'house'—as his *tendog*
(followers).

Adult housemates are expected to share responsibility for maintaining
the house of the *nakura' luma'* and for helping him to enlarge or rebuild
the structure should the house group outgrow it. In defining a house

TABLE 5.1
Household Composition

House No.	House Group Head	Total Persons		Generation Structure		Family Type
1	Musilhani (M)	10 {	M 7 F 3	0[a] (2)[b] : -1 (8) :	wife, HH 5 sons, 1 daughter; wife of son and husband of daughter—the latter are brother and sister	extended family, 2 generations depth
2	Sarabi (M)	11 {	M 5 F 6	+1 (1) : 0 (2) : -1 (8) :	wife's mother (widow) wife, HH 3 sons (1 divorced), 4 daughters; husband of eldest daughter	stem family, 3 generations depth
3	Jahali (M)	11 {	M 3 F 8	0 (3) : -1 (8) :	wife, wife's sister, HH 2 sons, 5 daughters, wife's sister's daughter	extended family, 2 generations depth
4	Baidullah (M)	19 {	M 9 F 10	+1 (1) : 0 (3) : -1 (9) : -2 (6) :	wife's mother (widow) wife, HH, wife's brother (widowed) 2 sons and wives, 2 daughters and husbands; wife's brother's son 2 grandsons, 4 granddaughters	extended family, 4 generations depth
5	Maharati (M)	13 {	M 8 F 5	0 (2) : -1 (9) : -2 (2) :	wife, HH 5 sons, 3 daughters, husband of one daughter 1 grandson and 1 granddaughter	stem family, 3 generations depth

6	Lamarani (M)	9	M 4 F 5	0	(3) :	HH (divorced), mother's sister's son and wife	extended family, 2 generations depth
				-1	(6) :	1 son and wife; mother's sister's son's son (1) and daughters (3)	
7	Jokarani (M)	9	M 3 F 6	+1	(1) :	wife's mother (widow)	extended family, 3 generations depth
				0	(4) :	wife, HH, wife's brother and his wife	
				-1	(4) :	1 son, 2 daughters and wife's brother's daughter	
8	Janati (M)	11	M 7 F 4	+1	(2) :	father, step-mother	stem family, 3 generations depth
				0	(2) :	wife, HH	
				-1	(7) :	5 sons, 2 daughters	
9	Umaldani (M)	9	M 6 F 3	0	(2) :	wife HH	nuclear family, 2 generations depth
				-1	(7) :	5 sons (1 divorced), 2 daughters	
10	Sariabi (F)	8	M 4 F 4	0	(2) :	HH (widow)	extended family, 3 generations depth
				-1	(4) :	2 sons, one son's wife, elder brother's son (divorced)	
				-2	(3) :	1 granddaughter, brother's son's son and daughter—latter married to second son of HH	
11	Selangani (M)	22	M 12 F 10	0	(2) :	wife, HH	extended family, 3 generations depth
				-1	(11) :	2 sons, 5 daughters;	

(continued)

TABLE 5.1 (continued)

House No.	House Group Head	Total Persons			Generation Structure	Family Type
					1 husband, 1 wife; wife's sister's daughter and husband	
				−2	(9) : 2 grandsons, 1 granddaughter; wife's sister's daughter's sons (5) and daughter (1)	
12	Gumanjil (M)	9	M 7 / F 2	0	(2) : wife, HH	stem family, 2 generations depth
				−1	(7) : 6 sons, eldest son's wife	
13	Awang (M)	12	M 5 / F 7	+2	(1) : wife's grandmother (widow)	extended family, 4 generations depth
				+1	(3) : wife's mother, mother's sister and husband	
				0	(4) : wife, HH, wife's mother's sister's son and daughter	
				−1	(4) : 2 sons and 2 daughters	
14	Isalhani (M)	8	M 4 / F 4	0	(2) : wife, HH	nuclear family, 2 generations depth
				−1	(6) : 3 sons, 3 daughters	
15	Gilang (M)	21	M 9 / F 12	0	(2) : wife, HH	extended family, 3 generations depth
				−1	(12) : 3 sons and 1 wife, 6 daughters and 2 husbands	
				−2	(7) : 3 grandsons and 4 granddaughters	

No.	Name	Total	Sex	Count	Gen.	No.	Members	Family type
16	Jikilani (M)	13	M	5	+1	(1)	wife's mother	extended family, 4 generations depth
			F	8	0	(4)	wife, HH, brother and brother's wife	
					−1	(6)	son and wife; daughter; brother's son (1) and daughters (2)	
					−2	(2)	1 grandson, 1 granddaughter	
17	Panglima Tiring (M)	22	M	9	0	(2)	wife, HH	extended family, 3 generations depth
			F	13	−1	(13)	4 sons, 6 daughters and 3 husbands	
					−2	(7)	1 grandson and 6 granddaughters	
18	Rugo-Rugo (M)	9	M	6	0	(2)	wife, HH	nuclear family, 2 generations depth
			F	3	−1	(7)	5 sons, 2 daughters	
19	Hajal (F)	14	M	6	0	(1)	HH (widow)	extended family, 3 generations depth
			F	8	−1	(6)	3 daughters and their husbands	
					−2	(7)	3 grandsons, 4 granddaughters (1 granddaughter by HH's son in House no. 11)	
20	Dessal (M)	11	M	7	0	(2)	wife, HH	stem family, 2 generations depth
			F	4	−1	(9)	6 sons, 2 daughters, eldest son's wife	
21	Sahalibulan (M)	15	M	5	0	(1)	HH (widower)	extended family, 3 generations depth
			F	10	−1	(12)	2 sons, 8 daughters, 2 husbands	

(continued)

TABLE 5.1 (*continued*)

House No.	House Group Head	Total Persons			Generation Structure	Family Type
22	Labu (M)	14	M 7	-2 : (2) :	(2 other daughters divorced) 2 granddaughters—by different daughters	extended family, 3 generations depth
			F 7	0 : (2) :	wife, HH	
				-1 : (5) :	1 son and wife, 2 daughters and 1 husband (1 daughter widowed)	
				-2 : (7) :	3 grandsons, 3 granddaughters; husband of 1 granddaughter	
23	Tandoh (M)	15	M 5	+1 : (1) :	wife's mother (widow)	extended family, 4 generations depth
			F 10	0 : (6) :	wife, HH, wife's sister and husband; husband's sister and husband	
				-1 : (6) :	2 daughters (1 divorced), 1 husband; wife's sister's daughters (2), husband's sister's daughter	
				-2 : (2) :	1 grandson, 1 granddaughter	
24	Malayhani (M)	15	M 6	0 : (4) :	wife, HH, wife's mother's sister's daughter and husband	extended family, 3 generations depth
			F 9	-1 : (8) :	1 daughter and husband; sister's daughter's sons (2) and daughters (4)	
				-2 : (3) :	1 grandson, 2 granddaughters	

No.	Name	Total	Sex	Gen.	Members	Family type
25	Tanjang Baru (M)	8	M 4 F 4	0 −1	(2): wife, HH (6): 3 sons, 3 daughters (1 daughter divorced)	nuclear family, 2 generations depth
26	Endemala (F)	7	M 4 F 3	0 −1 −2	(2): HH (maternal grandmother), paternal grandmother (0): connecting parents deceased (5): 1 granddaughter and husband, 3 grandsons	stem family, 3 generations depth
27	Sumarani (M)	9	M 3 F 6	0 −1	(2): wife, HH (7): 1 son, 5 daughters and 1 husband	stem family, 2 generations depth
28	Abdulkari (M)	11	M 7 F 4	0 −1	(4): wife, HH, brother and brother's wife (7): brother's sons (4), brother's daughters (2); son of sister (in House no. 29)	extended family, 2 generations depth
29	Barahim (M)	18	M 7 F 11	+1 0 −1	(2): wife's mother and father (5): wife, HH, wife's sister and husband; wife's brother (11): 1 son, 3 daughters, wife's sister's sons (2) and daughters (5)	extended family, 3 generations depth
30	Egoa (M)	6	M 4 F 2	0 −1	(2): wife, HH (4): 3 sons, 1 daughter	nuclear family, 2 generations depth
31	Tumpung (M)	9	M 7 F 2	0 −1	(2): wife, HH (7): 6 sons (1 divorced), 1 daughter	nuclear family, 2 generations depth

(continued

TABLE 5.1 (*continued*)

House No.	House Group Head	Total Persons		Generation Structure		Family Type
32	Muljarani (M)	20 {	M 10 F 10	0 (2) : −1 (9) : −2 (9) :	wife, HH 2 sons and 1 wife; 3 daughters and 3 husbands 4 grandsons, 5 granddaughters	extended family, 3 generations depth
33	Ebunghani (M)	9 {	M 4 F 5	+1 (1) : 0 (5) : −1 (3) :	mother (widow) HH (widower), 2 sisters, 1 brother; sister's husband sister's son (1) and daughters (2)	extended family, 3 generations depth
34	Timbangan (M)	18 {	M 11 F 7	+1 (2) : 0 (12) : −1 (4) :	wife's mother and father wife, HH, wife's sisters (3) and husbands (2), wife's brothers (3); wife's mother's sister's daughter and husband 1 son; wife's sister's sons (2) and daughter (1)	extended family, 3 generations depth
35	Jaharun (M)	6 {	M 3 F 3	0 (2) : −1 (4) :	wife, HH 2 sons and 2 daughters	nuclear family, 2 generations depth
36	Sarakil (M)	9 {	M 4 F 5	+1 (1) : 0 (2) : −1 (6) :	wife's mother (widow) wife, HH 3 sons, 3 daughters	stem family, 3 generations depth

ᵃThis indicates the generation relative to the house head (HH).

ᵇFigures in brackets are the number of persons in a given generation.
Kin, identified from the HH's viewpoint, follows the colon.

group, emphasis is placed on both co-residence—identification with a particular house and the leader who owns it—and the responsibilities which housemates share to maintain the structure and to recognize its owner as their leader and spokesman in village affairs.

'Those of one house' are not necessarily, or even usually, co-resident in the house continuously throughout the year. Families and married couples repeatedly disperse as boat crews, and while some house groups are comprised of a single family fishing crew, others contain more than one crew (see Table 4.1). Crews belonging to the same house are not always present in the village at the same time, nor do they necessarily travel together at sea. At any given time, part of a house group may be absent from the village. Housemates may also be joined by temporary visitors (*pasakai*). The presence of visitors is common, as the Bajau Laut frequently travel to other communities where they may expect to be lodged and fed by their kin. Visitors are distinguished, however, from long-term house group members. Thus Musahani (pseudonym) explained, in 1974, that following his elder brother's marriage, the latter became a member of his wife's father's house group in Sitangkai. However, he and his wife continued to visit Bangau-Bangau, staying, on their frequent visits in the house of his parents, often for a month or more at a time. Even so, Musahani stressed, no matter how often they visited Bangau-Bangau, the couple remained only 'visitors', their permanent 'house' being that of the wife's father in Sitangkai.

House groups vary in composition. Most are structurally complex, containing more than one conjugal family or married couple. Subsequent sections explore these matters in greater detail. Here it is sufficient to note that in Bangau-Bangau the largest house group in 1965 contained twenty-two people belonging to four families. Its members included the *nakura' luma'*, his wife, and their four dependant children; a daughter, her husband, and three children; a son, his wife, and one child; and a daughter of the house leader's wife's sister, her husband, and six children. At sea, three of these four families constituted separate fishing crews, while the husband of the fourth worked for wages outside the village. The smallest house group in the village contained only one family of six: a married couple plus their four unmarried children. This family comprised a single fishing crew. Most house groups fall somewhere in between these two extremes, although the majority have a multifamily composition.

Each house group is a single commensal unit.[2] While its members are present in the village, they prepare and eat their main meal of the day in common. But the *luma'* is not necessarily an exclusive commensal group, as family crews subsist separately at sea. In addition, small snacks eaten between meals are not necessarily shared. The principal daily meal is eaten in the early evening. Not infrequently, a common meal is also eaten, impromptu, when a family returns from fishing, even if this is late at night. When several married women live in the same house, they either cook together or take turns preparing the main meal by informal rotation (*magsilé*). As such women are usually sisters or a mother and her daughters, co-operation between them is generally well-established.

Meals are prepared in a separate cooking shelter called the *kusina*. This is normally attached to one side of the house and is reached either directly from the house interior or by way of the landing-stage. Cooking is done inside the *kusina* either over an earth-filled firebox placed on a low shelf or on a portable earthenware hearth (*lappohan*). Hearths are also carried at the stern of the *lepa* and are used to cook meals at sea. When food is being prepared for a large gathering, related women often set up additional *lappohan* on the open platform outside the house. Fish is nearly always the main dish (*lauk*). Cassava (*panggi kayu*) is the principal vegetable staple eaten with *lauk*. Only for ritual meals (*amakan*) is cassava replaced by rice. In preparation for cooking, cassava tubers are first peeled and grated (variously referred to as *li'is* or *angali'is*) and then spread on pandanus mats and dried in the sun. After drying, it is pressed into cakes and wrapped in banana leaves or sacking. These cakes may be stored for extended periods, and are carried by family crews at sea, providing, with fish, their chief provisions during fishing voyages. Cassava flour is prepared for eating either by frying in a wok (*kuali*) with coconut oil, the most common method, or by steaming to make a starchy cake called *putu'*, which is steamed inside a half coconut shell placed in the mouth of a round-bottomed cooking pot (*leppo'*) partially filled with water which is brought to the boil. As an everyday foodstuff, *putu'* is made either into thick cakes called *sanglag* (or *sinanglag*) or into thinner cakes called *tompah*. On the occasion of ritual meals, women frequently prepare long cakes of *putu'* mixed with rice flour and wrapped in *daun saging* (banana-leaf wrappers), called *bamban*. These are presented to departing guests to be eaten later. Men and the elderly are served first on public occasions, but at ordinary house meals the entire house group eats together.

Respect for age is marked in relations between house group members. The most senior woman of the house is ordinarily the final arbiter in the assignment of domestic tasks, including cooking and preparing meals. She and the *nakura' luma'* are also responsible for seeing that each married couple contributes its share to the group's common budget. In the case of an in-marrying husband, the senior couple ordinarily avoids open criticism. Normally, a degree of formality is expected and tends to characterize relations between a son-in-law and his wife's parents and her other senior kin. While this formality generally relaxes after several years of marriage, open criticism of a son-in-law is usually avoided, or is voiced indirectly through the wife. More troublesome are relations between in-marrying wives and the women born or raised in the *luma'*.

Houses vary in size. Most consist of a single rectangular room, averaging 4.5 metres wide and 6–9 metres long. Walls are made of thin planks or, less often, of '*kajang*' matting. Each wall contains at least one window. Most windows have wooden shutters that can be drawn closed at night, during rain, or when the members of the house are away from the village. The main doorway usually has a sliding wooden door, making it possible to seal up the house at night or when house members are absent. Low shelves are normally built along the side and rear walls of the house. Here, or in boxes beneath them, house group members store their personal effects. Except for an occasional wardrobe or cupboard, and in a few houses, a wooden bedstead (*kantil*), the interior is devoid of furniture.

Family members generally sleep on pandanus mats (*tépo*) and cushions spread on the floor. Until the age of four or five, children normally sleep on the same mats as their parents. Older children sleep separately. Adolescent and preadolescent girls generally sleep with their younger brothers and sisters, much of whose care is generally entrusted to them. Adolescent boys are allowed greater freedom of movement and may sleep by themselves or with small groups of companions, sometimes moving, night by night, from one house to another. Boys may also spend part of the night fishing with friends, returning home to sleep during the day. Each couple or family has an allotted sleeping space within the house interior and an area of wall space set aside for storing its bedding and other personal possessions. Older girls are generally responsible for collecting the family's bedding, rolling up the sleeping mats and cushions each morning, and storing them out of the way along the walls. Newly married couples often screen off their sleeping area with cloth hangings for privacy. Otherwise, house interiors are normally unpartitioned.

The living quarters of every Bajau Laut boat have a lateral *kokan*, or 'headside', the name deriving from the root word *kok* meaning 'head'. When people recline or sleep at sea, they lie crossways, with their head always at the *kokan* side of the boat.[3] In building houses, the Bajau Laut also erect them with a *kokan*. Houses preserve the same orientation as boats, with the entrance side corresponding to the stern, the opposite wall, the bow, and one of the two lateral walls as the *kokan*. At night, house group members are expected to lie with their heads toward the *kokan* and in the morning bedding is usually stored along the *kokan* wall. Observing the *kokan* orientation is said to be especially important when a pregnant woman is present. Lying obliquely or opposite to the *kokan* may cause the child the woman is carrying to become incorrectly positioned in her womb and so cause a breech delivery. These rules apply to everyone who sleeps in the house, including visitors. If a person moves in his sleep, he may be awakened or re-positioned by other family members, so that his body maintains its correct orientation. The *kokan* also has special importance for house group ritual.

At night, the house floor serves as a general sleeping area. On particularly sultry nights, couples may carry their bedding outdoors and sleep in the cooking shelter, particularly if the house interior is crowded. During the day, the floor is cleared of mats and bedding; cloth hangings are removed, and the interior is converted into a common space where visitors and friends are entertained and house group members relax or tend youngsters when not occupied with outdoor work. The open landing-platform is used for most outdoor tasks. These include drying fish, mending and drying nets, children's play, carpentry, boat-building, and the grating and drying of cassava flour (Plate 23). In hot weather, an open canopy of sails is sometimes erected over part of the platform to provide shade for those working on the *pantan*. Here, mainly in the evenings or at night, dances take place, public gatherings are held, including weighing rituals, weddings, circumcisions, and village litigation.

The House Leader (*Nakura' Luma'*)

The authority of the *nakura' luma'* derives in part from his position as house owner. In most instances, he is also the house group founder. On ritual occasions, the *nakura' luma'* sponsors major observances to which guests from other house groups are invited, and politically and jurally he is expected to represent the group in village litigation, normally championing his followers in inter-house group disputes.

In 1965, most *nakura' luma'* in Bangau-Bangau had begun their career as a house group founder. Twenty-four of the thirty-six house groups in the village were headed by *nakura' luma'* who first attained their position by founding a new house group. All were men. Typically, a founder leads a group of *tendog* to build a house which becomes the one with which they are identified. Less often, a man or woman becomes a *nakura' luma'* by inheriting a house and succeeding the former *nakura'* as the house group spokesman. In the remaining twelve groups—nine headed by men, three by women—the leader succeeded to his or her position through inheritance. A number of men, in the course of their careers as village leaders, have constructed more than one house.

Although most *nakura' luma'* are men, a woman may also head a house group. In 1964–5, three of the thirty-six *nakura' luma'* in Bangau-Bangau were women. Two were widows who inherited the house upon their husband's death (nos. 10 and 19) (see Table 5.1). In both cases, the husbands were said to have been the original *luma'* founder. In the third instance, a house group was co-headed by two elderly women. This group was anomalous in a number of ways. The two women were the mothers of a husband and wife who originally founded the group, but who died young, leaving four small children. In 1965, these children were still under marriageable age. The husband, Patak, was said to have originally built the house. He died shortly after his wife, leaving behind a house group that included his wife's mother, Liarah. Although an elderly woman, Liarah continued to look after her grandchildren and earned a small income by collecting shells and gathering and drying sea cucumbers (*bat*) for sale in Semporna town. Lacking a *lepa* and a resident boat crew, the house group was only partially self-sufficient, depending on other families for assistance and gifts of fish and other foodstuffs.[4] More recently, Patak's mother, Endemala, a sister of Panglima Tiring, joined the group, following her divorce from Lamarani, another house group leader. Although neither house owner nor founder, Endemala was, because of her forceful personality, generally looked to on public occasions as the group's spokesperson.

The other two house groups headed by women are both economically viable, and the widows who head them are active in village affairs, joining with their male counterparts in village mediation and factional disputes. One widow regularly calls on her son, an influential cluster spokesman who lives in a neighbouring house group, to speak for her on public occasions, although she herself is a major player in village factional politics. She and her house group followers are also important supporters of her son in wider village affairs.

The remaining nine house groups are headed by men who inherited their position from a former *nakura' luma'*. In four cases, the former *nakura' luma'* is still alive. In all others, including the three cases of female succession, the transfer occurred upon the death of the original *nakura' luma'*. Of the nine cases of male succession, seven took place from father-in-law to son-in-law, and two from father to son. This is consistent with the preference that daughters, rather than sons, remain in their original house group following marriage.

A house group leader is expected to be an effective public advocate. If not, he or she should be able to call upon persuasive cluster allies to present the views of the house group in public forums. Housemates never initiate public legal action against one another. In internal disputes, the *nakura' luma'* is expected to act informally in settling differences between his *tendog*. Dissension within the *luma'* is common, particularly in large house groups. If the *nakura' luma'* is unable to contain the dissension, the group is likely to split up, with some of its members defecting to other house groups. If dissension is serious enough, it may even spill over into the surrounding cluster, causing a realignment of cluster ties, a process generally marked by the tearing down of catwalks and occasionally the relocation of houses. Quarrels within the *luma'* tend to lead not to litigation, but, if they are serious, to the departure of some of its members. However, former housemates may bring legal action against one another, and indeed sometimes do. This often happens in divorce cases; the parties involved are likely to return to their own *luma'* and from there draw on the support of their *nakura'* in bringing legal action, possibly over property or the return of marriage payments.

The role of the *nakura' luma'* in village litigation is essentially that of a jural counsellor. His main task is to represent the interests of his followers and to gain the support of kin and village allies outside the group in the event of litigation with members of another house group. It is important to note, however, that each house group leader is likely to see the outcome of litigation in terms, not only of the interests of his housemates, but more generally, in terms of the wider relationships that exist between his own and other house groups. Consequently, a leader may persuade his followers to accept a judgement, or to scale down their demands, in order to reach a settlement acceptable to the leaders of other house and cluster groups in the village. House group leaders generally tend to play a moderating role in village conflicts. Finally, while the house leader is expected to uphold the interests of his followers, it needs to be stressed that jural rights attach in severalty to individuals, not to the *luma'* as a whole, which is not a 'corporate group' in a jural sense. Litigation always proceeds in terms of individual obligations and faults and the meshwork of relations that connect each of the separate parties involved.

House Group Composition

Table 5.1 provides detailed information on the composition of village house groups.[5] From this table, certain features of house group structure clearly emerge:

1. The house group is characteristically large. More than 55 per cent contain eleven persons—the median size—or more. Nearly 28 per cent have fifteen or more members, and there are four house groups with twenty or more members. Mean size is slightly more than twelve persons, and the range is from six to twenty-two persons (Table 5.2).

2. Coupled with its relatively large size, the house group typically contains more than two generations. More than 60 per cent of all house groups include three or four generations and none include less than two. Generational composition is summarized in Table 5.3.

3. The majority of house groups are structurally complex. As Table 5.4 indicates, lateral expansion is even more important than lineal depth. Nearly 60 per cent of all house groups contain an extended family unit, a group incorporating two or more families of procreation in the same generation, and a further 22 per cent contain a stem family, one incorporating a single family of procreation in two or more generations. Combined, the mean size of these multifamily house groups is fourteen persons.

4. The remaining 19 per cent consist of a single nuclear or conjugal family. All such families are numerically large, containing between six and nine persons. The mean size is slightly less than eight.

Underlying the composition of the *luma'* are two basic structural principles. The first is that a husband and wife never establish a separate house group of their own immediately after marriage. Instead, they live initially as subsidiary members in an existing house group, most often that of the wife's father. It is only after the pair has established a family of procreation of their own and their eldest children have reached, or are approaching, marriageable age, that they are likely to secede from the parental house group and set up an independent *luma'* of their own with the husband as founder and house group leader. Because secession is delayed, the couple's eldest children normally begin to marry soon afterwards. While some usually marry out, and so become members of other house groups, at least one child, and often several, remains to rear their children in the parental house group. As a result, most *luma'* soon develop into multifamily units. Except for a brief, initial period before the marriage of their eldest children, the majority of house groups contain a senior couple, plus possibly their still unmarried children, and the family, or families, of procreation of those of their married offspring who have chosen to remain in the parental *luma'*. As soon as dependant families are added to the group, its continuance is no longer dependent on the persistence of the founding couple. The house group is usually large enough at this point in its development to continue even if divorce or death ruptures ties within its founding generation. In theory at least, the multifamily house group is a potentially more stable unit, constituted

TABLE 5.2
Numerical Composition of Village House Groups

Number of persons	6	7	8	9	10	11	12	13	14	15	16	17	18	19	20	21	22
Frequency	2	1	3	9	1	5	1	2	2	3	0	0	2	1	1	1	2

Total number of house groups   36

TABLE 5.3
Generational Composition of Village House Groups

Number of generations	1	2	3	4
Frequency	0	14	18	4
Percentage of total house groups	0	39	50	11

TABLE 5.4
Genealogical Composition of Village House Groups

Genealogical Composition	Frequency	Percentage of Total House Groups
Nuclear Family		
Parents with children	7	19
Stem Family		
Married couple with parents	3	8
Grandparents, married child and grandchildren	4	11
Grandparents and married grandchild	1	3
Extended Family		
Parents with two or more married children	1	3
Two or more married siblings with children	2	6
Grandparents, two or more married children and grandchildren	12	33
Grandparents, married children, married grandchildren and great-grandchildren	4	11
First cousins with married children	2	6
Total	36	100

not simply of a single 'eye', but forming the node of an expanding meshwork of *mataan* relations, and so the basis, ultimately, of its own neighbourhood cluster.

The second principle is that the house group is only temporarily perpetuating. As the house founder and his wife reach old age and their grandchildren come to maturity, their children ordinarily depart to found new house groups of their own. By the time the last of their children is ready to make good its independence, the original dwelling is likely to be abandoned or dismantled. When this occurs, the family unit initially established by the ageing pair is typically dissolved. Occasionally, a house may be inherited by one of the couple's children, preferably the youngest, or the husband of the last-born daughter. But inheritance is only a temporary measure, adopted until the remaining husband, to whom control of the dwelling has passed, is in a position to build a new house and found a separate house group with himself, ideally, as its *nakura' luma'*.

The house group thus undergoes a regular cycle of growth, fission, and dismemberment, ending with its eventual dissolution and replacement by similarly constituted groups headed by persons who were once dependant housemates in previous *luma'*. Structural continuity is achieved not by the perpetuation of individual houses—as these are impermanent—but rather by the constant cycle of development that the *luma'* undergoes and by the processes of formation and fission that underlie its development through time (Sather, 1976).

The Developmental History of Village House Groups

The histories of individual houses are frequently complex. But in broad terms, these histories are roughly divisible into four main phases: (a) a conjugal phase in which the house group, at the time of its founding, is composed most often of a single conjugal pair plus their young children; (b) an expansion phase in which the founder's offspring are joined by in-marrying spouses; (c) a procreative phase in which grandchildren are produced; and (d) a hiving-off phase in which the *luma'* is partitioned as the families of the founder's children break away to establish separate house groups of their own. The term 'phase' is intentionally used here to indicate that overlapping or compression in the sequence is a normal occurrence. Thus, for example, while a pair's youngest children are still marrying, the eldest are very likely to have already established their independence.

The Conjugal Phase

New households are typically founded by a single married couple together with their still dependant children. Occasionally, aged or unattached relatives may be included in the group, or join it shortly after it is founded, particularly if its founding coincides with the dissolution of an established house group. These relatives are most often the husband's or wife's parents, a sibling, or a divorced child returned from his/her spouse's house group.

The conjugal family, at the point in which it emerges as an independent house group, is typically large, containing on average between seven and eight persons. Partition is normally delayed. Couples do not ordinarily establish their independence until they are well into their childbearing years. The reasons for this are chiefly economic. By the time families achieve independence by establishing themselves as separate house groups, most include at least three active working members of sixteen years of age or older. The house leader is an experienced fisherman and his older sons are a decided asset at sea. Some of his sons are likely to own their own fishing nets and other gear and at least one daughter is likely to be old enough to relieve his wife from at least some of the demands of routine child care, leaving her free to assist him in fishing or in managing the affairs of the house group.

Expansion Phase

The house group enters this phase upon the marriage of the eldest of the house leader's children. The phase continues as each of the couple's remaining offspring, preferably, for those of the same sex, in the order of their birth, takes a husband or wife. Marriage invariably entails a residence choice; one spouse or the other is required to leave his or her parental group and join the house group of his or her partner. The in-marrying partner obtains full rights of membership in the spouse's house group, including possible inheritance of the house. Marriage is therefore of crucial importance in determining the composition of the *luma'*. At least one in-marrying spouse must be added to the group if it is to continue into the founder's old age. In later sections of this chapter I discuss the factors that influence residence decisions, and in Chapter 8, I examine the relationship that exists between marriage and house group membership.

Procreative Phase

With the birth of grandchildren to the sons and daughters who remain in the house group following marriage, the *luma'* enters its procreative phase. The group loses the original unity it possessed as a simple conjugal family and becomes an internally differentiated, multifamily unit. At the time of marriage, a son is ideally provided with a boat, nets, and other gear. Thus he and his wife are able to operate as an independent fishing team. The wife ordinarily brings to marriage her own personal effects, including cooking utensils, sleeping cushions, and other domestic articles. Each family or couple comprises a separate productive group with its own capital assets and separate control over its earnings, and is able to exist as a separate domestic group during the time that its members live at sea. Within the *luma'*, each subsidiary family is allotted its own sleeping area and its members separately hold whatever property they acquire subsequent to marriage, or receive through inheritance, independently of both the house leader and their other housemates.

Partition or Hiving-off

This internal differentiation of the expanding house group foreshadows its eventual partition. Ideally, every man should head a house group of his own by the time he and his wife have reached, or are approaching, the end of their childbearing years. Most couples achieve this goal, provided they are able to form a stable marriage and bear children. First marriages often fail, thereby delaying the process. But eventually most couples succeed. Moreover, the goal of independence is viewed by the Bajau Laut as a legitimate aspiration, and nearly all house groups containing more than one subsidiary family eventually undergo partition.

Secession for the purposes of founding a new house group is called *pala'an* or *apinda luma'* and is seen as the inevitable outcome of family growth. Although it results in the dismemberment of the original parental house, secession is not considered to be a disintegrative or disruptive process, and is seldom accompanied by open conflict. What most villagers stress is the positive attraction of heading an independent house group, around which one can gather one's own children and grandchildren as dependants and supporters in the later years of life. Nevertheless, the ultimate lines of cleavage are evident from the moment the parental group loses its original unity as a single conjugal family and these lines are regularly marked by strain, even if not necessarily outright conflict.

Following marriage and the birth of children to the house founder's dependants, relations between the *nakura' luma'* and his children, and among the heads of the subsidiary families under his or her authority, come into sharp focus. As each family handles its own cash production, new and at times divergent interests are created. These produce an inevitable potential for conflict. For example, male housemates may come to feel that others are failing to contribute equitably to the common budget, are making excessive demands on their savings, or are holding back in times of need. Wives may quarrel over the apportionment of household chores, accuse one another of carelessness in the use of their cooking utensils, or of hoarding special foods for their children. As the house group grows in size, domestic arrangements are likely to become increasingly difficult. Problems arise not only from conflicts between the personal and joint interests of house group members, but also from simple crowding. In the largest house groups, living space is often cramped. For example, there may not be enough room, when all are present, for everyone in the house to eat together at the same time. While normally enjoying each other's company, the villagers often complain that a major drawback of living in a large house group is the lack of privacy and the involvement of others in one's personal affairs. The house leader is generally able to contain conflict for a number of years, until his authority begins to wane with his lessening economic contribution to the group and with the growing self-assurance of his dependants in village affairs. But even as secession occurs, the solidarity of the *luma'* is rarely shattered. Instead, relations between former housemates usually remain intact, and so form the basis of neighbourhood cluster alignments.

Thus new houses are typically built with the help of former house-mates and are generally located adjacent to the original dwelling. Consequently, as a house group undergoes successive partitioning, a cluster of adjoining houses is typically created, centred around the original dwelling, the main members of which are related, not only as kin and affines, but also as former housemates. While some realignment of families is likely to occur in the process, hiving-off is thus linked to the creation and subsequent consolidation of larger neighbourhood groupings. These, together with the individual houses that comprise them, constitute the basic social units of village society.

While interpersonal tensions appear inevitable as each house group grows larger this is not to suggest that conflict is necessarily rife or that there are not equally strong tendencies that work to hold the group together and delay the departure of its subsidiary families. The dispersal of family members on fishing voyages provides a periodic escape from household tensions. Also, young married men, particularly those with small children too young to be of help in fishing, are often economically dependent on the house leader, or other, older more experienced fishermen who live in the group, or in neighbouring houses within the same cluster. Housemates, particularly married women, value each other's companionship, and jointly sponsored rituals give recurrent expression to house group unity. Most importantly, the potential for conflict is reduced, and the movement of persons in and out of the *luma'* is made relatively easy when it occurs, by the absence of a corporate estate controlled by the group, or administered by the house leader, that might otherwise have to be divided, or left behind by those who secede from the group.

When secession occurs, the departing couple simply removes their belongings to the new house they have built for themselves. This is normally done with the help of their former housemates. It is usual for the *nakura' luma'* and his wife to settle property on their children as they leave the house, either at marriage or during partition. As a result, by the time that all but the last-born child have departed, most of the couple's heritable possessions (*pusaka'*) will have been bestowed, except for the house and a residual share of property reserved for the youngest child. Property bestowal is thus closely linked to out-marriage and the process of house group partition. It is also linked to gender. Heritable property is transmitted along gender lines, from man-to-man or woman-to-woman. As a result, there is no fusing of inheritance through marriage. Finally, the lack of a joint estate vested in the house group as a whole means that there are no compelling property interests to justify the continued membership of a subsidiary family once it is able to form a viable household unit on its own.

One final factor that tends to delay partition is that the construction of a new house represents a considerable investment. The founder must ordinarily purchase all of the necessary building materials himself, including hardwood piles, flooring, joists, posts, beams, sawn floor and wall planks, and roofing materials. In 1979, the average cost ranged from RM2,000 to RM5,000, with the median cost of materials being approximately RM3,000. Initial costs can be reduced by the use of poorer quality planks and posts, and possibly by substituting '*kajang*' siding for plank walls. Later, if the leader and his family prosper, these can be replaced by more substantial materials, and the dwelling can be enlarged by additional piling and extending the floors, walls, and roof. Most of the older houses in the village have undergone such enlargement, some several times. Similarly, as a household undergoes partition, sections of the dwelling may be dismantled and the materials used for repairs or in the construction of new dwellings erected by married couples as they secede from the group. Thus the house, as a physical structure, closely mirrors the economic fortunes of its members, particularly its leader, and the developmental processes affecting its composition.

House construction also entails a considerable outlay in labour time. Depending on the size of the work-force involved, construction is minimally spread over three or four months, with interruptions for fishing and marketing. Often the time involved is much longer. When I first arrived in Bangau-Bangau in 1964 there were two houses under construction which were still unfinished when I left the village eleven months later. Frequently, construction is suspended while the house founder works to set aside the necessary cash to purchase additional materials to continue the work.

As soon as the members of the founder's family occupy the new house, and establish a separate hearth—whether the house is totally completed or not—they are recognized as constituting an independent house group. The event may be marked by a small feast (*magkakan*) to which the family's close kin, particularly those who assisted in the construction of the house, are invited. Such a feast, however, is not mandatory.[6]

In order to better understand the way in which marriage and partition affect house group composition, it is useful to follow the history of one particular group in some detail. For this purpose I have chosen the house group of Dessal (no. 20), partly because it was one of the first to be established in the village, and so its history reflects nearly the full cycle of development, and also because it is fairly representative of most village *luma'* in terms of its size and composition.

In 1965, Dessal's house group contained eleven persons: Dessal, his wife Akbaraini, their six sons and two daughters, and the wife of their eldest son Karim (see Table 5.1). The first two houses to be built in Bangau-Bangau were those of Akbaraini's parents (no. 19) and her mother's sister, Amjatul and her husband, Panglima Tiring (no. 17). In 1958, with the help of his sons, Dessal built a small house next to that of Akbaraini's parents, within the original nucleus of the present pile-house village of Bangau-Bangau. Previously, Dessal's family had lived aboard his *lepa*. Shortly afterwards, Dessal's brother built a house (no. 12) next to that of their sister's husband, Selangani (no. 11), to form a new cluster to the south of the original group to which Dessal and Akbaraini had aligned their *luma'*. Selangani was a brother of Akbaraini's father, Panglima Atani, so the two clusters were closely related.

At the time of its founding, Dessal's house group consisted of a simple
nuclear family of nine persons: Dessal, his wife Akbaraini, and their
seven children. Later, a final child was born; Dessal and Akbaraini's eldest
daughter died; and Karim, their eldest son, married. Karim's first marriage did not last long. But late in 1963, he remarried and left the house
group to join his wife's family in Sitangkai. In 1965, while I was living in
Bangau-Bangau, Karim and his family rejoined Dessal's house group.
Shortly before Karim's remarriage, Akbaraini's father, Panglima Atani,
died and the original cluster which he headed split in two owing to
enmity between his widow Hajal and her sisters, including Amjatul,
Panglima Tiring's wife. As a result of this split, Dessal's house group was
now realigned, together with Hajal's, in a small faction separate from
most of the others that had belonged to the original village cluster, now
headed by Panglima Tiring as cluster spokesman.

Eight months after Karim's return, Dessal's second son Alkisun left
the village to work in Sandakan, where he was married for a short time
to a Chinese woman. In 1968, he returned to the village and he and his
brothers helped their father dismantle his old house and build a new one,
across the main walkway, facing the house of Selangani, the brother-in-
law of Akbaraini's mother Hajal and husband of Dessal's sister. The
move had long been contemplated and was made for several reasons.
The family's original house had been put up without ironwood pilings
and as a result, its foundations were no longer sound. Also, the breakup
of the original neighbourhood cluster had left Dessal and his family
physically isolated from their main village allies. The move thus realigned
the house group in a new and larger cluster.

Not long afterwards, Selangani, his health failing, retired from household leadership and was succeeded by his son-in-law, Salbangan, a son
of Hajal and Akbaraini's brother. Salbangan was, and remains, a man of
considerable ambition, and upon his father-in-law's retirement, he quickly
assumed leadership of the larger cluster now containing Dessal's family.

Shortly after this move, Karim and his family left Dessal's house
group and returned to Sitangkai, this time permanently. At the same
time, Alkisun remarried. For the next three years, Alkisun and his wife
alternated residence between Dessal's house group and that of his wife's
father. Several years later, Dessal's third son married. The marriage took
place despite the objections of Dessal and Akbaraini, who had begun
marriage negotiations with the family of another young woman, and the
couple were temporarily excluded from the house group. The son was
employed by the Public Works Department and during this time he and
his wife lived in the department's labour lines. Five months later, their
fourth son, Bagiti, married. His wife's parents were divorced and had
remarried, and so the wife had been raised, as a foster child, by other relatives. Consequently, there were no competing ties to claim the couple's
affiliation, and immediately following Bagiti's marriage, he and his wife
joined Dessal's house group.

When I returned to Bangau-Bangau in 1974, the household had
markedly changed, both in its internal structure and in its relations with
surrounding *luma'*. Two sons had married out, while two others had

remained in the house, adding to the group their wives and children, making it a multifamily unit. The house group was in the process of partition, as the eldest son still living in the house, Alkisun, was setting aside materials to build a new house adjacent to that of his father. Relations with nearby house groups were no less altered. Akbaraini had been reconciled with her mother's sisters, including the wives of Panglima Tiring and his brother Gilang. As a result, cluster alignments had been re-established along more or less the same lines as had existed at the time when Dessal first founded his house group sixteen years earlier. Cementing these realignments, Dessal's youngest son, Lunta, was betrothed to one of Gilang's daughters. In addition, Akbaraini was reconciled with her younger brother, Saharati, who, before the original split, had married into Panglima Tiring's house, taking as his wife the headman's eldest daughter, Ettoman.

Shortly after I left Semporna, Lunta married and joined Gilang's house group. Alkisun founded his own *luma'*, and Akbaraini was reconciled with the wife of her third son and he and his family rejoined Dessal's house group. (The circumstances surrounding this reconciliation are discussed in Chapter 7.) Three years later, the third son, Laiti, purchased Alkisun's house, while Alkisun built a new house close to that of his wife's parents in another part of Bangau-Bangau. Later, Laiti built a larger house beside Alkisun's former house. His wife's mother, now separated from her husband, moved to Bangau-Bangau with her remaining children and Laiti gave her the use of Alkisun's former house. One of her sons with his wife and children joined Laiti's house group as a dependant family. Early in 1979, the first of Dessal's two daughters married and her husband joined Dessal's house group.

When I returned to the village later in the year, Dessal's house group had entered the final phase in its development. The group was again undergoing partition. The last remaining son, with the help of his brothers, had just finished erecting the piling for a new house next to Laiti's and his father's. A new cluster was thus taking shape, formed primarily of the members of Dessal's original house group. Dessal's third son, Laiti, the most senior son remaining in the group, and economically the most successful, had already emerged as its effective spokesman. Laiti had also succeeded in adding to the cluster members of his wife's family. The marriage of Dessal's youngest daughter was being actively negotiated at the time and would probably soon be concluded. Dessal, now a senior *jin* (spirit-medium), was devoting much of his time to the practice of curing and had become increasingly dependent upon the economic support of his sons and son-in-law. Even so, the son-in-law living in his household was still a young man without children, and Dessal, barring serious ill-health, seems likely to remain the spokesman for his house group for a number of years to come.

From the viewpoint of the original house group, the hiving-off phase typically begins with the secession of the family of the founder's eldest child still resident in the group following marriage and continues over a number of years, normally as a series of successive partitions, until only the family of the youngest, or the last of the house founder's children to marry, remains in the parental house group. The process can clearly be seen at work in the case of Dessal's *luma'*, although it has yet to run its full course. It is generally felt that the family of the last-born child (*anak kabungsuan*) has a superior right to inherit the original dwelling upon the death or retirement of the founding couple. The basis of this right is the recognition that the couple's older children are better able to build houses of their own because they marry and establish families first, thus making simpler their earlier independence. Also, the villagers say that the youngest is likely to be the couple's favourite, and the most spoiled by its parents as a youngster.[7] In practice, there is a strong preference that the last remaining child be the founder's youngest daughter. The principal reason for this is that the couple who remain in the original house are responsible for caring for the ageing house founder and his wife until their death, and it is generally felt that a daughter is likely to be more attentive than a son or his wife. A daughter is said to be less likely than the son's wife to begrudge them food or complain of the extra work their presence causes. Also, household authority is said to pass more smoothly from a mother to her daughter than to a woman who, as an in-marrying wife, may be a relative stranger. The women involved are emotionally close and, as several villagers expressed it, approvingly, 'They are accustomed to each other's ways'.

The villagers repeatedly stress the importance of relations between women in house group succession. One of the two house groups in which succession to leadership took place from father to son is that of Janati (no. 8). The history of this group, in contrast to Dessal's, is somewhat exceptional.

Shortly before his marriage, Janati helped his father build a house. The family was living at the time in Janati's father's boat. When the house was completed, Janati's elder sister Hajima joined the house group with her husband and children, while Janati married and joined his wife's family in Sitangkai. Several years later, he and his new family returned to Bangau-Bangau and joined his father's house group. The group was further increased by Hajima's eldest daughter and her husband. Hajima's husband then built a house (no. 7) adjacent to Janati's father's house, where the couple were joined by Hajima's eldest daughter and her family, who moved from Janati's father's house. Later, when Hajima's youngest son married, the wife, too, joined this new *luma'*. In time, Janati's mother died, leaving his father a widower. Janati was the head of a growing family by now, with five children. His father eventually turned over to Janati the management of the original house group and ownership of the house he had helped his father to build.

Some years later, Janati's father married the widowed mother of Hajima's husband, who following the death of her husband had joined her son's house group and was thus living as a neighbour in the same house group cluster.

Because succession occurred after the death of Janati's mother, there was no senior woman in Janati's house group with whom his wife might otherwise have had to share responsibilities for the day-to-day running of the group. By the time Janati's father remarried, the transfer of authority was already established. Thus the potential source of conflict was absent. The second case is similar.

Ajainiha and her husband lived with their children in a small house (no. 33) near the northern edge of the village. Both were born in the Sibutu island group in the Philippines and neither had close relatives living in Bangau-Bangau when they first moved to the village. Later, two sons married into neighbouring house groups, aligning the family in a larger cluster, while a daughter married a man from Labuan Haji. Following the death of his wife, one son, Ebunghani, returned to his father's house group. Not long after his return, Ajainiha's husband died, leaving her with two small children to look after. Ebunghani took immediate charge of the house group and, although a young widower without children, is recognized by the villager elders as its *nakura'*.

As Ebunghani is without a wife, his mother, Ajainiha, continues to look after the internal affairs of the house, sharing housekeeping chores with her married daughter, Jubaidia. Again, the transfer of authority, although occurring from father to son, involved little potential conflict between married women.

Termination

As has already been stressed, each of the subsidiary families making up a larger house group functions as a primary productive unit, operating separately as a boat crew and managing its own cash income. Economically, the house group functions, secondarily, as a village commensal, housekeeping, and food-pooling group. The lack of an estate vested in the *luma'*, particularly in the form of fishing sites, boats, and other durable or relatively durable productive wealth, means that there are no compelling property interests that might otherwise preserve the authority of an ageing house leader once his physical powers begin to wane, with the partial exception of his house.

Houses, like fishing boats, are separately owned. Bajau Laut customary law (*addat*) stresses the rights of those who create property, and house ownership is therefore an important source of the *nakura' luma'*'s authority. Even as his powers begin to wane as a fisherman, an elder is still respected, and regularly consulted whenever important decisions must be made. As a result, even as his authority within the *luma'* declines, the transfer of leadership tends to be gradual and is often masked by relations of respect and an elder's increasing involvement in village affairs.

Finally, even though a house may be inherited, and the founder succeeded as house group leader by an heir, every *luma'* is eventually dissolved. Succession, therefore, is only short-lived, and houses are often dismantled several times within the house founder's lifetime. This can be seen for example in the history of Dessal's *luma'*.

Termination generally occurs when the dwelling initially erected by the founder is torn down. The maximum length of time a house remains occupied is ultimately limited by the physical durability of the structure itself. As a rule, the most durable parts of a house are the piles (*tu'ul*) on which it stands. These support the flooring and the main house posts and are made ideally of ironwood (*tabelian*). Under normal conditions, average sized piles are said to remain sound for thirty to forty years, perhaps longer. As long as they are serviceable, the upper structure of the house is usually maintained, so long as the owner or his widow is alive. Should the founder die or retire, his heir is likely to build a new house as soon as he can afford to. In doing so, he normally uses materials salvaged from the original dwelling. When this happens, the widow or the ageing parents, if they are still alive, ordinarily join the new house group to live out their remaining years. Occasionally, houses are dismantled even earlier, while the original house leader is still active. As in Dessal's case, this usually occurs as a result of disputes involving the members of adjoining house groups, resulting in the breakup of the cluster to which the group belongs, or to the realignment of cluster ties as new house group leaders emerge.

Even when a house is maintained, less durable materials, such as wall planks and roofing, require periodic replacement, much like boats. In the course of renovation, the structure may be enlarged, or parts of it pulled down, so that the size and state of repair of a house tend to reflect the numerical strength of the group that occupies it and the economic fortunes of its leader and other family heads. A well-run house tends to attract additional housemates. But no matter how successful a leader may be in maintaining a following, every dwelling is eventually pulled down, and when this happens, the house group founded when it was first erected comes to an end.

House Group Structure

From the preceding account of the house group's development through time, it should be clear that the Bajau Laut *luma'* is not, in any sense, a corporate or self-perpetuating group that persists from generation to generation. No such groups exist in Bajau Laut society. Instead, each house group takes its identity from a particular *nakura' luma'*. Its coming into being is a product of the skill of the *nakura'* in attracting and holding together a following and, from its founding onward, the composition of the *luma'* mirrors the cycle of growth, fission, and dissolution to which the family of the *nakura' luma'*, and the families of his house group dependants, are subject.

The Bajau Laut have no conception of the *luma'* as a social group that persists indefinitely in time, or which takes its origin from a remotely antecedent generation of ancestors. Although each house leader may seek to hold together a following for as long as he is alive, and perhaps increase its size if he can, there is no notion that the group should continue beyond his lifetime, preserving, in some way, the form in which it was founded. Even if a house is inherited, the house group that occupies it takes its identity from the new house leader. Thus the house group has a definite point of beginning and an end, limited ultimately by the active life span of its leader and by the physical durability of the house itself.

Even within these limits, groups disband, are reconstituted, and undergo repeated changes in composition, such that *luma'* are best thought of as contingent groups, in constant flux.

Even as an individual house group gains and loses members, it nevertheless preserves a similar structural form. It can be argued that it is this form, rather than the individual *luma'* that embodies it, which gives village social relationships their organizational continuity through time.

Despite the emphasis upon the personal links that join a house leader and his or her followers, every *luma'* is also a close-knit genealogical grouping. Links of allegiance are forged between close cognatic kin and affines. Structurally, the house group most often contains what Murdock (1949: 35) called a 'bilocal extended family'. Originally, Murdock (1949: 23–4, 33–5) applied the term 'extended family' to a unit comprising parents and the families of procreation of two or more married children. More specifically, he defined a 'bilocal extended family' as a family unit that 'unites the nuclear family of a married couple with those of some but not all of their sons, of some but not all of their daughters, and of some but not all of their grandchildren of either sex' (Murdock, 1949: 35). Later, Murdock (1960: 4) used the term 'extended family' somewhat differently. This inconsistency, or change of definition, will be considered later, but here it is sufficient to note that, in describing the structure of the Bajau Laut house group, the term 'extended family' is used with Murdock's original meaning, to refer to a group comprising parents and the families of two or more of their married children. An extended family in the Bajau Laut case rarely includes more than three generations. Only a small number of house groups include both grandparents and the family or families of procreation of their married grandchildren. Murdock (1960: 11) in his later writings replaced the term 'bilocal' with 'ambilocal'. The meaning, however, is the same. Either a son or a daughter, 'depending upon the circumstances of the particular case', may remain after marriage (cf. Murdock, 1949: 35). In other words, residence may be either virilocal or uxorilocal, but not exclusively one or the other, with the choice determined by 'circumstances'.

The structural composition of the house group, following an initial phase of expansion, is typically that of a bilocal or ambilocal extended family in the sense just discussed. Founded by the house leader and his wife, most house groups expand within a short time to contain the families of those of their married sons or daughters who have not married out, nor yet seceded from the group; the couple's still unmarried children, if any remain; plus possibly other persons, with or without offspring, chiefly children, grandchildren, or siblings. The Bajau Laut kinship system is bilateral, and the structural unit that most commonly comprises the house group may be termed 'bilocal' in the sense that sons and daughters have the same rights of membership in the group and that either, or both, may equally remain following marriage.

In most families, at least one or two children marry out, and because of age differences of those who remain, older children often make good their independence by the time their younger brothers or sisters are beginning to marry and rear families of their own. As a result, few house groups contain, at any given time, more than two or three dependent families. This can be seen from the history of Dessal's house group. Although six of Dessal's seven children married during the period in which we traced the house group's history, never more than two subsidiary families were co-resident in the *luma'* for any prolonged period of time. In 1979, twenty-one years after the house group was founded, two children had married out, three had set up households of their own or were in the process of doing so, one married child remained in the house group, and one had not yet married. In 1965, only two house groups in the village contained more than three dependent families, or couples still without children, in addition to the house leader and his wife. One contained four, another five couples. In 1975, the household of Gilang, after the marriage of Dessal's youngest son into the group, included for a time, six married couples, four with children. Households of this size are unusual, however. More often, older children depart as younger brothers and sisters marry, keeping generally within two or three the number of dependent families present at any given time.

Additional people may occasionally be incorporated in the house, or later rejoin it but even with the subsequent inclusion of such people, the basic structural form of the group remains the same. This form is essentially that of a pyramid of interlocking nuclear families or married couples—'eyes' (*mataan*) in the Bajau Laut metaphor—each family or married pair typically at a different stage of maturity, with the house founder and his wife at the apex, and extending through three, occasionally four, generations each successively linked by parent–child ties. It is this formal pattern that persists rather than individual house groups themselves.

Murdock (1960: 2), in defining the principal features of 'bilateral societies', argues that one of their chief characteristics is the structural prominence of a 'small domestic unit' based generally on the 'elementary' or 'nuclear family'. Murdock sharply distinguishes the 'elementary family' from the larger 'extended family'. The former consists of parents and unmarried children, the latter, following his original definition (Murdock, 1949: 33–5), comprises parents plus the families of procreation of two or more married children. Murdock lays stress on the bilateral nature of the elementary family. He characterizes it as 'fundamentally a bilateral kin group ... organized without the use of any lineal principle' (Murdock, 1960: 3). In contrast, he treats the extended family as a 'minimal descent group'. Thus, he argues, 'an "extended family" ... must necessarily be based on a lineal principle—either patrilineal, matrilineal, or ambilineal—rather than exclusively bilateral filiation. An extended family is essentially a minimal clan or localized lineage ...' (Murdock, 1960: 4). For Murdock (1949: 23–4, 33–5), the extended family exists only as a localized unit in a larger structure of descent groups, and, like the latter, is characterized by indefinite continuity through time provided for by lineal affiliation. An extended family is inherently incompatible, in this view, with a bilateral form of social organization (Murdock, 1960: 4).

Murdock's treatment of the family and of bilateral social systems generally raises a number of serious conceptual difficulties (Sahlins, 1963). As several writers have observed (Fallers and Levy, 1959; Bender, 1967; Yanagisako, 1979), Murdock fails to distinguish between the concepts of 'family', 'household', and 'domestic group'. The first is basically a kinship unit, the second a residential group, and the third a unit whose members share common tasks related to child care and the provision of food and other basic necessities. In any particular society, the three are not necessarily identical (Bender, 1967). In addition, Murdock's treatment of the family is static and ignores variations that arise from the development cycle that family groups undergo. Finally, in distinguishing between different types of families, Murdock is inconsistent in the definitions he employs. This is particularly so in the case of the 'extended family'. In his later writing, Murdock (1960: 4) reserves the term 'extended family' for a unit 'which embraces two or more married siblings in its senior generation'. His original 'extended family' becomes a 'lineal family', a name Murdock himself acknowledges as inappropriate. As I have argued elsewhere (Sather, 1978: 192), not only does this altered usage exclude from consideration the overwhelming majority of 'extended families' in the ethnographic literature, but represents what can only be interpreted as an attempt by Murdock to classify himself out of a theoretical impasse created by his own insistence that the 'extended family' exists in perpetuity as part of a more inclusive structure of descent groups.

A close analysis of the Bajau Laut *luma'* makes it evident that, contrary to Murdock, an extended family system can exist, and function within the context of still wider kinship alignments, without the recognition, or necessary use, of descent as a principle of organization. Clearly, the Bajau Laut house group is not a 'descent group', minimal or otherwise. Although the house leader and his wife are typically the senior members of the group, their position depends, not on descent as such, but on the leader's role as house owner, his senior generational status, and the position he occupies among his dependant housemates as their principal spokesman in village affairs. Eligibility to house group membership is established, not by successive genealogical affiliation, but by marriage and bilateral filiation, that is, by parent–child ties, traced directly to the *nakura' luma'* or his wife, or through their immediate dependants, most often their children. While the Bajau Laut recognize descent lines, called *turunan*, and use them in tracing genealogically remote relationships, these lines are traced independently of house group membership. House groups are not, in any sense, defined by such lines. As far as kinship is concerned, it is not successive genealogical affiliation, but rather particular filiative ties, or serial ties, that are important and individually used to associate dependants with a particular house owner or his wife.

In this regard, part of the difficulty inherent in Murdock's treatment of the extended family derives from his failure to distinguish between 'descent' and 'serial filiation', a distinction clarified by Scheffler (1966). So far as the Bajau Laut 'extended family' system is concerned, ties between successive generations are based not on descent, but on serial filiation, traced maximally through four generations. Moreover, serial continuity is only temporary, for, with the passage of each generation—and often within the same generation—new house groups are formed and old ones dissolve, and, at the same time, individuals and nuclear families repeatedly move between these groups.

Filiation, by its nature, is bilateral and its use as a principle of house group organization is fully consistent with the bilateral organization of Bajau Laut kinship generally. Moreover, neither filiation nor marriage alone automatically 'ascribes' an individual to membership in a particular house group. Instead, they provide the basis, on the one hand, for claims to eligibility and, on the other, obligations on the part of the house leader and others to accede to these claims. While most housemates acquire membership at birth, through partition, or by in-marriage, others who previously belonged to other *luma'* may claim admission by pressing these claims, or they may rejoin the group after having once relinquished membership. An element of choice is always involved. Thus claims must be pressed and acceded to, and in all cases, they must be accompanied by actual residence sustained over a prolonged period to amount to membership.

It is these basic principles of affiliation by which claims to eligibility are established that give the house group its stable structural form. Bilateral filiation and marriage are by far the most important. Less important, but requiring brief mention, are two minor principles—adoption and fosterage, and the incorporation of affines.

Every individual owes his house group membership to one of these four principles. He or she may be either the house group founder or a member of the group by right of filiation; an in-marrying spouse, including the founder's husband or wife; an adopted or foster member; or an incorporated affine. Thus it is possible to classify each person under one of four headings:- filiation, in-marriage, adoption or fosterage, and incorporation (Table 5.5).

Filiation

Nearly every Bajau Laut child is a member of one particular house group by birth. The main exceptions are those whose families continue to live on boats. In principle, this group may equally well be the house

TABLE 5.5
Principles of House Group Composition

Principle of Membership	Number of Individuals	Percentage
Filiation	335	76.10
Marriage	81	18.24
Adoption or Fosterage	8	1.80
Incorporation	16	3.60
Total	440	100.00

group of the child's father as that of its mother. In practice, it tends more often to be the latter, particularly if the child is the first-born. Uxorilocal residence is the expected norm during the first few years of marriage, or until after the birth of the couple's first child. Of all village marriages, 71 per cent are uxorilocal during this period, 24 per cent virilocal, and 4 per cent other (Table 5.6). Subsequently, most couples continue to live with the wife's parents until they establish their independence, but the percentage of uxorilocal residence declines to 57 per cent after the birth of the couple's first child; virilocal residence increases to 28 per cent, while other forms of residence make up 16 per cent of all marriages (Table 5.7). These other forms consist of residence with grandparents, one of the husband's or wife's siblings, or a sibling of one of the couple's parents. The couples involved are in most cases those whose parental house group has dissolved or whose parents are dead or separated. As long as one parental house group remains intact, most married couples (85 per cent) continue to live with one or the other's parents until they establish a *luma'* of their own.

An element of choice is always involved in residence. While the factors that influence choice tend to favour residence with the wife's family, it must be stressed again that, in principle, filiation is strictly bilateral. Sons and daughters have identical rights to remain in the house group and for children these rights are the same whether they are acquired through the mother or through the father. There is no jural or terminological distinction made between them.

Regardless of which house group a child is born into, it does not usually come to maturity in its natal *luma'*. Parents generally leave the original house group during the hiving-off phase, as their eldest offspring reach marriageable age. By accompanying its parents, a child relinquishes membership in the house group into which it was born, and becomes a member of the newly founded house group established by its parents during the partition of the original *luma'*. It is normally into this house group or, in the case of those who marry out, into a similar group founded by its spouse's parents, that its own offspring are born and acquire their initial house group membership.

By right of birth, a child most often belongs to the parental group of one or the other of its parents. The choice is made by the parental couple and the leaders of their respective *luma'*. While a degree of choice, or option, is involved, once a particular residence decision is taken, it is, in

TABLE 5.6
Initial Residence after Marriage

Couple's Place of Residence	Incidence	Percentage (approx.)
Wife's parental house group	15	71
Husband's parental house group	5	24
Wife's mother's parents	1	4
Total	21	100

TABLE 5.7

Later Residence after Marriage

Couple's Place of Residence	Incidence	Percentage (approx.)
Wife's parental house group	27	57
Husband's parental house group	13	28
Husband's brother's house group	1	2
Wife's brother's house group	1	2
Wife's sister's house group	1	2
Husband's father's brother's house group	1	2
Wife's mother's sister's house group	3	6
Total	47	100

Firth's terms (1957: 5), definitive, that is, it assigns an individual to membership in one, and only one, house group. However, the choice is always reversible (Firth, 1957: 5). An individual is never permanently bound to it, but may change his group membership several times during his lifetime. The first change regularly occurs in childhood when his membership is transferred to the new house group founded by his parents upon their secession from the original *luma'*. Membership is thus acquired at birth, or is later transferred as secession occurs, by virtue of bilateral filiation. Following Freeman (1956: 87–8; 1958: 26–8), the system is more specifically one of utrolateral filiation, in that membership is established initially in either the husband's or wife's parental house group, but never in both. However, the Bajau Laut system of filiation differs from that of the Iban described by Freeman in that neither of these house groups is ordinarily either spouse's natal *luma'*. This is because filiation is not only optionally reversible, but is regularly and systematically revoked in each generation. This difference in filiation is of fundamental structural importance. House group membership is transferred in every generation from an existing group to a newly founded one, with the result that, from the perspective of the original house group, there is an inevitable break in filiative links between successive generations. While this break may be temporarily averted by the short-term inheritance of the house, affiliation is, nevertheless, eventually transferred to a new house group and the original *luma'* is dissolved. The difference can be summarized by saying that the Bajau Laut system is one of discontinuous, as opposed to continuous filiation. While the house group is self-replicating, it is not, unlike the Iban *bilek*-family, a self-perpetuating group that continues from one generation to the next.

All children have identical claims to membership in the house group into which they are born, or grow to maturity, except in so far as the youngest daughter is granted, in practice, a superior claim to succeed the house founder or his wife upon their retirement or death. The emphasis in defining these rights is on parentage. The central relationships that unite house group members are those between parents and children and between siblings of the same parents, mirroring internal *mataan* relations. Collectively, persons standing in these relations to one another are termed *tai'anakan* (see Chapter 8) and the relationships that exist between them form the relational core, not only of the house group, but also of family boat crews, neighbourhood clusters, and of nearly every other social grouping of significance at the village level. As a house group expands, successive filiative links, and their collateral extension through relations of siblingship, are temporarily included in its composition. This inclusion is relatively short-lived, however, as filiative links of membership are eventually revoked or transferred to other *luma'* in the ensuing process of house group partition and dissolution. Relations traced maximally through three successive filiative links define, both ideally and in practice, the effective limits of eligibility to house group membership. With very few exceptions, no one outside these limits is accorded house group membership, apart from in-marrying spouses.

What needs to be stressed is that not all people related within these limits are necessarily members of the same house group or even of the same cluster. Ties of filiation establish rights of eligibility, but actual membership additionally requires prolonged residence and acceptance of the responsibilities that membership entails, including recognition of the house leader's authority. Furthermore, ties of filiation provide an individual with multiple and overlapping claims of possible admission to more than one house groups. While most claims to membership are acquired by birth or are transferred from one group to another in the process of house group partition, further changes in residence occasionally take place after a house group is founded. Additional persons may subsequently gain admission to the group on the basis of ties of filiation other than the house founder's offspring. Such persons most often include brothers or sisters of the *nakura' luma'* or his wife, their children, or one of the pair's widowed or ageing parents. Such movement usually comes about as a consequence of divorce, death, quarrels between housemates, or the dismemberment of an existing house group. The breakup of marriage as a result of death or divorce is by far the most important factor. Only ten of the thirty-six house groups in the village have not, at some point, gained or lost members in this way. Divorce is the most common cause of such movement and its frequency is primarily a reflection of a relatively high divorce rate, particularly during the early years of marriage. During the study period, there was one divorce in Bangau-Bangau for every two marriages, giving an aggregate divorce rate for the community of 50 per cent (Barnes, 1949). In the great majority of cases, the widowed or divorced spouse simply rejoins the parental house group he or she left at the time of marriage. Thus there is no real change in house group composition. Dessal's eldest sons, Karim and Alkisun, for example, both returned to their father's house when their first marriages ended in divorce. For both, the return was only temporary. Later, Karim joined his second wife's house group, while Alkisun eventually built a house of his own, his second, this one within the cluster containing his wife's parents.

Occasionally, new members may join the group by virtue of filiative ties, particularly if their parents are dead or are no longer in active management of a house group. For example, after she was divorced, Endemala joined the house group originally founded by her daughter Baydati and her husband Patak, both of whom had died some years earlier. The house group (no. 26) contains Endemala's four grand-children and Patak's widowed mother, Liarah. Endemala's parents are both dead and her only other child, a recently married son, Mandal, continues to live with his father, Lamarani. Another example is that of Salbayani, a brother of Dessal's wife Akbaraini. Salbayani quarrelled with his mother Hajal over the care of his children by a first marriage. When his second marriage failed, Salbayani joined the house group of his father's sister, Sariabi (no. 10), taking a son with him. His daughter had earlier chosen to remain in Hajal's house under her grandmother's foster care. Such cases are relatively infrequent. Only twelve house groups (33 per cent) contain members admitted on the basis of ties of filiation who are not the children of the house founder and his wife, grandchildren born into the group, or others such as parents or younger brothers and sisters present at the time of its founding. Included are forty-four people (13 per cent) accorded rights of membership on the basis of filiation.

While the entry of other kin is comparatively infrequent, their presence nevertheless emphasizes the element of choice inherent in house group membership, and that filiation provides potential opportunities for admission to more than one house group. Choice is made in terms of specific residence decisions, and once an individual elects, accompanies his parents, or joins a spouse to take up residence in a particular house group, his membership is unambiguously defined, even though he may later on found a group of his own, or join another, already established *luma'*.

The combined outcome of numerous individual acts of choice is the emergence of relatively stable, albeit fluid, house groups. At the same time, the overlapping nature of eligibility provides each individual with a characteristically large field of potential claimants and sponsors through whom alternative lines of affiliation may be sought or accorded, as village house groups and larger clusters are founded, gain and lose members, and dissolve.

Marriage

Residence is clearly important in determining the house group to which each individual belongs. In this regard, marriage constitutes the principal occasion on which a residence choice results in a change of house group membership.

Filiative claims are generally established by birth, or are transferred from one house group to another in the process of partition. While some additional reshuffling of persons may occur, due chiefly to the breakup of marriage, the incompatibility of housemates, or the pull of an effective leader, such occasions, involving the entry of additional kin into the *luma'*, are comparatively infrequent. Marriage, on the other hand, invariably entails a residence choice. Moreover, it is one that nearly every individual must make at least once in the course of his or her lifetime. In Bangau-Bangau, of 138 people twenty-five years of age or older, all but one have, at some time, been married (Table 5.8). The one exception is a woman in her thirties, crippled by a severe birth deformity. Even though she has never been married, she has borne, and is currently rearing, a daughter. This exception aside, all normal individuals marry at some stage in life. However, because women generally marry at a younger age than men, in later years, a number of women enter a state of permanent widowhood. The marital status of adult villagers is shown in Table 5.8.

Marriage requires that one marriage partner leaves his or her parental *luma'* to live in the house of his or her spouse, normally that of the husband's or wife's parents. The Bajau Laut have a special term for this move, *paukum* or *paukum ma pamikitan*, literally, 'to join' or 'to join with one's affines (*pamikit*'). Husbands and wives who marry into their partner's house group attain full rights of membership in the group, including in the case of an in-marrying husband, the right to inherit the dwelling and succeed the original house founder as *nakura' luma'*. When house succession occurs, it is typically an in-marrying son-in-law who inherits. Six of the thirty-six house leaders in Bangau-Bangau originally married into the group they now head. By leaving his parents' house group, the partner who marries out abandons for the time being equivalent rights in his or her parental house group. This follows from the principle that an individual may belong to only one house group at a time. The only way in which marital rights differ from those established by filiation is that they are contingent upon the continued existence of a marriage relationship. Should death or divorce sever this tie, the in-marrying spouse is expected to return to his or her own kin. In most cases, this means that the individual rejoins the parental house group he or she left at the time of marriage, as did, for example, Karim and Alkisun.

A first marriage is ideally arranged by the couple's parents, their related cluster elders, and other senior kin. Later marriages are generally contracted directly by the couple themselves. A discussion of marriage arrangements, and of the economic and ritual aspects of marriage, are

TABLE 5.8

Marital Status of Individuals 25 Years of Age and Over

Marital Status	Number of Individuals	Percentage (approx.)
Married	117	84.8
Widow/widower	16	11.6
Divorced and living with offspring	4	2.9
Divorced with no children	–	–
Unmarried	1	0.7
Total	138	100.0

taken up in Chapter 8. The rules that apply to marriage primarily concern alliances between cognatic kin. While non-cognates (*a'a saddi*, literally, 'other people') may marry, their union is neither frequent nor favoured, and cognatic marriage is the norm, both preferred and actual. For cognates, marriage and sexual relations are prohibited as incestuous (*sumbang*) within limits defined by two concepts: *dabohé'* and *bai pinaduru'*. The term *bohé'*, meaning 'water' or 'fluid', refers in this connection to semen, regarded by the Bajau Laut as the primary generative element in procreation. The union of those who are *dabohé'*, 'of one semen'—that is, a father and his children and full- and half-siblings of the same father—is strictly prohibited, as *sumbang*. Also considered *dabohé'* are the offspring of brothers, that is, immediate patrilateral parallel cousins. More distant patrilateral ties are generally ignored. *Bai pinaduru'* means, literally, 'having been nursed from the same breasts (*duru'*)'. Relations are counted as 'incestuous' between a woman and any child she has nursed, and between those who were nursed by the same mother, real or adoptive—that is, full- and half-siblings by the same mother (or nurse). In addition, marriage is generally avoided between all cognates, through the range of first cousins who are not of the same generational level, although exceptions do occur.

The most stringent prohibitions apply to primary kin and to children and their parents' siblings. Under no circumstances may such persons marry. Outside these limits, marriages are allowed, although between patrilateral parallel cousins, marriage requires a prior ritual payment to negate what are considered to be the spiritually deleterious consequences of such a union. Intergenerational marriages may be arranged if there are compelling reasons for doing so, and if the husband and wife are relatively close in age. Thus Lunta, the youngest son of Dessal, married Gilang's youngest daughter, Bunga Rampai, although the girl is Lunta's *babu'* or aunt, as Bunga Rampai's mother and Lunta's mother's mother are sisters. However, Bunga Rampai is several years younger than Lunta and their marriage, described briefly in connection with the history of Dessal's house group, served to re-establish a cluster alignment broken years earlier by enmity between Lunta's grandmother and Bunga Rampai's mother. Thus there were compelling reasons for the marriage, which was meant to mend relations between neighbouring house groups and capped a process of cluster realignment a number of years in the making.

With the exception of the children of brothers, all other cousins are strongly preferred marriage partners. Nearly 80 per cent of all unions in Bangau-Bangau are between *kampung* (presumed or actual cognates); most are between *kaki* (persons related, or presumed to be related, as cousins of some degree) (see Chapter 7). Marriages between first and second cousins are particularly important structurally, as they serve to maintain relations between persons classed as 'close' kin.

There is no marriage prohibition within either the house group or the cluster, provided the union is not incestuous in the sense of *sumbang*, as just described. Marriage between housemates is highly unusual however, owing to the structural composition of the *luma'*. In most cases, the only persons of marriageable age are brothers and sisters. The only exceptions are house groups that contain other kin, in addition to the house group founder and his family, who joined the group sometime after the *luma'* was founded. In Bajau Laut terms, such house groups are said to comprise more than one *mataan*. Typically, one or the other partner is a more recent member of the *luma'*. Marriage, in this case, tends to reinforce ties between the founder's family and those who join the group later. This is illustrated by the following case, the only example in 1965 of intra-house group marriage in Bangau-Bangau.

Baidullah, with the help of his son, Buyung, built a house (no. 4) near the landward edge of the village. Two years later, his family was joined by Ganti, an older brother of Baidullah's wife, Laisia. Ganti joined the house group after his wife's death and was accompanied by a small son and his youngest daughter, Rubiah (Figure 5.1). Soon after joining Baidullah's house group, Rubiah married Dessal's eldest son Karim, to whom she was already betrothed, and within a year the couple joined Dessal's house group. Her departure is said to have come as a disappointment to Baidullah, who also feared the departure of his own son, Buyung. He therefore proposed to Ganti that he call his daughter back to the house and arrange for her remarriage to his son Buyung. Rubiah, who was then not yet fourteen years old, at first refused. Several weeks later, Karim and his father's family left Bangau-Bangau on a fishing voyage. Rubiah remained behind to look after the house with two of

FIGURE 5.1

Composition of Baidullah's House

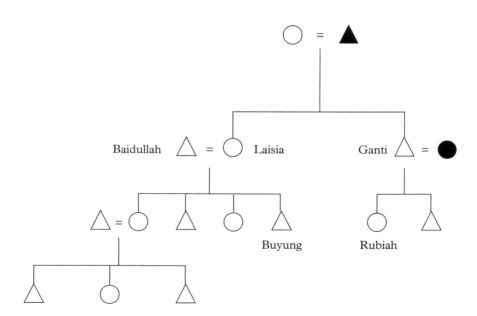

Dessal's sons, who were then attending school in Semporna town. Taking advantage of the opportunity, Baidullah and Ganti went to where the girl was staying and again tried to persuade her to leave her husband. This time they succeeded. Rubiah returned to Baidullah's house and was immediately married to Buyung.

Rubiah's remarriage was arranged in violation of *addat* which requires that at least one full month (*dabulan*) elapse before a woman remarries after a divorce. As soon as Karim and his father Dessal returned to the village, they brought legal action against Baidullah and Ganti. In the end, Rubiah's remarriage was upheld, but Ganti was required to make full restitution of Karim's bride-wealth and other marriage gifts. The remarriage, however, served its purpose. It both ensured the couple's continued presence in the house group and cemented Ganti's relationship with Baidullah. In 1979, when I returned to the village, Buyung and Rubiah were still living in Baidullah's house, where they and their children had become as the senior subsidiary family in the *luma'*.

While intra-house group marriage such as this may be rare, marriages within the larger cluster are common and are frequently arranged by the elders or the couple's parents as a way of preventing the attenuation of close cognatic ties between cluster allies. While a single marriage may suffice, a double marriage is sometimes arranged (see Chapter 8). This occurs between a son and daughter of a pair of sisters or of a brother and a sister. Double marriages not only consolidate the cognatic meshwork that links cluster members, but have the additional advantage of ensuring that one couple will reside in each of the two intermarrying house groups. As a result, neither group loses members as a consequence of marriage and both have an equal stake in preserving the relationship.

From the point of view of the house founder and his wife, whether a child marries out or remains in the house following marriage is of considerable importance. At the time a house group is founded, the founding couple have usually already passed their main childbearing years. At least one of their children must therefore remain if the house group they head is not to be totally dismembered before their death.

Understandably, conflicting pressures are often brought to bear on children by their parents and other kin anxious to secure their presence after marriage. The Bajau Laut are well aware of these pressures and deal with them in several ways. One way is by giving preference, in seeking marriage partners, to the offspring of close cognates living in the same cluster. Such marriages not only keep children within neighbouring houses, but also avoid the dissipation of resources in the form of bride-wealth (*dalaham*) among possibly unrelated families. Another way is for the couple's parents to decide during marriage negotiations in which house group the pair will live after marriage. Such decisions are particularly sought by parents who have only one or two offspring and are often secured with financial concessions, such as additional marriage gifts or reduced bride-wealth. Thus, when Laiti married Tia, he was required to pay an exceptionally large *dalaham* in order to gain her parents' consent to remove her from their house group in Sitangkai. He had also to pledge Tia's father that he would arrange for her return as soon as she became pregnant so that she might bear her first child in his house. For most newly married couples, a permanent residence choice is often deferred for several years and preceded by what may best be termed an initial period of 'trial residence'.

The marriage ceremony is held in the bride's parents' house or in the house of the man who acts during the arrangement of her marriage as her formal guardian (*wakil*). Afterwards, all couples are expected to remain with the wife's parents for the first two years or so of marriage, or until after the birth of their first child. Just over 70 per cent of all marriages are uxorilocal during this initial period (see Table 5.6). Although generally living with the wife's parents, the couple are expected to make occasional, and sometimes prolonged, visits to the husband's family. As a result, unless a prior agreement has been made between their families, most couples alternate for a time between the two parental house groups before establishing themselves permanently in one of the two groups. This practice of moving back and forth is called *magpinda-pinda*. It gives newly married couples an opportunity to discover which set of housemates they find most compatible, and allows their parents and other kin time to reconcile themselves to their final decision. It also helps create the basis of a later pattern of visits.

The importance of personal compatibility is stressed by the villagers. It is felt that anyone who joins a house group should be able to get along with his or her fellow housemates. This is particularly so for women, since they must work together daily. It is said to be less important for men, provided they are diligent and contribute their share to the group's budget. Divorce is frequent during the early years of marriage; most cases involve incompatibility, not only between husband and wife, but also between spouses and the members of one or both families. The villagers are aware of this, and a number insist that divorce is less frequent among boat-dwelling couples because they are under less pressure to accommodate to an extended group of kin. Unfortunately, I was unable to collect marital history information from enough boat-living couples to make a meaningful comparison possible, but this view may well be correct. Later, continued incompatibility may cause a family to withdraw from a cluster, as in the case, described in Chapter 6, of Umaldani and Bengani. Only when a couple are into their childbearing years, and it is clear that their marriage is likely to last, does residence enter what may be called, by comparison, a 'permanent phase'.

During this later phase, residence is more variable, as can be seen from Table 5.7. It nevertheless continues to be predominately uxorilocal. Daughters are twice as likely as sons to remain in the parental house group following marriage. As a consequence, village domicile groups, both houses and neighbourhood clusters, have a markedly matrilateral composition with uterine ties as the predominant genealogical relations, even though these ties have no special jural status.

There are several reasons for this. The one most often mentioned is the close emotional bond that is said to exist between a mother and her

1   View of the main canal at Sitangkai with moored house boats, 1965.

2   Aerial view of Bangau-Bangau, 1965; bridge on stilts links village to shore.

3 Removing detachable harpoon-head from dolphin.

4 Tandoh, a Bangau-Bangau house group leader and medium, poling over coral terrace watching for fish.

5 Part of Ligitan reef complex at low tide, showing vein of igneous rock. In the foreground, nets drying and in the background, a fishing party waiting for the change of tides.

6 Village girls setting off by *boggo'* on a gathering expedition.

7 Careened *lepa* showing roofed living quarters, carved bowsprit, poling-platform, and *sa'am*.

8 Fire-treating *lepa* with palm-frond torch.

9 Constructing a new *lepa*; an adze is used to shape the *bengkol*.

10 Drying nets at sea from poles erected along the sides of the *lepa*. Note the rays drying at the rear of the vessel.

11 *Linggi*' nets hanging from drying rack on Ligitan Island.

12 Replacing *selibut* floats.

13 *Anakop* netting: a diver flushing fish from area of coral enclosed by a double circle of netting.

14 *Anakop* netting: diver removing coral fish from netting.

15 *Magambit* netting: fishermen manoeuvre net encirclement into shallower waters. Note the boat registration numbers painted on the prow of the *lepa*.

16 *Magambit* netting: swimmers tighten the inner circle of nets.

17 *Magambit* netting: boats heavily laden with fish and nets hauling in inner encirclement of netting.

18 *Magambit* netting: couple in *boggo' (foreground)* watching start of net hauling.

19 *Magambit* netting: spearing escaping fish from boats drawn up around outer circle of nets.

20 *Magambit* netting: fleet temporarily disbands at the conclusion of a drive.

21 Village pile-house under construction.

22 Bangau-Bangau at low tide showing the arrangement of houses in clusters.

23 The open landing-platform is used for most outdoor tasks such as: (a) preparing strips of pandanus for weaving; (b) drying fish; (c) recreational activities; (d) grating and drying cassava flour.

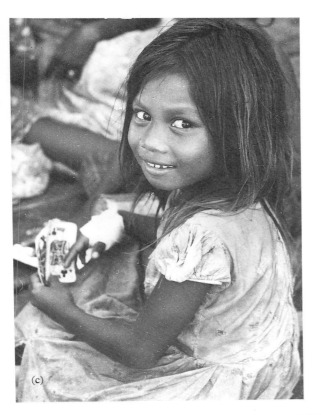

(c)

(d)

24 The bride being ritually bathed by her future mother-in-law on the morning of the wedding.

25 A bride and groom during the *magsanding* ceremony.

26 Guests dancing in honour of the bride and groom during *magsanding*.

27 *Mandi sappal:* (a) a village medium directs a group of women and children as they assemble at the bathing site; (b) using a winnowing tray, the medium throws water over the group.

28 Burial party arriving at the cemetery island; the centre boat carrying the body of the dead flies a white flag from the stern indicating that the deceased is a woman.

29 Part of the deceased's property being buried in the grave with the body.

30 Inserting a temporary stake on the headside of a newly filled grave. Holding the stake, the *imam* recites the *dua'a tulkin*.

31 A wooden gravemarker replaces the temporary stake.

32 A woman serving rice and fish for a *magmaulud* gathering inside the house.

33 *Magtimbang*: person being weighed sits in a sling while being blessed by an *imam*. The counter-weight is chiefly made up of bananas, coconuts, and firewood.

34 *Magtimbang*: plates of rice cakes placed below the central pivot of the beam by members of the sponsoring group.

35 *Anambal*: a curing session.

36 *Magpai baha'u*: mediums and their assistants prepare rice offerings.

37 *Tampat* Si Bangai-Bangai, a large coral rock believed to be the home of a local resident spirit known to villagers as Si Bangai-Bangai.

daughters. The importance of this bond is particularly marked during the first years of marriage and, above all, at the time of the daughter's first pregnancy. Women are typically young, between twelve and sixteen years of age, when they marry for the first time. Many continue to feel a need for their mother's presence and close emotional support. Several women told me that if they married into their husband's house group, they would have no one to confide in, or to take their side if they quarrelled with their husband or his family. During her confinement, a woman should be attended by her mother, or by an older sister. Sisters should also be present to maintain the fire that is kept burning by her bedside, to prepare the special rice porridge (*mistan*) she is fed following delivery, and in general to care for her during the several weeks of her recovery. Even if her parents agree to a daughter's marriage into another house group, it is sometimes stipulated, as a form of vow (*janji'*), that she returns to her parents' *luma'* for her first delivery. The complications which Laiti's wife Tia experienced during her first pregnancy were attributed to Laiti's failure to fulfil such a pledge made with Tia's father. In this instance, a boat had to be quickly dispatched to Sitangkai to bring Tia's parents to Bangau-Bangau so that they could be present at her delivery. After a woman has successfully gone through childbirth, the mother's presence is no longer felt to be so important. Even so, most women say that they take comfort from her presence. The assistance of sisters may normally be fulfilled even if they live in different house groups. Even so, their proximity is valued.

TABLE 5.9

Effect of the Wife's Parental Ties on Residence

Type of Residence	Number	Percentage
Uxorilocal residence		
Both parents alive	16	70
Mother dead, father alive	2	9
Father dead, mother alive	5	22
Both parent dead	–	–
Insufficient data	4	–
Virilocal residence		
Both parents alive	3	30
Mother dead, father alive	4	40
Father dead, mother alive	2	20
Both parents dead	1	10
Insufficient data	3	–
Other residence		
Both parents alive	2	40
Mother dead, father alive	2	40
Father dead, mother alive	1	20
Both parents dead	–	–
Insufficient data	2	–
Total	47	

In general, ties between a woman and her mother, and, secondarily, between sisters, remain close, even for older women with grown children. The importance of these ties, coupled with the need for compatibility among the women living in the same house group, strongly favour uxorilocal residence and the cohesion of groups formed around a core of related women. The significance of mother–daughter ties as a determinant of residence can be seen from Table 5.9. As long as a woman's mother is alive, she and her husband will generally continue to live in her parents' house group, at least until they establish their eventual independence. In 91 per cent of all cases of uxorilocal marriage, the woman's mother is still alive, and in 70 per cent, both parents are still living and present in the same house group. In sharp contrast, in 85 per cent of all cases in which the woman's mother is dead, she lives outside the parental house group, either with her husband's parents or with other kin. A father's death has much less influence on a woman's residence. Following the death of their father, the majority of women continue to live in the house founded by their parents for as long as their mother is present (Table 5.9).

There are only three cases in which a woman whose parents are both alive resides virilocally. In one case, the woman's parents divorced while she was still young and she was raised as a foster child by other members of her family. In the other two cases, the women's parents are boat-dwelling. Thus there is no alternative house in which the pair might live. The mother of one woman is a sister of her husband's mother and the wife stressed, in discussing her marital history, that her mother-in-law had always behaved 'like a mother' (*buat enggo'*) to her, from the time of her wedding.

A husband's parents also exert a strong influence on the couple's place of residence. If both are alive, the couple is much more likely to reside virilocally than if one or both are dead. In 73 per cent of all cases of virilocal residence, the husband's father and mother are both alive. However, as many men whose parents are alive reside elsewhere as live in their parents' house. Thus, while the husband's ties with his parents are important, they are clearly much less so than the wife's ties to her mother and sisters.

In addition to the emotional bond that exists between a mother and her daughters, there are significant structural and economic factors that favour uxorilocal residence. Each married man's primary economic concerns are with the management of cash production and the private interests of his immediate family. The social relations most important to these concerns are both narrower than the house group—centring, instead, on the family fishing unit—and also wider—involving outside fishing partners, other workmates, and village supporters. In contrast, a woman's concerns centre to a much greater extent in her immediate house group and house group cluster. Thus, women are responsible for distributing fish for food gifts, for housekeeping, and the preparation of common meals. Their chief work relations are consequently with other housemates and women of neighbouring house groups. So there are marked advantages in preserving established female work groups. These

TABLE 5.10
In-marrying Spouses per House Group

Number of In-marrying Spouses per House Group	Incidence	Percentage
0	–	–
1	12	33.3
2	14	38.9
3	3	8.3
4	4	11.1
5	3	8.3
6 or more	–	–
Total	36	100.0

TABLE 5.11
Composition of the House Group Labour Force

Manner of Recruitment	Number of Persons	Percentage
Filiation	94	52.5
Marriage	77	43.1
Adoption and Fosterage	1	0.6
Incorporation	7	3.9
Total	179	100.0

same advantages do not apply to men, or at least not as decisively. Male work relations are generally more extensive, and the ties involved can usually be maintained even if a man changes his residence from one house group to another, as long as he continues to live in the village. Food sharing and relations of everyday co-operation are conducted largely by women and so provide, as a result of uxorilocal residence, the principal points of connection in the personal networks that internally unite house group and cluster members.

In the thirty-six house groups comprising Bangau-Bangau, there are eighty-one in-marrying members, making up 18.4 per cent of the total population of the community (Table 5.10). These individuals include both the wives of house leaders (twenty-five women) and those who entered the house group as husbands or wives of the leader's children or other dependants. Reflecting the prevalence of uxorilocal residence, thirty-four (61 per cent) are in-marrying husbands and twenty-two (39 per cent) are in-marrying wives. The number of in-marrying members per house group is shown in Table 5.10.

These figures do not indicate, however, the decisive role those who marry-in play in the domestic economy of the village. While in-marrying members constitute only 18.4 per cent of the total population, they constitute a much more significant 37.4 per cent of the adult population (those sixteen years of age or older). In-marrying husbands and wives make up 43.1 per cent of all economically active housemates. Those actively engaged in fishing or wage work are shown in Table 5.11. As those who join a house group in marriage typically do so at the start of the most productive phase of their life, and the majority are men, the economic significance of marriage to the house group can be appreciated. In 53 per cent of all house groups, in-marrying husbands make a significant contribution to the house group budget, and in nearly 20 per cent of all house groups, they are the principal source of economic support and play the dominant role in managing the house group's affairs. Finally, when a house is inherited, they are the most likely to succeed the founder as house leader.

Adoption and Fosterage

An additional, although infrequent, way of claiming house group membership is by adoption (*angipat*); adopted children are known as *anak i'ipat*. *Angipat* means, literally, 'to care for' or 'nurture'. Adoptive relations are established by a formal verbal agreement, sealed by a payment (*pangnipatan*) made to the child's natural parents by the adoptive family. *Addat* stipulates that this payment should include an item of permanent heritable wealth, ideally gold jewellery (*dublun*). The remainder is generally paid in cash. The Bajau Laut say that if nothing is paid, the adopted child's life will be shortened. More importantly, the payment bears witness to the agreement between parents and the gift of *dublun* explicitly signifies—as in the case of marriage where a similar payment is made—a transfer of jural rights in an individual from one family to another. With adoption, the child assumes the same jural rights as a natural child of its adoptive parents.

In contrast to a number of other Bornean societies (Freeman, 1958: 28–9; 1970: 16–22 on the Iban), adoption is infrequent among the Bajau Laut. There were only three cases among the 226 children under sixteen years of age in 1965. Only one house group in twelve included an adopted member. In 1979, the figure had increased to one in eleven, but clearly adoption remains uncommon. Childlessness is cited as the primary reason for adopting a child, and the infrequency of adoption appears to be related to the extremely low infertility rate among the Semporna Bajau Laut in 1964–5 (again, in contrast to the Iban). Adoption is nearly always arranged between close kin. It ideally takes place while the child is still an infant, and is sometimes agreed to prior to the child's birth, with the formal transfer of the youngster taking place soon afterwards, while the infant is still being nursed.

Fosterage is slightly more frequent. Foster children are called *anak ilu* and may be either orphans (*anak dodos*) or children who, for a variety of reasons, prefer to live with other relatives in preference to their own parents. All foster children in Bangau-Bangau are either orphans or youngsters whose parents have remarried. Typically, while living with one parent, the child quarrels with its step-parent. An example is provided by Bayani (pseudonym), whose troubled marital history is discussed in Chapter 6 in connection with neighbourhood cluster relations.

Bayani and his first wife were said to have been unusually close, and her unexpected death in childbirth came as a great personal loss. Later, Bayani remarried and built a house in a cluster formed by his second wife's father and married brother. His second wife had children by a previous marriage and also bore Bayani a child. Living in their house were also two daughters and a son by his first marriage. The two girls often quarrelled with their stepmother. In time, the eldest married and went to live with her husband in his boat. On their return to Bangau-Bangau, the couple anchored in another part of the village. Bayani's behaviour became increasingly erratic, and at times violent. Sometimes he sided with his daughter, Bunga Randam, and quarrelled with his wife over her treatment of the girl; at other times, he punished his daughter when she complained or argued with her stepmother. In order to escape her father's beatings, the girl often took refuge with her father's relatives, particularly with her widowed grandmother Hajun (pseudonym).

Bayani often came to Hajun's house to take his daughter home. Finally, one day he struck her several times with his fists. Hajun, who until then had not interfered, cursed her son and demanded that he leave the girl in her house. She would care for her. Since then, Bunga Randam has remained under the foster care of her grandmother.

Foster children, particularly orphans, are normally brought up by a brother or sister of one of the child's parents; by a grandparent or grandparents; or by an older, married sibling. Unlike adopted children, who have the same jural status as their adoptive parents' natural children, foster children continue to be counted as the offspring of their natural parents. Thus Bunga Randam remains, in jural terms, Bayani's daughter. A final case of fosterage can be cited to illustrate this distinction.

Borneo, some years after the death of his first wife, married Julmania, the eldest daughter of Muljarani (no. 32). Borneo and Julmania are both middle-aged. Julmania's previous husband drowned in a fishing accident, leaving her with two children,[8] the eldest a son of eleven. Borneo had three children by his first marriage, including a daughter of marriageable age, named Tolah. After his wife's death, Tolah looked after the two younger children and took over much of the responsibility for her father's family. It was therefore perhaps inevitable, as several villagers later suggested, that she and her stepmother should quarrel. Muljarani, although a highly respected village elder and cluster spokesman, could do little to reconcile the pair. Eventually, Borneo was forced to ask his daughter to leave the house group, and she went to live under the foster care of Borneo's brother in another part of the village.

Not long afterwards, shortly after my arrival in Bangau-Bangau, Tolah was abducted by her cousin Mandal, the son of Lamarani, and brought to the headman's house. As is customary in cases of abduction, the headman attempted to bring the couple's families together to arrange a marriage. Borneo, because of his estrangement from his daughter, at first refused to take part in the negotiations. However, as Panglima Tiring pointed out, as long as he is alive, Tolah's marriage required his consent. That Tolah lived as the foster child of his brother did not alter the fact that, in terms of *addat*, he remained the young woman's father. Marriage can only be concluded with a transfer of bride-wealth from the husband to the wife's father, for which the latter must give formal acknowledgement. In the end, Borneo consented. The marriage took place, and the couple even stayed for two days in Muljarani's house before moving into the house of Mandal's father (no. 9).

As this case illustrates, fosterage, unlike adoption, does not involve a transfer of jural rights of parentage. The foster child, however, is expected to live as a member of its foster parents' house group. It is not uncommon during childhood for a youngster to stay for a short time with other families, due to quarrels, or in order to avoid punishment for misbehaviour but, like adoption, cases of long-term fostering are infrequent. In 1965, there were only five children living in what the villagers regard as a state of long-term fosterage, including Bunga Randam. Tolah was no longer a foster child, but lived as the wife of Mandal in Lamarani's house. Three of the five children are orphans who live under the foster care of a married sister of their deceased mother.

Incorporation

There is one final principle of house group membership that remains to be mentioned. This I call 'incorporation'. Incorporation arises directly from marriage and may come about in two ways. Occasionally, those who marry into a house group bring with them children from a previous marriage. Should the marriage prove enduring, such children acquire the same rights of membership in the group as children born directly into it. The numbers involved are small. Of 226 children under sixteen years of age, only nine gained their house group membership in this way, four as a result of a single remarriage. Incorporation may also come about when an individual who joins a house group on the basis of a kin tie to the house leader or his wife is accompanied by a husband or wife. The latter is similarly incorporated as a member of the house group like other in-marrying affines. Only seven persons, four husbands and three wives, gained their current house group membership in this way.

Leadership and the House Group as an Economic and Ritual Unit

Most men, as they grow older, take an increasing interest in legal matters, as well as, very often, ritual and curing. Frequently, as their authority within the house group lessens, elderly leaders assume a greater involvement in village affairs, acting as legal counsellors and spokespersons for the members of their house group and other village kin and cluster allies. Elderly leaders are regularly consulted on questions of *addat*, legal precedent, and the past history of house group relations. Standing to some degree above the partisan rivalries of younger leaders, their views tend to carry weight. Thus the declining economic contribution of elderly leaders tends to be offset, at least to some degree, by their increasing involvement in village litigation and public discussions.

Every senior house leader is expected to have a knowledge of *addat* and of the jural obligations associated with kinship, marriage, and promissory agreements. He is also expected to listen to his housemates' complaints and remind his followers of their duties towards housemates and kin. In the case of serious disputes, cluster spokesmen and house elders act as legal counsellors. When disputes involve other house groups, house group leaders may be able to work out an informal settlement without involving the headman, acting generally as mediators. Breaches of *addat*, and serious disputes that cannot be resolved informally, are referred to the village headman for formal litigation.

Litigation is organized primarily in terms of house groups, clusters, and *mataan* ties. Disputes between housemates are regarded as an internal house group matter and are ordinarily left to the *nakura' luma'* to resolve. Formal village hearings usually concern disputes between members of different *luma'*. Former housemates may bring suit against one another only after one party has withdrawn from the *luma'*.

Every adult villager is individually responsible, in a jural sense, for his or her own conduct and for any debts or contractual obligations he or she assumes. Nevertheless, the house group as a whole, and to a lesser degree the cluster, comprise important units of legal action. Housemates are expected to back each other in village litigation. However, if an individual is clearly at fault, his housemates are likely to urge him to accept a settlement in the interest of restoring goodwill. All settlements arrived at through village hearings are to some degree 'political' in Gulliver's terms (1971: 179), in the sense that their outcome is influenced by the relative strength and solidarity of support that each party can bring to bear. While the headman can call disputants together, and can see that they discuss their differences, he has little power to impose a settlement against their will. The responsibility of each house leader is to galvanize support among his housemates, present his follower's case, and, if necessary, seek added support among his own and his dependants' kin living in other house groups. In seeking outside support, wider village interests come into play. In protecting the jural rights of his followers, a *nakura' luma'* must reconcile this goal with the more general interests of his *luma'* and of the network of kin and cluster ties in which the members of each group are enmeshed. These interests, coupled with a respect for *addat*, work to preserve the fabric of village relations in the face of frequent contention and intense factional rivalry.

In a large multifamily house group, each conjugal family or married couple represents, in economic terms, a subsidiary group. Its members function as an independent unit of economic process, managing their own assets and separately acquiring and expending wealth. Most family heads own their own boat and fishing gear, conduct their own trading activity, or engage separately in outside employment. Income from employment, and from the sale of fish, belongs to the family alone, rather than to the larger house group. Such income may be retained either in the form of a cash reserve managed by the wife, or disbursed to individual family members for their own personal use.

Such families are not self-contained groups, however. An important part of the labour and income of family members goes for household purposes, to meet the general needs of the house group as a whole.

Family members contribute labour in performing housekeeping tasks, in helping prepare meals, sharing in child care, or in aiding the house leader in making repairs to the dwelling. In addition, part of each family's catch is set aside for general consumption, as 'cooking fish' (*amilla' daing*), and is shared out between housemates and, secondarily, presented as gifts to kin living in nearby *luma'*. Families also contribute cash income for the general use of the household and to pay for ceremonies sponsored by the house leader on behalf of individual house group members.

In this respect, there is a fairly clear division between subsistence and cash elements of fishing, reflecting, on the one hand, the joint interests of the house group and localized village kin and, on the other, the private interests of each subsidiary family within the *luma'*. Before fish is sold, food-sharing obligations must generally be met. Called *binuanan daing*, their fulfilment takes the form of gifts of 'cooking fish'.[9] These are distributed, not by the fishermen themselves, but by their wives. Food sharing is thus channelled by women and takes place primarily between related married women living in the same and neighbouring house groups. These gifts reinforce the matrilateral skewing of relations within these groups. Through the sharing of fish, each family is enmeshed in a wider network of distributive obligations. Families and married couples are involved in a personal network of exchanges which, while limited in each individual case, when taken together with those of other families, have the combined effect of binding, not only house groups, but the whole village in a complex, overlapping series of distributional ties running across house and cluster boundaries.

Any fish remaining after these food-sharing obligations of *binuanan daing* have been met are marketed. The income received belongs to the family separately for the personal use of its members. Such income is variable, but is generally received in small increments, realized at the end of each fishing voyage. From this income, the family head ordinarily sets aside a cash reserve for reinvestment in fishing gear, for example, future ceremonial expenses, or for larger purchases required by family members. At times, a family's need for cash may exceed what it holds in reserve or can realize immediately through its current income from fishing. On such occasions, the family head turns to his housemates and village kin for assistance. Thus, while a family's cash reserve is intended primarily for the use of its members, each family is under obligation to respond from time to time to requests for aid from its housemates and other village kin. In contrast to food sharing, family interests are kept to the fore and careful accounts are kept of such monetary gifts. Each donor family expects a future return, and requests for assistance imply a promissory commitment of return on the part of the recipient. Transactions of this nature are a central part of relations between housemates and village kin, and are conceptualized in terms of an idiom of reciprocal debts and credit.

The balance of private and joint interests that characterizes house group and wider relations reflects on both the nature of Bajau Laut fishing and important characteristics of village social structure. Fishing entails a considerable element of unpredictability. Voyages are not always successful. At times, landings are insufficient to market; at other times, they yield an income well beyond the immediate needs of the family. Food sharing, and the existence of a wider network of distributive obligations, tends to ensure that each house group receives a relatively adequate supply of fish for daily use and lessens the risks of short-term failure that is otherwise a characteristic feature of the fishing economy. While a few households suffer chronic scarcity, the support of allied house groups lessens its hardships. The house co-headed by Liarah and Endemala, without a fishing crew of its own, receives regular help from others. Similarly, within the house group, young couples, as well as the aged, are likely to be supported by the more active, experienced fishermen and their families. Young men generally acquire experience as fishermen while they are still house group dependants. Only after attaining some measure of personal success, as the head of a subsidiary family fishing crew, do they establish their independence as separate house group leaders by building a house of their own. Later on, the greater the degree of economic success a leader enjoys, the larger the number of house group and cluster dependants he is likely to attract and retain. Through the use of private means, ambitious men are thus able to secure a wider degree of influence within the village while, at the same time, food sharing reduces the risks of short-term failure in the case of the less experienced and elderly.

The house group, for all of its importance, is not, as we have stressed, a persisting group. Its membership alters, and the group itself is eventually replaced by others as its once subsidiary families establish their independence. The eventual dissolution of the group is closely linked to the balance of joint and private interests emphasized here. The members of each subsidiary family possess their own assets, such as fishing boats and nets, and there is no common house group estate in which they acquire a shared interest. This situation facilitates house group partition because, as each family withdraws, its members have only to take their personal effects with them. In addition, natal members generally receive at the time an individual inheritance from their parents. There are no shared property interests to complicate the process of partition. Similarly, without a joint estate under his management, a house group leader lacks the means to maintain rigid authority over the affairs of the house group into old age. As a consequence, the transfer of house group leadership tends to be gradual and is closely connected to the increasing economic contribution of the next generation of married members. By managing their own cash affairs, subsidiary families preserve considerable economic autonomy, making relatively easy their eventual secession and the ultimate replacement of the original group by the new *luma'* they establish.

As long as he is recognized as *nakura' luma'*, the house leader is expected to bear a major share of the expenses involved in managing the household. Other men—the leader's married sons, for example, or his sons-in-law—are expected to contribute, but the principal burden generally falls on the *nakura' luma'*. With advancing age, this burden gradually shifts to the younger, more active male members of the *luma'*, and effective leadership also passes increasingly into the hands of the active younger generation. There is thus a gradual relinquishing of effective control over the internal management of the *luma'* and its budget. Even so, until the older man's death, he is treated with respect and generally acts as the group's spokesman on public occasions.

House group unity is given moral sanction and the group is maintained as a common venture through its members' participation, as a group, in ritual. Dissension between housemates and disrespect towards the senior members of the *luma'* are believed to provoke *busung* ('spiritual calamity'), from which all house group members may suffer. Outwardly, *busung* is expressed through sickness, possibly death, accidents, and economic failure. The memory of deceased housemates should be revered, and, as discussed in Chapter 10, former house group elders, as ancestors (*mbo'*), are believed to take a continuing interest in their living descendants. Vows (*janji'*) are frequently made to their souls by those seeking special favours. In return, favoured housemates may dedicate themselves to a specific act of remembrance, or of personal piety. Vows are also to be made to God (*magjanji' ni Tuhan*). Although intended to secure a favour for a particular individual, their fulfilment normally requires the co-operation of the vow-taker's entire house group. The most common form of repayment is sponsorship by the *luma'* of a scriptural reading. As illustrated by the example below, failure to fulfil such vows may imperil the entire *luma'*.

Ordinarily, vows are made to God (*Tuhan*) in what are considered to be serious circumstances. Their fulfilment takes the form of a rite of thanksgiving (*magmaulud*), described at greater length in Chapter 10, in which male guests are invited to the vow-taker's house to read from the scriptures. *Magmaulud* is carried out by the house group as a whole under the sponsorship of its *nakura'*. Failure by the group to fulfil its terms of the vow is regarded as a serious ritual offence, which places the entire group in a state of jeopardy (*kabusungan*). In this particular case, a chain of events began when two house leaders sought to sponsor a joint rite of thanksgiving but could not agree in which of their two houses the ritual should be held.

Gardinus's infant daughter was taken seriously ill and appeared for a time to be close to death. Gardinus swore a formal vow to God that should the girl recover, he and the members of his house group would sponsor a *magmaulud* rite. Shortly afterwards, the infant's health began to improve. At the same time, Gardinus and his family rejoined his father's house group. Prior to this, they had lived in a house group headed by Gardinus's wife's uncle, Baidullah (no. 4). Although belonging to different house clusters, the two groups are closely related as Baidullah and Gardinus's father, Labu, are brothers. Ganti, Gardinus's wife's grandfather is also Labu's wife's father and a member of Baidullah's house group. In view of these ties, Labu and Baidullah agreed to share the cost of a joint *magmaulud*. However, the two men could not agree on where it should be held, since both wished to act as sponsor. Moreover, each had a legitimate claim, as Gardinus was now living with Labu, but had made the promise when he was still living in Baidullah's house.

Impatient with the delay, Gardinus and his father decided to hold the rite without Baidullah's help, and proceeded to purchase rice and invite the heads of other house groups to attend. This angered Baidullah, who let it be known that he would not take part. On the appointed evening, I accompanied Panglima Tiring and his sons to Labu's house (no. 22). When we arrived, we found the house in darkness and the members of the household loudly arguing. Gardinus's wife had sided with her uncle, according to neighbours, and just before the rite was to begin, had returned to Baidullah's house taking their daughter with her. Since the participation of the mother and daughter is essential, Labu was left with the embarrassing task of announcing the postponement of the *mag-maulud* and of sending home the guests as they arrived. Many, as we returned to our homes, commented on the gravity of the situation.

Two days later, Gardinus's wife and daughter returned to Labu's house. However, Labu and Baidullah remained unreconciled. A week later, a new-born infant in Baidullah's house group, the child of another niece and sister of Gardinus's wife, died suddenly. The death was a great blow to Baidullah. It was widely interpreted as a sign of *busung*. Greatly shaken, Baidullah personally carried the infant's body to Labu's house, where, in a dramatic gesture, he and the rest of his house group joined his brother's *luma'* to mourn its death. During the night's vigil and sub-sequent rites of bereavement, the two house groups came together, forming for a time a single ritual unit.

In this case, the bonds that existed between the two house groups were reaffirmed in the most dramatic manner possible. For a day and a night, the two house groups were united in a common act of mourning which, some said, was also an act of atonement meant to free Baidulah's *luma'* of *busung*.

Flagrant disregard of *addat*, and grave moral sins (*dusa*), such as incest, impiety, or ritual defilement, are thought to create a state of spir-itual danger characterized by 'heat' (*pasu'*). Not only is the guilty person endangered, but 'heat' is believed to envelop his house group, possibly even the village, or the entire region in which he lives. 'Heat' upsets the natural order, and, in the most general sense, is thought to disrupt rela-tions between mankind and the natural world, calling down a variety of disasters, such as epidemics and droughts. In a much more limited sense, a variety of acts involving others in everyday social relationships are thought to provoke a limited form of spiritual 'heat'. Here, again, the danger involved may extend to others, and the entire house group is believed to be liable, in a spiritual sense, for the actions of its individual members. This may be illustrated by a second example involving, in this case, the house group of the village headman, Panglima Tiring.

In her later years, Panglima Tiring's mother, Kamsiniha, broke off ties with her son. In July 1965, the old woman died. In cases of this sort, the villagers usually attempt to bring about a reconciliation, because it is believed that the dying should not leave this world still harbouring ill-feelings towards their living kin. Those who are the object of such feelings are believed to be endangered. On such occasions, the Panglima himself is usually the person who conducts the reconciliation ritual (*magkiparat*). However, Kamsiniha died suddenly, before the headman could be summoned.

Within an hour of her death, the Panglima's grandson fell from the landing stage of the headman's house and severely gashed his leg on the platform ladder. With this, no one was permitted to leave the house. Although a guest, even I was advised to remain indoors. For the rest of the day, no one in the headman's house ventured out. Only in the evening, after Kamsiniha's burial, did life in the house group return to normal.

Every ritual observance an individual undergoes, from birth to death, takes place in the house and is sponsored by his or her *nakura' luma'*. These observances are described at length in Chapter 9. Some are minor and attended by only the immediate members of the house group and a few invited guests from other houses; others are major rituals attended, ideally, by representatives of all, or most, house groups in the village. All major observances, including *magmaulud*, are accompanied by a feast (*elotak*) served to the male guests and prepared by the women of the group plus female kin and cluster neighbours. Small gifts may also be given to the principal guests representing other *luma'*. In the case of weddings, there may also be larger invitational gifts presented beforehand to other house group leaders in order to assure their attendance.

Frequently, the expenses involved in sponsoring such rituals are beyond the immediate means of a single family or married couple. Although the rites are normally held on behalf of individual members, all housemates are expected to assist, contributing money and time, and the role of the *nakura' luma'* as ritual sponsor includes that of marshalling the combined resources of the group and of seeking additional aid, if necessary, from among his own and his wife's kin living outside the house. If the house leader is still economically active, he is likely to bear the major share of these expenses. Ritual activity, together with litigation, are the principal occasions for house group co-operation. Through ritual, housemates acknowledge the leadership of the *nakura' luma'* and give tangible expression to their shared concern for one another's fate and physical well-being.

1. See Chapter 4.

2. In 1979, one village house group had divided its hearth, with part of the group withdrawing to set up a separate cooking area. The group was rent at the time by squabbling, and the division was seen as the first step toward the group's partition into two *luma'*. In 1965, all house groups made use of a single hearth.

3. See Chapter 4. Only a corpse is laid lengthwise on the deck of the *lepa*. The same is true of the house. The physical orientation of the body inside boats and houses thus signifies states of life and death (Waterson, 1990: 94). The *kokan* is also the chief locus of house group ritual (see Chapter 10).

4. As mentioned in Chapter 4.

5. This information relates to August 1965, the time of my second village census. House numbers correspond with Map 5.1, which shows the location of each of these house groups within the village.

6. None were held while I lived in Bangau-Bangau and I am relying here on the accounts of informants.

7. See Chapter 7.

8. In harpooning a giant ray, his foot became entangled with the harpoon cable and he was dragged overboard.

9. See Chapter 4.

6
Clusters, Village Leadership, Enmity, and Reconciliation

Lamak poté' tulutin, da'a patugutin.

When the white sail fills with wind, don't pull taut the mainsheet.
(From *Kalangan tebba*, a traditional Bajau Laut song)

ALL social groups in Bajau Laut society—including family boat crews, house groups, and clusters—are identified with, and take their name from, a particular leader or group head. To a large degree, groups are the creation of individual leaders. At the same time, they are also the focus of ties that enmesh each individual within the larger village community.

The House Group Cluster (*Ba'anan*)

Every house group in the village, with one exception, the house of Lamarani (no. 6), is aligned with from one to six others in a tightly aggregated group of neighbouring pile-houses.[1] These larger, aggregated groups are called *ba'anan* (or *tumpuk*), meaning literally 'cluster'. In 1965, there were nine house group clusters in Bangau-Bangau. Their locations are shown in Figure 6.1. The largest (Cluster D) consisted of seven houses, including that of the village headman, or 101 people, and the smallest (Cluster H), of two houses, or fifteen people. Most other clusters contained between three and five houses, or thirty-five to fifty-five people. The average number of houses per *ba'anan* was four, and the average size was forty-seven people. In Sama, the term *ba'anan* describes any grouping or clustering of objects, including living things, most commonly 'schools' of fish (*ba'anan daing*). The verbal form, *magba'an-ba'an*, describes the process of 'clustering'.

In most cases, the houses making up a cluster are not only built close to one another, but are usually connected by planks, secondary bridges, or catwalks. In four instances, they share a single landing-stage (see Figure 6.1). Thus the existence of a house group cluster is readily apparent even to an outside observer visiting the village for the first time. When an existing cluster splits, as occurred, for example, when

FIGURE 6.1
Village Clusters

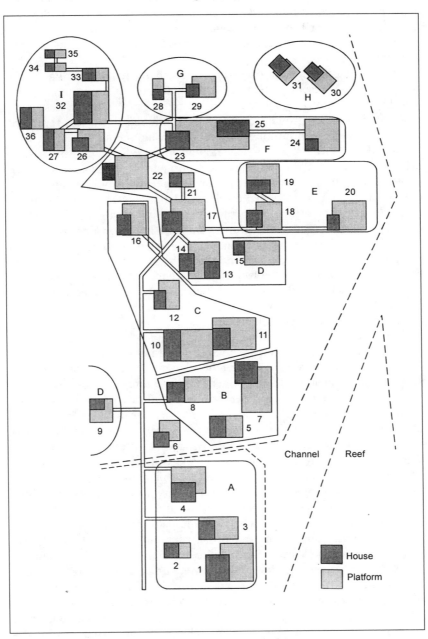

Note: Figures correspond to the house numbers in Table 5.1.

Akbaraini's mother Hajal quarrelled with her sisters, the result is at once apparent in the dismantling and relocation of secondary walkways and plank bridges. Exceptions exist in the case of newly established clusters, most near the outer edge of the village. Here where additional houses are planned or under construction, the outline of cluster alignments is often less obvious.

Neighbourhood clusters originally emerged from pre-existing family alliance groups present at the time of Bangau-Bangau's founding. Those who built their houses together were, in most cases, families belonging to the same alliance group (*pagmunda'*). In this sense, clusters represent a direct crystallization out of earlier moorage alignments.

With the abandonment of boat nomadism, the formation of clusters became linked to the process of house group partition.[2] As a house group undergoes partition, the seceding families generally build houses in a group surrounding the original dwelling. Alignments are generally maintained, at least for a time, with the cluster to which the original house founder belonged. But if the group of *luma'* (house groups) formed in the process of partition is large enough—or is able to attract additional allies—fission is likely to occur, and the new group formed through partition may break off, possibly bringing others with it, to form a new *ba'anan*. Cluster boundaries tend to be redrawn with the emergence of each new generation of house leaders. The process is also linked to the rise of influential cluster spokesmen.

The core members of most clusters include, as a consequence of house group partition, persons who are related not only as close cognatic kin and affines, but also as former housemates. Similarly, the relations that join house group leaders are generally the same as those that maximally unite house group members themselves. In each generation, cluster alignments centre, in particular, on from one to four interrelated sibling sets. For example, the connections that exist between the senior members of the largest cluster in the village (Cluster D) are shown in Figure 6.2. Basically the group is organized around three sibling sets interrelated by marriage, and, in two cases, by parent–child ties. Figure 6.2 also shows the genealogical relationships of the principal members of the remaining eight clusters. Relations in most of these latter groups are less complex, but all show essentially the same pattern of organization, with sibling ties and marriage as the principal bonds linking house group leaders within each cluster. Occasionally, the siblings or parents of an in-marrying spouse may also join the *ba'anan*, but as children are born, and often as additional marriages are arranged with established cluster members, affinal ties tend to be converted to consanguineal ones, with the result that each individual's personal network of cognatic relations tends to be densely focused within his or her cluster. Thus clusters can be described, in a loose sense, as localized kindred groups. Hence, every *ba'anan* member, with the possible exception of in-marrying spouses, belongs to the personal kindred of every other member, and relations within the group have the nature of a dense node or 'cluster' (J. A. Barnes, 1968: 118) of tightly interwoven cognatic ties.[3]

(continued)

FIGURE 6.2
The Main Genealogical Connections Uniting Clusters

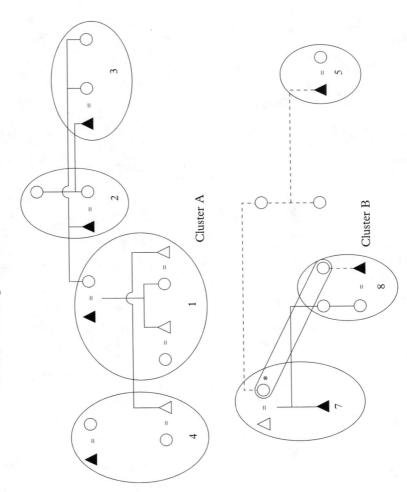

192

FIGURE 6.2 (continued)

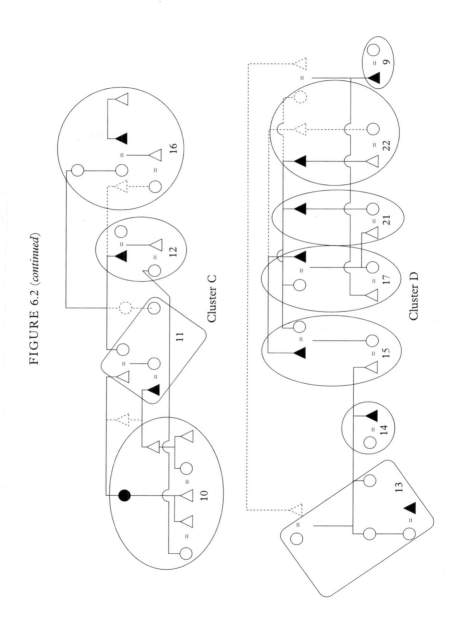

Cluster C

Cluster D

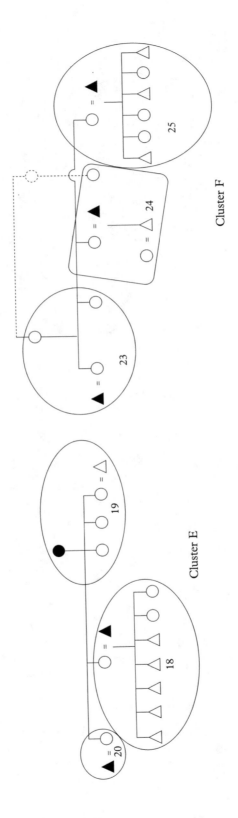

Cluster F

Cluster E

(continued)

194

FIGURE 6.2 (continued)

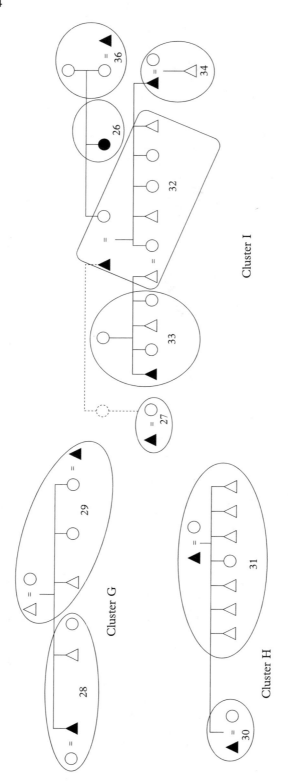

Cluster I

Cluster G

Cluster H

O = Female
△ = Male
●▲ } Nakura' luma'

Notes: Figures correspond to house numbers in Table 5.1.
*This woman is remarried to the grandfather of her son's wife.

Adult members of the cluster visit each other almost daily, and village work groups are regularly made up of people from neighbouring house groups. The majority of any fisherman's roster of regular fishing partners belong to the same cluster. Although partnerships include at least several men from other clusters, the initial planning of most voyages is done by roster-mates living in the same and neighbouring houses. For most men, cluster members are also their principal source of fishing information. Even so, most families regularly fish with others living in different clusters, and for husbands who have recently married into the group, their principal partners are likely to live elsewhere, at least until they have had time to develop close working ties with their new *ba'anan* members. Women, in general, are more restricted in their work relationships and are less free to move about the village than men. Although women are not excluded, men generally represent the house group at public gatherings, and males alone participate as guests in house group-sponsored rites held outside the cluster. Women rarely attend ceremonies held in other clusters unless their immediate kin are involved; their participation in most cases is limited to lending utensils and assisting the women of the sponsoring house group to prepare and serve food. Thus, the women's regular working companions are almost always drawn from within the immediate cluster. On the other hand, the relationships involved tend to be especially frequent and intimate. Because of the prevalence of uxorilocal residence, the composition of the *ba'anan*, like that of the house group, tends to be markedly skewed in favour of uterine ties. Thus women are less likely than men to have married into the group, and generally have a greater number of their close kin present, very often including their parents, sisters, and married daughters.

Every individual also has relatives living in other clusters. There are always some who have married outside the group, and others who have married in from other *ba'anan*. Although ties of mutual interrelatedness tend to be heavily focused within the cluster and, in the case of long-established groups, are often reinforced by intermarriage, the group is by no means isolated in terms of the personal kin ties of its members. Nearly every cluster includes what may be described as 'pivotal house groups'. These are groups whose members, while identified with one particular cluster, have especially close ties with the members of one, or possibly several, other groups belonging to different clusters. Such house groups create an important relational bridge between village *ba'anan*. In some cases, relations between two, or possibly three, clusters are almost equally close. Although the Bajau Laut give no special name to such house groups, their importance is well recognized, particularly when a wider degree of co-operation is sought. Pivotal house groups are especially important in the management of conflict within the village. House group members frequently play a moderating or conciliatory role when disputes occur between the different clusters bridged by their members, and their presence generally works to prevent the community from splintering into antagonistic factions. The position of the leader of a pivotal house group is very much like that which the village headman occupies within the community as a whole. The headman's effectiveness as a mediator depends upon his use of a widely extended network of personal kindred and marriage relations. In a very real sense, the headman's house group serves as a pivotal *luma'* for the entire village.

The senior house leaders and their wives make up an informal body of elders (*matto'a*) who exercise a strong influence over their *ba'anan* followers and mobilize their assistance on occasions when common action or material aid is called for on a larger scale than a single house group or family can supply, or when the economic or political interests of the group are challenged. One leader is generally recognized as the principal spokesman for the cluster, and like houses, clusters are identified by name with individual leaders. The position of the cluster spokesman is more informal, however. Each house leader is expected to settle differences among his followers and represent their interests in village hearings and other gatherings. In general, the *ba'anan* spokesman is turned to only when a wider degree of support is sought, or when a house leader feels that he lacks sufficient legal skills, knowledge of customary law (*addat*), or personal persuasiveness to represent his followers effectively in village litigation. On the other hand, *ba'anan* elders exert considerable influence and are generally involved in the planning of major house group undertakings. Food sharing is centred mainly in the cluster and, for weddings and other major ceremonies sponsored by the head of an individual house group, cluster members are expected to assist with monetary gifts, and the women of the group to help in preparing food or in making ready the house to receive guests from other clusters. Those with special skills, particularly *ba'anan* elders, may also be asked to oversee the ritual aspects of the ceremony. Younger members are expected to provide entertainment or serve food. In the case of death rites, the assistance of cluster members is especially important, for the immediate family of the deceased is expected to remain in total mourning throughout the initial rites of bereavement (see Chapter 9). Children tend to form play groups within the cluster and are generally supervised by any adult who happens to be present. Although cluster members provide each other with daily help and companionship, there are few activities that are performed by the cluster as such. Instead, assistance is called forth and rendered between individuals on the basis of their particular personal ties with one another. While similar ties may extend outside the *ba'anan*, obligations entailed by relations within the group, supported by its spokesman and elders, are viewed as particularly binding, with the result that clusters tend to constitute highly cohesive support groups.

Like the house group, the cluster is not a permanently enduring group of constant membership. Its composition changes over time, reflecting similar changes in the membership of its constituent house groups, shifts in alignment between house leaders, and the founding and dissolution of individual *luma'*. While every cluster is typically organized around a core of married siblings, or several interrelated sibling sets, and tends to split along sibling lines when fission occurs, alignments between house leaders are possible on the basis of any of the same cognatic and affinal links that provide the basis of house group association. As a result, the cluster similarly affords its members multiple lines of possible affiliation, graded in terms of social and genealogical 'closeness' (*magsékot*). Thus, the closer the tie, in both a personal as well as a genealogical sense, the more likely it is to form the basis of an alignment. Personal compatibility, and the attraction of a persuasive *ba'anan* spokesman, may, as in other contexts, be as important a determinant as kinship.

The continued existence of each neighbourhood cluster depends upon the individuals who comprise it. The groups themselves are fluid. Individual housemates are expected to co-operate with one another in various undertakings. In the same way, neighbourhood ties are also important, and the members of neighbouring house groups are similarly expected to co-operate in domestic tasks and food sharing. Failure to fulfil these expectations leads to the breakup of the *ba'anan* and the realignment of house and cluster relations in terms that directly reflect individual ties of co-operation and support. This process can be seen by looking again at the history of Dessal's house group, this time from the point of view of its wider cluster relations.

At the time when Dessal first built his house, it formed part of a cluster that included his wife's mother, Hajal and her husband, Panglima Atani. The latter was then government-appointed leader of the local Bajau Laut community in Semporna.

The cluster was dominated at that time by a sibling set consisting of Hajal, a brother and his wife, and three sisters and their husbands. The cluster expanded as other children of Hajal and Atani, in addition to Dessal's wife Akbaraini, added new houses to the original *ba'anan*. Among them was Hajal's eldest son Umaldani, his wife Bengani, and their children. Umaldani built a house beside Dessal's and Panglima Atani's. However, Bengani and her mother-in-law soon began to quarrel. While, in retrospect, housemates on both sides tended to interpret these quarrels in terms of personal animus between the two women, it was apparent that these quarrels were also related to a growing political split within the emerging generation of Hajal's children just coming to house group leadership.

Umaldani's position of seniority as the eldest of the sibling set was being increasingly challenged by a younger brother, Salbangan, whose political ambitions were openly favoured by their mother. Hajal's favouritism was exacerbated by her intense dislike of Bengani. Salbangan's first marriage failed, but soon afterward he remarried. This time he married the daughter of Panglima Atani's brother, an ally of the Panglima, and the head of an adjoining neighbourhood cluster. When this marriage took place, Umaldani pointedly failed to attend or take any part in the negotiations leading up to it.

This brought the strained relations between the two brothers into the open. In the years that followed, the two men ceased speaking and severed all recognition of social obligations, becoming *bantah* (formal 'enemies').

Hajal and Bengani grew increasingly estranged. Finally, in 1963, when Hajal was about to leave on a dangerous boat journey to the Philippines, Umaldani and his wife refused to press Hajal's hands, as a sign of love. This refusal provoked a crisis within the cluster. Akbaraini and her mother tore down the catwalks joining their houses to Umaldani's, leaving the latter's house physically isolated from the rest of the village. In addition, Hajal brought suit against her son.

With this, Umaldani and his family dismantled their house. For a time they lived in Labuan Haji, where Umaldani's eldest son had married, but eventually they returned to Bangau-Bangau, building a new house (no. 9) in another part of the community. For a brief period, during the time that I was living in the village, Umaldani realigned himself with Panglima Tiring's cluster group (see Map 5.1). Eventually, however, as his married children established *luma'* of their own, he became the leader of a new cluster.

This break between Hajal and Umaldani strained relations between Hajal and her sisters, who sought to distance themselves from their quarrels. Without Panglima Atani's restraining presence, dissension became increasingly open following his death. Again, it was generally interpreted as conflict between related women, originally provoked by the presence of an in-marrying wife. But strained relations were also linked to the emergence within the group, once again, of a new cluster leader. Following Atani's death, Panglima Tiring became its principal spokesman. He was the eldest of three brothers, two married to sisters of Hajal, another to her niece, and all heading allied house groups in the cluster. They formed a major core of support. Added to this core were two of the headman's wife's brothers, Labu and Sahalibulan. The headman also gathered to his following three of the children of one of Panglima Atani's brothers. A second brother, Selangani, headed the adjacent cluster into which Salbangan had married.

As a result of this strain, Hajal and her daughter Akbaraini withdrew from the cluster, together with a second married daughter, her husband Rugo-Rugo, and their family. These three *luma'* formed a new and much smaller *ba'anan*. While his wife tended to side with her mother and sister, Rugo-Rugo, who was a younger brother of Panglima Tiring remained neutral and, following the split, his house group assumed a pivotal position, maintaining links in both clusters. As a fisherman, Rugo-Rugo and the headman remained regular roster partners, together with a third brother, Gilang, who then lived with his family in the headman's cluster. Eventually, the presence of this pivotal group proved crucial in reconciling Hajal and her sisters, bringing about a reconsolidation of the cluster under Panglima Tiring's leadership. This reconciliation was preceded, however, by the withdrawal of Akbaraini and Dessal.

The split between Hajal and her sisters left Dessal increasingly isolated from his closest village kin. Dessal was born in the Tawitawi island group. In the early 1920s, when he was still a child, his parents joined the main Semporna band while the community was still boat-living. Later, Dessal's sister married Selangani, a brother of Panglima Atani, while he himself, after an unsuccessful first marriage, eventually married

Akbaraini, a daughter of Atani. Some years later, Dessal's only brother Gumanjil founded a neighbouring house group (no. 12) within Selangani's cluster. In 1963, Dessal's eldest son Karim married and moved with his wife to Sitangkai. The next year, his second son, Alkisun, moved to Sandakan to work. In 1968, Alkisun rejoined Dessal's house. At this point, Dessal and his sons dismantled the original house and built a new one, across the main village walkway, facing Selangani's house, thereby realigning themselves in Selangani's cluster, together with Dessal's brother and sister and Akbaraini's brother, Salbangan.

Over the period of twelve years since its founding, Dessal's house group had been aligned in three different clusters and his house had been rebuilt once. Following the relocation of his house, Dessal's house group began to undergo expansion and partition, becoming itself the focus of an emerging neighbourhood grouping.

Shortly after Dessal had realigned his house group in Selangani's cluster, Selangani retired due to declining health, and was succeeded by his son-in-law, Salbangan. A persuasive public speaker and the wealthiest man in the village, Salbangan emerged as a powerful cluster spokesman. For a time he became the principal political rival of Panglima Tiring. Later, following his mother's reconciliation with Amjatul, Panglima Tiring's wife, Salbangan and the headman patched up their differences and became political allies. Following the reorganization of native administration, Salbangan became Wakil Ketua Kampung and to further cement relations, a marriage was arranged between his eldest daughter and Hati, a son of Panglima Tiring.

Sometime after Selangani's retirement, Alkisun and his wife joined Dessal's house group. A short time later, Dessal's third and fourth sons married, and the fourth son and his wife joined Dessal's house group. In 1975, Alkisun completed a new house next to his father's. Later, the third son, Laiti, rejoined his father's group with his wife Tia. In 1978, Laiti bought Alkisun's house, while his older brother built a new house in a cluster elsewhere in the village close to his wife's father's house. Laiti then built a new and much larger house for himself, giving Alkisun's house to his wife's mother and her children. Later, one of Laiti's wife's brothers, his wife, and family joined Laiti and his family in the new house Laiti had constructed.

By 1979, Laiti was clearly emerging as the leader of a new cluster containing Dessal's house group, now in the final stages of its development. In 1980, Dessal's youngest son married a daughter of Gilang, joining his father-in-law's house group, thereby re-establishing a relationship severed years earlier by the split between Hajal and her sisters. At the same time, the first of Dessal's two daughters married and her young husband joined Dessal's house group. Following this marriage, Dessal's fourth son and his family built a house close to those of Dessal's and Laiti's, in the emerging cluster now headed by his older brother. Later, Dessal's youngest daughter married, also bringing her husband to join his house group.

In this final development of Dessal's *luma'* is seen the process of cluster formation as it is linked to the partition of Dessal's original group and the emergence of his son Laiti as house leader and a cluster spokes-man. Having received a secondary education, Laiti had advanced to a senior position within the Public Works Department. As a consequence, he is now one of the wealthiest and most respected villagers, who is able to funnel favours and public services, including piped water and em-ployment, to other village members. Having only an adopted daughter in 1980, Laiti has augmented his cluster by incorporating, in addition to his parents and younger brother and sisters, a number of his wife's rela-tives, thus gathering together a sufficient number of followers to form an effective cluster.

While sibling ties form the relational core of every cluster, not all siblings normally live together in the same *ba'anan*. Some generally marry out, like Dessal's sons Karim and Lunta, or build houses in other clus-ters, like Alkisun. Those who live elsewhere are not lost to their brothers and sisters. Instead, they provide links of possible wider support and potential avenues for future realignments should new cluster spokesmen emerge or enmity split existing groups. In addition, some sibling sets are too small or fissiparous to serve as the basis of an effective cluster of their own. Whether a sibling set forms the core of a larger cluster or not depends, in the final analysis, not only on its size, but on the presence of an effective sibling leader, like Laiti, Panglima Tiring, or Salbangan, able to hold together a coalition of related house group leaders.

Within a sibling set, the position of the eldest is generally one of respect, both for brothers and sisters. The eldest of a sibling set is referred to by special terms of address.[4] Ordinarily, siblings maintain close relations, even if they live scattered through the village in non-allied house groups, as do, for example, Laiti and Alkisun. One of their number is usually acknowledged as sibling leader. This is often, al-though not always, the eldest brother. As in the case of his nephew Laiti, the career of Salbangan illustrates the significance of sibling leadership to the emergence of a village cluster. Like Laiti, Salbangan was not the eldest of his sibling set.

Umaldani was the eldest of Hajal's children. Salbayani was two years younger, while Salbangan was the third son. There were also two younger sons and three daughters, including Laiti's mother, Akbaraini. One of Akbaraini's sisters was married to Rugo-Rugo, a brother of Panglima Tiring, while the youngest son married Panglima Tiring's eldest daughter, Ettoman.

After his marriage, the second son, Salbayani, joined his wife's father's house group. Unexpectedly, while bearing a sixth child, Salbayani's wife died in childbirth. For the Bajau Laut this was perceived as a form of 'bad death' (*patai sabil*).

Salbayani was distraught and attempted several times to take his life. During the mourning period he had to be carefully watched by his kin and following his wife's burial, he refused to leave her graveside. Instead, he remained on the cemetery island for two nights before he would allow his own and his wife's kin to bring him back to the village. After this, the villagers say, his behaviour changed. Previously, he had been hard-working and a devoted father. He now became a gambler, with few friends. He seldom fished, but lived, instead, on the charity of his brothers and sisters. He was moody and given to bouts of violent temper. According to his sister, Akbaraini, even his appearance changed. He lost most of his hair, becoming almost totally bald.

In 1963, Salbayani remarried. His new wife was an older divorced woman, with children by a previous marriage. For a time, Salbayani appeared to have regained something of his former personality. With the help of his brothers and his wife's kin, he built a substantial house for his family in the small cluster formed by his new wife's father and brother at the seaward edge of the village. Soon, however, his behaviour became erratic again. When his children by his former wife complained of their stepmother's treatment, he beat them severely.

These beatings continued despite the open objections of other villagers, until his daughter fled to the house of her grandmother, Hajal. While I was living in the headman's house, Salbayani came to his mother's house on a number of occasions to take back his daughter. Each time, however, she ran away again. Finally, in taking back the girl, he flew into a particularly violent rage. As two of his sisters caught hold of the girl in order to hand her over to her father, Salbayani struck her several times with his fists, knocking her to the floor of the house. At this, Hajal, who until then, had not intervened despite the girl's pleadings, lost her temper. Tearing the girl out of her son's hands, she cursed him. As other villagers, drawn by the noise, gathered on the nearby landing-stages, Hajal ordered Salbayani to leave the girl and not come back to her house again. The girl subsequently became Hajal's foster-child.

By this time, the relatives of Salbayani's new wife had become alarmed. A few weeks later, they persuaded her to leave Salbayani, and she returned with her children to her father's house, which adjoined her husband's. However, she later returned to Salbayani. But after a series of quarrels, she again left him and rejoined her father's house group. Less than a week later, despite the strong objections of her father and brother, she once again returned to her husband.

Her return so outraged her brother that he and his family tore down their house and moved to the opposite, landward side of the village. Within a few days, he began to set down piles for a new house. When I met him on the main village bridge carrying planks, he told me that he had moved so that he would 'never have to look on Salbayani and his sister again'. Later, as his new house began to take shape, his father and his family also abandoned their house and joined him.

Following the departure of his brother-in-law and his family, Salbayani, whose behaviour many of the villagers now began to fear, quarrelled with the husband of his second oldest daughter. While her young husband was absent from the village, Salbayani forcibly removed the girl from her husband's boat where the couple lived and took her to his house. At the first opportunity, however, she ran away and rejoined her husband.

The second time this occurred, Salbayani began a search of the village, looking for the couple, armed with a knife. As he began his search, alarm spread through the village. People climbed on to the roofs of their houses or took refuge in their fishing boats. One man was cut slightly when he tried unsuccessfully to disarm Salbayani.

As this was happening at the seaward side, Salbangan, acting as sibling leader, quickly called a meeting of the rest of the sibling set at his house near the village centre. Even Umaldani attended, the seriousness of events overriding their enmity. All agreed that Salbayani had to be stopped. Backed by his sibling's support, Salbangan confronted his brother. Taking up a position at the centre of the main village walkway, armed with a steel-headed harpoon, Salbangan called to Salbayani and, as he approached, told him that he must stop his search and return home. Otherwise, Salbangan said, he would kill him. He also promised Salbayani that if he left the matter in their hands, his brothers and sisters would bring the question of his daughter's marriage before a village hearing. As the rest of the village looked on tensely, Salbayani finally agreed and, after arguing with his brother for a time, returned home.

After this incident, Salbayani's wife left him permanently, taking her own children with her. Salbayani then abandoned his house in what had been the cluster of his wife's kin and moved with his youngest son into the house of his father's sister and her husband, into which his eldest daughter Enna had married some years earlier.

In all, Salbayani's actions contributed to the breakup of one entire cluster; the dissolution of three house groups, including his own; and the reconstitution of another headed by his wife's brother and containing his second wife and her father. His actions had become so dangerous that, to forestall retaliation and possible blood-feud, only his siblings could intervene. From these events, Salbangan's ascent as principal sibling leader was affirmed through his decisive action in galvanizing his brothers and sisters; in subsequent years, he further consolidated this position.

True to his promise, Salbangan brought the marriage of Salbayani's daughter to a village hearing and succeeded in arranging for her divorce and remarriage. Several years later, Salbangan and Umaldani were re-conciled, following the death of Umaldani's wife, Bengani. Later, as a widowed elder, Umaldani himself became a cluster leader and an ally in the village affairs of both Salbangan and Panglima Tiring. After the opening of the Semporna district by road, Salbangan increasingly turned his energies to business ventures, particularly to fish-marketing and carrier trade, in doing so forming important business links outside the village. He and Panglima Tiring, now reconciled, reaffirmed their kin ties by arranging a marriage between their children.

While clusters may, potentially at least, be more enduring than house groups, their composition alters with each successive generation, as established house groups dissolve and as new ones are founded, and as relations between cluster allies become attenuated, or are ruptured as a result of death or contention. Additional changes occur, as illustrated by the history of Dessal's alignments, as individual house leaders reorient themselves around the *luma'* of dependable allies, and as new sibling leaders—men of wealth or forceful personality like Salbangan—who are able to attract and hold together a larger coalition of supporters emerge. Indeed, it can be said that clusters exist only as long as they contain an effective spokesman capable of holding together a coalition of house group elders and followers.

Village Leadership, *Addat*, and Litigation

In the past, when the Bajau Laut were entirely boat-dwelling, political leadership within each band was vested chiefly in its 'elders' or *matto'a*, comprising its senior generation of active family heads. With the development of village life, the *matto'a* have, if anything, increased their pre-eminence. Respect for seniority applies to unrelated villagers as well as to family members, kin, and cluster allies. Within the village, 'elders' include, most notably, senior house group leaders, family heads, and cluster spokesmen. The majority are elderly men, but senior women are also included. As a group, the *matto'a* are responsible for mediating disputes, safeguarding *addat*, and protecting the interests of their followers out of, it is said, a sense of 'love', 'compassion', or 'pity' (*ma'asé*). In return, respect for the elders is sanctioned by the concept of *busung* and a notion that after death, elders remain, as ancestors (*mbo'*), a continuing source of possible favour or reproach.

The village is also represented by a village headman (Ketua Kampung). The title is conferred by the government, through the Pegawai Daerah or District Officer, and the incumbent is directly accountable to the native chief with jurisdiction over the community. The headman represents, in formal terms, the primary link between the village and the district government. In 1979, the Ketua Kampung was chosen by community election from among the senior house leaders of the village, subject to ratification by the Pegawai Daerah and the district and native chiefs. Once chosen, the headman remains in office until death, removal for misconduct, or voluntary retirement. The headman of Bangau-Bangau in 1965, Panglima Tiring bin Hawani, has served as Ketua Kampung for over thirty years, since shortly after the village's founding. He succeeded the first government-appointed leader of the original Pasar Laut band, his wife's brother-in-law, Panglima Atani, following the latter's death. In 1979, the Ketua Kampung received a stipend of RM100 per month, paid quarterly, in compensation for the time he spent on official duties. In 1964–5, headmen were officially referred to as Orang Tua. Most, including Panglima Tiring, were unpaid, except when required to attend native court sessions. In 1979, because of the large size of Bangau-Bangau, Panglima Tiring was assisted by two unpaid assistant headmen (Wakil Ketua Kampung). Like the Panglima, both are also senior cluster spokesmen. Whenever the headman is absent from the village, one or the other assistant assumes his duties.[5]

The headman's position is largely an external creation. Within the village, such authority as the Ketua Kampung possesses is an extension of his status as a senior cluster spokesman and the representative of an exceptionally large and extended network of cognatic kin. As noted previously, political leadership within the village is exercised by senior house and cluster leaders and, as I have argued elsewhere (Sather, 1978), no separation can be sustained between domestic and politico-jural relations in this regard. Authority within the community is a function of domestic ties, and political support is marshalled and exercised within, and between, house groups and clusters. Village-level politics and domestic relations are, in this regard, inseparable.

Panglima Tiring was one of thirteen children. Five of his brothers head village house groups of their own, while a sister, Endemala, co-heads a sixth group. His wife's family is almost equally large, and three of Amjatul's brothers and one sister head four additional house groups. In addition, the Panglima and his wife have thirteen children. In 1965, two of their sons were also house leaders, while six other children were married into other house groups. Partly as a result of these ties, the headman is the spokesman of the largest house group cluster in the village. Together, he and his wife have close personal ties of kinship and affinity with individuals living in every other village cluster, and more than two-thirds of the individual house groups in the community. Thus his house occupies a central position within a wider network of inter-community relations. His chief duty is to maintain peace between house groups and clusters. His ability to do so clearly depends upon his domestic status and the extensive network of personal ties that he and his wife maintain with other house group and cluster elders. Like others, the headman is expected to be a man of good sense and experience. The villagers frequently express a conviction that every group—from the smallest fishing party to the entire village—requires a 'leader' (*nakura'*) who can 'reason' and so make decisions on behalf of his followers. The headman should possess intelligence, and when decisions are called for, his views should be well thought out and persuasive.

A major responsibility of the Ketua Kampung and other village elders is to safeguard the body of socially binding rules, canons of behaviour, and sanctions, described collectively as *addat*. Cognate notions, similar to the villager's concept of *addat*, are a widespread feature of socie-ties of the Malayo-Indonesian world. Such notions, particularly those of '*adat*' law, are the subject of a vast descriptive and interpretive litera-ture (Ter Haar, 1948; Hooker, 1972). In reference to Borneo, discus-sions of '*adat*' have assumed at times an almost mystical character. The classic example is Sharer's treatment of the Ngaju Dayak concept of *hadat*, which is described by Sharer as a 'divine cosmic order and harmony ... that rules the whole of life and thought, and all relations between man and the cosmos' (Sharer, 1963: 74–5). Implied in this view is a notion that any infraction of *hadat* disturbs this cosmic order and so creates a state of disequilibrium in man's relations with the rest of the universe. For the Bajau Laut, while compliance with *addat* is seen as having ramifications in terms of natural phenomena, health, and physical well-being, the actual applications of *addat* in village life are very different.

The most significant difference is that the Bajau Laut tend to think of *addat* in highly personalized terms. Each individual, in order to live at peace with other community members, must act according to the specific provisions of *addat*, as these relate, in different situations, to himself and others. In practical terms, the Bajau Laut see disagreements and dissension as an inevitable part of human affairs. Harmony, in the villagers' view, is not, by any means, the usual condition of existence. The presence of *addat*, however, makes reconciliation and the containment of dissension possible. Those who repeatedly breach the rules of *addat*, or refuse to submit to conciliation, endanger the social fabric and are believed to invite calamity (*busung*), both upon themselves and others. While actions contrary to *addat* are felt to be imperilling, what absorbs the interest of the villagers is not abstract notions of cosmic order, or equilibrium, but rather specific acts of wrongdoing; the individuals who commit and are affected by these acts; and, even more, the specific measures required to redress their effects and bring about reconciliation and repair of the social fabric. In this respect, every act of redress is seen as a triumph of *addat*.

Very generally, the term *addat* covers all the various norms, rules, and injunctions that guide an individual's conduct, and the sanctions and forms of redress by which these rules are upheld. Virtually every sphere of human activity has its own particular *addat*. Thus the villagers talk of marriage *addat*, the *addat* of greetings and leave-taking, mourning *addat*, and the *addat* of food sharing. Unlike many Borneo people, the Bajau Laut distinguish between *addat* and *ugama* (religion). The rules of ritual, prayer, and propitiation are all a matter of *ugama*, as distinct from *addat*. Although individual rules of *addat* may be believed to have a religious charter, and should, in all cases, be consistent with religious tenets, *addat* and *ugama* are, nevertheless, thought to refer to separate normative domains. The headman and other elders are the principal stewards of village *addat*, while the *imam*, whose role as ritual officiators is examined in Chapter 9, are looked upon as the chief stewards of *ugama* within the community. The rules of *addat* regulate interpersonal relationships and define the obligations that exist between persons standing in different relationships to one another. *Addat* also defines property rights, rules of inheritance, and the manner in which tangible goods may be transferred from one person to another. Like the English notion of 'custom', *addat* also describes personal habits. However, *addat* has a strongly normative connotation; its rules refer essentially to what an individual ought to do, not necessarily to what he or she does. In this sense, the Bajau Laut distinguish from *addat* social and personal conventions that lack a moral or normative basis. Such conventions are called *pantun*. The villagers often speak of individuals as possessing a personal *addat*. Reflecting its moral basis, such *addat* is frequently spoken of as 'good' (*ahap*) or 'bad' (*alaat*). To have 'good *addat*', implies that an individual's behaviour not only accords with specific rules of *addat*, but, more importantly, exemplifies more abstract moral ideals, such as generosity, sensitivity to duty, compassion, or responsiveness to the needs of others. Thus *addat* embodies more general moral values and provides a measure by which personal conduct may be judged in moral terms. Finally, while not all rules of *addat* are externally enforceable, where means of enforcement exist, and there are recognized sanctions for specific offences, these rules and the sanctions that enforce them are also included, and described by the villagers as part of the community's *addat*.

Every senior house leader is expected to have a knowledge of *addat*. He is expected, moreover, to use this knowledge in settling disputes between his followers and in upholding their interests in village litigation. The villagers say that most household quarrels are between women. While there appears to be some truth in this, perhaps because of the preponderance of related women among housemates and cluster allies, quarrels between men are often more serious and are likely to lead to house group dismemberment unless resolved. In the case of serious quarrels, cluster spokesmen and other elders may be called in to help find a settlement. Where disputes involve the members of other house groups, the leaders representing these groups may seek to work out an informal settlement between themselves, without referring the dispute to a higher level of leadership. Failing this, quarrels are referred to the village headman for settlement or, depending on their nature, are taken directly to district authorities.

Unlike other elders, the headman has the power to convene an informal meeting of the parties involved in a quarrel, or to call a more general village hearing in the event of a serious breach of *addat* or a dispute that threatens community peace. In the case of a minor dispute, the headman ordinarily invites the parties to his house for an informal, face-to-face meeting; each side is usually represented by its house leader. Most meetings are held at the request of an individual *nakura' luma'*, who also takes part in the discussions. The headman acts chiefly as an arbiter and public witness (*saksi'*) to any agreement reached by the parties. If the two sides cannot find an informal solution, and particularly if their families are divided by a long history of mutual grievances, or if the matter brought to the headman's attention is a serious one to begin with, the dispute is almost certain to be brought before a village hearing for litigation. The villagers distinguish between two types of hearings. The first is called *sinalassai*, or *magsalassai*, and is generally considered to involve less serious matters, usually quarrels, including marital disputes, insults, acts of disrespect, or personal grievances. The emphasis is usually upon reconciliation, and fines are not ordinarily levied. The second, called *maghukum*, generally involves more serious matters, where there is ordinarily a clear violation of *addat*, a more explicit attribution of wrongdoing, and, frequently, the imposition of a fine or the award of compensation. More generally, a breach of *addat* is called *sa'*, and redress, *kasa'an*.

All hearings take place in the evening in the house of the village headman or, if a large number of spectators and witnesses have gathered, on the headman's house platform. Anyone may attend, raise questions, and express an opinion, but the proceedings are normally dominated by house leaders and other *matto'a*, including the principal cluster spokesmen. The headman generally opens the hearing by stating that its purpose is to settle a dispute, or to hear a complaint. He then outlines the nature of the complaint and stresses that those taking part should seek to restore goodwill between the litigants and their kin. In this way, he calls attention to the purpose of the hearing and the overriding responsibility of everyone present to restore amicable relations between the parties involved. Hearings are sometimes heated, and it may be necessary for the headman to remind those voicing opinions of their responsibility to see that goodwill is re-established. The basic purpose of all hearings is described by the villagers as *magsulut*, meaning essentially mutual accord, or reconciliation. In order to achieve *magsulut*, settlements often call for mutual concessions by both parties.

The first hearing I attended in Bangau-Bangau well illustrates this point. The case involved two adolescent girls who came to blows after calling each other names. Ordinarily, the situation might have been ignored except that the girls' families became involved. In the course of their struggle, one girl claimed to have lost a bracelet; the other had an earring broken. The decision of the hearing was to require the family of each girl to restore the property of the other. The outcome was seen as a compromise in which each family came off more or less equal (*tabla'*).

Village hearings, as well as more informal mediation sessions conducted in the headman's house, deal most often with marital disputes. Before a couple are granted a divorce, they are usually called to an informal meeting with the village headman, who first attempts to bring about their reconciliation. A reconciliation that averts a divorce is called *amahilala'*, literally, 'putting matters to right'. If the headman and other elders taking part find either the husband or wife at fault, they may issue a warning called *batang-batang*. Such a warning indicates that if the guilty party persists, and the marriage ends in divorce, he or she is likely to suffer an adverse judgement in the subsequent settlement of marriage payments. If reconciliation proves impossible, and the marriage was formally registered, the couple are referred to the district *imam* to initiate a formal divorce. Usually there are no further legal proceedings unless there are difficult property issues that cannot be resolved directly by the couple's families. If such issues exist, the matter may be brought before a village *hukum* presided over by the headman, who acts as mediator and witness to any settlement the two sides conclude. Other frequent subjects of *maghukum* hearings include sexual delicts and elopement, disputes over debts, property loss or damage, and personal insult, slander, or acts of discourtesy. Verbal bickering is common, and sometimes results in accusations of insult or public discourtesy. Hearings may be called in order to bring about a public retraction of an insult, or an exchange of apologies. In the case of hearsay slander, or a charge that one person has secretly cursed (*panukna'*; *anukna'*) another, the accused may clear himself by swearing a public oath (*magsapah* or *anapah*) while touching the Koran in the presence of witnesses.[6]

After the headman has opened a hearing, litigants and witnesses are called upon to present the facts of the case as they see them. Once both sides have had an opportunity to present their evidence, and possibly answer questions posed by the headman and others, the session is opened to an exchange of views as to how the matter can best be resolved. The headman has little authority over those who are not members of his own house group, except by dint of personality and through his personal relations with the litigants and their kin. He cannot, in most situations, impose a judgement unless it is mutually acceptable to both sides. It is here that *addat* and the elders' knowledge of past settlements are likely to be of special importance. If a case can be linked to a specific rule of *addat*, as interpreted through past settlements of a similar nature, the correctness of a settlement is likely to be widely accepted, and it is difficult for either party to reject it out of hand. Moreover, should they do so, the other side has a strong case to refer to the native court, where the outcome is likely to be more punitive, since the court possesses the power of judgement and is less compelled to compromise. The concept of *busung* also enters as an important support of judicial process. Those who reject the verdict of a hearing, swear falsely, or break off proceedings before a settlement can be reached, are believed to lay themselves open to *busung*, in the form of sickness or ill-luck.

Litigation is relatively frequent. During the initial study period (1964–5), the headman called an average of one formal hearing and two or three informal meetings per month. Most house groups are involved in some form of litigation at least once a year.

The Bajau Laut consider themselves a peaceful people, particularly by comparison with the shore people living around them. Even so, in the case of a serious dispute there always exists a danger that the injured party will resort to self-help, or direct physical retaliation against the culprit or his family. Traditionally, physical retaliation was considered a legitimate form of redress in a number of offences, including adultery, sexual relations with unmarried women, physical injury, and homicide. Cases involving physical injury, including homicide, are now usually handled by the police and the state and district courts.[7] Minor accidental injuries are usually dealt with by a separate convention called *diat*. Traditionally, the threat of retaliation was limited by the acknowledged right of the headman and other community leaders to provide sanctuary to anyone involved in a dispute or accused of wrongdoing. The provision of sanctuary is still important, primarily in cases of elopement, or the abduction of a woman. By granting sanctuary, the offence for which the person is accused is automatically brought under judicial review, through mediation overseen by the headman, and potential retaliation or open feuding within the community is thereby forestalled, at least temporarily.

At present, the right of the headman to intervene in disputes in order to preclude self-help is supported by the state, but it is clear that the institution of sanctuary is one that has long existed among both sea- and shore-dwelling Bajau. Early colonial writers frequently wrote in condemnation of what they saw as the practice of Bajau leaders of providing shelter to fugitives from the law, commonly interpreting the practice as an expression of their collusion with outlaw elements.[8] While collusion may well have been involved in some instances, what these writers failed to understand was that the responsibility of providing sanctuary was an inherent obligation of leadership in Bajau society and formed a vital element in the operation of the traditional legal system. The institution was, and still is, an effective curb against possible violence among those who acknowledge the authority of a common leader. Those involved in a serious dispute may take temporary refuge in the headman's house. In doing so, they place themselves under the headman's protection. Any attempt to remove them by force becomes, in effect, an attack upon the headman and his supporters. The granting of sanctuary is said to be an expression of the headman's feelings of 'compassion' towards those whom he 'protects'. It does not necessarily imply his support for their actions. When the parties come together to settle their differences, the headman is expected to remain neutral. Essentially, the institution is meant to preclude feuding by placing the accused party under the protective care of a leader until the matter for which he is accused can be arbitrated peacefully or, failing a village settlement, can be referred to a higher level of authority for judgement.

Another means by which retaliation was traditionally averted was to pledge an item of inherited property (*pusaka'*), usually a gong (*agung*), to the injured man's family as a sign of good faith. The pledge was retained until the injured man showed signs of recovery and was then returned to its owners. Like the granting of sanctuary, the pledge secured a temporary assurance against resort to physical retaliation and signalled the intent of both sides to avert bloodshed.

While the headman can intervene and call disputants together to discuss their differences, a power sanctioned today by the state government, he cannot compel them to accept a judgement. He must rely instead on house and cluster leaders to secure their compliance with decisions reached through mediation or by informal discussions conducted in his house.

Diat and Blood-money

There are two forms of traditional indemnification in Bajau Laut society: (a) *diat*, paid as a token of solicitude in the case of a minor, usually unintentional, injury; and (b) *bangun*, blood-money, paid, if the dead man's kin are willing to accept it, in the case of homicide.

The Bajau Laut regard as serious any injury, however minor, that causes bloodshed. A powerful cultural aversion operates, and if one member of the village causes, or in some way is responsible for, a bleeding injury to another, the situation is considered of utmost seriousness and is handled directly by a formal convention known as *diniatan*. Most cases resolved in this way involve accidental injuries or those attributable to negligence. Common examples are when a person falls from the house platform belonging to another *nakura' luma'* or is injured by the collapse of a poorly maintained catwalk.

Diat is seen by the villagers as a symbolic token of concern. It consists of a small monetary indemnity, usually in the late 1960s and early 1970s of RM0.50–3.00, depending on the seriousness of the injury and the extent of culpability. Its actual value is considered less important than its symbolic intent as a sign of apology. The Bajau Laut also believe that its payment has a curative virtue; without it, the injury, it is said, will not heal properly. Payment of *diat* is called *diniatan*, or, less commonly, *mayad diat* ('to pay *diat*'). The individual responsible for causing the injury, or a parent or other house group elder in the case of a youngster, carries the *diat* to the house of the injured person, together with a large dish (*lai*) filled with water. The water is used by the person performing *diniatan* to wash the wound. While doing so, it is customary to recite a brief blessing, for example: *Murah-murahan kapahap bo' ka diniatan* [Hopefully, with this *diat*, may you soon recover]. The injured person must eat his meals from the dish for three consecutive evenings. If the injury is serious, the person responsible is expected to show his concern by regularly visiting the injured person during his recovery. On the fourth day, the dish is returned to its owner.

In most cases, the injury compensated by *diat* is minor. In a typical case, a young girl named Norija threw a bottle out of the window of her father's house just as a young married man, Binsali, passed by on the village walkway. The bottle struck him and opened a small cut on the side of his head. Norija's mother, on behalf of the house group, at once brought *diat* to Binsali's house. Another case, which occurred several years earlier, represents a somewhat more serious incident. This involved a gang of village boys who were playing at night. One boy, Algunda, threw a fish spear at a cat sitting on a stack of planks. The spear missed the cat, grazed off the planks, and went through an open window. Inside the house a youngster, Dandam Rindu, was sleeping on the floor and the spear pierced her ear. Not knowing this, Algunda jerked the spear back through the window. In doing so, he tore the child's earlobe. Her screams roused the house. The boys were quickly rounded up and made to confess to what had happened. In this case, the boys were clearly at fault, and their parents were also deemed to have been negligent for not supervising them more closely. Feelings ran high in the injured child's house group. As a special sign of penitence, *diat* was carried to the house by Algunda's father, accompanied by the other members of his house group. Parents of the other boys also showed their concern by visiting the girl and her parents during her recovery.

Ordinarily, *diniatan* concerns only the families of those directly involved. The headman intervenes only when these parties are from different villages. Such cases are unusual, but one occurred in 1964. It developed out of a stone-throwing fight between schoolboys, in which one was slightly injured, and was resolved through the intercession of the headmen of Bangau-Bangau and a second village, who acted as intermediaries in arranging the payment of *diat*. Under ordinary circumstances, *diniatan* is initiated by the person responsible for the injury, or by his house group. Its acceptance signals the willingness of the injured family to put the matter behind them and resume amicable relations. The primary purpose of giving and accepting *diat*, the villagers say, is the same as the goal of village hearings, namely *magsulut*, meaning 'conciliation' or 'putting aside differences'. *Diniatan* is usually concluded by a mutual exchange of vows.

Diat is paid only in the case of a non-fatal injury. Traditionally, a deliberate homicide was said to have required the taking of a life in retaliation. The aggrieved family was expected to take reprisal not only against the culprit, but also any member of his family who offered him support, shelter, or aided his escape. Bloodshed could only be averted, upon the agreement of the aggrieved family, by the payment of blood-money. It was here that a village leader might intercede, offering sanctuary until this payment could be negotiated. The act of payment is known as *binangunan*. In the past, blood-money was usually accepted only in the case of unintentional homicide, where there existed a close relationship between those involved, or when there were mitigating or justifiable circumstances. Today, all forms of homicide are referred to the police. Even so, in the case of deliberate homicide, there remains a strong feeling in favour of retaliation. This feeling is partly an expression of a principle, also reflected in litigation, that the resolution of conflict can come about only by re-establishing 'equality' between the parties involved. Neither side should be seen as having bested the other. Thus a murder should be repaid with the murderer's own life or, failing that, with the life of another member of his family who assisted him to escape.

An aborted attempt at blood-money payment occurred during my last fieldwork in Bangau-Bangau in 1979. The case began over a year earlier with the murder of a group of six men by pirates near Sitangkai in the Philippines. After the murders, the pirates, who were not Bajau Laut, scattered and went into hiding. The father of one of the men killed lived in Bangau-Bangau. After the bodies were found floating in the sea, he travelled to Sitangkai to identify his son. By the time they were found, the bodies were badly decomposed, and he was able to recognize his son only by the shape of his feet. After months of patient tracking, two of the pirates were located in Jolo, where they had joined the Philippine armed forces. They were ambushed and killed by brothers of the murdered men. While I was staying in Bangau-Bangau, the third, and last surviving, pirate appeared in Semporna, where he tried, through intermediaries, to arrange for payment of *bangun*. However, news of his appearance reached the police and he was arrested. The son of the state assemblyman paid his bail, presumably using part of the blood-money, and also, it was suspected, after receiving a bribe. The murderer was released and escaped once more to the Philippines. Despite this setback, the father vowed that he, or the others, would eventually get their revenge.

A village leader might traditionally intercede by granting sanctuary to a man who committed homicide until the payment of *bangun* could be negotiated, provided there were mitigating circumstances and that both parties were members of his community. If the murderer came from outside his village, or from another band, he was likely to join the victim's family in seeking retaliation. In the past, if the life of a Bajau Laut was taken by an outsider, the community generally looked to its patron for retaliation. The former mayor of Sitangkai, a Tausug politician who, during his rule, closely fitted the traditional role of a patron, told me that he took revenge on behalf of his Bajau Laut followers several times in the past. Generally, pirates are tolerated in Sitangkai provided they do not attack local people. An example he described concerned a pirate group that violated this rule and attacked a Bajau Laut family living in a small, isolated pile-shelter located half a kilometre from the main Sitangkai settlement. As the pirates approached the shelter by boat, one of the group threw in a grenade, which exploded killing everyone except for a young woman, who was thrown free by the blast. Although injured, and totally naked, she managed to swim to Sitangkai, unseen by the attackers. Here she identified the pirates, who were well-known locally. The mayor and a party of his armed retainers set out at once and apprehended the group just as they were reaching an outer island that served as their hide-out. The pirates were bound by the ankles with rope and dragged behind the mayor's boat back to Sitangkai. Upon arrival, all were found to be drowned and their bodies were placed on the bridge that spans the main Sitangkai canal. Here they were displayed for two days under armed guard, to prevent the men's families from recovering their bodies until they had begun to decompose. By taking such action, the mayor insisted, his Bajau Laut followers were seldom troubled as long as he was in office. Today, he claimed, the young educated man who took his place as mayor has no idea of how to 'protect' his people, with the result that Sitangkai is now, he claims, a far more dangerous place, with murders and robbery common, and seldom punished.

Enmity and Ritual Reconciliation

Not all dissension between village members is successfully resolved. Two persons may, as a result of a personal grievance, sever all contact including speech, by declaring themselves formal enemies (*bantah*) (see Chapter 7). Two examples have already been mentioned in the previous chapter, Panglima Tiring and his mother Kamsiniha, and the brothers Umaldani and Salbangan. Those who are *bantah* can only be reconciled by ritual means.

The rite by which formal enemies are reconciled is called *magkiparat*. Enmity, in general, is believed to be a source of *busung*. Consequently, friends and relatives of *bantah* are likely to try to persuade the two to undergo *magkiparat*. This is particularly true if one of them falls ill, appears close to death, or faces a situation of physical danger. For example, when Laiti's wife Tia became pregnant, she and Laiti's mother, Akbaraini, underwent a ritual reconciliation. The two women had earlier become *bantah* as a result of Akbaraini's opposition to Tia's marriage to her son. *Magkiparat* was performed in this case ostensibly to avert any possible complications that might arise in connection with Tia's pregnancy. It also reflected the desire of Laiti's parents to make it possible for Tia to deliver her child in their house. During the two women's enmity, Laiti and Tia had been forced to live in temporary quarters provided by the Public Works Department. Similarly, it is not uncommon for a village curer, in treating a patient, to ask that he or she seek reconciliation with all his or her *bantah* as a precondition for full recovery. Under such circumstances, the latter are almost certain to agree; otherwise, they may be held responsible, should the patient die, or fail to improve. Above all, the villagers say, an individual should not go to his grave unreconciled with his *bantah*; when a person appears to be near death, a determined effort is normally made to clear away, through *magkiparat*, all outstanding relations of enmity that may exist between the dying man or woman and other villagers.

In Bangau-Bangau, the rite of *magkiparat* is usually performed by the village headman. The two persons to be reconciled are made to sit side-by-side, facing westward (*kasoddopan*), in the direction assumed in prayer (*sambahayan*), while the headman stands behind them.[9] Each participant is required to provide a small number of coconuts. Holding one of these in his left hand, the headman splits it with a knife, opening the shell just enough for the water inside to run out. While pronouncing a prayer, the headman allows the water to flow over the heads of the pair seated at his feet. The empty coconut is placed on the house platform, where the rite is held, and split in two with a single sharp blow. The two halves of the coconut must turn the same way, either face upward or face downward. Otherwise, the procedure is repeated, using another coconut, until the required results are obtained.

As soon as the rite is over, the two are bathed, and then join the members of their families and other invited guests in public prayers (*magdua'a*) followed by a feast (*elotak*). Until the rite is concluded, the two are not permitted to speak to one another. The final act of resuming speech (*maghilling pabalik*) marks their resumption of normal relations, including social obligations as kin or neighbours, that they may have renounced during their enmity.

1. The numbering of house groups corresponds with Table 5.1.

2. In 1964–5, a small number of boat-living families still made Bangau-Bangau their home anchorage. The incorporation of boat-dwelling families thus continued to play a small part in the growth of village clusters. This role, however, had become a very minor one compared to house group partition. Between voyages, boat-living families generally tied their boats to a house platform belonging to village kin. Although I have not counted these families as house group or cluster members, they tended to be considered in every-day village relations as the followers of the particular house group and cluster leaders with whom they regularly moored. Others, however, moored separately and so continued to live in traditional family-alliance groups. These latter families remained highly mobile and were frequently absent from the village.

3. Chapter 8 examines how marriage is used as a way of consolidating these 'nodes'.

4. See Chapter 7.

5. As noted in Chapter 2, the former village of Bangau-Bangau has now been divided for administrative purposes into two communities, Bangau-Bangau and Sri Kanangan, each with a separate headman, assistant headmen, and village development committee.

6. A common oath formula is *Sapahanku embal hinangku pabalik* [I hereby swear (*sapah*) that I shall never do it again].

7. See the case of Erol in Chapter 8.

8. A number of these complaints can be found in the *British North Borneo Herald*.

9. See Chapter 3. The rite is held just after sunrise, in the early morning hours when the sun is near the opposite horizon.

7
Kinship

Magdindingan kita yuk samin betapa, saga bangka yukna abaya'na kello' ania' gi' ma kita suku' saga si'it ku saga usba'-waris ku. Anambungna misala si Mohamed Asara yukna missa' kata'uanku. . . . Bud lintik-lintikan, ma bud tinalitikan. Magsai yukna amaya'na maka runggu' parukla'na suku' saga si'itna pi'itu kam palua'na. . . . Magkawin kita . . . Sa'na buat napa'in, yukna panji na siga bangsa Malayikat nai. Bang pakayab panjina, panjina bang pakayab. Tabinggil antuhilas urabi Malayikat. Patenggé yukna panjina endawin gi' bansa Malayikat.

'If you wish to ask for my hand,' she says, 'you must call together my in-laws and my kinsmen and obtain their consent.' 'But I do not know them,' answered Mohamed Asara. . . . Now she arrives with her kin. You can recognize her by the trimmed and decorated eyebrows. By the dots along her brow. . . . So it is, he says, raise up the banners as a sign of respect to the race of angels. The flags wave, fluttering in the wind, the flags of the angels. (From *Suli-Suli Jin*, a traditional Bajau Laut *kata-kata* sung by mediums)

THE preceding chapters have described the main groups comprising village society—house groups and neighbourhood clusters—and the role of house and cluster leaders in resolving conflict, marshalling support among their followers, and in giving direction to a variety of common undertakings. Between housemates and cluster members, leadership and interpersonal relations of support are channelled primarily through ties of kinship and marriage. This chapter examines the nature of village kinship ties; the schema of social expectations that they embody; and the values that underlie them, particularly notions of reciprocity, debt, credit, and vow-taking. It also looks at the ritual mechanisms by which kin ties may be repudiated and, if severed, the ways in which kinsmen may re-assert them through ritual reconciliation.

Kinship

Kinship constitutes a fundamental idiom of Bajau Laut life. For every individual, kin ties come to the fore on occasions of crisis and special significance. The villagers turn to their kin for comfort in times of adversity, look to relatives for care when they are sick or infirm, and seek their support when they are involved in serious conflict and require reliable allies. Work relations are formed chiefly between kin and for most villagers, everyday life is spent largely in the company of relatives.

While kinship structures most areas of village life, every individual also has frequent dealings with non-kin, persons who are unrelated in a genealogical sense or by ties of marriage.

In Bangau-Bangau, all village members, whether related or not, are personally known to one another and meet often, both at sea and in the course of frequent village gatherings. The village itself is not a kin group and for any individual the community contains both kin and non-kin. Frequent occasions exist for non-kin to meet, and strong friendships regularly develop between village age-mates whether these persons are related or not. Such friendships typically begin in childhood and usually last throughout adult life. In childhood, most boys form an extensive network of friends. Girls are more restricted in their contacts, but they, too, tend to form strong personal friendships while young. At low tide, girls organize parties of 'companions' (séhé'), much like the fishing parties formed by boys, to collect crabs and shellfish. At her wedding, a woman's former girlfriends attend to her, help her to dress, and entertain her during the period of seclusion that immediately precedes the wedding. Occasionally, in order to strengthen a bond of friendship, young men may swear ritual 'blood friendship' by *maginum laha'*, literally 'drinking blood', thereby pledging to come to one another's aid in the future, regardless of circumstances or personal risks.[1]

After marriage, a man's concerns are expected to turn increasingly to his own and his wife's kin, and for most villagers friendships formed in childhood tend to recede in importance. Nevertheless, friends frequently exchange evening visits and are expected to attend the circumcisions, weddings, and other ceremonies held on behalf of one another's children. As a final expression of affection, friends, both men and women, are expected to attend each other's death and memorial rites.

The significance of friendship was demonstrated two months after I arrived in Bangau-Bangau in 1964, when Panglima Tiring's lifelong friend Luma'ang died.

At the approach of death, the headman was one of the first persons to be notified. He contributed a major share to the funeral expenses and helped supervise the bathing and shrouding of his friend's body. He also went aboard the boat that carried Luma'ang's body to the cemetery, an act reserved for closest friends and the immediate family of the deceased, and he and another friend, Muljarani, assisted with Luma'ang's burial. Muljarani, like the headman, is an elderly cluster leader. At the graveside, Muljarani recited the main graveside prayers (*dua'a tulkin*) and conducted the *addat* invocation for the dead man's soul.

Both men were genuinely grieved by their friend's death. Panglima Tiring told me afterwards, as we returned to the village, that it had been especially important for him to take a part in Luma'ang's funeral. This, he explained, was not only because of their friendship but also because Luma'ang belonged to an older generation that had now all but passed away. All of Luma'ang's close relatives, including his brothers and sisters, were already dead, so that no one but his friends remained to grieve for him and see that he was properly mourned.

As Panglima Tiring stressed, friends should remain loyal, even taking the place of kin, if need be, as he and Muljarani had done in mourning Luma'ang. The ideal friend is like a close relative in the sense that his support can always be counted on. But friends are allies by choice. In this sense, friendship is as important between kin as it is between unrelated persons. Consequently, when men are both friends and kinsmen, they tend to stress their friendship first, as a way of emphasizing the genuineness of their concern and personal regard for one another.

Despite the significance of friendship, an individual's most important and frequent relations are normally with kin. Kinship is traced bilaterally by the Bajau Laut and, in formal terms, equal importance attaches to relations between an individual's father's and mother's kin. In practice, however, a person's circle of active relatives generally contains a greater number of his or her mother's kin because couples more often reside among the latter, rather than among the husband's kin. Residence thus acts as a prime determinate of effective kin relations, and active co-operation tends to be channelled mainly through kin relations traced between women.

The significance of this is important in terms of the form such co-operation takes. In everyday village life, its principal form is food sharing, child care, and housekeeping. Here women are the principal transacting parties. For men, ties of co-operation, while involving housemates and cluster allies, are likely to extend beyond these groups in the form, for example, of fishing partnerships and wider village relations of jural support. In this respect, marriage is important as a form of social partnership, because of the different and essentially complementary ways in which men and women employ kin ties in relations of work, leadership, and support.

Kampung

Collectively, all known or presumed kin of an individual are termed *kampung*. The term refers to all persons to whom an individual acknowledges a cognatic relationship, whether the precise nature of this relationship can be traced or not. A strong assumption exists that those who live close together are related to one another, so that the term is frequently extended to neighbours as well. It is common for people to say, *itui saga kampungku*, 'all those hereabout are my *kampung*', or *dakampung kami*, 'we are all of one *kampung*'. There are no genealogical limits beyond which cognates are no longer counted as *kampung*; the boundaries of the category are indefinite and vary from person to person. Few villagers, however, know the identity of all of their second cousins, and third cousins constitute, for most, the collateral limits of those whom they regularly acknowledge as *kampung*.[2]

An individual's *kampung* thus comprises a personal field of kin which no two individuals, even full siblings, entirely share. Ego's *kampung* might best be described as his or her 'cognatic kin of recognition' (Peranio,

1961: 95). Within this field, relations are traced equally through males and females. Affines are excluded unless they are also related as cognatic kin. Collectively, affines are referred to as *pikit-mamikit*. All persons who are not considered *kampung*, that is to whom no form of relationship is thought to exist, however distant, are referred to as *a'a saddi*, literally 'other people', hence non-kin.

While the term *kampung* refers to all of an individual's known or presumed cognatic kin, in practice the term is usually applied only to those who are regarded as 'distant' (*magta'ah*). Those who are 'close' (*magsékot*), while counted as *kampung*, are, in practice, placed in a number of more finely discriminating categories, such as 'mother', 'father', 'sibling', and so on. The term *kampung* is seldom applied to cognates within the collateral range of first cousins (*kaki mentedda'*). In the case of 'distant kin', precise genealogical connections frequently cannot be traced. Often individuals count each other as *kampung* simply because their parents considered each other cognates. Such relations have very little social significance. Sometimes they are noted with favour when marriages are contemplated or families take part in common social gatherings. Otherwise, there are no specific obligations that *kampung* have toward one another, either as individuals, or collectively. There is a feeling, however, that *kampung* should not be treated as total strangers. In the case of sea voyaging, or in paying visits to other settlements, distant kinship often serves as the foundation for friendship and hospitality. The villagers say a person will generally find it easier to establish social contacts with distant kin, should the need arise, than with 'other people'.

Dampo'onan

Between kin, numerous descent lines, called *turunan*, are recognized, leading back to particular ancestors (*mbo'*). However, recognition of ancestry is generally shallow, and is rarely reckoned beyond four or five generations. However, when collateral branches are added, acknowledged cognatic connections ramify widely, and the number of persons to whom an individual can potentially trace some form of relationship is often great. For the Bajau Laut, the significance of descent lines is that they provide the means by which genealogical relationships can be traced and individuals may be placed in more specific classes of relationship.

All descendants, through both males and females, of an individual's two sets of grandparents constitute a narrower category of cognatic kin called *dampo'onan* or *dampalanakan*. In Bangau-Bangau, the two terms are used interchangeably. Informants say that the term *dampalanakan* describes a set of 'descendants' (*anak*) traced from grandparents to 'grandchildren' (*empu*). The term *dampo'onan* derives from the root word *po'on*, meaning 'tree', 'stem', 'origin', or 'source'. Here the analogy, a familiar one in the Austronesian world (Fox, 1971), is with the trunk or central stem of a tree. In contrast to *kampung*, a person's *dampo'onan* (or *dampalanakan*) are regarded as genealogically 'close'.

Dampo'onan thus defines a limited subset of cognatic kin; its limits are fixed by reference to one or another of an individual's known ancestors. Essentially one's *dampo'onan* consists of the two stocks formed by an individual's grandparents. By 'stock' is meant, following Radcliffe-Brown (1950: 22), 'all the descendants of a man and his wife counting descent through females as well as males'. Specifically, *dampo'onan* comprise an individual's four grandparents and all their descendants down to Ego's own generation: Ego's parents, parents' siblings, his or her own siblings, and first cousins. There are variations in individual usage, however, and additional kin may also be included, provided their ancestry can be traced and they are considered 'close' in social terms. Moreover, the term for grandparents (*mbo'*) may be used in a classificatory sense to include further ascendants, for example, great-grandparents and the immediate collaterals of Ego's lineal grandparents, whether living or dead. As a consequence, the category may include, for particular individuals, more distant kin, so long as they are able to trace their connection through *turunan* lines to common 'ancestors'.

Although descent provides the basis for recognition of *dampo'onan* relationships, it is the collateral axis of relationships that is most important in terms of everyday social interaction, aid, leadership, and cooperation. Among the most active generation of village members, aid is characteristically given, fishing partnerships are formed, and support is sought between collateral kin of the same generation, especially siblings and their spouses, rather than lineal kin of different generations. Except for parents and children, transgenerational ties are far less significant than those between persons of the same generation.

Dampo'onan relations are, at once, both Ego-centric and ancestor-delimited. Consequently, their composition and significance alters in the course of the lifetime of the individual from whose perspective they are defined. As an individual enters the grandparental generation, kin of his own and antecedent generations are reduced in number through death, and so his own *dampo'onan* recedes in importance, with elderly relatives becoming, more importantly, the points of departure for new *dampo'onan* recognized by their descendants. Hence, the significance of *dampo'onan* ties varies as one enters and eventually passes beyond the most active generation or village cohort.

The recognition of *dampo'onan* ties throws light—in much the same way as does the presence of 'extended family' domestic groups—on the role which descent may play in a bilateral society like that of the Bajau Laut, which lacks descent groups and is essentially non-lineal in its constitution. In this regard, the tracing of descent lines provides a way in which kin can be identified and the schema of social obligations between them maintained, or brought into play, provided the individuals involved choose to recognize and implement these ties. Sometimes, elderly relatives are consulted for genealogical information, and when strangers meet, they often question one other in order to find a common ancestor by way of tracing their *turunan* lines.

Dessal's son Laiti described an experience which illustrates this process at work.

One afternoon, a family of strangers arrived in Bangau-Bangau from Sitangkai. They were looking for relatives in the village. The husband walked along the village walkway, while his wife and children stayed in his boat, which was tied to the walkway pilings. I hailed him and invited him to my house platform. He was a bit shy to question people directly. But as we talked, he outlined his own ancestry and questioned me about mine. He also asked about my wife Tia, who was born in Sitangkai. He asked about her parents, her parents' brothers and sisters, and her grandparents, and discovered that he and Tia had the same great-grandfather, Si Go'oh. He exclaimed, 'We (your wife and I) are *dampo'onan*!', and was very pleased. After this, I invited his family to my house, and now, every time they visit Bangau-Bangau, they stay with us, and Tia and I treat them as close kin.

Ordinarily, *dampo'onan* ties are not traced back as far as this, as the names of distant ancestors tend to be forgotten in time, particularly when their descendants live in different villages or, in the past, when they identified themselves with different boat anchorage groups. Even the names of grandparents who have been dead for a number of years may be forgotten unless their descendants have reason to maintain close ties with one another. It is interesting to note that Laiti himself is also descended from Go'oh. However, he only learned of this later, when his brother Alkisun worked out, with the help of his grandmother, his own and his brothers' genealogies, after I had questioned them about their ancestry. Previously, Laiti and Tia had reckoned their relationship as second cousins (*kaki mendua*) by way of another line of ascent. The villagers say that by tracing *turunan* they are able to avoid 'losing' their *dampo'onan*, and if they are 'lost', of rediscovering them, as Laiti and Alkisun did when they re-established their genealogical connection with Go'oh, and so with his living descendants, including the family of Sitangkai visitors.

Generally, in following lines of ascent, persons seek to discover an ancestor, or set of ancestors, they share in common. Occasionally, collateral branches are used when the names of common ancestors have been forgotten, or exact relationships can no longer be remembered. Such links establish *kampung* ties. For *dampo'onan* relations, knowledge of genealogical ties makes it possible to place individuals in more specific classes of relationship.

Tai'anakan

Within each individual's *dampo'onan*, primary kin are distinguished as *tai'anakan*. The category includes an individual's parents, his brothers and sisters, and his own children. The category therefore distinguishes, for the Bajau Laut, the most intimate of all kinship ties.

Kinship Terminology

All kin are placed in a limited set of terminological categories defined primarily by sex, generation, and collateral distance. Specific expectations attach to each of these categories, which, in total, provide Ego with a guide to the behaviour expected in most person-to-person relations with kin.

Consanguineal Terms

The classification of kin is bilateral; primary kin are distinguished terminologically from all others, and relationships are structured chiefly by generation.[3]

Ego's primary kin (*tai'anakan*) are set apart by separate terms: father (*mma'*); mother (*enngo'*); siblings (*denakan*); and child (*anak*). Siblings are most often referred to by terms that indicate relative age: elder sibling (*siaka*) and younger sibling (*siali*). Gender is not distinguished. The eldest of a sibling set may be referred to as *siaka to'ongan* ('true eldest sibling'), the youngest as *siali to'ongan* ('true youngest sibling'). Half-siblings with the same father but different mothers are referred to as *denakan magdabohé'* ('siblings of one semen'), while those of the same mother but different fathers, as *denakan magduabohé'* ('siblings of two semen'). Children are referred to either as *anak* or *ondé*. *Ondé* may be used for children generally, while *anak* denotes the existence of a specific genealogical relationship, that of biological offspring. Nursing infants are called *anak duru'an* ('breast children'). The eldest or first-born child is called *anak siaka*; the youngest, or last-born, *anak kabungsuan*, and birth order may be specified by the use of numerical terms.

Kinship terminology is basically of an Eskimo type (Murdock, 1949: 228). Outside primary kin, all cognates are designated by six basic terms: grandparents, their lineal ascendants and collaterals (*mbo'*); parents' siblings and collaterals of their generation, male (*bapa'*) and female (*babu'*); cousins (*kaki*); children of siblings and cousins (*kamanakan*); and own grandchildren and children of *kamanakan* (*empu*) (Figure 7.1).

The term for grandparents (*mbo'*) is extended to the siblings and cousins of lineal grandparents as far as relations can be traced and to further ascending generations, that is, great- and great-great-grandparents. The terms *koktu'ut* ('knee') and *kéngkéng* ('little toe') may be used to indicate generations removed from Ego in the case of both grandparents and grandchildren. Thus *mbo' koktu'ut* refers to great-grandparents and *mbo' kéngkéng* to great-great-grandparents. These terms are rarely used in practice and when they are, they are generally reserved for lineal ancestors or descendants. In the second descending generation, the term for grandchild (*empu*) is similarly extended to all collaterals and descendants as far as relationships can be traced.

All cousins, whether cross or parallel, patrilateral or matrilateral, are designated by a single term, *kaki*. Degrees of collaterality may be specified by the use of numerical terms, that is, *mentedda'*, *mendua*, *mentellu'*, literally 'once', 'twice', 'thrice', and so on. Third cousins (*kaki mentellu'*) are regarded as 'distant kin' (*kampung*) and tend to form the limit to which collateral ties are normally traced. The children of cousins are called *kamanakan kaki*. If they are close to the same age as Ego, they are treated as cousins, rather than as nephews or nieces. The terminology facilitates this shift and reflects the fact that age and generation may be out of phase. Thus an individual may marry a *kamanakan kaki* of the same age, despite their being of different generations. The marriage of Dessal's youngest son, Lunta, and Bunga Rampai, a daughter of Gilang,

FIGURE 7.1

Bajau Laut Kinship Terminology: Terms of Reference

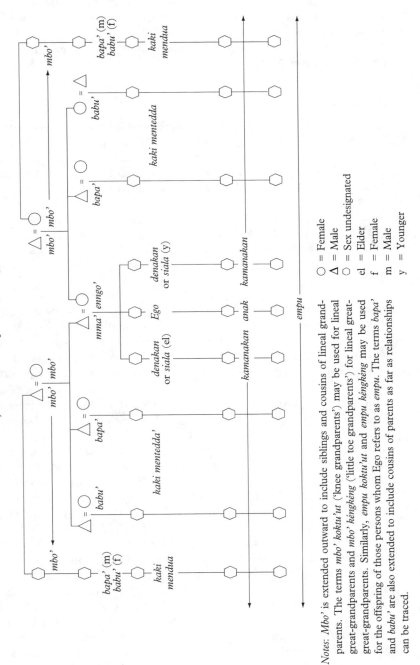

Notes: Mbo' is extended outward to include siblings and cousins of lineal grandparents. The terms *mbo' koktu'ut* ('knee grandparents') may be used for lineal great-grandparents and *mbo' kéngkéng* ('little toe grandparents') for lineal great-great-grandparents. Similarly, *empu koktu'ut* and *empu kéngkéng* may be used for the offspring of those persons whom Ego refers to as *empu*. The terms *bapa'* and *babu'* are also extended to include cousins of parents as far as relationships can be traced.

described in Chapter 5, is an example. Such marriages are not uncommon. Once they occur, and a corresponding adjustment in kinship terminology is made, age and generation among collateral kin and their descendants are brought back into alignment in successive generations. While there is a general avoidance of intergenerational marriage, this avoidance, except for parents' siblings and their children, does not prevent such marriages from being concluded, and when they are, from being accommodated by a terminological shift.

The sex of any relative may be specified by the addition of *lella* ('male') and *denda* ('female').

Affinal Terms

Affines are referred to collectively as *pikit-mamikit* and are never merged terminologically with cognates. *Pikit* means, literally, to stick, join together, or adhere. To be related by marriage is *magpikit-pikitan* or *pamikitan*. The general categories *kampung*, *dampo'onan*, and *tai'anakan* include, as a rule, only cognates. A separate set of reference terms exists for affines; the same terms are never used for both one's own and one's spouse's cognates. In this, terminology reflects social behaviour.

The principal affinal terms are seven in number: parents-in-law (*mato'a*); sibling-in-law (*ipal*); spouse of siblings (*bilas*); child-in-law (*ayuwan*); husband (*hella*); wife (*handa*); and co-parents-in-law (*ba'i*) (Figure 7.2).

Affinal terms, except for those used between spouses and between their parents are extended to spouse's relatives. All cognates of Ego's spouse in the first, second, and further ascending generations, regardless of their sex or degree of collaterality, are referred to as *mato'a*. However, if such persons are also related as cognatic kin, they are included in the appropriate kin category for cognates. Given the preference for endogamous marriage, this is frequently possible. As a result, the number of affinal relatives recognized is kept to a minimum. In one's own generation, the term *ipal* is used for both spouses of one's siblings and cousins and the siblings and cousins of one's spouse. The term *ayuwan* is used as a reciprocal of *mato'a* to refer to the spouses of Ego's children as well as to the spouses of all of those cognates whom Ego refers to as *kamanakan* and *empu*. Additional terms may be used in the case of *ayuwan* and *ipal* to specify exact genealogical relationships. A spouse of one's grandchildren, for example, is referred to, more specifically, as *ayuwan menempuan*.

The spouses of siblings refer to each other as *bilas*. The relationship between them (*magbilas*), particularly those of the same sex, is a socially important one in that *bilas* are frequently housemates or live in neighbouring house groups, as cluster allies. As a term of address, *bilas* is often used reciprocally between unrelated friends or distant kin to connote a relationship of familiarity and reciprocal support.

Tili' is used as a descriptive marker to designate step-relations. A stepchild, for example, is referred to as *anak tili'*; a stepmother as *enngo' tili'*; and a stepfather as *mma tili'*. Stepchildren are also referred to as *anak benoa*. *Benoa* (or *amoa*) means literally 'bring with' or 'carry'.

FIGURE 7.2
Bajau Laut Kinship Terminology: Affinal Terms

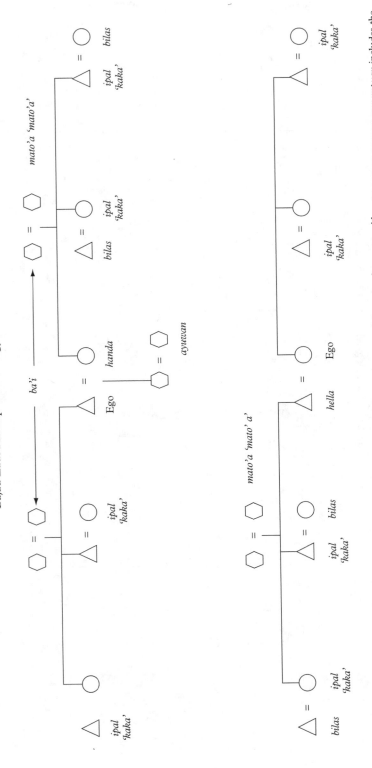

Notes: Quotation marks indicate terms of address. Where none exist, personal names or nicknames are used. *Mato'a* is extended to include siblings and parents of the spouse's parents. Also *ayuwan* or *ayuwan menempuan* includes the spouses of grandchildren and *ipal* or *ipal menkakian* the spouses of cousins.

224

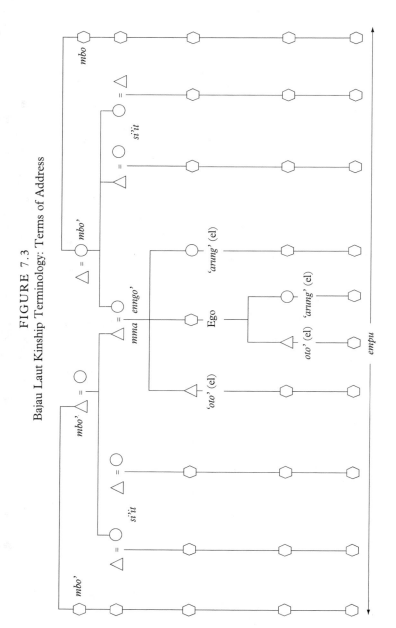

FIGURE 7.3
Bajau Laut Kinship Terminology: Terms of Address

Notes: Where no terms are listed, personal names or nicknames are used.
(el) = elder

Terms of Address

Terms of address are limited and reflect generation, relative age, and respect: grandparents and elders generally, including house group and village leaders (*mbo'*); father (*mma'*); mother (*enngo'*); parents-in-law (*mato'a*); parents' siblings (*si'it*); eldest son or eldest brother (*oto'*); and eldest daughter or eldest sister (*arung*) (Figure 7.3).

The terms *oto'* and *arung* are particularly important. Parents use the terms to address their eldest son and daughter, respectively, and they are also used by siblings for the eldest brother and sister of a sibling set. The position of the eldest sibling is a socially significant one, with the eldest brother or sister generally expected to act on behalf of the younger members of the set as sibling leaders. *Oto'* and *arung* are also used as general terms of respect for those of the same or younger generations. During weddings, the bride and groom are addressed, respectively, as 'Si Arung' and 'Si Oto' by their kin, as terms of special respect.

Where address terms are lacking, personal names (*on*), or nicknames (*danglai*) are used, preceded, in formal address, by a vocative marker, *si*. In general, members of senior generations, particularly parents-in-law, are not, out of respect, addressed by personal names.[4] There is, however, no formal name avoidance.

Dyadic Relations

There are no corporate kin groups in Bajau Laut society comparable to clans and lineages. However, *dampo'onan* relations and ties between primary kin form, within each local community, the relational core of both house groups and neighbourhood clusters. The significance of these groups is that they impose a form of 'closure' upon each couple's meshwork of interpersonal relationships. By living together, housemates and cluster allies are singled out for participation in daily transactions based on long-term expectations of reciprocal support, as sanctioned by moral values, and upheld by the authority of house and cluster spokesmen (Sather, 1976).

While neither the house group nor the cluster coincides entirely with Ego-centric categories of 'close' kin, ties outside these groups are only selectively recognized, and may at times be ignored. In contrast, relations between house group and *ba'anan* members are constantly evoked. Support can be withheld only by renouncing house group or cluster membership. By combining kinship, marriage, and residential association, stable groupings of supporters are created, coalescing around individual leaders. As a result, the categories by which the Bajau Laut conceptually order their cognatic and affinal relations reflect not only individual social behaviour, but also provide a framework of ties around which cohesive groups emerge, if only temporarily.

Parent–Child Relations

The relationship that exists between parents and children is said to be the closest and most intense of all dyadic bonds. The Bajau Laut describe the relationship in terms of *kalasaan*, a state of selfless, devoted love. The villagers say that in no other relationship does one experience the same sense of unquestioning love as exists between parents and children. While married couples, and brothers and sisters, ideally love one another, their love (*lasa*) is conditioned by practical responsibilities. The love that parents feel for their children—and children for their parents— is, by comparison, unconditional and total. No one is more pitied than orphans, or those who are childless, or have lost their children in infancy, for it is said that the love which such persons have been deprived of can never be regained or found in any other relationship.

As small children (*ondê*), infants receive almost constant attention; are addressed by special terms of affection, or pet names (*senangbai*), and enjoy close physical contact with their parents. Until the age of four or five, they normally sleep on the same mat as their parents. If they cry or are fretful, they are generally suckled or held by their mother. The Bajau Laut value the open expression of feelings, and both fathers and mothers frequently fondle and caress their children. During these early years, the pleasure of intimate physical contact appears to be a significant part of the relationship that develops between parents and children. As a sign of affection, a child is often stroked on its back, shoulders, and the top of its head. Affection is often expressed in this way even when the youngsters are grown, for example, when parents and children meet after a long separation.

As soon as they begin to walk, children are taught to swim. They are held in the water by their parents, who support them with their hands, while encouraging them to paddle and kick with their arms and legs. Instruction continues until children reach the age of three or four. By then they are usually adept in the water and begin to join other children swimming around the platforms and catwalks at high tide. Still, young children must be watched to keep them from falling into the water and drowning. Parents with youngsters who are able to crawl or just beginning to toddle usually fence off the open bow and stern sections of their boats, or nail boards across the lower half of the doorway to their houses, to prevent infants from wandering into danger.

When children are about five or six years old, physical expressions of affection become rarer and much of their daily supervision is entrusted to an adolescent daughter or niece. By this time, children are expected to perform a variety of minor chores around the house or in the family boat. They are also taught to obey their parents and show respect towards elders. Discipline is extremely mild, however. One of the few cases of suicide in the community, which is said to have occurred in Sitangkai a number of years before I began fieldwork, involved a father who, in anger, struck his young son on the back. The boy went to the stern of the family boat, lay down and apparently fell asleep. A short time later, the father discovered that he was dead. Grief-stricken, the man went berserk (*magsabil*) and, before he could be restrained, took his own life. Physical punishment is unusual, and parents normally rely on scolding or verbal threats to make children obey.

By adolescence, boys enjoy considerable freedom of movement. They usually play in groups of boys of the same age. At the same time, they are encouraged to involve themselves in the work of the family at sea. By seven or eight, most boys begin to accumulate their own fishing gear and by their early or mid-teens are usually of considerable help to their father. Girls are expected to stay closer to home and are usually restricted in their companions to girls of their own and neighbouring house groups. They spend much of their time in the company of their mother and sisters, from whom they generally learn to cook, sew, mend clothing, and keep house. In multifamily house groups, most of a girl's instruction takes place within her immediate family.

Birth order is important to the kinds of relationships children develop with one another. As noted, special terms of address are used for eldest son and daughter by both parents and younger siblings. The position of the eldest entails special responsibilities. The eldest daughter is expected to look after her younger brothers and sisters, to feed them at times, change their clothing, and watch over them while they are at play. The eldest son is expected to protect his younger brothers from being bullied, and later to safeguard the reputation of his sisters.

Siblings

Relative age and respect for seniority are also stressed in sibling relationships. Ideally, love should also be present. Special terms of endearment are used for younger children by other members of the family. On the other hand, elder siblings should be shown respect. Later—as they are the first to marry and become active house leaders—older siblings are normally looked to as spokesmen by their younger brothers and sisters. One sibling is acknowledged as their principal leader; this is usually, but not always, the eldest brother. His house typically serves as a common meeting place. Here siblings gather to discuss matters of mutual concern, such as marriage plans, house-building, or the financial arrangements for weddings and other house group undertakings. An older brother or sister usually attempts to settle differences between younger siblings and to foster close support within the group. Ties are strongest, as a rule, between siblings who live in house groups within the same cluster. When several brothers and sisters live close together, in the same *ba'anan*, the individual who acts as sibling leader is generally also the principal spokesman for the cluster as a whole. This can be seen in the case of Laiti, Dessal's son, whose emergence as a cluster leader was discussed in Chapter 6. In the course of the partition of his father's house group, Laiti emerged as the leader of a cluster that contains, in addition to his parents, his younger brother and two younger sisters and their families. To this group, Laiti has also added his wife's younger brother, their mother, and several other unmarried brothers and sisters. He has thus attracted to the group a large part of his wife's sibling set as well as part of his own.

In practice, the eldest brother does not always emerge as the leader of his sibling set, nor is he always the spokesman for the cluster in which his other brothers and sisters live. Laiti's eldest brother, Karim, married into Sitangkai, where he now heads a house group that is part of a cluster made up chiefly of his wife's kin. His second brother, Alkisun, also married out and built a house in another part of Bangau-Bangau, in a cluster headed by his wife's father. However, he remains close and is a frequent visitor to the houses of his father and brother. As a reflection of their closeness, Alkisun and Laiti sometimes joke about the fact that they have both married wives with the same name (Albitia).

Because of the prevalence of uxorilocal residence, brothers, as for example, Karim and Alkisun, are frequently dispersed among their wive's kin. As a result, a sibling leader may, as in Laiti's case, be a younger brother. He may even live separately from his other brothers and sisters. Salbangan, who married the daughter of his father's brother, Selangani, left the cluster of his brothers and sisters to join his father-in-law's house group. Later, Salbangan succeeded his father-in-law as house and cluster leader, becoming in the process the acknowledged leader of his sibling set. His rise to sibling leadership was marked by the withdrawal of his eldest brother Umaldani from the cluster containing their mother and married sisters. Shortly afterwards, as cluster boundaries were redrawn, Salbangan emerged as principal cluster spokesman for a *ba'anan* allied to, but separate from, the cluster occupied by most of his other brothers and sisters. None the less, his house, like that of Laiti's, remains a common gathering place, even though it is located within a different cluster from those of his siblings.

Some groups of siblings lack an effective leader, while others are too small or too dispersed to form a viable house cluster or smaller alliance unit on their own.

Sibling ties are characterized by close solidarity, tempered in the case of elder brothers and sisters, with respect. Relative age is noted even in the case of twins (*kambal*). The Bajau Laut consider the first-born of a pair of twins to be the younger (*siali*) and the second to be the elder sibling (*siaka*). This is because younger children, out of respect, are expected to walk in front of their elders, and so, by analogy, are thought to precede their elders out of the womb. Older siblings are expected to look after their younger brothers and sisters. Once Laiti was explaining how, as a very small child, he almost drowned.

My two older brothers, Karim and Alkisun, and I were the only children in our family at the time, except for a sister who later died in childhood. Our father was using *tuba* poison and everyone was in the water collecting fish. I was the only one left in the boat. I must have leaned over the side to watch what was going on and fell (overboard) unnoticed by the others. My brothers say when I was discovered missing, the family began to search, and I was found by Karim in the water beneath the boat, nearly drowned. I was much too small to remember anything of what happened myself.

At this, I turned to Karim, who was sitting next to us and I asked whether he remembered this incident. He answered immediately, 'Yes, of course, I remember it all. I was the eldest. The eldest must always look after the younger children in the family.' The incident clearly helped to create a strong bond between the two brothers. Had Laiti died, his older brothers, and particularly Karim, would have failed in their responsibility. By acting quickly, Karim had not only saved his brother's life, but had made up for his momentary inattentiveness. Even more than thirty years later, a sense of relief was still evident in Karim's answer.

Should their parents die, married siblings may be expected to take their place, caring for their younger brothers and sisters until the latter are able to marry and establish families of their own. Similarly, should they themselves die prematurely, a brother or sister may be expected to look after their children.

The position of the youngest or last-born child is, like that of the eldest, unique. The youngest in a sibling set is referred to as the *anak kabungsuan*. The villagers say that it is usually the parents' favourite. It is often nursed longer than its brothers and sisters and tends to be treated with greater indulgence by the other members of the family. The youngest, particularly the youngest daughter, is the child most likely to remain in the parental house after the rest have left, and so normally assumes primary responsibility for the elderly couple's care.

At their parents' death, children are expected to withdraw totally from everyday affairs for one or two days and observe a period of complete mourning. Before the body of a parent is shrouded for burial, children are called forward one at a time to kiss the forehead as a final sign of their *lasa*.

From childhood, brothers and sisters are expected to stand as one in quarrels with 'other people'. They are expected to confide in one another and take each other's side in village litigation, whether or not they are housemates or live in the same cluster. Brothers and sisters should love each other, but their relationship is seen, above all, as one of *tabang* or 'help'. During childbirth and recovery, sisters have customary responsibilities to attend the new mother. Brothers and sisters should visit each other in times of sickness and bereavement, come to each other's aid financially, and attend the rituals that the others sponsor. In sum, brothers and sisters represent each individual's first line of call in times of need.

An illustration of the strength of sibling ties can be seen in the confrontation between Salbangan and Salbayani described in Chapter 5. Although Salbangan threatened to kill his brother if he persisted in searching the village, their confrontation acknowledged the ultimate responsibility that siblings bear for one another's conduct. In this case, less closely related villagers were reluctant to intervene. Curbing Salbayani's behaviour rested ultimately with his siblings, in particular with the leader of the sibling set. If others intervened, Salbayani's siblings might be compelled to come to the latter's defence, just as Salbangan did, afterwards, in the matter of the divorce of Salbayani's daughter and her remarriage.

The Bajau Laut differentiate primary kin from more distant collaterals. The terminological merging of cousins and siblings, or their merging in specific contexts, is a common feature of many Bornean and Philippine kinship systems (Frake 1960; Appell, 1965). The assertion of Murdock (1960: 2–3, 13) that their differentiation reflects the functional importance of the nuclear family and their merging the importance of an 'extended family', or of ambilineal descent, has sometimes been accepted as a structural correlate to these terminological differences. The case of the Bajau Laut and other groups within insular South-East Asia suggests that the issue is more complex. In the case of the Subanun, for example, relational terminology merges cousins and siblings, yet domestic units are based exclusively on the nuclear family (Frake, 1960). In contrast, the Bajau Laut possess extended family based house groups, yet consistently differentiate cousins and siblings. As an explanation of this apparent paradox, among the Subanun, Frake (1960: 61) suggests that since

both Ego and his siblings ultimately marry out of their common family of orientation, establishing independent families of their own . . . it is only the parental members of a family, upon whom its existence depends, who receive distinctive kinship designation. Siblings become parental members of independent families collateral to Ego's, and Ego's patterned relationship with families founded by siblings is not significantly different from those with families founded by cousins.

The situation is radically different in the case of the Bajau Laut. Some siblings typically remain in the parental house group following marriage, and even as they eventually establish their own house groups, their ties to one another remain much closer than those with cousins, being very often the basis of cluster alignments. Moreover, within the house, each nuclear family remains an identifiable economic unit and, in the normal course of events, the eventual source of a new house group. Thus, primary kin form a structurally distinct category, separate from more distant collateral kin. Finally, the marital status of siblings and cousins are diametrically different; the one being prohibited as marriage partners, the other preferred.

More Distant Kin

Relations with kin outside Ego's *tai'anakan* are generally modelled on those between primary kin. Ideally, cousins behave like brothers and sisters. In practice, close ties rarely extend beyond first cousins, and the importance of these relations tends to depend upon factors other than kinship, such as residence and personal friendships. Those who live together in the same or neighbouring houses are usually close. Cousins are often included among a man's regular fishing partners, and five of the thirty-six house groups in Bangau-Bangau contain the families of married cousins. The chief difference is that cousins, in contrast to siblings, are preferred marriage partners and are generally given first consideration when parents decide upon suitable mates for their children.

Similarly, uncles and aunts are expected to behave like parents, and nephews and nieces like sons and daughters. A particularly close sense of identity is said to exist between children and their father's brothers and mother's sisters. Occasionally, a man may inherit property from his father's brothers, or a woman from her mother's sisters. At marriage, a woman's paternal uncle generally acts as her guardian and may later assume jural responsibility for her welfare should her father die.

The relationship between grandparents and grandchildren is often a bond of unusual warmth and affection. It is almost always a relationship of easy familiarity despite the difference in age, and grandparents are expected to be more tolerant of a youngster's misbehaviour than parents or parents' siblings. Children frequently take refuge with their grandparents when they are in trouble or are threatened with punishment by their parents. In discussing ties between grandparents and their grandchildren, the villagers sometimes point to cases in which children have chosen to stay with a grandparent in preference to their own parents or have, in later life, faithfully attended their grandparents in sickness and failing health. Several villagers told me that their first experience of deep personal loss occurred at the death of a grandparent. Often a grandfather has a favourite grandson to whom he passes on much of his knowledge of protective spells or magical lore. The oldest villager in Bangau-Bangau in 1965 was a man of uncertain age known as 'old' Lailané'. He was totally blind and able to get about only by crawling. Despite his frailty, Lailané' was at the time the most respected 'seer' (*ta'u nganda'*) in the village. During the time that I lived in Bangau-Bangau, he was training his youngest grandson, Ratu, a boy of fourteen, in the lore of 'seeing'. The boy was his favourite and he and the old man, whom other villagers regarded with awe, spent long hours together in intimate conversation.

Husband–Wife Relations

The villagers say that a husband and wife should be drawn together by both love or affection (*lasa*) and physical longing (*makahandul atai*). Like siblings, their relationship should also be one of compassion and mutual concern (*ma'asé'*). The villagers believe that some couples are fated to marry. This is called *suratan*, or *magtiggup suratan*. Such persons, it is said, know from the moment they meet that they are destined for one another. However, in most marriages, a young wife is thought to develop feelings of affection for her husband only after they have been married for some time. At first, a husband should be patient and allow his wife time to accustom herself to their relationship. Later, the marriage may be annulled by mutual consent if such feelings fail to develop.[5]

· Couples whose marriage survives the first three or four months are generally expected to develop a close personal bond. After the birth of a child, divorce becomes increasingly unlikely. It is commonly said that half the love which a husband and wife originally felt for each other is transferred to their children when they become parents. Children are typically the objects of intense affection. In this regard, husbands and wives sometimes quarrel over their treatment. For example, a husband may feel that his wife does not spend enough time with their children,

failing to see them properly fed or watched over. Similarly, a wife is
likely to quarrel with her husband if he gambles, or spends money foolishly without regard to the needs of their children. On the other hand, as
Amjatul said, 'No marriage is complete without children. Why else does
a husband and wife work so hard, if it is not for the sake of their children?' Barrenness, although rare, is recognized as grounds for divorce,
and if, after two or three years, a couple remain childless, they generally
divorce and remarry, trying their luck with new partners.

Marital ties tend to grow stronger with time. With the birth of
children, a couple and their offspring form a subsidiary unit within the
larger house group. At times, marital ties may conflict with kin loyalties.
This may be seen in the case of Umaldani, discussed in Chapter 6.
Umaldani's break with his mother came about largely because of
quarrels between Hajal and his wife. Tiring of the trouble, he withdrew
from the house cluster to which his mother belonged shortly after
Panglima Atani's death. Rather than allying himself with Hajal and two
brothers and a sister as part of the new cluster they formed, he dismantled his old house and built a new one in a different cluster into which
a second sister had previously married. In doing so, he relinquished his
former position of principal sibling leader. Umaldani's wife was unrelated
to her husband or to anyone else in the original house cluster in which
they lived, and it is partly to avoid conflicts of this sort that the villagers
say that it is better to arrange marriages with close kin, particularly with
women already known to the husband's female kin.

While the husband is the recognized head of the family, his wife has
charge of the family budget and together with other senior women is
responsible for the day-to-day running of the house group. The
husband makes most decisions regarding fishing, is generally responsible
for marketing and the disbursement of the family's savings, and
represents the group at public gatherings. Whenever it is necessary for
the family to visit the village of another Sama-speaking group, or the
market stalls and shops in Semporna town, the husband usually goes
alone or accompanied by his sons while his wife and other children wait
for him in their boat or remain in the background. However, the couple
co-operate in virtually all economic undertakings. The wife owns and
inherits her own personal property and is consulted whenever important
decisions affecting the family's welfare must be made. While the sexes
tend to separate for rituals, feasts, and at times of relaxation, a man
always eats with his wife and children within the privacy of his house or
boat, and the couple are constant companions during fishing voyages.
At sea, there is a marked division of labour. Men set and haul nets, dive,
sail, and handle the boat; women prepare food, tend the younger
children, collect shellfish, and assist in preparing fish for drying. Women
often take a hand in poling or in holding the boat steady while men set
out their nets, and both sexes share in the work of mending and drying
nets. Basically, the husband–wife relationship is one of mutuality, and
the common interests and complementary activities of husbands and
wives within the house group and at sea afford ample occasion for
developing strong bonds of affection.

Other Affinal Relations

The nature of village dyadic ties can only be understood when considered in terms of the relative independence of the nuclear family and its intermittent existence as a separate domestic unit. The strong bonds developed between siblings in a family persist and later provide the basis for house group and netting fleet alliances, and for the creation of food-sharing networks.

The husband–wife relationship, on the other hand, provides the basis on which new family units are created. At marriage a couple are said to form a new *mataan*, distinct yet connected to the *mataan* originally formed by their parents into which they were born. Likened to the mesh of a fishing net, each *mataan* is regarded as the constituent of a larger meshwork of relationships. Marital ties are essentially symmetrical and require that each partner perform complementary tasks that are together necessary for the family's survival. For the first few years, these ties tend to be precarious and are generally viewed as secondary to pre-existing kin relations. Later, with the birth of children, marital ties become increasingly permanent and assume a prominent place in village social relations as the basis on which *mataan* ties are founded, extended, and consolidated. From this point onward, the subsequent stability of the marriage tends to depend on how well the couple perform their responsibilities as parents and family members and on the success their in-laws have in developing amicable relations.

Marriage establishes a union between two sets of cognates, or if the spouses are already related, as they usually are, it superimposes affinal relations on an existing series of consanguineal ties. Once marriage is concluded, the couple's parents are brought into a new relationship and refer to one another as *ba'i* ('co-parents-in-law'). Their relations are likely to be strained at first owing to the desire of each to secure the affiliation of the couple in their own house group. For this reason, the villagers feel that it is of great practical benefit if at least two of the couple's parents are siblings or close cousins. Otherwise, while their relationship is likely to be correct and formal, there is always a chance of conflict which may jeopardize the couple's marriage. Moreover, since the couple's parents are likely to be called upon by their children for assistance, there is considerable advantage to their being relatives, and so allies who can work together closely when called upon for aid by their children. Where individuals are both affines and cognates, the Bajau Laut stress their kinship connection and attempt, as far as possible, to assimilate affines into appropriate categories of kin relationship, thereby minimizing the number of those they count as affines.

A degree of formality normally exists in relations between a man and his wife's parents. He should not raise his voice in their presence or discuss their private affairs with others. However, like other affinal ties, there is considerable individual variation. After a number of years of marriage, a man may become as close to his wife's parents as his own; husbands often fish with their wife's father and succession to leadership within the house group most often passes from father-in-law to son-in-law.

Marriage creates a series of sibling-in-law relationships (*ipal*), which often become important ties of mutual support. If *ipal* are housemates, or live in adjacent houses, their relationship is likely to be close, ideally much like that of brothers and sisters. Thus brothers-in-law may be expected to help each other financially and frequently co-operate in fishing.

At marriage, an individual is linked to his spouse's network of personal kin and is expected to participate in the exchange of goods and favours that takes place between them. For a man who marries into his wife's house group, ties with her parents and their kin are almost certain to become his principal relations of support, at least until such a time as he is able to found a house group of his own. His presence is certain to be important, and the economic success of the group and its internal harmony are likely to largely depend on his contribution and ability to co-operate with his father-in-law, his wife's brothers and her sisters' husbands. If a husband proves to be industrious (*ahungun*) and gets along well with his wife's relatives, her parents are likely to do all they can to see that the couple remain together. They may even support him in marital quarrels with his wife. One woman, whose husband worked outside the village as a boat-hand on a coastal freighter, took a young lover who visited her at night in her father's house during her husband's frequent absences from the village. The husband was a Tidong from another district, and so had no village kin to alert him to the situation. In private, other villagers said that the woman was behaving foolishly, but reserved their strongest criticism for the woman's father for not taking his son-in-law's part and putting a stop to her infidelity since the husband got along well with the rest of the house group, held a steady job, and was a good provider. If, on the other hand, a husband is quarrelsome, or fails to contribute his share to household expenses, the woman's father retains the right to dissolve his daughter's marriage, provided she accepts his decision, by simply asking her husband to return to his own family and by letting it be known to his own kin that he wishes to arrange for his daughter's remarriage.

Inheritance and Economic Relations

In describing the nature of village fishing teams, and the relationship that exists between family and house group interests, some basic principles of economic ownership were discussed in Chapter 4. Here I expand upon this discussion by relating these principles to relations of kinship, marriage, and inheritance.

Like many traditional fishermen, the Bajau Laut regard the fishing grounds they exploit as an 'unowned resource'. Although they possess considerable traditional knowledge of the behaviour of fish and other marine life, fishing remains, as an economic activity, very much like hunting-gathering in the sense that the Bajau Laut lack significant control over the principal ecological variables involved (Anderson and Wadel, 1972: 153–4; Leap, 1977: 258). A set of norms exist that regulate the use of fishing sites in ways that safeguard the rights of temporary users, but the sites themselves are unowned in the sense that exclusive rights of access are not vested in individual families or communities, but are available equally to all fishermen.

The absence of such rights exerts a powerful influence over the nature of social relationships within the community. Thus there are no permanent economic resources vested in any of the social units that make up Bajau Laut society. Major assets, such as houses and boats, are durable only to a limited degree and all require eventual replacement. As such they are only partially heritable. Transgenerational ties based on inheritance have therefore little structural significance. The importance of this fact can scarcely be overemphasized. The absence of corporately managed property effectively limits the authority of house group leaders and means that there is no long-term basis for a cultural concern with house group continuity. In contrast, rights in property are defined in such a way as to allow for the maximum independence and mobility of the individual families that make up the house group.

Boats and fishing gear are individually owned. During his active lifetime, a man is likely to replace his fishing boat at least twice. Traditionally, boats were not inherited. At the death of the owner, his boat was taken apart and the solid keel section was cut in two for use as a coffin. With the acceptance of more orthodox Islamic teachings, from the late 1960s onward, this practice is no longer followed, and boats are occasionally inherited, provided they are still seaworthy. Sons have first rights of inheritance. The heir is generally determined by need, the owner's prior wishes, or is decided upon as part of a general division of a man's estate. Boats are rarely, if ever, owned by women, so that if a man lacks a son, his boat generally passes to a brother, a brother's son, or grandson. In practice, boats are, even now, rarely inherited. Those who are elderly, or in ill-health, usually retire from fishing or join the family crew of a younger man, and so frequently cease to maintain a boat during the last years of their life.

Houses are also male property. However, a widow may assume temporary trusteeship of a house after her husband's death, generally until a successor is able to take over the management of the house group, rebuild the dwelling, or erect a new one. The successor in most cases is a son-in-law (see Table 5.5). Although houses are more durable than boats, and more often inherited, they are by no means permanent, and, as with boats, their inheritance is only temporary. Every house group leader is therefore expected to eventually build a house of his own.

Every individual possesses a stock of personal effects. For men, these include clothing, tools, and fishing gear. Traditionally, at least a part of this property was buried with its owner. For purposes of inheritance, the Bajau Laut distinguish between two general classes of property (*a'as*): *magkaat* and *pusaka'*. Literally, *magkaat* means 'worn out' or 'in disrepair'. Additionally, the term describes all property destroyed upon its owner's death. In contrast, *pusaka'* refers to any property, tangible or intangible, transmitted through inheritance.

In 1964–5, most of the deceased's personal belongings were treated as *magkaat*, unless they were relatively unused or had been set aside by the owner for a particular heir. In conformity with more orthodox Islamic practice, by 1979, it was unusual for any kind of property to be buried with the dead. The villagers gave a number of reasons for the earlier practice. Some said that seeing the deceased's possessions reminded them of their sorrow. More commonly, it was said that the dead have need of their belongings in the hereafter. While I was living in Bangau-Bangau, a number of persons described dreams in which a dead kinsman appeared to ask that a particular object be returned and placed on their grave so that they might use it. The objects requested included three fishing nets, a metal adze, and a kerosene lantern. In all cases the request was complied with. In addition to personal effects, more valued property which is ordinarily inherited might be buried with its owner if there was no suitable heir, or if the owner failed to name the person to whom he wished the property to pass. Once when an elderly woman was being buried, a fine set of gongs (*kulintangan*), originally acquired as *pusaka'*, was placed in her grave. Harka, then a young unmarried man who was helping to fill in the grave, observed jokingly that there would be music and dancing in the graveyard that night. Finally, in addition to providing for the needs of the dead, some informants argued that property treated as *magkaat* normally has little value, and so it is better disposed of, if not bestowed beforehand, rather than risk possible squabbles between the dead person's heirs.

During the death rites, a village *imam* or a group of *imam* is engaged to pray for the dead and to lead the members of the deceased's house group in morning and evening prayers. Each *imam* receives for this service a shirt (*baju*), sarong (*hos*), and other gifts, including articles taken, or paid for, out of the deceased's estate.

A woman's personal belongings include her clothing, cooking utensils, bedding, and jewellery. At marriage, a woman is customarily provided by her parents with a full set of cooking utensils, including a wok, cooking pot, spatula, plates and bowls, glasses, and a kettle. In addition, her husband's family is expected to furnish her with sleeping sarongs, a full set of new clothing, and a dower gift of gold jewellery. These articles, as well as any further gifts presented by her husband during their marriage, become her personal property. If inherited, they are treated as female property, devolving on her daughters or other kinswomen, usually by bestowal. As a man, her husband has no claim on them.

All forms of inherited property are normally described as *pusaka'*. Included may be houses, boats, tools, personal belongings, and in general any asset received from another person through inheritance. *Pusaka'* typically also includes both tangibles and intangibles that seldom change hands except by inheritance. Included in this class of *pusaka'* are brassware, particularly betel-nut cases (*selappa'*) and pedestal bowls (*garul*); musical instruments; especially valued household furnishings, particularly wooden wardrobes and four-poster beds; and certain types of esoteric knowledge. Brassware devolves through males, normally by individual bestowal. Musical instruments consist of gongs (*agung*) and drums (*tambul*), which are male property; and xylophones (*gabbang*) and kettle gongs (*kulintangan*), which are female property. In the case of musical instruments, the choice of an heir is often determined by evidence of proficiency in playing the instrument. Jewellery is also commonly treated as *pusaka'*, although it is generally acquired in ways other than by inheritance. Typically included are gold rings, bracelets, brooches, ear-rings, and tortoiseshell combs. Finally, heritable property may include protective charms, spiritual formulae, knowledge of herbal cures, and spells. Some types of spells, particularly the curative spells (*tawal*) employed by professional healers (*ta'u anawal*), are specifically non-heritable. They may be taught only upon receipt of payment, generally payment in kind rather than in money. Others, however, including verbal formulae used for spirit placation (*guna-guna*), spells for self-protection (*sihil*), invisibility (*haligmun*), or invulnerability (*panglias*), form a carefully guarded body of esoteric knowledge transmitted as *pusaka'* only among closely related kin. Such knowledge is highly valued and, as a rule, is imparted to a son or grandson only when the latter is old enough to comprehend its importance and not betray what he has learned to strangers.

Husbands and wives own property separately and neither acquires an interest in the assets which the other inherits or owned prior to marriage. All inherited property is associated with either males or females and so never becomes the joint possession of a married couple, much less of the larger house group, but is held separately and devolves independently through heirs of the same sex. Thus, at death, the surviving spouse has no claim in his or her partner's estate. Property acquired in the course of marriage from family earnings becomes the personal property of the family member for whom it was purchased, and is ordinarily retained by the owner in the event of divorce or the husband's or wife's death. In times of extreme need, a wife's jewellery may be pawned or redeemed through a local goldsmith, but only with her consent. Similarly, a man may be forced to sell or pawn a piece of brassware or other *pusaka'*. However, this is done only in extreme adversity. In particular, a wife is likely to be reluctant to part with her jewellery as it represents her principal source of economic security in case of divorce or widowhood. The only assets which may be described as jointly held are the family's cash savings, which are seldom inherited. Should either the husband or wife die, they are generally used to meet the resulting funeral expenses.

Where there exists heritable forms of property, these are clearly limited and do not ordinarily take the form of productive assets employed by the family in earning its livelihood. A family may be well-off and yet its members possess very little, if any, *pusaka'*. As a consequence, the economic fortunes of individual house groups vary markedly through time, and depend almost entirely on the success of their currently active members. Moreover, there is no corporate control of such heritable assets as do exist. Rather, these are individually owned, even assets that are jointly used or purchased by a couple from their joint income. Such property as is inherited is typically bestowed by parents on their children as the latter marry or depart from the parental household. Inheritance allows for the easy independence of family members, and is closely connected to the process of house group partition and the transfer of economic and jural responsibilities within the *luma'*. Most importantly, the absence of significant relations of inheritance means that the ties of kinship and marriage that tend to be of greatest importance, those among the economically active, are generally between collaterals of the same generation. Thus it is chiefly between siblings, their spouses, and other close collateral kin that house group alignments are forged, netting fleets are organized, and food sharing and reciprocal exchange of favours and support takes place.

Kinship Values

Reflected in the expectations that exist between specific classes of kin and affines are more general moral values and collective perceptions of character and motive.

When one kinsman or housemate comes to the aid of another, the action is frequently spoken of as an expression of *magbuddi*. The term *buddi* connotes awareness of responsibilities, sensitivity to obligation, compassion, or even kindness. As in any society, the Bajau Laut have a schema of social roles and their attendant expectations which are internalized, enter the consciousness of individuals, and become subjectively real as attitudes, motives, and life goals. The notion of *magbuddi* relates primarily to this internalized dimension of social expectations. Concretely, expressions of *magbuddi* may take many forms. But all have generally the nature of voluntary gifts or offers of assistance made between persons who share some degree of mutual responsibility as kinsmen, housemates, neighbours, or friends. For example, when a man sponsors his son's circumcision, others may display *magbuddi* by attending the celebration, by offering monetary gifts if they are men; or by helping to prepare the food provided on such occasions if they are women. It is also *magbuddi* to visit those who are ill, and to help their families, or those who are widowed or destitute, with gifts of food and money, provided that such help is given voluntarily, out of an inner sense of responsibility, love, or compassion.

When an individual fulfils a formal obligation, meets the terms of a contractual agreement, or discharges a prescribed duty, his actions are not generally spoken of as *magbuddi*. Instead, *magbuddi* is looked upon by the Bajau Laut as an expression of inner feeling, as an act prompted from within. The inner feelings that prompt *magbuddi* are most commonly described in terms of two notions, *ma'asé'* and *magkalasa*. Both are complex concepts with many shades of meaning. *Ma'asé'* means primarily pity, concern, gratitude, sympathy, or compassion. *Magkalasa*, or simply *lasa*, means chiefly love, affection, honour, or respect. The villagers say, for example, that a husband should show both *ma'asé'* and *lasa* towards his wife. Otherwise he takes her for granted, even while fulfilling his duties to her as a husband. Similarly, he should show *ma'asé* towards his own kin. If a man cares for his ageing parents and looks after their comfort when they are no longer able to provide for themselves, he should do so from a sense of *ma'asé*, an inner feeling of responsibility, compassion, or gratitude, thereby showing *ma'asé* toward those who attended to his own needs while he was still a child and in need of their care. At the same time, he should also attend them out of love or *magkalasa*. Similarly, if a brother, sister, or a cousin is in need, he or she should be shown *ma'asé* and not be left to suffer want alone. Services, favours, or aid rendered from a sense of *ma'asé* and *lasa* are all described as examples of *magbuddi*.

If possible, an act of *magbuddi* should be reciprocated in kind. The Bajau Laut, like the Tausug (Kiefer, 1972b: 66), describe *magbuddi* as 'love repaid by love', using precisely the same expression. But it is recognized that those who receive aid may not always be in a position to reciprocate. Even so, aid, as an act of *magbuddi*, should be given. In contrast to *magbuddi*, *puhung* or *amuhung* is the giving, out of self-interest, in order to gain something from others, even presenting gifts where they are not needed in order to profit or curry favour. While even the humblest are expected to display *magkalasa* or 'love', the feeling should be exemplified, above all, by those whom life has favoured—the prosperous (*dayahan*) and those who are village leaders, house group heads, or cluster spokesmen. It is in this connection that *magkalasa* sometimes assumes the form of *ma'asé*, finding expression as 'pity' or 'concern', particularly in reference to the feelings of a leader toward his followers, of elders or senior kin toward those who are younger, or of those who are well-off toward those who are less favoured. It is felt that those who enjoy respect, have the power, or possess the necessary means to do so, should, out of an inner sense of compassion, love, and affection, be willing to come to the aid of kin, friends, and neighbours who are less fortunate, or who are in special need of their support.

The notion of *magbuddi* is closely associated with kinship and house and cluster membership in the sense that an individual's primary responsibility is always towards his nearest kin, fellow housemates, and neighbours. Whenever granting favours or responding to the needs of others, these people should be an individual's first concern. At times, however, aid may be extended to others. In this way, new relationships may be established. A man may side with another in a quarrel, and in return be invited to the latter's house, addressed as a friend (*bagai*), and possibly receive a vow of similar support in the future. Those who can, may offer *magbuddi* to others as a way of expanding their circle of support to unrelated friends and distant kin. Men of ambition may extend their influence in this way, provided they attend first to the needs of their nearest allies and dependants.

To render aid is called *nabang* (or *tabang*). The term covers the hundreds of minor favours exchanged between housemates and village kin. It also includes food sharing, gifts of fish or money, the lending of property, labour help, attendance at ceremonies, and political backing.

Aid received should be returned. This principle of reciprocity is called *tabang-manabang*.

Tabang-manabang is generally thought of in terms of the actions of creating and repaying debts. Women living in neighbouring houses may ask to borrow serving dishes or cooking utensils for a feast; or they may ask the help of others in preparing food for a large gathering. A man may borrow another's boat or outboard engine or enlist his help in repairing his house platform.[6] Here the recipient normally requests a service, gift, or loan. Once it is received, he incurs a 'debt' (*utang*), which remains outstanding until he returns the property he has borrowed or repays the gift or service he has received. The process of incurring and discharging debts is described as *magutang*. What is extended, owed, and returned is *nabang*, 'aid' or 'help'.

Magbuddi may thus be thought of as a special case of *magutang*. The recipient of an act of *magbuddi* should acknowledge his gratitude by some form of return favour. However, the terms of repayment are never specified, and a return, while expected, cannot be demanded, but must be given, as was the original favour, out of *magkalasa*. The exchange is basically unsolicited. Among kin and housemates, the granting and repaying of favours involves, in most cases, more explicit obligations. Favours are usually requested, and impose on the recipient a clear obligation of return, either inherent in the request or verbally acknowledged at the time it is made. Nevertheless, *magbuddi* is the ideal. There is a saying, 'When you aid others in adversity, what you perform is *magbuddi*' (*Bang ka' anabang mundusia asusa', onna magbuddi*). In other words, kinsmen and other allies should ideally volunteer their help and come forward readily in times of need. Similarly, requests for aid should be acceded to out of an inner sense of responsibility and be given as an expression of feelings of concern, love, or caring. By the same token, a return should be made as a sign of gratitude or affection. Underlying such transactions should be mutual expressions of *ma'asé* and *magkalasa*.

Related to the notions of *magutang* and *magbuddi* is another concept of special importance, that of *magjanji'*. The term *janji'* (or *najal*) refers to a pledge or vow, and when used in connection with an exchange of aid, reflects, to some degree, the opposite of *magbuddi*. Favours, valued services, goods, political support, and moral backing, all classed as forms of 'aid', are typically exchanged within the context of *magutang*, that is through the actions of creating and discharging 'debts' between individuals—kin, affines, neighbours, cluster allies, or friends. Exchange is initiated by offers or requests of help and is kept in motion by obligations of return. These obligations may, at times, be backed by a verbal pledge or vow. It is this vow that the Bajau Laut describe as *janji'*.

Janji' may take many forms. In the case of a monetary debt, it may consist of a simple verbal promise of repayment. For a personal favour, it may consist of a general assurance of future support or a more specific pledge to undertake some particular line of future action on behalf of the individual granting the favour. Often, pledge-taking has the nature of a formal promissory agreement of future payment or the transfer of property, as in the case of bride-wealth negotiations or arrangement for the future division of a personal estate. On such occasions, an outside witness (*saksi'*), such as the village headman, may be called upon to be present when the agreement is concluded. Here the pledge takes the form of a promissory contract to which both parties may declare themselves bound by mutual vows.

In the past, such promissory contracts formed the basis of deferred trade between Bajau Laut fishermen and traditional shore-dwelling artisans, such as blacksmiths, potters, boatwrights, and *kajang*-makers. Goods were not generally kept in stock, but rather were produced and paid for according to terms pledged by both the artisan and the buyer. Only after receiving the buyer's pledge did the artisan begin to fashion the goods requested. The buyer took delivery after paying the agreed price. In the case of promissory contracts of this nature, obligations are secured, not by sentiments of 'love' or 'pity', but by a verbal pledge.

To the Bajau Laut, sanctity attaches to the pledge. Failure or refusal to fulfil its terms is believed to invite calamity (*busung*) in the form of sickness, accidents, or ill-fortune. When a pledge is witnessed, there are also legal safeguards to secure compliance. The more pious Bajau Laut consider God to be the ultimate guarantor of all pledges. Unlike *magbuddi*, which is upheld by social sanctions, fear of shame, or possible withdrawal of support, *magjanji'* may carry the force of a legal contract and is believed to be upheld by spiritual sanctions that punish non-compliance.

Magjanji' (pledge-taking) often takes the form of a ritual vow. In its simplest form, an individual may make a vow with himself. This is called *magjanji' ni kandi* or *najalanku*. If a person is in need, he may commit himself to an act of piety should a relative or friend come forth with an offer of help. For example, he may be involved in litigation with another family. If a cousin or brother provides decisive backing, he may, as a sign of gratitude, perform an act of devotion, such as a period of daily prayer, or make a special contribution for the upkeep of the village mosque. In this case, God is thought to be a party to the vow and, by determining the course of events, makes possible the favour, even though it was performed by another person. Although it is somewhat unusual, an individual may also make a vow to another person, usually to a parent or, less often, to a brother or sister. Such vows take the form of a pledge of mutual support or a promise of respect in return for a personal favour. Vows may also be made to those who are dead, particularly to deceased parents or grandparents. In this case, spiritual favours are sought in return for a special act of remembrance, such as clearing around the dead person's grave, erecting a tomb shelter, or constructing a cloth covering over the grave. In each case, what the pledge-taker seeks is generally an act of *magbuddi*, a voluntary proffering of help on the part of another person. Through the intercession of God, prompted by a vow, acts of *magbuddi* are called forth in times of need, in return for which the pledge-taker commits himself to a return favour, an act of personal devotion, or both. Finally, vows may also be made directly with God (*magjanji' ni Tuhan*), as a ritual act, without the intermediation of others.

Social relations in Bajau Laut society centre on reciprocal support, mutual help, and the exchange of goods and favours. The cloth of social life is woven of multiple threads of reciprocal aid conceptualized in terms of the notions of *tabang-manabang*, *magbuddi*, and *magutang*. Aid may be offered voluntarily, as an expression of love or from a sense of responsibility, moral duty, or compassion, or else it may be solicited from those for whom there exists customary expectations of support. In either case, aid given and returned creates a web of credits and debts enmeshing kin, affines, housemates, neighbours, and friends. At times, those seeking aid, or involved in an exchange of goods or favours, may secure their transaction with a vow. In doing so, they sometimes extend the web of credits and debts beyond the confines of village society, to unrelated trading partners and beyond, ultimately making God and the ancestors a party to their transactions.

Enmity and the Repudiation of Kin Obligations

A man has the right to expect aid from a kinsman. For 'distant kin' (*kampung magta'ah*), this expectation has little binding force, and may on occasion be ignored. However, for close kin and certainly for those a person considers to be his *tai'anakan*, in particular his house- or cluster-mates, it is felt to be axiomatic of their relationship.

The only way in which a person may legitimately repudiate the claims of a close kinsman or cluster-mate to his support is by declaring themselves parties to a relationship of formal enmity. Such a relationship is called *magbantah*. Those who stand in such a relationship refer to each other as *bantah* (personal enemies). The relationship is a dyadic one and *bantah* are described as persons between whom there exists a serious grievance or, more likely, a series of grievances. These may include the withholding of support or even of an expected display of compassion or love. Hajal and Umaldani are said to have become *bantah* when Umaldani refused to press his mother's hands when she was about to depart on a difficult boat journey to Sitangkai. Hand-pressing is a gesture of inner concern expected of family members on such occasions. Its refusal is seen as a major act of emotional repudiation and indifference. In this case, the act involved, for Umaldani, the breaking of relations not only with his mother, but with his brother Salbangan as well, and led to the eventual dismantling of Umaldani's house and the realignment of his house group in another cluster.

In almost all cases, *bantah* are, like Umaldani and his mother, close kin. Non-kin, should they have unreconciled grievances, may readily ignore one another or pursue their differences through village litigation. These options are not available to close kin, particularly to house- and cluster-mates.

Magbantah is a recognized jural category, and those who are *bantah* to one another are entitled to disclaim any obligations that might otherwise exist between them. Indeed, such repudiation is at the very heart of *magbantah* relations. Characteristically, *bantah* sever all contacts with one another, including speech. Under ordinary circumstances, the function of village mediation is to clear up grievances dividing community members. In the case of *bantah*, however, such grievances are not amenable to normal adjudication and may be resolved only by ritual means through a rite of reconciliation called *magkiparat* conducted by the village headman. Once this rite is concluded, normal obligations and responsibilities can be resumed.

The significance of *magbantah* is that it allows kin who do not get along with one another, if not to erase their relationship, at least to repudiate all obligations towards one another as kin. Its effect is to void all claims to each other's aid—severing in a social sense their mutual ties as kin.

Declarations of enmity affect not only person-to-person relations, but often have important ramifications for house group and cluster alignments. If enemies were formerly cluster allies, the result is almost certain to be the withdrawal of one party or the other from the cluster, such as in the case of Umaldani. When formal enmities occur, the members of other house groups may take sides. If this happens, the cluster itself may fragment, with some house groups aligning themselves with one antagonist, others with his rival, and with perhaps one or two seeking to preserve a pivotal position in the resulting realignment by remaining neutral.

Often, enmity marks the final repudiation of relations between former allies that have become strained over the years or are characterized by growing antipathy. Thus Umaldani's final break with his mother followed a long history of bickering and open complaints between the older woman and his wife. It may also mark the end of relations that have become attenuated as senior kin or cluster leaders have died, new leaders have emerged, and as families have realigned themselves around new house group and cluster allies. Also involved in Umaldani's case were the death of Panglima Atani, the original cluster leader; the death of Umaldani's own father, as *nakura' luma'*; his mother's support of his rival Salbangan, and the founding of new house groups containing Umaldani's own children. In a situation where there tends to exist multiple links of interrelationship between the members of different house groups, relations of enmity serve the highly important social function of defining cluster boundaries, of making it clear in many cases, where these ties overlap or intergrade, who are in actuality one's allies and who are not, and who stand in a position to act as intermediaries between allies and antagonists. Thus, relations of *magbantah* are, in a sense, the converse of *magbuddi*. They define ties of antipathy and non-support, particularly where these override contrary expectations, and so are expressive not of 'love' or 'sympathy', but, conversely, of its absence in relations, particularly where love and sympathy ought otherwise to be expected.

1. They do not actually 'drink' blood (*laha*') in a literal sense, but each makes a small cut in the skin, usually on the arm, which they press together while pledging friendship.

2. When I was collecting genealogies, Dessal's second son, Alkisun showed unusual interest and was able to compile a complete genealogy from his eight great-grandparents to his own and his brothers' and sisters' children. This he did with the help of Hajal, his grandmother and sole living grandparent. The names of only two of his great-great-grandparents are still remembered. My impression in collecting genealogical information from other informants is that Alkisun's knowledge of personal ancestry is unique and much greater than that possessed by most persons of his age (forty-seven years at the time). It might thus be considered a case of maximal recognition. On the other hand, most adults know the names of all of their first cousins and most of their second cousins whether they live in the same village or not. For elderly villagers, such as the headman and his wife, the number of known living cognates runs from 200 to 300.

3. Nimmo (1972: 93–4) asserts that kinship terminology has become 'more classificatory' among house-dwelling Bajau Laut in southern Sulu than it was traditionally among boat-dwellers. He does not substantiate this assertion, however, and in the Semporna district I found no evidence that house-living Bajau Laut employ kin terms any differently from those who live in boats.

4. For an account of naming and the use of names, see Chapter 9.

5. See Chapter 8.

6. A special term exists to describe a reciprocal exchange of labour service: *magdangin*. Such labour exchange is employed in the village chiefly on the occasion of house and platform construction or repair. Shore groups employ it, mainly between related house groups, largely in farming.

8
Marriage

Pindahanta yukna sulita ina'. Ania' maitu' bai tita man paglahat aluha. Gom aku pasinta, aho', pahé ni Babau Junya, bai tabantug i aku lella ania' kono denda, si Bujang Kawasa. Gom yukna palik sa'ta. Ta'abut yukna dapitu' na anambut ma matana si Bujang Kawasa, sarang-sarang denda.

Let us hear a new story, mother. For there are many tales told in this wide country. I wish to journey, yes, to the Shallow World for I have heard a man say that there is a woman there named Maiden Kawasa. I wish to find out if this is so. In seven days time he saw with his own eyes the Maiden Kawasa, who was, indeed, fair. (From *Suli-Suli Jin*, a traditional Bajau Laut song sung by mediums)

Types of Marriage

FAMILIES, house groups, and clusters all include members related by marriage. Whereas childbirth focuses concern inward, on the mutual interdependence of family members, marriage turns attention outward, in what is frequently a major realignment of kin and intergroup relations.

Ideally, marriage is arranged by the couple's parents, by their cluster elders, and other senior kin, through a formal process of negotiation called *magpahanda* (wife-taking). Such marriage is called *kawin magpahanda*. There are exceptions, however. Marriage may also be precipitated by elopement (*maglahi*), a girl's abduction (*magsinaggau*), or by a public declaration made by the couple of their intention to marry (*magpolé*).

With adolescence, a marked degree of public separation enters into relations between the sexes. At feasts and public gatherings, there is little mixing. Women and youngsters ordinarily sit together outside the house or in the kitchen area, preparing food, gossiping, eating, and chatting among themselves, while men and youths sit inside praying, feasting, discussing village affairs, or talking about fishing and other matters of interest. In everyday life, within the house group, there is, in contrast, easy familiarity between men and women, but a marked separation of labour, so that relations tend to be basically mutual, rather than equal.

Although marriage negotiations are conducted, ideally, by a couples' parents and other village elders, courtship among the young, called *angagap*, exists and is accepted provided it is carried out well out of public notice and its outcome does not conflict with parental wishes. The Bajau Laut are not a puritanical people. However, open expression of sexual intimacy, even among married couples, is considered shameful. The villagers regard sexual gratification as a natural and important part of marital happiness.[1] It is viewed, however, as a purely private matter between a husband and his wife. Intercourse generally takes place during the night, when the other members of the house are asleep, and is said to be performed quickly so as not to awaken other housemates. Newly married couples are said to take advantage of the periods they spend at sea to engage in more prolonged lovemaking. During periods of rainy weather, when fishing is suspended, those at sea sometimes retire to the privacy of their boats to sleep, and couples may use the occasion to engage in intercourse, which is otherwise avoided during the daytime, with little fear of being disturbed. One village elder jokingly told me that most youngsters in Bangau-Bangau were conceived by couples at sea during storms or periods of rainy weather.

For unmarried men and women, opportunities exist for courtship and secret meetings. In the evenings, young people often gather on one of the village house platforms to play the bamboo xylophone (*gabbang*) and exchange joking song repartee, which often has an amorous element. Couples may also meet clandestinely, usually by prior arrangement, on an unfrequented section of the village walkway or in a deserted kitchen. Such meetings usually take place at night. Frequently, younger brothers or sisters are used as message-bearers. Less often, a man may visit a girl's bed at night by pre-arrangement. Parents may countenance such meetings provided they are not opposed to the couple's union and that the meetings are carried out discreetly. Otherwise, if a man is discovered alone with a woman, or is found visiting her secretly at night, he is liable to legal action by her father. Touching, or being in close proximity without the presence of others, is interpreted as an admission of sexual intimacy or a preliminary to intercourse. Once it comes to public notice, it cannot be ignored. If the circumstances are particularly compromising, the couple may be compelled to marry. Such marriages have the status of marriage by abduction.

Negotiated Marriage

Following a boy's circumcision, his parents normally begin setting aside money for his marriage. Later, he is asked to consider a suitable bride. Generally, parents suggest the names of daughters of close kin, but the boy's personal wishes are also taken into account. The villagers distinguish between love, in the sense of affection (*lasa*), and physical passion that arouses emotions of longing (*makahandul atai*), and consider both as being essential to a happy marriage. Without the latter, it is said that no marriage is likely to last for long, no matter how advantageous it might appear from the point of view of the couple's kin.

Once the boy's wishes are known, his parents inform their kin and cluster elders. The girl's parents are then approached, usually by the boy's mother, both parents, or by a deputized go-between. This first meeting, which is called *anuna'*, generally takes place in the evening, just after dark, and is conducted discreetly, in order, the villagers say, to protect both families from possible embarrassment (*iya'* or *maka'iya'*) should the suit be rejected. It is also called *magtilau* ('to ask' or 'propose'). Unless the two families are closely related, or the parents are close personal friends, the boy's parents or their representative is expected to observe a number of formalities, including the use of indirect speech in expressing the purpose of the visit.

The villagers say that such visits, which always precede *maghanda*, are rarely unexpected. Most parents appear to have a fairly accurate idea of which young men have shown an interest in their daughter and have usually given some thought to which of these might make a suitable husband. Consequently, the boy's representative is generally informed at once if the match is unacceptable. However, etiquette requires that this be done in a way that does not imply a direct rejection. Usually the girl's parents will explain, for example, that their daughter is still too young to marry, or that she has already been promised to another.

If the proposal is acceptable, the girl's family usually suggests a second meeting, generally in three or four days' time. Unless the families are intimately related, they also refer the boy's parents or their representative to an appointed go-between (*suku'*) who is charged with conducting all subsequent negotiations on their behalf. During the intervening period, the girl's parents set about consulting their own kin. If the latter approve of the match, the girl's father fixes the amount of the bride-wealth (*dalaham*). Although he generally reserves a major share for himself, it is customary to divide a portion among the girl's senior close cognatic kin (*dampo'onan*). There are no set rules that govern this division. Each relative must make a special claim, based principally on past gifts made to the girl's father. The latter takes note of these claims and, after some compromising, arrives at a total figure acceptable to those of his own and his wife's kinsmen who agree to take part in the negotiations. The amount of any additional gifts (*sokat*) that may be requested of the boy's family is also fixed at this stage. In addition, the girl's father is expected to name a guardian (*wakil*) to act on his behalf as a formal witness to the marriage agreement. Customary law (*addat*) stipulates that this should be a patrilateral kin, if possible, preferably one of the father's brothers. Most often, the *wakil* is the father's eldest brother, or the leader of his sibling set.

The girl is generally excluded from the preliminary discussions that take place between her parents and their kinsmen, and is informed of the proposal only when her parents are on the verge of reaching a final decision. Generally, daughters are expected to accept their parents' choice with little comment. One reason is that women are typically young at the time of their first marriage, often only thirteen or fourteen years old. As Amjatul, the headman's wife, observed, 'At that age, they know nothing of men and are embarrassed by any talk of marriage.' As with men, sexual attraction is considered important to a woman's marital happiness.

One mother, explaining the reason for her daughter's recent divorce, said simply that the girl had 'no desire' (*embal bilahi*) for her husband. At the time when her initial marriage is planned, most women are expected to be too naïve to have formed any clear comprehension of such attraction. Sometimes, however, women openly voice objections to a particular choice, or show their displeasure by refusing to eat, or even threatening suicide (*magsabil*).[2] As a final resort, a woman may secretly agree to elope with a man more to her liking. Ideally, a daughter should accede to her parents' wishes. This, the villagers say, is because her parents are devoted to her happiness and, owing to their greater experience, are better able to select a suitable partner than she herself.

If the girl's kin object to the match or, less often, if it is opposed by the girl herself, her family will dispatch their go-between to inform the boy's representative. If, on the other hand, no one is sent during the three- or four-day period requested by the girl's parents, the boy and his family can be relatively certain that their proposal has been accepted.

Consequently, the second meeting (*magpahanda*) is typically a ceremonious affair. On the morning of the appointed day, the boy's go-between, his parents, and other kin wishing to take part form a procession and, accompanied by the music of gongs and drums, proceed through the village to the girl's house, or that of her representative as specified during their first meeting. Here they are formally received by the girl's kin. After gifts for the girl are presented, and received by her parents, the two sides sit down to face-to-face negotiations. These are generally conducted by go-betweens unless the two families are closely related. In the latter case, the financial terms of the marriage are usually agreed to informally beforehand, and this public meeting serves essentially to ratify them in the presence of witnesses. Go-betweens are expected to be quick-witted and skilled public speakers. Negotiations take place under the guise of verbal play and joking. The villagers say that the hallmark of the go-between's art is *pinangilang*, meaning, literally, 'getting close to something'. The exchange between the go-betweens always draws an appreciative audience; the skilled go-between hiding his meaning, and the gravity of what is being deliberated by indirection, wit, and word play. As with the initial proposal, neither the future bride nor groom attends this second meeting. When an agreement is finally concluded, the boy's kin distribute *sireh* and betel-nut among the girl's relatives; their acceptance of these gifts serves as a token of consent. A date is then set for the couple's wedding (*kawin*) and a period of engagement (*tunang*) is announced.

The engagement period is seldom longer than two or three months and may be as brief as three or four days. During this time, the boy is free to visit his future wife and is expected to bring her small gifts (*pagbuan-buan*) and perform a variety of minor chores around her house, such as cutting firewood or supplying her house group with drinking water. Collectively, these gifts and services are described as *anunggu' tunang* ('looking after (one's) fiancée'). He continues to live with his own family, however.[3] Should he be absent from the village for any length of time, he is required to make a relatively substantial gift to her family both before he leaves and upon his return. Ordinarily, none of these gifts are returnable should the engagement be broken off. One of the reasons for the briefness of the engagement is that providing these gifts is considered an added financial burden.

Marriage by Elopement

During the 1964–5 period, nearly 40 per cent of all marriages were precipitated by the actions of the couple themselves. Most of these cases involved elopement. The term for marriage by elopement is *kawin maglahi*, from the root word *lahi*, meaning literally 'to run'.

When a couple elope, they generally flee the village and take refuge with relatives in another community. Sometimes, they find temporary refuge on an agricultural estate, in a timber camp, or rented quarters in a city, where they are not likely to be known. Very often, the couple are aided by age-mates who act as emissaries to inform them when tempers have cooled sufficiently to make possible their return to the village and reconciliation with their families. If disapproval of the match is strong enough, the girl's family may try to recover her by force, in which case the matter is almost certain to end in litigation. Otherwise, the couple are quietly married upon their return, usually in a modest ceremony. Mostly, elopement occurs because of parental opposition, or as a means of escaping an unwanted match favoured by the couple's kin. In most cases, the period of elopement is brief. If sexual intimacy occurs, the girl's parents may be able to claim compensation, or, during the marriage negotiations, they may be offered gifts (*sokat*) by the boy's family, besides the *dalaham*, in order to regain their goodwill.

Frequently, elopement results in litigation. This is illustrated by the case of Hali and Mambang (pseudonyms) heard by the village headman not long after I began my first fieldwork in 1964. The circumstances of the case were somewhat unusual in that the couple had lived together, out of wedlock, for most of a year before they returned to Bangau-Bangau.

Hali and Mambang eloped to a timber camp in the Lahad Datu district. Mambang's father, Pana, brought a complaint against Hali to the village headman. At the time, the two families were both boat-living. Once the couple's whereabouts were discovered, friends were dispatched to arrange for their return to the village. As soon as they returned, Panglima Tiring called a public hearing (*maghukum*). Pana accused Hali of living immorally with his daughter; Hali replied by saying that he wished to marry Mambang, but that he and his parents did not have enough money to pay the bride-wealth that Pana and his kin had demanded.

During elopement, as during the engagement, sexual relations should not take place. As the headman later explained to me, the question of whether a violation of *addat* had taken place, as seemed likely, hinged on whether or not the couple had had intercourse during the months that they lived at the timber camp. Therefore, the headman called upon Hali and Mambang to testify in turn. When they confessed to having had sexual relations, Panglima Tiring observed that this placed Hali plainly in the wrong, for he had not married Mambang and had paid nothing to her father for the right to sleep with his daughter. On the other hand, he added, it was clear Hali wished to marry Mambang. He then asked Hali's father how much he and his son could afford to pay as *dalaham*. After a brief conference, Kaling, Hali's father, set a figure, consisting mainly of Hali's timber camp earnings.

The Panglima then suggested to Pana that he accept this amount and consent to the immediate marriage of Hali and his daughter. However, he added, Hali had wronged Pana and his behaviour could not go unpunished. He therefore suggested that Hali and his father pay Pana an additional compensation soon after the marriage was concluded.

The most pressing matter, Panglima Tiring later explained to me, was to arrange for the couple's marriage as quickly as possible in order to avoid further trouble arising between the two families. Their elopement had already caused considerable anger, and clearly the couple were intent on living together. Panglima Tiring managed to accomplish his aim by having Pana lower his daughter's bride-wealth to a sum that Hali could afford to pay immediately. At the same time, *addat* had been breached and Hali must not be allowed to feel that he had profited by his actions. Thus a fine was levied against Hali to be paid off in the future. The amount settled upon was roughly equal to the difference between the bride-wealth that Hali and his father were able to pay and that which Pana had originally demanded. The settlement was a reasonable compromise, and relatively satisfactory to both sides. In addition, the obligation to pay future compensation placed Hali in his father-in-law's debt. He and his own father would be compelled to attempt to regain Pana's goodwill. Otherwise, Pana might bring about the couple's divorce, causing Hali to lose the bride-wealth he had agreed to pay. On the other hand, if Hali proved himself a diligent provider, it was likely the Pana might be willing to overlook at least part of the compensation owed to him. So the stage was set for possible future concessions which would likely strengthen the ties between the two families strained by the couple's elopement.

Marriage by Abduction

Less often, marriage is precipitated by abduction. This is known as *kawin magsinaggau*, from the root *sinaggau* ('to catch').[4] Typically, a boy captures the girl he wishes to marry and, usually aided by a group of age-mates, holds her hostage in the village headman's house until the couple's parents agree to consider their marriage. The headman's house is considered a neutral sanctuary where persons accused of wrongdoing may find temporary refuge, and so avoid retaliation, until a formal hearing can be called. By bringing the girl here, her abductor places himself, in effect, under the jural protection of the headman. Once this happens, a gong is sounded; the two families involved are notified, and the fathers and other kin representing both sides are summoned to the headman's house to begin deliberations. The headman's responsibility is to convene the two families and to act, during their deliberations, as the boy's guarantor, seeing that they negotiate in good faith.

The danger of retaliation is always great in the case of abduction. The girl's kin may make a determined effort to gain her release. Her brothers and their friends may attempt to rush the house where she is being held and free her by overpowering her captors. The result is sometimes fist-fights. When an abduction occurs, the headman is additionally expected to appeal for calm. In this, he is usually joined by village religious leaders and other elders. Generally, the girl is released and allowed to return home as soon as her family agrees to participate in discussions with the boy's family. In most cases, these discussions end with an eventual marriage agreement, but often at the price to the boy and his family of a substantial compensatory gift (sokat) being demanded by the girl's kin.

Marriage by Declaration

A couple may appear before the village headman, or less often before a respected spiritual leader (imam), and make a public announcement of their desire to marry. Marriage as a result of such a declaration is called kawin magpolé.

As in the case of abduction, once an announcement is made the headman (or imam) is expected to act on the couple's behalf, convening the pair's kin and acting as a guarantor of their interests during the deliberations that follow. In this way, the institution provides a means by which the headman may intervene, as a neutral third party, in a situation that is otherwise very largely an intra-family concern and represent the young couple, who otherwise have little legal voice except as represented by their parents and house leaders. Until married, an individual's legal status is essentially that of a minor. To a degree, the institution provides a check on parental authority in a situation in which there may exist strong conflicts of interest between parents and their children. In addition, the villagers believe, that some marriages are preordained by fate (suratan). An announcement by a couple, or their elopement, is often interpreted as evidence of suratan, suggesting that the couple's marriage was predestined from the beginning. As a result, parents generally give way, in most cases eventually accepting a union formed against their wishes.

The chief reason for a public declaration is to circumvent parental opposition or to forestall the arrangement of an unwanted marriage. In addition, the villagers say, rivalry in courtship is sometimes involved. In August 1979, a couple who had met only a few days earlier made a sudden declaration before Panglima Tiring of their desire to marry. Both were engaged (magtunang) to other partners. The young man had only recently arrived in Bangau-Bangau from Sitangkai to participate in the death rites for his father who had died during a visit to Semporna. For the woman, the declaration was seen as providing a convenient way out of an earlier betrothal that, it was said, she had later come to regret. Shortly after the announcement was made, the girl suffered a brief spell of hysteria and, while I was present in the headman's house, was treated by Dessal, as a medium. It was widely believed that, out of jealousy, she had been cursed (*jinuhilak*) by her village fiancé.

The villagers say that a public declaration is usually prompted by the woman, or is made at her urging, and a woman may appear alone before the headman if she fears that the man she wishes to marry is wavering in his interest. Thus she may precipitate a union by making a public announcement, much as a young man may take direct initiative, forcing a marriage by means of abduction.

Choice of Marriage Partners

Most parents consider the successful arrangement of marriage to be among the most important obligations they have toward their children. The future happiness of the young is said to depend in large measure upon the wisdom with which their parents fulfil this obligation. In addition, marriage brings about a realignment of relationships between family and kin, and is validated by what is usually a major financial transaction. Not surprisingly, parents attempt to secure for themselves as decisive a voice in these arrangements as possible. In the case of a daughter, village *addat* upholds the subsequent right of the girl's father to intervene, should she complain later of mistreatment by her husband, or inadequate support. The girl's family by no means surrenders all responsibility over her future welfare to her husband and his kin upon her marriage.

In various ways, the power of parents to control marriage arrangements is limited, although ideally children should defer to their parents' judgement. Once children reach puberty, parents, particularly those with daughters, are expected to be vigilant. Their predicament is expressed in a village saying that 'fish and daughters are alike; both must be disposed of quickly least they spoil'. A girl may be promised in marriage at any age, and are occasionally betrothed in infancy. This is called *kawin paksa*, literally, 'forced marriage', in recognition of the fact that betrothal occurs before the girl is old enough to be consulted. However, marriage does not take place until after the young woman's first menstruation. Forced marriages, although they occurred in 1964–5, were not widely favoured. Parents generally begin considering eligible suitors soon after a girl's first menstruation and most girls are married for the first time soon after they reach puberty, usually between the ages of thirteen and sixteen. Men should be older, usually between eighteen and twenty. At the time of marriage, a man must be old enough to support his wife and himself. Additionally, a man's marriage may be delayed by family illness or other unforeseen demands upon the family's cash reserves otherwise set aside for his marriage. The age discrepancy between spouses should not be greater than five or six years in the case of first marriages. In subsequent marriages, age differences are often much greater.

If possible, parents attempt to arrange their children's marriages so that a daughter's bride-wealth can be used to help finance a son's marriage. For this reason, it is usually desired that a family include children of both sexes. A special term, *elotan*, exists for a child preceded and followed by children of the opposite sex. Such children are especially welcome. A girl may marry before an older brother, but siblings of the same sex should marry strictly in the order of their birth. This is particularly so in the case of brothers since each son's *dalaham* must be drawn from the same family resources. If a girl marries before her older sister, the bridegroom is expected to present the older girl with a compensatory gift called *kalkaran*.

The Marriage Ceremony

The marriage ceremony generally lasts for two days and is opened by the formal presentation of the bride-wealth to the girl's *wakil* or guardian. This is called *anud dalaham* ('to pay *dalaham*'). The bride-wealth—part of the dower gifts[5] intended for the bride-to-be—is carried to the house of the *wakil* in a special container covered in fine cloth, by a large party of the groom's relatives accompanied by musicians playing gongs and drums. Traditionally, the party was borne through the village in boats decorated with cloth banners (*panji*).[6] Now they usually form a procession and travel by the village walkways and platforms. The party is welcomed by the *wakil*, who receives the bride-wealth and other gifts. They then proceed to the girl's house where they take possession of the bride-to-be and escort her back to her *wakil*'s house where she remains until the wedding ceremony is concluded.

Later in the afternoon, the groom's relatives return to the *wakil*'s house to attend a wedding feast (*amakan*), followed after sunset by dancing (*magigal*) and entertainment (*magtangunggu'*) provided by musicians hired by the groom's kin.

During the feast and festivities that follow, the bride-to-be is expected to remain out of sight, at the rear of her *wakil*'s house. Here she is attended by unmarried age-mates, friends, and close female relatives who remain with her until the conclusion of the wedding. Although a girl may sometimes slip away secretly to sleep in her parents' house, by custom she should remain isolated from her family from the time she is escorted from their house until the wedding is concluded. Her separation can be interpreted as an expression of her 'liminal' status (Turner, 1967: 94–110), no longer a maiden (*bujang*) nor yet a wife *(handa)*. The bridegroom, too, is excluded from the *amakan*, and usually spends the night before his marriage with his age-mates in the house of a close relative.

At sunrise on the following morning, the girl is led outside to the *wakil*'s house platform where she is bathed by her future mother-in-law (Plate 24). Although this ritual was no longer observed by 1965, the girl was traditionally bathed while seated on her future mother-in-law's lap. As on other occasions, the girl is seated facing eastward (*kaluwa'an*) while she is bathed. After the bathing, she is wrapped in a dry sarong and led to the inner headside (*kokan*) of the house where her attendants begin combing her hair and applying white lotion (*borak*) to her face. By 1979, the ingredients used for facial adornment were replaced by commercial powder and rouge, but in 1964–5 adornment was still elaborate and supervised by a female specialist. After the girl's face is whitened, her eyebrows are trimmed to a fine line and then traced in black with soot (*buling*). Above each eyebrow, a line of dots called *lintik* is drawn. A second fine line is traced in black across her forehead ending at each temple in a barbed design called *soso' sangkil* ('harpoon barbs'). While the bride's face is being adorned, her hair is combed up and fastened in place with paper flowers and an ornamental tiara. She is then dressed in wedding garments provided by the bridegroom and his family. As she is being dressed, her mother is likely to pay her a furtive visit. The fingers and toes of both the bride and groom are stained with henna (*magpassal*). The stain remains visible for some months, and it is commonly said that should a bride become pregnant while her fingers and toes are still stained with henna, it suggests that the couple began sexual relations before their marriage was concluded.

In the traditional song cited at the beginning of the chapter, which is sung by mediums during curing sessions, a poetic description of the bride's adornment is given that brings out clearly its powerfully emotive associations in a society that values emotions, or conditions of the heart (*atai*).

Someone says, 'All is now ready. The time for the wedding has come....' Her mother speaks. 'We must authorize the most powerful medium (*jin*), the most powerful priest (*imam*), to perform the wedding. We shall also ask the *kural mata*, Pearl, the handsome maid, Maiden Intan Nara, to attend upon the bride. She is skilled in these arts beyond all others....'

In the morning, Kawasa comes from the house and is bathed. She smiles and laughs. Some play gongs, some dance, as others scrub the fair Kawasa. Her friends soap her. After this fresh water is poured over her as she sits straight upright. She puts on a fresh sarong, as her wet sarong is changed. After she has changed into a dry sarong she is led into the inner headside (*kokan*) of the house. She is led to where her eyebrows are to be trimmed. A woman exclaims (*amanyabat*), 'Come to us Maiden Kawasa....'

Then speaks the *imam*, an *imam* from the rainbow, who says that he has come to this world (*Babau Junya*, the 'Shallow World') to see how people on earth perform these matters.

Now Intan Nara is holding Maiden Kawasa by the chin. She passes the single-bladed knife just above her brow. With one stroke she makes the maiden seven times more beautiful. Her face is as radiant as a pearl, her eyebrows are like the new moon on the second night that it appears. Then the skilled medium praises Intan Nara, saying that she is truly adept.... 'Yes, that is so. Truly, I have trimmed eyebrows since I was a young maiden.... Now, as you can see, I am already old and people must help me to get about, supporting me with their hands.'

She then takes up the knife again, and with a single stroke over the eyebrow from the right, the face glows like gold, the eyebrows smooth as a levelled *gantang* measure, and curved like the new moon. Then with a single stroke from the left, the face glows like gold, the eyebrow smooth as a levelled *gantang* measure.... Then she bends the head so that she can appraise the back of Maiden Kawasa's neck. Bending so that she can see it, she trims her neck with the knife. Her skin is like the flesh of the coconut, like the new moon the second night that it appears. After trimming her neck, she combs her hair. Again, she loops her hair; she winds it three times. Then she fastens it up in two loops at each side of her head like the hammerheadshark (*paminkungan*). Then she powders the face of the fair maiden. Her beauty bursts the chest (*makatungkas daggaha*).

Around midday, when the sun is near its zenith, the young man is brought by a party of his relatives to the *wakil*'s house. Here he is received by the girl's kin and made to sit on mats opposite the *imam* engaged by his family at the centre of the circle of male guests assembled inside the house. After prayers, the *imam* begins the wedding proceedings by asking the *wakil* whether or not he has received the young man's *dalaham*. When the *wakil* answers in the affirmative, the *imam* takes the young man's hand in his own and the two place their left feet together, with their large toes interlocked, while one of the guests covers their joined hands and feet with a cloth. The *imam* then asks the groom to repeat after him the marriage formula (*batal*) and calls upon the *wakil* to act as witness. The groom's pronouncement of the formula (*mag-batal*), in the presence of the *imam* and *wakil*, together with the payment of *dalaham*, formally legitimize the marriage.

As soon as the bridegroom has pronounced the *batal*, the cloth covering his hands and feet is removed and he is led by the *imam*, or by a chosen guest, to the headside of the house where the girl is shielded from view by a cloth partition held in place by her female attendants. While this is done, the guests and attendants chant (*magsa'il*). As the chanting ends, the cloth is parted and the groom is led to where the bride is sitting with her face to the *kokan* wall, her back to the guests. The groom's right index finger is placed on her forehead and she is then turned until she faces the guests, who are arrayed facing the *kokan* wall. This turning of the bride forms the dramatic climax of the wedding ceremony and is accompanied by joking and verbal encouragement from the guests. The bride is expected to remain expressionless, with eyes averted. A raised seat is prepared for the couple, decorated like a throne, made either inside the house of chairs or of a four-poster bed, or, in more elaborate weddings, outside on a raised dais erected on the house platform. As soon as the bride is turned about, the groom is conducted by the *imam* to the seat prepared for him. The bride is then led by her attendants, usually with some show of resistance, to where the young man is seated and is made to sit by his side. This sitting of the couple side-by-side is called *magsanding* (Plate 25). For the girl it represents, the villagers say, her moment of glory. Guests gather around the pair to dance in their honour or simply admire them (Plate 26).

A second night of dancing may be held following the couple's *magsanding*. The newly married couple sometimes spend their first night in the *wakil*'s house. More often, however, they return immediately to the house of the bride's parents where they remain for the next four or five days. After this period, it is customary to pay a brief visit to the man's family. Notice is given in advance so that his relatives can prepare refreshments. Sometimes a second *amakan* is held attended by the woman's relatives. Such visits usually last for several days. Afterwards, the couple is expected to take up residence in one or the other natal house and to settle into the normal domestic routine of the house group (*luma'*).

Some time later, usually within a few weeks, the two families meet the district *imam* and officially register the couple's marriage.

Economic Aspects of Marriage

In terms of village *addat*, the most important element of the marriage ceremony is the payment of bride-wealth. The pronouncement of the marriage formula in the presence of the *imam* is seen as a promissory commitment on the husband's part to provide for his wife and to 'cherish her' according to the expectations of the marriage relationship. The transfer of bride-wealth, on the other hand, signals an assumption of jural responsibilities with respect to the wife and rights of filiation in any children she may subsequently bear. A man may take a mistress (*kirida*) without paying her family *dalaham*, but the relationship has no jural status except as an economic contract involving monetary support in return for sexual favours and confers no rights on her children, as heirs or legal kin.[7] In contrast, transfer of bride-wealth creates a complex of jural obligations, linking not only the husband and wife, but also their kin, and establishes through her offspring, potential ties of kinship between both parties to the transaction.

The payment of bride-wealth confers on the husband potential rights as father to any children the woman may bear. It also grants exclusive rights to his wife's sexuality. The existence of these rights is explicitly recognized in the event of divorce. Should a marriage be terminated without consummation, the husband may claim return of the full amount of the *dalaham*. However, should he enjoy the woman's sexual favours, the amount is correspondingly reduced, and should the woman bear him one or more children, her parents have ordinarily no further financial liability. The main exception is in the case of her infidelity. If the wife is guilty of adultery, her husband may demand from her family twice the amount of the bride-wealth, as compensation for the alienation of these rights. The woman and her family have no equivalent claim in the case of the husband's infidelity, although his adultery is recognized as grounds for divorce.

The payment of bride-wealth confers only partial rights *in rem* over a woman (Radcliffe-Brown, 1950: 50). The wife's father, or her *wakil*, retains the right to intervene, and possibly to dissolve a woman's marriage, should he feel that her husband is not adequately fulfilling his responsibilities toward her, as his wife. Several examples have been cited in earlier chapters. He is expected to show grounds, however. If the woman leaves her husband, with due cause, and returns to her parents' household, or the man returns to his own family after quarrelling with his wife, the father may expect a small gift from the husband, in compensation, upon their reconciliation. Should the woman commit adultery, the father and his kin remain liable, as well as the man with whom she committed adultery. Finally, since the recognition of kinship is bilateral, a woman's children remain the kin of her own family, as well as kin of her husband.

The payment of bride-wealth, besides its social and jural significance, is also a major economic transaction. The burden of assembling the necessary wealth falls principally on the bridegroom's father. Rarely are he and his sons able to raise the needed wealth alone, but must turn to the bridegroom's *dampo'onan* for aid. The exchange of gifts made at the time of marriage is, as a rule, the most important single transaction to affect the balance of debts and credits existing between kin.[8] In assembling the necessary wealth, the boy's father not only makes use of what is often several years' savings, but acquires, in the process, a series of debts that are likely to require years to repay.

In addition to the bride-wealth, the groom's kin are responsible for the wedding expenses which, in the case of an elaborate marriage, may exceed the value of the bride-wealth. In the past, prior to marriage, the boy's father was expected to provide his son with a fishing boat and other gear. While no longer expected, the investment traditionally represented a considerable additional expense.

There are also a number of other payments, or expenses, entailed by marriage. In the case of a first marriage, the bridegroom and his kin are expected to provide the following:

1. *Pagbuan-buan.* These are the small gifts, usually cash or foodstuffs, presented by the boy to the girl's family during the period of the couple's engagement. In 1965, they ordinarily ranged in value from RM5 to RM40, depending on the length of the couple's engagement. In 1979, families generally calculated their value at around RM50 per month. They are generally considered as maintenance payments, although they may include gifts of clothing and minor jewellery.

2. *Sokat.* The *sokat* is best regarded as a payment for the goodwill of the bride's kin. In the Bajau Laut legal system, the *sokat* serves the highly important function of clearing up past grievances between the two sets of kin; it includes compensation for current or past grievances which the girl's kin feel have not been adequately repaid in fines or through past litigation. If the marriage is precipitated by elopement or abduction, compensation for the boy's actions may be included in the *sokat*. Uncollected debts may also be included. The size of the *sokat*, like that of the *dalaham*, is fixed by prior negotiation. If the two families are closely related, and on amicable terms, *sokat* may be waived entirely or only a token payment may be asked. In 1965, the *sokat* was paid either in cash or purchased foodstuffs, typically in several instalments, presented during the weeks preceding the wedding, and was distributed among the girl's kin in accordance with their prior claims.

3. Invitational gifts. During the 1964–5 period, members of the boy's family were expected to distribute small gifts of rice and sugar to each house group invited to attend the wedding. According to the

villagers, these gifts were to free the members of recipient houses from the necessity of fishing. This practice is no longer followed. Instead, each guest is expected to make a small gift to the groom's family. These gifts, usually of RM5 or RM10, are used by the latter to defray wedding expenses (*balanja'*).

4. *Balanja'*. The term *balanja'* covers all the expenses incurred in connection with a wedding. One of the most notable changes in marriage between 1965 and 1979 was the enormous increase in the cost and scale of village weddings. The *balanja'* now frequently exceeds the value of the bride-wealth and ancillary gifts. On the other hand, the recent custom of guests making gifts to the groom's family, rather than receiving invitational gifts as in the past, eases the burden somewhat. The village group leader (*nakura'*) say that it is usually possible for the groom's family to recoup as much as half of the *balanja'* through these gifts.

Marriage serves as a means of highlighting the wealth and prestige of the groom's family, so that considerable social pressure exists to mount as lavish a wedding as possible. Correspondingly, the amount of *balanja'* depends upon the family's means and their ability to tap the resources of their kin.

Included in the *balanja'* is the cost of food served at the *amakan*; cigarettes, soft drinks, *sireh* and betel-nut, and other refreshments served to the guests, and kerosene for the pressure-lamps used to illuminate the dance platform. In addition, if public entertainment is provided, the groom's family pays the hired musicians. In 1979, a troupe of musicians charged around RM150 per night, plus expenses. The *imam* is also paid a small fee (*talma*), and additional small gifts are presented to the girl's attendants, the woman who supervises her adornment, and others who assist with preparations. The groom must also provide the girl with cloth for her wedding clothes and, in addition, purchase a new set of clothing for himself, as well as sleeping sarongs and bedding. At the conclusion of the wedding, he and his family pay the fee (RM50 in 1979) for registering the marriage with the district *imam*. In 1964–5, the total *balanja'* averaged RM75 to RM150; in 1979, the average was around RM1,000, but may be as much as RM1,800.

5. *Dalaham*. Because of its social and jural significance, the *dalaham* must be paid in full before the wedding takes place. Its payment occurs in a separate ceremony (*anud dalaham*) immediately prior to the wedding. If the two families are closely related, a larger payment may be credited to the groom's family than is actually made, or some portion of the *dalaham* may be returned for use as *balanja'*.

The total *dalaham* consists of two main elements, *mahalna* and *basingan*. *Mahalna* is a monetary payment, the bride-wealth proper. *Basingan* is made up of gold jewellery, such as ear-rings, bracelets, brooches, and expensive cloth. *Basingan* is best described as a 'dower gift'; it becomes the bride's personal property following marriage.[9] It should include at least one gold coin or brooch (*dublun*). In 1965, each *dublun* was valued at RM50. In 1979, its value was RM200. The monetary payment is ordinarily divided between the bride's father and his kin, although a father may sometimes make over part of his share to his daughter.

The size and composition of the *dalaham* is arrived at during negotiations between the two families and depends upon a number of factors. The most important of these is kinship. If the couple are closely related, the *dalaham* is almost always reduced and may involve only a token payment to signal the transfer of jural responsibility. Wealth and social standing are also important. If the bridegroom's family are wealthy, they will ordinarily be asked to pay a larger *dalaham*. Similarly, if the girl's family is wealthy, they will normally request a larger *dalaham*. The girl's reputation, physical appearance, health, and personal character are also taken into account and figure, at least implicitly, in negotiations.

In 1965, the total value of the *dalaham* ranged from RM25 to RM800, the average being between RM150 and RM350. In 1979, the average was RM1,000. The largest *dalaham* paid during the year was RM2,000, paid by the village headman Panglima Tiring at the marriage of his son to a daughter of Salbangan. Both fathers are leaders of major neighbourhood clusters and the marriage of their children was arranged for the purpose of bringing about an important realignment of village political relations, uniting two related, but previously rival, factions.

Secondary Marriage and Polygyny

The marriage ceremony differs somewhat in the case of secondary marriages. First marriage is a rite of passage. In social terms, it marks the end of youth and the beginning of adulthood for both partners. Prior to marriage, young women are called *bujang*, young men *subul*. Following their marriage, the couple create a new *mataan* and should their union be ended by death or divorce, they never return to their previous status again. Men and women who are widowed are known as *balu* and those who are divorced, as *bituanan*. Usually, both *balu* and *bituanan* take a leading role in arranging any subsequent marriage they may contract and later unions are generally entered into with minimal formality.

For secondary marriages, preferences are the same as in the case of first marriages, with one exception. Families occasionally favour a form of sororate union, known as *pinalisig*, in the event of the death of an elder daughter. If the woman's husband has proven to be a good provider, and the two families are on friendly terms, they may arrange for the widower's marriage with a younger sister of his deceased wife. *Pinalisig* is said to be a traditional practice among all Sama-speaking groups in the Semporna district, including the Sama Dilaut.[10] Actual instances are relatively rare, however. As in the case of Tia, discussed below, its arrangement is sometimes met with opposition, particularly if there is a large age difference between the widower and the younger sister.

Tia's father died when she and her nine brothers and sisters were still young. The eldest in the family, a sister named Daylawan, was newly married at the time. With their father's death, Daylawan's husband took over the care of the younger children. When Daylawan died, their relatives wished to preserve their close relationship with the widower, who had raised his wife's brothers and sisters like a father. By the time of Daylawan's death, the second daughter was already married, so that the choice fell on Tia, the third daughter in the family. But Tia refused. The main reason, as she told me later, was that she looked upon the man as her father. He was many years her senior and had cared for her since she was a small child. She felt that it would be 'incestuous' (*sumbang*) to become his wife, and she threatened to kill herself if their kin insisted on arranging the marriage against her will. The widower, who, she said, was a kindly man, came to her aid, saying that he shared her feelings. Under the circumstances, the marriage would not be fitting, and he would prefer, he said, to find his own wife.

A major reason cited for arranging a widower's marriage with a younger sister is to ensure that the older sister's children are not taken from the family and brought up by possible strangers should the father remarry. The headman's youngest brother and frequent fishing partner, Kubang, married his wife's younger sister upon the former's death, and so remained allied with his wife's kin, and reared a daughter by the elder sister together with his children by his present wife. *Pinalisig* marriage is seldom arranged unless there are children involved. The converse possibility of levirate, a woman's marriage to a brother of her deceased husband, is not practised by the Bajau Laut.

As long as a man or woman is still young, remarriage is expected. However, once a woman passes the age of forty, it becomes increasingly unlikely that she will marry again should she be widowed or divorced. It is generally easier for older men to remarry, and for this reason, and because women marry younger and so tend to outlive their husbands, women in 1964–5 greatly predominated among those of widowed and divorced status, particularly the former (Table 8.1).

Bajau Laut *addat* permits polygyny, but instances are rare. In 1965, there were no cases of polygyny in Bangau-Bangau. In 1979 one villager, Tia's mother's brother, had two wives who shared the same household. In addition, three women were second wives of non-Bajau men. Two lived in separate houses, and one shared a house with her co-wife. Few men can afford to support more than one wife; usually

TABLE 8.1
Widowed and Divorced Status by Sex

Marital Status	Men	Women
Widowed (*balu*)	2	12
Divorced (*bituanan*)	6	7
Total	8	19

only women whose families are poor consent to polygynous marriage. All but one of the village women who were co-wives (*maru*) in 1979 were recent refugees from the Philippines and all came from poor families with few social ties in the community.

Divorce

Divorce (*magbutas*) is relatively frequent. During the study period, the ratio of divorce to marriage was 1 : 2. From genealogies and marital histories, the ratio appears to have remained relatively constant during the last two generations.[11] While nearly half of all first marriages end in divorce, only two villagers in 1965 had been divorced more than once. Divorce generally occurs within the first two years of marriage. After that, it becomes increasingly unlikely, and secondary marriages tend to be relatively stable.

Many marriages end within a few weeks, frequently without consummation, and are simply annulled by mutual agreement of the two families and the return of bride-wealth and other marriage gifts, with the exception of *pagbuan-buan* and *balanja'*. Otherwise, divorce begins with the return of the husband or wife to his or her natal *luma'*. Although formal legal rights in divorce belong chiefly to the husband, most separations are initiated by women, mainly because of the structural nature of the house group. To initiate a separation, the wife simply places the personal belongings of her husband outside the house, on the house platform, or returns them to the house of her husband's parents.

If the house leader, or the couple's parents, is unable to bring about a reconciliation, the couple are referred to the village headman. The headman then arranges for a discussion with the estranged pair, either together or individually. If the headman is also unable to persuade them to settle their differences, they are generally referred to the district *imam* if their marriage was officially registered. The *imam* usually agrees to hear their case only with the assurance that the pair have already consulted local community leaders. If they remain determined upon divorce, the district *imam* ordinarily issues a temporary certificate, not making the divorce final for several months, during which time the couple are urged to attempt a trial reconciliation. If this fails, he legally terminates their marriage with a formal certificate of divorce (*surat taluk*).

If the marriage is not registered, divorce may be granted by a village *imam*, provided similar evidence exists that a serious effort has been made at reconciliation.

If property division cannot be arranged by mutual agreement, the matter is brought by the headman before a formal village hearing. The headman and other elders act as witnesses to the agreed terms of the division. If the couple have children, they usually stay with the mother, especially if they are small and still in need of maternal care. Older children are permitted to choose which parent they would prefer to live with. In some cases, they may choose to place themselves under the foster care of another relative, particularly if their parents remarry. As part of the divorce settlement, a father may be asked to provide a small sum for the maintenance of his children until they are old enough to look after themselves or until their mother has remarried. Upon remarriage, the woman's new husband is expected to make a small payment to the children's father in order to transfer jural rights to himself as their stepfather.

Divorce may lead to disastrous consequences if strong feelings of jealousy are involved as illustrated by this case.

Erol (pseudonym) married a daughter of Duahali (pseudonym), a senior house leader in Bangau-Bangau. The marriage was stormy from the beginning. After little more than a year, the couple were divorced and both returned to their parents. However, Erol soon decided that he wanted his former wife back. But by this time she is said to have fallen in love with someone else. Determined, Erol brought the case to a village hearing. Dissatisfied with the outcome, he took the matter to the native court, which, upholding the village hearing, decided against him. It ruled that the couple's divorce was valid, that they had been living apart, and that during this time Erol had not supported Narah (pseudonym), his former wife. Embittered, Erol told friends that if he was not to have Narah, no one would.

Early one morning, Erol hid beside the path to Semporna, where it ran through a tract of forest (*talun*). When Narah passed with a sister and a girlfriend, Erol came out on to the path behind them with a bush-knife. He struck Narah across the head and hands, causing her to fall to the ground. The other two women ran screaming for help in the direction of the village.

The next person on the path was Lagong (pseudonym), a cousin of Narah, who ran towards the sound of the screaming. Later, in recounting events, Lagong said that if the women had stayed and not run, they might have saved Narah's life, as the force of the first blows knocked the knife from Erol's hand. By the time they returned to her, Erol had recovered the knife and stabbed Narah to death. He then fled into the forest. Lagong ran to Semporna town to summon the police. By the time the police inspector arrived with the doctor from the district hospital, Narah was dead.

Erol remained in hiding for three days. Unlike many younger men of his age, Erol had taken up fishing and was well known as a story-teller. He had sought out the most knowledgeable old people and had made himself a master of traditional story-telling forms. He was also believed to be magically adept, having mastered a variety of magic (*sihil*) by which he was thought to have gained the power to make himself invisible and to move rapidly from place to place. During the next three days, he appeared in many different parts of the district, quickly disappearing again. Finally, he appeared at Tongkalloh village, on Bumbum Island. Here the villagers fed him while secretly sending word to the police, who arrived and arrested him without a struggle. Erol was then taken to Tawau, where he was tried and convicted of murder.

Narah was buried in the village cemetery the night following her death. Fearing trouble from Erol, who was still at large at the time, the villagers buried her body well after dark, about ten o'clock at night.

Erol's case is exceptional. Divorce is mostly uncontested. If the former husband and wife are still young, they usually find new partners, as Narah had apparently done, and remarry within a few years.

After divorce, a woman is not permitted to remarry for a month, until after her next menstruation. This provision is intended to eliminate uncertainty about the paternity of any child she may bear.

Incest and Endogamy

Marriage provides a significant means by which the cognatic composition of house groups and, more especially, of clusters is maintained. The rules of preference that apply to marriage concern primarily endogamous unions between cognatic kin. While non-cognates may marry, their marriage is neither frequent nor favoured, accounting for less than 20 per cent of all village marriages. Cognatic marriage is the norm, both preferred and actual (Table 8.2).

Marriage between kin is favoured provided that it does not violate rules of incest. These rules are defined by reference to two concepts: *dabohé'* and *bai pinaduru'*. *Bohé'* refers to semen; hence those of the 'same semen' (*dabohé'*)—brothers and sisters of the same father, father and daughter, and the children of brothers—are prohibited from marriage and sexual relations. *Bai pinaduru'* means, literally, 'having been nursed from the same breasts (*duru'*)'.[12] Hence, a mother and any son she has nursed, and children, real or adopted, nursed by the same woman, are prohibited as marriage partners. Incest is believed to imperil the natural order. Traditionally, those who committed incest were said to have been punished by drowning, with the guilty pair bound in nets weighted with rocks and thrown into the sea (*ni labuan*). In the case of the children of brothers, harm may be averted, and their marriage permitted, provided ritual expiation is performed. Here a substitute, in the form of objects of gold, is thrown into the sea. More distant patrilateral ties are generally ignored.

Among close kin, intergenerational marriage is avoided between children and parents' siblings. Outside this range, it is permitted unless generational differences coincide with marked discrepancies in age. Children of cousins are referred to as *kamanakan kaki*, literally, 'nephew/niece-cousin', and are generally treated as cousins (*kaki*) if they are of similar

TABLE 8.2
Relationship of Marriage Partners

Category of Relationship	Frequency	Percentage
Dampo'onan (first cousins)	17	28
Kampung (more distant cousins), *kamanakan kaki*, and presumed kin	34	56
A'a saddi (unrelated)	10	16
Total	61	100

age and as nephews or nieces (*kamanakan*), if they are younger. Marriage between *kamanakan kaki* of the same age is not uncommon.[13]

The categories of *dampo'onan* and *kampung* both figure in marriage arrangements. Table 8.2 shows the incidence of cognatic and non-cognatic marriage. The most favoured marriage is between eligible *dampo'onan*, that is, first cousins (*kaki mentedda'*), with the exception of patrilateral parallel cousins (the children of brothers); 28 per cent of all marriages fall within this category. Included is one marriage between the children of two brothers (*anak sumbang*). The husband, a senior cluster spokesman, explained the reason behind his marriage in the following manner:

My father and his brother were close. After my first marriage ended in divorce, he suggested that I marry his brother's daughter. He told me at the time that the marriage would be a good one, for, he said, 'if I die, you will still have a man you can look to as a father'. Some years later he did die, and since his death, my father-in-law, with whom I live, has treated me like a son.

In this case, the marriage proved to be a particularly advantageous one. Because of his close ties with both his own and his wife's kin, the husband has been able to play a double role as the cluster spokesman for his wife's relatives while acting as the leader of his own sibling set. However, he confided near the end of my stay in 1965, he sometimes felt that the frail health of his wife and their failure to have more than three children was a sign that their marriage was 'hot'. Ten years later, however, his wife, whose health had improved, unexpectedly bore two more children in quick succession.

The remaining sixteen instances of first cousin marriage include twelve cross-cousins and four matrilateral parallel cousins.

As Table 8.2 indicates, most marriages are between *kampung*. Included in the category are second and more distant cousins, *kamanakan kaki*, and more remote kin whose precise relationship cannot be traced. By far the most frequent are marriages between second cousins (*kaki mendua*). Such marriages account for twenty-two of the thirty-four cases of unions between *kampung*, or 36 per cent of all village marriages for which I collected reliable genealogical information. In a sense the figure is actually greater, as all *kamanakan kaki* marriages occurred between individuals who, in a classificatory sense, counted each other as second cousins. In some respects, second cousin marriage is the most important form of cognatic union because first and second cousins form the collateral limits of an individual's 'close kindred' (*dampo'onan*). By arranging a marriage between their children, first cousins bring their descendants (*empu'*) back within the circle of those counted as 'close kin'. Without intermarriage, their genealogical relationship becomes attenuated and is likely to be forgotten. Together, first and second cousin marriages comprised over 60 per cent of all village marriages in 1964–5.

The villagers cite a number of reasons for preferring cognatic marriage. First, it is said to make easier the personal adjustment of the couple, allowing them to fit smoothly into the existing network of relations between housemates and cluster allies, as they are already well known to one another. Cognatic marriage is also said to be more stable because if the husband and wife quarrel, their families will usually intervene to put pressure on them to settle their differences. This is particularly so if they have children, due to a fear that, should they divorce, their children will be taken away and possibly brought up by 'other people'. According to Laiti, if a married couple are unrelated, 'the wife can easily run away, or the husband can return to his own family, even if their quarrel is only a trivial one. On the other hand, if they are related, their fathers will try to bring them together again, and the woman's brothers may even beat her, if they think she is acting foolishly.'

In 1993, following the marriage of Panglima Tiring's son Hati to Salbangan's daughter Mambang, the latter discovered that her husband was still visiting Salasa, a woman he had courted as a bachelor. Upon learning of this, she removed his personal belongings from her father's house (where the couple were then living) and returned them to the headman's house. Mambang's grandmother, who is the senior woman in Salbangan's house, and Hati's mother, Amjatul, are sisters, and the two women immediately intervened. Although relations between the couple continue to be strained, their families have managed to keep them together. At least for the time being, Amjatul has prevented her son from taking out divorce papers, so that neither he nor Mambang is able to remarry. In this case, there are also political considerations involved. In extreme cases, parents may refuse to accept a child back into their house, as a way of forcing a reconciliation.

Secondly, marriage negotiations are made easier if the couple's parents are closely related. Proposals may be discussed openly when parents consult with cluster elders, rather than through go-betweens, provided the families are also on close social terms. Thirdly, marriage payments are retained largely, or entirely, by close kin, rather than passing to outsiders. To the extent that the couple's immediate kin overlap, claims may be cancelled out, and the total *dalaham* is generally reduced, sometimes to a token payment of RM25 or RM50 exclusive of dower gifts (*basingan*).

Most significantly, cognatic marriage serves to consolidate kinship ties and to prevent the attenuation of relations between the children of current village allies. The villagers clearly recognize the importance of marriage in these terms. It is said that kin, by arranging marriages between their children, 'keep their offspring from growing apart'. Intermarriage, in other words, 'brings them together again'. The term used to describe the process, *magtiggup*, means, literally, 'to close up' or 'shut' and is used to describe the action of a bivalve, such as a clam, when it draws its shell closed. What is meant in this connection is that kin who are beginning to draw apart are pulled together again by endogamous marriage. Their children and grandchildren are brought back within the meshwork of 'close' kin relationships as *dampo'onan*. Without marriage, they would otherwise pass into the category of 'distant kin'. Close cousin marriage thus brings about a consolidation of stocks within the kin networks of the couple's children and grandchildren, and if continued generation by generation, produces an increasingly close-knit cognatic meshwork. Reinforcing this meshwork is particularly important in the case of relatives who are allied within village neighbourhood groups and is looked upon as a way of ensuring the continuation of their alignment through time. In the Bajau Laut idiom, this process is likened to the mending or re-weaving of fishing nets and, in some cases, to the tying together of separate nets, or *mataan*, to form still larger meshworks.

Magtumbuk Sengkol

Two families may affirm their ties through a double marriage involving a son and daughter from each family (Figure 8.1). This practice of arranging consecutive marriages between families is called *magtumbuk sengkol*. *Sengkol* refers to the wooden cross-members set within the hull of a fishing boat that support its removable decking planks (see Figure 4.1). The etymology of the phrase is obscure, but some informants suggest an analogy, likening a double marriage to the *sengkol* reinforcing the two halves of a boat's hull. *Tumbuk* refers, literally, to the action of striking the sea with a pole, in order to drive fish from the deep water into the *angan*, or reef rim, during netting. *Magtumbuk sengkol* marriages are frequent in Bangau-Bangau, and always involve families that are close kin and village allies. The two marriages need not take place at the same time; more often, the second marriage is arranged some years after the first, with the timing depending on the ages of the sons and daughters involved.

Shortly after the founding of Bangau-Bangau, the first two house groups established in the village (nos. 17 and 19) were united by a double marriage.[14] This pair of marriages has remained critical to the political history of the village ever since. The wives of the two house group leaders, Amjatul and Hajal, are sisters and the marriages involved a daughter and son of each woman. Each daughter remained in her

FIGURE 8.1

Magtumbuk Sengkol

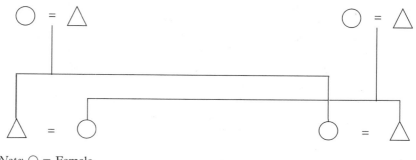

Note: ○ = Female
Δ = Male

parent's house, Amjatul's daughter with Amjatul and her husband, Panglima Tiring, and Hajal's daughter with Hajal and her family. The marriages thus took the form, in essence, of an exchange of sons between the two house groups. Shortly afterwards, Hajal arranged a second double marriage with her brother Sahalibulan, the village *nakura' jin* (leader of the community's spirit-mediums) (see Chapter 10). By this time, Sahalibulan had established a house in the same cluster (no. 21) close to the houses of his two sisters. At the time, all three siblings were close allies and the marriages were intended to ensure continued co-operation among their children. In the prior generation, Amjatul's own marriage was part of an earlier *magtumbuk sengkol* union, which also involved her husband Panglima Tiring's brother, Gilang, and a third sister, Maharingdang. Finally, bridging the two generations was still another marriage, between a younger brother of the Panglima, Rugo-Rugo, and his *kamanakan kaki*, Nasarayni, a daughter of Amjatul's sister, Hajal. The first cluster in Bangau-Bangau was thus organized around two sets of siblings, knit together and reinforced by no less than seven *magtumbuk sengkol* marriages. Two of these double marriages predated the founding of the original neighbourhood cluster; the other five were arranged after it was established.

Later, after the death of her husband, a falling out occurred between Hajal and her sisters Amjatul and Maharingdang. Eventually, Hajal and the two women became *bantah*. As a result, the original cluster was split for a time into two factions. Even so, all seven marriages remained intact, and, while the system of food sharing broke down, as it depended on female co-operation, the sister's husbands, their sons, and brothers remained largely neutral, preserving close personal ties across factional lines. For example, Panglima Tiring and his brother, Rugo-Rugo, remained fishing partners, even though Rugo-Rugo's wife generally sided with her mother Hajal against the Panglima's wife, Amjatul. Twenty years later, the breach between Hajal and her sisters was healed, and the larger group was reunited, and even enlarged as the result of the partition of several of its original house groups. Significantly, marking this event, intermarriage was once again resumed. An additional five marriages have been arranged within the cluster since and it is possible, even likely, that at least several of these marriages will eventually develop into further double *magtumbuk sengkol* unions, as more sons and daughters reach marriageable age.

A number of advantages follow from the practice of *magtumbuk sengkol*. First, it eliminates potential conflict by ensuring that one couple will reside after marriage in each of the two intermarrying house groups and that, in both cases, the offspring will be reared among close village allies. Second, the bride-wealth paid in the marriage of a son, although seldom identical, is returned in the marriage of a daughter. The nett transfer of payments between the two families is thus kept in balance (*tabla'*). Finally, and most importantly, it establishes, even more than a single cognatic union, a strong bond between, or within, local alignments of village kin. In this case, *magtumbuk sengkol* is said to express a particularly strong sense of solidarity, and through the children that result, ties of kinship are renewed, and the descendants of present *ba'anan* allies are drawn closer together through a merging of their personal cognatic networks. In this way, the dense focusing of relations is reinforced and preserved, and the pre-existing meshwork linking village allies is not only maintained, but strengthened.

1. Sexual attraction outside of marriage, referring to both pre- and extra-marital relations, is distinguished separately as *magkarom*.

2. The term *sabil* has a variety of meanings. For example, the death of a woman in childbirth is called *patai sabil*. The term *magsabil* means to run amok, to go beserk, attacking others and possibly oneself because of some unbearable grief, or shame, which the person committing the act has suffered. Later in this chapter I describe a case of homicide in which a man attacked and murdered his former wife. Most villagers also regarded this as a case of *magsabil*. In another example, Bayani (pseudonym) attempted to take his life following the death of his first wife in childbirth by refusing to return from the cemetery after her burial. More often, *magsabil* is used, as here, to describe an actual or threatened suicide. Threats of suicide are most commonly made when parents arrange a marriage against a son's or daughter's will or contrary to the latter's choice. Such threats are seldom carried out—none in living memory in Bangau-Bangau—but when they are made, they tend to be taken seriously and may cause parents to give way and accede to their child's wishes.

3. Traditionally, among shore groups in Semporna, the young man begins to live with his future wife's family at this time.

4. Among other local Bajau-speaking groups in the Semporna district, the term for abduction is more commonly *magsaggau*. Some shore groups are said to recognize an additional way of contracting marriage called *magsarahakan* in which a young man presents himself to the girl's father bearing a knife (*bari'*) and asks that he either be granted the girl's hand or be put to death.

5. For usage of the term 'dower', I follow Mair (1971: 68–9), who notes, 'Etymologically the words *dowry* and *dower* are associated with an endowment of somebody with property. Dower ... is used for the gift of property made to a bride from her husband or his kin in Islamic societies' (italics in original).

6. See the opening song text to Chapter 7.

7. It is unusual for parents to permit a daughter to become a mistress. Only those who are very poor are likely to do so. A man's wife is also likely to object to his taking a mistress, although she may find the relationship more tolerable than his taking a second wife. To my knowledge only one man in Bangau-Bangau, a well-to-do house leader, maintains a *kirida*. The woman, who has borne a child, continues to live in her parent's house. It is possible that there may be others, however, as the relationship is generally not made public.

8. See Chapter 7.

9. See n. 5 for a discussion of the notion of 'dower'.

10. In 1979, the Member of Parliament for Semporna, Datuk Sakaran, now Tan Sri, followed the practice and married the younger sister of his deceased wife.

11. See Chapter 5.

12. See Chapter 5 for a discussion of these notions in relation, more specifically, to marriage within and between house groups.

13. See Chapter 7.

14. See Chapter 2 for a description of the founding of these first two houses and the development of the original village house group cluster.

9
Ritual, Prayer, and the Life Cycle

Atui ondé-ondé inan angemmal i danau. Atui amassa ondé-ondé inan, amassa magsapaat i Tuhan. Atui kineséyan kelat-kelat inan. Atui ondé-ondé inan iluna pangajagaku. Ondé-ondé arak amatai, bo' ania' sukudna embal amatai. Atui pagpaléyang.

The boy then went to the lake to seek magical powers. There he called upon God for help and cleansed his magic rope. Then he resumed fighting. He was almost killed, but it was not his fate to die, and he flew clear. (*Kata-kata Ania Ondé-ondé inan*, a traditional Bajau Laut folk-tale)

Good and Evil and God's Omnipotence

THE Bajau Laut believe that the universe is dominated by two forces, both eternal and present since the beginning of time. The first can be described as a force for good that emanates from God (*Tuhan*). The second is a force for evil that derives from the spirits (*saitan*). Ultimately, God is believed to be omnipotent and places evil in the world in order to test man's determination to be good. Man must therefore submit to the will of God and honour Him with prayers and other acts of personal devotion. In this way, an individual gains favour and repays God for the blessings that he or she has received. In addition, most villagers feel that it is also necessary to come to terms with evil. In order to avert misfortune, the majority therefore propitiate the spirits, at times even enlisting their aid to escape danger or avoid ill-fortune.

Prayer

In Bajau Laut ritual practice, prayer represents the most basic expression of the villagers' faith in God's omnipotence. Two forms of prayer are distinguished: *sambahayang*, which is obligatory and fixed in form, and *dua'a*, which is voluntary, variable, and is addressed to God on a variety of special occasions.

Five daily prayers (*sambahayang lima waktu*) are one of three obligatory religious acts, known to the villagers as *wajib*, that are expected of every adult man. Women may also perform daily prayers. In practice, however, only a few do so, except for the major prayers performed at the village prayer-house (*maskid*) each year at the conclusion of the fasting month. The other two obligatory acts are observance of fasting (*puasa*) and alms-giving. Alms are customarily given in Bangau-Bangau during fasting month in a form called *jakat pitla'*. Daily prayers, fasting, and alms-giving are three of the five pillars of Islam (*rukun Islam*). The other two are the profession of faith, which is known to most adult villagers, and the pilgrimage to Mecca. The latter is counted as a commendable act (*sunat*), rather than an obligatory one, and is expected only of those who are wealthy enough to be able to afford the journey. Until 1979, no Bajau Laut from Semporna had made the pilgrimage (*haj*). Since then, several have done so, including the headman, Panglima Tiring and his son Wayijal, the village *khatib*.

Daily prayers are performed at set times, signalled, since the construction of the village *maskid*, by the sounding of a wooden drum kept in the community's prayer-house. These times are: *sambahayang subu* (sunrise), *sambahayang duhor* (midday), *sambahayang ashar* (afternoon), *sambahayang magrib* (sunset), and *sambahayang isha* (evening). As a rule, prayers are performed only in the village, rarely at sea, and the prayer ritual is generally simplified unless prayers are performed in public, in the village *maskid* or at house group gatherings. Only elderly men and those who are especially pious observe all five daily prayers on a regular basis. On Friday, midday prayers are customarily performed in the village prayer-house. These are followed by a reading from the Koran or sacred commentaries (*Kitab*), either by the prayer-house leader (*imam*) or the *kati* (*khatib*). In addition, a special prayer, known in Bangau-Bangau as *sambahayang mayat*, is performed for the dead as part of the death rites. Following burial, an *imam* or a group of *imam* may be invited to lead morning and midday prayers in the deceased's house as part of the memorial rites for the dead called *bahangi*. When performing *sambahayang*, no matter what the occasion, the supplicant stands, facing in the direction of Mecca and generally first makes a brief aspirational prayer (*hajjat*), followed by the *takbir* or phrase *Allahu akbar* ('God is great'), and concludes with the *fatihah*, or opening verse of the Koran. In its complete form, the *fatihah* is followed by the *ruku'*, a deep bow and prostration.

The voluntary prayer, or *dua'a*, is the central feature of nearly every house group-sponsored ritual. It has the nature of an informal petition directed to God, which varies from occasion to occasion, and is performed in a seated position with the palms upraised. It is accompanied by a reading from the Koran or commentaries and is followed by refreshments or a meal served to those who take part. Nearly every event of significance to the members of a house group is celebrated with a *dua'a*. Such events include recovery from illness, the birth of a child, a son's circumcision, the memorialization of the dead, or the reconciliation of former enemies (*bantah*). There is also a special form of *dua'a* performed at the graveside. The general purpose of all forms of *dua'a* is to accrue merit in the hereafter and secure peace in this world and freedom from misfortune.

The Village Prayer-house (*Maskid*)

In 1965, there was still strong opposition among the Semporna congregation to the entry of Bajau Laut into the district mosque ('*masjid
daerah*'). By 1979, as discussed in Chapter 2, this opposition had largely
disappeared. The social and religious consequences of this change,
particularly as they apply to death rituals, are reviewed at the end of this
chapter. In 1979, a few elderly villagers occasionally attended Friday
services in the district mosque. Otherwise, most communal religious activity is centred in the Bangau-Bangau *maskid*.

The first *maskid* was built in Bangau-Bangau in 1967, and rebuilt and
enlarged in 1969, with village labour and materials supplied by the state
government. The events leading up to the *maskid*'s construction and its
consequences were far-reaching.[1] Upkeep of the *maskid* and arrangements for celebrations held there are the responsibility of a village prayer-
house committee, which includes three appointed officials: the principal
imam, or spiritual leader of the village congregation; the *khatib*, who is
responsible for Friday sermons; and the *bilal*, or muezzin.

The term *imam* is used by the villagers to refer, in a more general
way, to all men, including these three *maskid* officials, who have demonstrated competence in religious matters; who are able to recite from the
Koran, lead *dua'a*, and conduct life crisis rites, such as weddings, circumcisions, and funerals. In 1965, there were seven acknowledged *imam*
in Bangau-Bangau. All but one were senior house group leaders. There
were also a number of younger men receiving religious instruction from
the district *khatib*, including Panglima Tiring's eldest son, Wayijal. In
1979, Wayijal became the village *khatib* and in 1990, he and his father
went on the pilgrimage to Mecca, the first Bajau Laut from Semporna to
do so. A number of younger children were also enrolled in 1965 in the
Koranic school in Semporna town. As a result, by 1979 the *imam*
included a larger number of younger men. In general, the *imam* are held
in high esteem by other villagers. It is not necessary that a house group
leader become an *imam*—and most, indeed, do not—but most senior men
try to acquire enough religious learning to be able to recite the Koran
and participate in *dua'a*. While any man who is able to lead others in
prayers and scriptural readings may be called an *imam*, the villagers say
that the term should be reserved more specifically for those who are also
capable of conducting public rituals, such as marriages and circumcisions. Most house leaders have a favoured *imam* whom they regularly
consult on questions of ritual observance and call upon from time to
time to preside over house group-sponsored rituals. Such *imam* generally
live within the same cluster and act, in effect, as the group's chief
spiritual leader.

While house group and cluster leaders concern themselves chiefly
with the practical affairs of their village followers, the *imam* minister
mainly to their ritual needs. To a degree, the two roles overlap in that most
imam are also house group leaders. But the *imam* are fewer in number,
and most house group leaders are not *imam*. As a general rule, men tend

to turn to ritual roles late in life, while secular leaders are generally younger men, mainly those in their most active middle years. The position of the *imam* is a part-time one. Most hold other jobs, and being mainly elderly, in 1965 most *imam* were fishermen. However, those who act as *imam* are partially supported by gifts (*sarakkah*) received for the services they perform, which are believed to confer merit on the givers, and by annual alms (*pitla'*) presented by the house group leaders they advise.

The Annual Ritual Calendar

As noted earlier, the Bajau Laut year is punctuated by a succession of prevailing winds, defining four principal seasons.[2] Within this larger annual round, the basic calendar of village social and religious activities is defined by a succession of 'moons' (*bulan*) and by the nightly sequence of lunar phases corresponding to the moon's cyclic waxing and waning. The moon serves as the primary measure of time. As lunar phases are linked to the alternation of tides and currents, and to the constant renewal of the sea itself, they impose a basic periodicity on village movement and economic activity. A final temporality derives from the sequence of night (*sangom*) and day (*allau*), and from the daily transit of the sun, out of darkness from the east (*kaluwa'an*), and its passage through the zenith of the sky, to the west (*kasoddopan*), from rising to setting and back into darkness. Fittingly, this smaller 24-hour interval begins, not at midnight, but at sunset. Its chief divisions are: (a) night, (b) sunrise, (c) midday, and (d) sunset. Within the village, each of these times is the appropriate occasion for particular social and ritual undertakings.

For religious purposes, the Bajau Laut make use of the Islamic calendar which divides the year into twelve lunar months. Punctuating the year is a series of calendrical observances. Five are regularly celebrated and three of these are major village observances: (a) *Bulan puasa*, Ramadan or fasting month; (b) '*Hari Raya Puasa*', or *hailaya puasa*, a feast-day marking the end of fasting, on the first day of the month of Shawwal; and (c) *Mandi sappal*, a celebration held on the final Wednesday in the month of Safar (*bulan sappal*). Minor observances are held by some village families to mark (d) '*Hari Raya Haji*', or *hailaya hajji*, on the tenth day of the month of Zu'lhijjah; and (5) *Maulud*, the birthday of the Prophet Muhammad, on the twelfth day of the month of Rabia-al-Awwal.

Religiously, by far the most important period of the year is the fasting month. The beginning of the month of Ramadan is determined by state religious authorities and is announced over the radio and by local religious officials. In addition, the villagers say, as with other lunar changes, it is possible to predict the beginning of Ramadan by following the nightly phases (*hali*) of the moon and by watching for the appearance of *pa'-pa'*, white sea-foam floating on the surface of the sea, which is said to mark the end of one lunar month (*patai bulan*) and the beginning of the next (*sahali bulan*). Most adult men attempt to observe the fast at least partially, but only the very pious, as a rule, totally abstain from food and drink between sunrise and sunset for the entire month. When family members are not away at sea, the main house group meal of the day is eaten after *sambahayang magrib*, that is, following sunset. If the family can afford it, this is generally more elaborate than meals eaten at other times of the year. Later in the evening, after dark, men and older boys gather in the village *maskid*. Here, after *sambahayang isha*, they perform special prayers called *sambahayang teraweh*. These involve the full prayer formula, pronouncement of the *fatihah*, and the *rakaat* (or *ruku'*), deep bow, prostration, rising to the knees, and prostration again, repeated ten to twenty times. The families of those who have gathered bring cakes and sweetened coffee which are shared out among those present after prayers. Later, the *imam* and many of the older village men are likely to remain in the prayer-house to read from the Koran or commentaries, often staying until sunrise.

Because of this great outpouring of prayers the villagers consider *bulan puasa* to be a month of special auspiciousness. The souls of those who die during the month are said to be hastened in their ascent to heaven, while the living, protected by prayers, are safeguarded from misfortune. As a force for evil, the spirits are thought to be largely quiescent during *bulan puasa*. It is also a time when an individual is likely to petition God directly for special favours as God is believed to be particularly attentive. The blessings most often sought for are health (*selamat*) and a long life (*umul ata'ah*). Fasting month is also, to some degree, a time of night and day inversion. Gatherings of house group members and of village men inside the prayer-house take place after sunset or before sunrise, while during the daylight hours, the villagers, particularly those observing the fast, often sleep.

Near the end of Ramadan, each house group presents alms (*jakat pitla'*) to one of the village *imam*. The choice is a matter of family preference, but the villagers say that the *imam* chosen is the one generally called upon by the house leader to officiate during the year at household-sponsored observances and to lead his guests in prayers. The head of the house group carries the *pitla'*, which generally consists of a '*gantang*' of rice plus a small amount of money, to the house of the *imam*, accompanied by other members of his house group. The alms are presented to the *imam* on a tray. As it is handed over, the house leader makes a brief speech, saying that this *pitla'* is presented to him for God and the Prophet Muhammad (*kerena Allah, kerena Muhammad*). As he receives the gift, the *imam* blesses the house leader and his followers. He then leads the men of the house in prayer (*dua'a*). *Pitla'* is viewed as a charitable gift, and the same term is used for small gifts made to widows or others who are destitute.

The fasting month ends only when the next new moon is sighted. As with the beginning of the fasting month, this is determined by state religious authorities and is announced in the same way. The first day of Shawwal, the month following Ramadan, is marked by '*Hari Raya Puasa*', a day of general feasting. It is the one day of the year when every family seeks to be home in the village. During the feasting period, boat-living families frequently stay with their house-living relatives. On the morning of 'Hari Raya Puasa', a special service is held in the village *maskid*. This is the one occasion village women regularly attend, standing at the back of the prayer-house which is typically thronged with families. As the service ends, women from each house group bring to the *maskid* trays of rice cakes (*pannyam*) and turmeric rice (*buas banning/bianing*), topped with saltfish wrapped in banana leaves. The celebration strongly emphasizes village solidarity. The food is shared out so that the members of each house group return home with rice and cakes prepared by other village families. As they leave the *maskid*, the men bless each other and clasp hands (*salam*). Later in the day, the villagers, dressed in new clothes, call at the houses of their friends and relatives, where they are served sweetened drinks, cakes, and other refreshments. The exchange of visits continues until the eighth day of Shawwal, although on a much diminished scale after the first two days, as most families, out of necessity, return to regular fishing.

In 1979, a series of mishaps cast a pall over the annual 'Hari Raya Puasa' celebrations in Bangau-Bangau. First, the night before, the walkway in front of the prayer-house collapsed into the water under the weight of the great crowd of people attempting to come to the *maskid* to pray. Later, a toddler from a boat-living family, perhaps unfamiliar with the open house platform, fell into the water beneath the house in which his family was staying and drowned before he could be rescued. The usually attentive womenfolk, preoccupied with preparing food, failed to see him fall. A night vigil was held for the infant, who was not buried until after *sambahayang ashar* on 'Hari Raya Puasa' itself. Prior to burial, while these mourning observances for the infant were still being held, the villagers, even those who were not related to the house group with whom the child's family was staying, were reluctant to enjoy themselves openly, and it was several days before the festive air and round of visits and well-wishes characteristic of 'Hari Raya Puasa' returned to the village.

The third major calendrical celebration, *Mandi sappal*, unlike Ramadan and 'Hari Raya Puasa', is not wholly sanctioned by state religious authorities. In variant forms, it is none the less practised by Muslims throughout the Malayo-Indonesian world, including other Sama speakers (Wulff, 1974–5). It is held locally on the final Wednesday of the month of Safar. This month (*bulan sappal*) is thought to have, in some respects, the reverse nature of Ramadan. Hence it is also known to the Bajau Laut as the 'month of misfortune' (*bulan bala'*). It is a period when the spirits are believed to be especially active. Some say that during the month the souls of evil-doers leave hell and invade the living world, bringing with them misfortune and suffering. Those particularly endangered are said to be women, infants, and young children. Because of the connection of the celebration with a belief in spirits, district religious officials have in recent years tended to discourage its observance with some success. In 1965, every family in the village took part; but in

1979, only a small number of houses, much less than a quarter of the village, participated.

Mandi sappal is a ritual bathing (*mandi*) performed over women and children for the purpose of warding off evil. On the night before it is held, an *imam* may be invited by the house leader to write verses from the Koran on slips of white paper. These are called *selamun*, and are placed inside one of the large jars (*kibut*) in which the house group's drinking water is stored. The next day, women and children, many of the women carrying infants in their arms, gather at sunrise in the shallows at the edge of the bay near the village. Here they are showered with water by the village *imam* and spirit-mediums, using special plaited cane winnowing trays called *ligu* (Plate 27). Before the bathing begins, an *imam* recites the *bang*, or call to prayer, and, while showering water over the bathers, both the *imam* and spirit-mediums pronounce blessings and call upon God to dispel any evil that might threaten them. This bathing is also called *magtulak bala'*, literally 'driving away misfortune'. After the bathing, everyone returns to the village. Here the bathers change into dry clothing, and in the houses where *selamun* were placed in the water jar, household members drink water drawn from the jar. Afterwards, a small festive meal is served, sometimes shared with neighbours and close kin.

In the houses of the village *imam* and more pious villagers, the Prophet's birthday and '*Hari Raya Haji*' may be observed with prayers and a special meal, but these observances are not widespread.

Rites of Transformation and the Life Cycle

Each of the following rites takes place in the house group, under the sponsorship of the house group leader. Some are attended only by family members; others represent major village gatherings.

Rites of Birth

As soon as a woman knows for certain that she is pregnant (*abettong*), she is expected to begin observing a series of dietary restrictions.[3] She may not eat octopus (*kohita*), or any type of red fish (*daing kéat*). She must also avoid a kind of banana called *saging hinugan* and any banana that is doubled or fused (*kambal*); otherwise, it is believed, her child may be born deformed. Later, there are other prohibitions that apply during puerperium and still others during nursing. In the seventh month of pregnancy, a woman is said to crave (*angiram*) special foods, particularly sour fruits, which her husband is expected to obtain for her.

Once a woman's menstruation ceases for certain, a village midwife (*panguling*) is engaged to perform the delivery and to look after the mother's health and that of her child through the months immediately before and after delivery.[4] As with the *imam*, she usually comes from the same cluster. Around the fifth or sixth month, the woman is called to the house of the *panguling* so that the latter can 'feel her stomach' (*ni hilut*). An experienced midwife can judge in this way how long it will be before delivery takes place. The woman is asked to return for increasingly frequent visits until the *panguling* feels that the child has descended, or 'fills the womb'. It is then known that delivery is imminent. The woman is asked to remain in the village and so begins her confinement.

The moment the amniotic fluid bursts (*kamba' bohé'*), the midwife is summoned. By custom, an expectant woman should be assisted by her mother and married sisters, but other women generally help as well. Men are usually excluded, unless complications arise that call for the attendance of a curer or medium. The woman reclines on the floor, with her back supported by an elderly attendant, most often her mother, while the *panguling*, reaching under her sarong, takes hold of the child as it is delivered. An abnormally prolonged delivery (*elotok*) inevitably causes grave anxiety and is often described as a form of *busung* (ill-fatedness). If the delay continues, someone is sent from the woman's house to the house of the *panguling*, carrying the family's betel box filled with areca nut, lime, *sireh* leaves, and other materials necessary for chewing (*pinapa'*). The *pinapa'* are distributed among the *panguling*'s housemates, who are asked to chew. The act of chewing a betel quid is believed to hasten delivery. Alternatively, the betel box may be taken to a villager who is thought to have special powers in dealing with *elotok*; there were several in Bangau-Bangau in 1965. If the *panguling* or her husband, or the villager with special knowledge of *elotok*, is a medium, as is usually the case, the person coming from the expectant woman's house is also likely to bring a small gift, such as a dollar note or a bundle of *sireh* leaves, to put inside the medium's medicine box. If the delivery is still delayed after the betel quid has been chewed, a medium or curer is summoned and asked to diagnose the cause of difficulty and treat it, so that the infant can be delivered and the mother's life removed from danger.

As soon as the child is delivered, the midwife blows water from her mouth over its body to begin its breathing. She then ties the umbilical cord with a white thread (*sarban*). This is done, the villagers say, to prevent the child's breath (*napas*) from 'escaping' (*palawas*) through the navel. Breath is, for the Bajau Laut, a major life principle. The midwife then hands the new-born infant to one of the women attending the delivery, who bathes it (*kinosé'an*) in warm water, wraps it loosely in cloth, and places it beside the mother. The umbilical cord is not cut until the placenta is delivered. It is strongly felt that the placenta should be expelled as quickly after childbirth as possible. The mother's belly is usually held to prevent its reflex into the womb. Once delivered, the afterbirth (*tamuni*) is also washed, wrapped in white cloth by the *panguling*, and placed inside a special coconut shell receptacle (*ba'ung*), which is then bound securely. Later, the afterbirth is disposed of by the house group head, the child's grandfather, or another respected male elder. It may be buried, set adrift at sea, or, very rarely, hung from a tree. Burial is by far the most common mode of disposal.[5] The person disposing of the afterbirth must look straight ahead while carrying the receptacle; otherwise, it is believed, the child may grow up wall-eyed (*alibat*). As soon as the afterbirth is expelled, the *panguling* cuts the umbilical cord using a sharp bamboo sliver. The cord is left long and allowed to drop off on its own. Once it does so, it is hung from the top of the infant's cradle. Some families say that care should be taken that the umbilical cord is not lost; otherwise the child may grow up to be forgetful.

Throughout the next three or four days, until the mother can leave her bed, the midwife carefully follows her progress, calling on her from time to time. The recovery period normally lasts from three to seven days.[6] During this time, a fire is kept burning by the woman's bedside in a portable hearth (lappohan). This period of 'warming' is known as magamak. For its duration, the new mother is fed a special rice porridge (mistan) prepared by the women who are attending her, normally her sisters. Her body is also rubbed regularly with fresh green leaves of the bangkuru tree (Morinda citrifolia). These are similarly thought to 'warm' her body like the bedside fire. At the end of the recovery period, if the mother is strong enough to walk, she is bathed (pinandi) by the panguling. After bathing, or, in some cases, following delivery, the midwife receives a small payment, consisting usually of RM5 and a tin of talcum powder (santah). After being bathed by the panguling, the mother may begin to eat again with the rest of the house group.

Bathing is an important ritual act; in this connection it marks the woman's safe transit through what the villagers see as a difficult and dangerous passage. Village curers similarly bathe patients following their recovery from a particularly grave illness or following some other life-endangering experience, such as being lost at sea or near drowning.

As soon as a child is born, the father is expected to prepare a hanging cloth cradle, usually made of fine batik cloth, which is suspended from the house rafters over the wife's sleeping place, or, in the case of a boat-living family, from the centre beam of the covered living quarters. The Bajau Laut call this cradle buahan. Among neighbouring strand Bajau in Semporna, it is known generally as rundangan or dundangan. Among strand groups, the first time the child is placed inside the cradle is an occasion for a brief but important ceremony called magisi ni rundangan, literally, 'filling the cradle'. The cradle is decorated with pannyam and other cakes. Seven sarongs are placed inside the cradle, one on top of another in seven layers (pitu magsusun). The new-born infant is then laid on cushions. Candles are lit, and, one at a time, seven guests invited to assist take up a candle and one of the sarongs, and carrying both, circle the dundangan, ending by placing the sarong on the cushions beside the child. When all seven sarongs have been removed from the cradle, the child is placed inside. As this is done, an imam leads the men present in a dua'a and reading from the Koran, Kitab, or Bejanji. Afterwards, a small meal is served to the guests. Among the Bajau Laut, this ceremony is usually much abbreviated, or is omitted altogether, although a brief blessing for the child's health is normally pronounced when it is first placed inside the cradle, witnessed by a small house group gathering.

Within a month or so after birth, some families invite an imam or an especially pious elder to perform a brief ceremony called kinamatan. Ideally, this should be done before the child has started to eat solid food.

Like all rites associated with infancy, it is performed at sunrise. A relative other than the child's parents, of the same sex as the child, whose own parents are still alive, is invited to hold the child. The *imam* places a small piece of sugar (*gula batu*), or other solid food, in its mouth. This signifies its introduction to solid food, and is usually witnessed by a small gathering of guests. Afterwards, refreshments are served.

Kinamatan is sometimes followed, if the family can afford to do so, by a haircutting ceremony called *ginuntingan*. In the same way, a relative of the same sex, whose parents are still alive, is asked to hold the child. First, the *imam* leads the men in prayers, after which they all stand chanting in a circle surrounding the child. The attendant carries the child and a pair of scissors (*gunting*) on a plate around the circle. Each man cuts a small bit of hair and blesses the child. The child's father follows, and gives each man a small gift (*sarakkah*), usually RM1. Afterwards, a feast is served, prepared by the women of the house group. By village standards, the *ginuntingan* ceremony is expensive and is held only by those who are relatively well-off. To reduce expenses, it is often combined with the *kinamatan* rite. In addition, a number of related children, usually from the same cluster, may undergo the ceremony at the same time, with their families sharing the expenses.

As soon as the infant is able to crawl (*magtamba'*), the mother and child, often accompanied by the father and other members of their house group, pay a call on the midwife to present a second customary payment, consisting of five green coconuts, a ripe coconut, and a betel quid (*mama'*).

Later, the mother and child may again visit the *panguling*, bringing with them the ingredients for betel chewing (*pinapa'*) and possibly other small gifts, should the infant develop a head rash called *buruk*. Among the Bajau Laut, the midwife is closely associated with mediumship, and every *panguling* is believed to be aided by a tutelary soul called the *sumangat panguling*. Some say this soul causes *buruk*. The rash is treated by the midwife in a minor rite known as *pinatemmu*, in the course of which the child's head is rubbed with coconut oil while the midwife chants over it. The treatment is often lengthy and is sometimes spread over several days. Adults may also suffer *buruk*. When this occurs, they may be advised by a curer or medium to visit a midwife for treatment. Relations between the mother and her midwife tend to be very close, typically persisting throughout both women's lifetime.

Girls have their ears pierced while still very young, between the ages of two and three. In the past, both sexes underwent tooth-filing (*lagnas*) between their seventh and tenth years. By 1965, only the most elderly villagers could still remember having heard stories of tooth-filing, which had already ceased before their own childhood.

Circumcision (Magislam)

Between the ages of ten and sixteen, all boys are circumcised in an elaborate village ceremony called *magislam*. Among the Semporna Bajau Laut, there is no comparable operation performed for girls. As a rule, three or four boys undergo circumcision at the same time. Their parents are always close kin, frequently members of the same house group or cluster allies, and in this way, the expenses, which in 1965 averaged between RM100 and RM200, are shared. The operation is preceded by a procession through the village in honour of the boys, prayers, often dancing, and a major feast held on the evening before the operation, followed by further prayers and a minor meal.[7]

Circumcision is performed in the morning, shortly after sunrise. The boys are first taken to the kitchen shelter (*kusina*) or the open platform, where they are bathed by the *imam*, attended usually by their fathers and brothers. As in the early morning bathing that precedes marriage, the young men are made to face eastward (*kaluwa'an*), toward the rising sun. They are then led back to the house, dressed, and seated in a row on the floor facing the officiating *imam* and other male guests. A large gong covered with cloth is placed on mats (*tépo*) spread over the centre of the floor. Each boy in order of age, beginning with the eldest, is seated on the gong while the operation is performed to the accompaniment of drumming and chanting. One man, standing behind the boy, holds the young man's head upright as the operation takes place, while other attendants, standing in front, screen off the area from view with cloth. As soon as the operation is over, each boy returns to his place on the floor. A tray of rice is placed before him and blessed by the *imam*, who concludes his prayer by throwing a small handful of rice into the boy's lap. This is said to aid healing. Afterwards, the guests are served light refreshments of cakes and coffee. The boys spend the following night in the house of the specialist who performed the operation (*mudin*), almost always in 1965 Panglima Tiring or his friend Muljarani. This is done so that he can attend them should any complications arise. For his services, the *mudin* receives from each boy's family a gift of *pitla'* consisting of a coconut and a tray of uncooked rice. Today, money is also given. Depending on the family, in order to avoid infections and other complications, a medium (*jin*) may also be invited to assist the *mudin*, the two men sitting side-by-side facing the boys.

The villagers frequently describe *magislam* as the preliminary step to a son's eventual marriage. It marks the beginning of a boy's transformation to full manhood. When it is over, the young man's parents are expected to begin planning for the eventuality of marriage, and the young man himself is expected to work diligently, preparing for the day when he will have a wife and family to support. If he takes a job outside the village, he is expected to entrust part of his wages to his parents to be put aside for his marriage expenses.

Naming

Children are given a personal name (*on*) within a week or two of birth, conferred usually by their parents, or possibly, as a special courtesy, by a grandparent or other elder among their close kin. It is believed to invite harm to a child to leave it unnamed beyond the first few weeks of life. Each name should be unique, a distinguishing mark of its bearer's personal identity, not borne by anyone else, living or dead. Ideally, no two Bajau Laut names are the same.

Names are derived from varied sources, and because of the requirement that each be unique, are often imaginative. In 1965, one village youngster was named Halikoptar (helicopter); another Jansun ('Johnson' for the outboard engine), and a third Gasuling (gasoline). Today, many names derive from Arabic. Most names are undifferentiated by gender. A few women's names, however, are compounded of two elements, one feminine, such as Entan, 'diamond', Musa, 'pearl', or Lasa, 'love'. Occasionally, parents give all their children names beginning or ending with the same syllable, such as, for example, ja- or -hati.

In addition to personal names, most individuals acquire during their lifetime at least one, and often several, nicknames (*danglai*). Occasionally, a person may become better known by his *danglai* than by his personal name. One house leader in Bangau-Bangau is known to everyone in the village as Domag. While many people realize that Domag is a *danglai*, I found that no one outside his immediate circle of close kin knew his original personal name (Bagunal), or how he came to be called Domag. Many commonly used *danglai* are a shortened form of the individual's personal name. Laiti's wife Albitia is generally known as Tia. Others have the nature of a familiar name, used only within the immediate family circle. Their use connotes a strong sense of intimacy, or personal warmth. Other *danglai* can be described as friendship or joking names, and are used exclusively between close friends, or within a peer group. Such *danglai* often make a humorous reference to some peculiarity of a person's character or appearance, or commemorate some jointly experienced incident. One young man in Bangau-Bangau, who is unusually fat, is known to his age-mates as Gajamina, 'sea cow'. Such names are usually conferred between youngsters, but close friends may continue to use them throughout their later life, as a mark of special affection.

The Bajau Laut are without formal name avoidance. However, out of respect, the villagers rarely address those who are older than themselves, or of a senior generation, by personal names. If two persons are related, kin terms are preferred, and in many cases relational terms of address are used between persons who are not genealogically related. Elders, and house group and cluster leaders are addressed, respectfully, as 'grandparents' (*mbo'*).[8] Age-mates commonly address each other as *séhe'*, 'companions', or by the reciprocal term *bilas*, 'co-brother/sister-in-law'.

Death Rites

At the approach of death, close kin are summoned. Boats are dispatched to call back (*binangun*) those who are away fishing or who live in other villages. Paying final respects to the dead is felt to be one of the most solemn obligations that exists between kin.

As soon as breathing stops (*abakkat napas*), the immediate family shows its grief by wailing (*magdohong* or *maglindu*). At the same time, a gong is slowly beaten to signal the individual's passing to the rest of the village. The immediate survivors of the deceased (his or her spouse, children, parents, and siblings) are expected to give themselves over entirely to mourning and the open expression of grief, and the elders among the deceased's more distant kin, outside the immediate circle of close relatives (*tai'anakan*), are expected to make all the practical arrangements on their behalf for the subsequent death rites. A collection is generally taken and a small party is sent to market to purchase supplies, such as white cloth, incense, rice, sugar, and coffee, for the night vigil and the washing and shrouding of the corpse. The *imam* who advises the house group is called for to see that all of the necessary arrangements are correctly carried out. His first act is to turn the body of the dead person so that its head no longer points toward the headside (*kokan*) of the house or boat. This simple act of reorientation, positioning the head and feet of the body perpendicular to the 'headside', so that they are now in line with the entrance and back wall of the house, or with the bow and stern of the boat, signifies death and the departure of the deceased from the world of the living. The body is no longer a 'body' (*baran*), but, as a consequence of reorientation, becomes a 'corpse' (*bangkai*).

Expressions of grief are often intense and the survivors must also be looked after. The Bajau Laut believe that strong emotions should not be repressed or bottled up. Hence, those who were close to the deceased, such as children, or husbands and wives, should be allowed to give way to their feelings in order to come to terms with the sense of loss they have experienced. On one occasion when I was present during a woman's funeral, her widowed husband, in his grief, attempted to impale himself on a fish-spear which he had fixed upright on the house floor and had to be subdued and calmed by his kin and neighbours. More often, particularly during long, sleepless vigils, the surviving kin fall unconscious or become hysterical, and the attendance of a medium is often required.

The first task that must be performed following death is the washing and shrouding of the corpse in preparation for burial. This is called *amahilala' a'a amatai*. The term *amahilala'*, or *mahilala'*, has the general meaning of 'putting in order', 'repairing', or 'making right'. It is most often used to describe the ordinary task of housekeeping, or cleaning and putting a house in order, or of repairing an object, such as an outboard engine. It is also used, to describe the reconciliation of a previously estranged husband and wife. Here the term is used with the meaning of 'putting the dead person (*a'a amatai*) in order'. After it is completed, the body of the deceased is referred to by a special term, *mayat*, and is no longer looked upon as a source of defilement. The task of washing and shrouding the body must be performed by someone of the same sex as the deceased, from outside the immediate family circle. In the case of a man, an experienced *imam* is often called upon for this purpose, usually assisted by others. Assistants are often affinal kin of the deceased, or relatives by marriage of other members of his or her house group.[9] The task of 'putting death in order' is a complex one, divided into a number of separate stages.

In the first stage (*pinasungi'*), the bowels and bladder are emptied by pressing down on the stomach. Next, all of the orifices of the body are cleansed. The second stage (*tinampoyo'an*) consists of preparing the shroud from white cloth, which can be neither cut with scissors nor sewn.

The third stage (*pinandi*) involves a thorough washing of the entire body. Fresh water and soap are used. This stage is highly important, as the Bajau Laut believe that the body of a dead person must be perfectly clean; otherwise it will not be admitted to heaven, where everything is said to be spotless and without blemish. While the body is bathed, a piece of white cloth is placed over the face and around the waist. In the fourth stage (*kinottoban kukku*), the nails (*kukku*) are cut and all dirt is removed from under them, beginning with the fingers and ending with the toes.

During the fifth stage (*pinasium*), members of the deceased's house group and other close relatives are invited to come forward, kneel, and kiss (*pasium*) the deceased on the forehead. The *imam* supervising the death rites calls on the deceased's kin to come forward one at a time. This is an emotional moment; and many break down and weep. When kissing the deceased, the face must be dry, so tears are carefully brushed away. The villagers describe the kiss as a sign of love (*kalasa*) and a final token of farewell.

The body is then washed again. If the family has the means, a special water called *bohé' siam* is used. This is purchased from one of several *imam* in Bangau-Bangau, and is blessed and strained through white cloth. Otherwise the body is washed with ordinary fresh water, as before. In the next stage (*pinindah*), the body is moved from the place where it was bathed and laid out on its back on a length of white cloth. Finally, the body is enshrouded (*engkotan*) in three layers of white cloth. Narrow strips of cloth are torn from the hem of the shroud and tied around the wrists of the members of the deceased's immediate family. These strips are believed to secure the survivors' life-souls and so prevent them from following the soul of the deceased in death. It was also customary to wrap the shrouded body in a sleeping mat or mats secured with additional strips of shrouding cloth. In 1979, these latter practices were no longer followed and the body was simply shrouded or, if wrapped in a *tépo*, this was removed at the graveside and no longer buried with the dead.

According to Islamic convention, barring exceptional circumstances, the body should be buried within 24 hours of death. The preferred time of burial is in the late afternoon, shortly before sunset, between afternoon (*sambahayang ashar*) and evening prayers (*sambahayang magrib*). Occasionally, however, burial takes place the following morning or on the afternoon of the day following death. Such delays may be necessary in order to allow time for close kin to arrive from other villages or to call back those who were away fishing at the time of death. While the body remains in the village, social gatherings such as weddings or village hearings should be postponed; musical instruments, such as the xylophone (*gabbang*), should not be played; and all loud laughter and shouting should be avoided, particularly within hearing of the mourners. If death occurs in the afternoon or evening, the body is kept in the village overnight for burial the following day. When this happens, a night-long vigil or wake is held in the house where the body has been laid out in readiness for burial. During the vigil, guests generally come and go, although some kin and neighbours always remain with the immediate survivors to look after them and receive others coming to pay their respects. Except for the immediate family, the vigil is far from solemn. Coffee and sweets are served, and the guests freely gossip and joke with one another. In the morning, those remaining in the house are served a simple breakfast.

Before the body is removed from the village and taken to the cemetery for burial, the *imam* supervising the death rites, usually with a company of other men, goes to choose a suitable grave site. This is usually done after consulting with the deceased's family, as there is often a strong preference that the deceased be buried near a former spouse, close to the graves of his or her parents, or in some other specific area of the cemetery. Once a site is chosen, the *imam* recites prayers which are believed to soften the earth and magically remove stones, making it easier to prepare the grave. Once this is done, the party of men who accompanied the *imam* begin to dig the grave, while the *imam* returns to the village to oversee the carrying of the body to the cemetery.

Before the final removal of the body from the village, special prayers are performed by a group of *imam* or pious elders over the shrouded body. These prayers are called *sambahayang mayat*. Each man who takes part in the prayers afterwards receives from the deceased's kin a sarong (*hos*) and shirt (*baju*), as *sarakkah*. As soon as the prayers are concluded, the body is carried to the cemetery, accompanied by the surviving family and close kindred. As the body is removed, a gong is again sounded to announce to those remaining behind that they may now resume their ordinary activities.

Under the influence of district religious authorities, Bajau Laut death rites, more than any other ritual observance, have undergone dramatic change. In 1964–5, the dead were transported to the community's burial island by boat, according to detailed ritual rules. The boat transporting the body flew a white banner, from the bow if the deceased was a man, from the stern if a woman, and varying in size depending on the age, small for a child, and large for an adult (Plate 28). More importantly, signifying death, the body was laid out lengthwise, head to the bow, feet to the stern, rather than toward the lateral headside of the boat. As soon as the body was carried ashore, it was held aloft and the members of the deceased's immediate family were led back and forth beneath it. This was done as a final act of parting, in order to sever all remaining earthly ties with the dead. Traditionally, if the deceased was an adult fisherman, his boat was dismantled, and the sideboards or keel section were used to fashion a coffin in which his body was buried, with wood below and above it to prevent direct contact with the soil. Also, as described in Chapter 7, part of the deceased's property, known as *magkaat*, was placed with the body inside the grave and buried with the corpse (Plate 29).

Now, the body is carried to the grave in a simple litter, and is buried without a coffin or wrapping of mats in the communal Muslim cemetery on the outskirts of Semporna town or in the new community cemetery near the village. Burial in these new sites, rather than on the former burial island, reflects not only a change in burial practice, but also a dramatic alteration in the status of the Bajau Laut, marking their acceptance by neighbouring people as Muslims. Also absent from the current death rites, or at least not as marked as previously, are notions of spiritual danger once prominently associated with death and with contact with the dead, including a series of ritual acts meant to safeguard the souls of the survivors and safely commit the soul of the deceased to the hereafter. The traditional death rites ended, following the return of the burial party to the village, in a final rite of exorcism in which the deceased's soul was sent from the house or boat in which the death rites took place and dispatched, with appropriate instructions, to the cemetery.

Once the body is lowered into the ground and covered with earth, the *imam* recites the prayer for the dead (*dua'a tulkin*), which, the villagers believe, has the effect of awakening the deceased, as if from sleep, and bringing about the realization that he or she is dead and no longer has a place in the living world. In the past, this was followed by a brief exhortation addressed to the dead directly to accept his or her fate and not trouble the living. Just before the body is covered with earth, the immediate survivors remove the strips of white cloth tied around their wrists and cast them into the grave. Once the grave is filled, a small stake is inserted in the earth directly over the head of the body (Plate 30). As with the lateral orientation of the house and boat, this stake indicates the 'headside' of the grave. As he recites the *dua'a tulkin*, the *imam* faces this stake, after which water is poured over it. This water is described as 'provisions' (*lutu*) for the dead. It is also said to 'cool' the body, reflecting a belief that the body, in its journey to heaven, is in danger of being consumed by the fires of hell owing to impurities it has absorbed while its owner lived in this world. With this done, the burial party returns to the village. Upon their return, the *imam* leads the mourners in a reading of the Koran and prayer (*dua'a*). This is followed by a brief meal (*amakan*). Before the guests return home, members of the deceased's household are expected to make known to those present, on how many subsequent days they plan to hold commemorative rites for the dead (*bahangi*). The number depends on the age of the deceased, his or her social importance, and the economic means of the house group.

Memorial Rites for the Dead (Bahangi)

Up to five commemorative rites may be held, ending with one or another of the following: *bahangi tellu*, three days after death; *bahangi pitu*, seven days after death; *bahangi dua' mpu*, twenty days after death; *bahangi empat pu*, forty days after death; or *bahangi dahatus*, one hundred days after death. Very few house groups attempt to undertake the full series of rites till the hundredth-day ceremony. The first seven days are thought to be the most important. When the deceased is buried on the day following death, there is sometimes a discrepancy in the way in which days are reckoned, some households counting from the day of death, others from the day of burial.

Until either the three-day or seven-day rites are held, the *imam* is asked to come to the household each day, at morning and evening, to read from the Koran or commentaries and to lead the men of the house group in prayers. Following each reading, coffee and biscuits are served.

The seventh-day celebration is marked by a larger gathering of guests and is followed by a meal of rice and fish. For the first seven days, a sleeping mat is left spread on the floor of the house, near the headside, where the body of the deceased was placed prior to burial. Cushions and pillows are stacked around the sides of the mat. On these are placed sarongs, shirts, and other gifts to be presented to the *imam* and others who took part in the prayers following the conclusion of *bahangi pitu*. At this time, the *imam* is also presented with a small monetary gift in payment for leading the morning and evening prayers. With the conclusion of either the *bahangi tellu* or *bahangi pitu*, the immediate family of the deceased ends total mourning and resumes normal life. The *bahangi dua' mpu* is usually a more modest observance than the seventh-day celebration, while the *bahangi empat pu*, if it is held, is normally the largest and most elaborate of the memorial rites.

Within a few weeks after burial, the stake placed temporarily over the head of the deceased is replaced by a wooden marker (*senduk*) (Plate 31).[10] Symbolically, the act of placing this marker at the headside of the grave represents the final separation of the dead (Kiefer and Sather, 1970). Later, the *senduk* also serves as a point of contact. Here, facing the marker, the deceased's kin make offerings and invoke the dead. When they do so, they generally pour water over the *senduk*. The marker itself is positioned directly over the head of the deceased and represents, in symbolic terms, a gendered replica of the human body (Kiefer and Sather, 1970). After this, should the ghost of the deceased, or its lingering life-soul, continue to visit the family, it is likely to be suspected that the preceding death rites were improperly carried out. In particular, these signs suggest that the body was inadequately washed. In extreme cases, should these visits persist, the washing of the corpse may be 'repeated' by bathing the *senduk* itself and the corpse 'cooled' by pouring water over the grave. Through the *senduk*, the living are able to remain in contact with the transcendental soul of the dead, are able to show their remembrance, and gain the continued favour of the dead, now transformed as ancestor (*mbo'*).

Typically, Bajau Laut grave sites are congested, and often in digging a new grave, bones from previous burials are uncovered. These are wrapped in white cloth and reburied. Pious elders are especially believed to possess special, carefully guarded knowledge that allows them to ascend directly to heaven after death, rather than remain in their graves until judgement day. In 1974, when I was present, villagers digging a new grave uncovered an earlier burial thought to be that of a pious elder named Alalbimbang. Despite a thorough search, Alalbimbang's bones could not be found. This the villagers saw as a sign that the pious elder had entered directly into heaven.

Graves are sometimes covered with an open shelter (*luma'-luma'*), consisting of a simple roof set on four corner-posts. Under ordinary circumstances, graves are avoided because of their connection with death. However, the ancestral dead are conceived of as generally beneficent figures, although they may also punish, and their graves are often visited in order to seek special favours or blessings. Offerings may also be made to the ancestors and placed by the *senduk*, usually in response to a dream, or upon the advice of a seer or spirit-medium.

1. See Chapter 2.

2. See Chapter 3. In the past, for boat-dwelling bands, these seasons also marked a possible shift in moorage location as families moved to the lee of prevailing winds.

3. After, the villagers say, she has missed two consecutive menstruations.

4. Among neighbouring shore Bajau, the *panguling* is also called the *pandai*.

5. Among neighbouring shore groups in Semporna, the *tamuni* is buried in the earth and traditionally a sprouting coconut (*pangsutan*) is planted immediately above it. The resulting palm that takes root over the *tamuni* is believed to be mystically related to the new-born and may not be felled or disturbed, representing in a sense his or her plant counterpart.

6. Among shore people it traditionally lasted for forty days and was calculated by the use of white lime tally marks.

7. It should be remembered that evening marks the beginning of the day on which the operation is performed.

8. See Chapter 7.

9. Performing these tasks connected with death is one of the roles strongly associated with in-marrying house group and cluster members.

10. Elsewhere, in a comparative paper written with Thomas Kiefer (Kiefer and Sather, 1970), I have discussed at some length symbolic elements associated with the placement of these markers and their carved design features.

10
Fate, Luck, and the Ancestors

Bai angindam bai magpapinjadi kita.

How we were created, so we become. (Traditional Bajau Laut saying)

Ritual Vows (*Janji'*)

THE vow or pledge (*janji'*) is a notion of fundamental importance in Bajau Laut social relations. But the vow also has a religious component and so additionally forms the most frequent basis on which village ritual observances take place.

Interpersonal relations between village kin and neighbours take the characteristic form of linked transactions that, through the rendering and return of 'help' (*tabang*), have the cumulative effect of creating and discharging 'debts' (*utang*). The obligations of reciprocity involved in these transactions are frequently backed by a pledge or verbal promise. But more than this, the pronouncement of a pledge is thought to solemnize, and impart a religious significance to any form of promissory agreement (*magjanji'*) that one person enters into with another. As a result, failure to fulfil the terms of a pledge is said to invite *busung* (calamity). Besides the forms of *magjanji'*, associated with kinship and related directly to an exchange of social favours and support, there are other forms of vow-taking that have a more overtly religious nature.

An especially pious elder, Lamarani, once explained to me why a feeling of sanctity tends to characterize promises by saying that all human existence involves, at its heart, a promissory relationship between humankind (*mundusia*) and God (*Tuhan*).

We, as human beings, enjoy the gift of life from God. We also enjoy His special favour, namely, the Prophet and his teachings. For these gifts, we, as their recipients, must repay God by living in accordance with His wishes. These wishes are revealed to us through the Prophet's teachings. Otherwise, if we refuse to live as God wishes, we will suffer misfortune in this life and eternal damnation in the next. In addition, a person may also gain merit in the eyes of God by behaving properly. In this way, by his actions, he benefits both himself and others.

What Lamarani implies here is that God Himself is the source of all vows. As the ultimate bestower of gifts, most notably the gift of life, God is also, in a final sense, responsible for vouchsafing the terms of all promises. Agreements sealed with a promise are therefore sanctified, and their violation is an act of impiety, ultimately punished by ill-fatedness and the loss of God's favour.

As a ritual vow, the act of *magjanji'* may take several forms. The simplest is called *magjanji' ni kandi*, and consists of a promise which an individual makes with himself. If, for example, a person is in difficulty he might wish that someone—a relative or friend—would come forward with an offer of help. If such help does materialize, he is expected to perform an act of devotion or piety, as a promised sign of thankfulness in fulfilment of the vow he made with himself. Even though help may come from another person, the Bajau Laut say that it is God who controls such events. Therefore it is God who should be repaid, as well as the person who provided the help.

An individual may also make a vow with another person, normally a close kin, such as a father (*magjanji' ni mma'*) or mother (*magjanji' ni enggo'*). Such promises have the form of a pledge of mutual support, or a promise of special respect or honour, in return for a personal favour. Vows may also be made to places believed to be imbued with special power (*tampat*). Some are thought to be capable of granting blessings to those who visit them for the purpose of vow-taking (*magjanji' ni tampat*), in return for offerings and other signs of respect or promises of acknowledgement. Graves are often treated as *tampat* and visited by those seeking special favours. Other *tampat* are believed to be the dwelling-place of spirits. Anyone who disturbs such a *tampat*, or gives offence to the spirit or spirits that make the *tampat* their home, is likely to fall ill or suffer an accident. When this occurs, a promise may be made at the site pledging a petition of forgiveness in return for the victim's recovery. Relations with spirits (*saitan*) are somewhat different than those involved in other forms of vow-taking because spirits are believed to be essentially malevolent beings, intent on, in most cases, causing injury and testing a person's faith in God. As a result, vows are intended to persuade the spirits to withdraw their attack and so provide a means, not so much of obtaining blessings, as of curbing misfortune and securing temporary protection against danger.

The most frequent vows are those which are made directly with God Himself. These are called *magjanji' ni Tuhan* and take the form of a promise that, in return for a special favour, the individual will dedicate himself to an act of piety or devotion, as a sign of thanksgiving (*magsukul*). Many kinds of favours may be sought in this way. For example, God may be asked to deliver someone from danger, or to bring him home safely from a difficult journey. If a fishing party fails to return to the village when expected, or is caught in a storm at sea, those at home may make a vow promising a rite of thanksgiving in repayment for its safe return. Vows may also be made by those who find themselves in danger. Frequently, vows are made by people seeking success in fulfilling a personal ambition. However, God should not be petitioned simply for material wealth or worldly profit. There was a case, which was cited several times as an example, in which a shore Bajau is said to have won a large lottery as a result of a promise to God. Although it was said that the man contributed a share of his winnings to the district mosque fund, his example was pointed to as an improper use of vow-taking. It was noted that he soon frittered away his fortune and was left even poorer afterwards than he had been before.

The greatest number of vows made with God are in connection with childbirth and illness. The Bajau Laut believe that human life is itself a divine gift. The power to grant, prolong, or withhold life rests ultimately with God. Every individual has a singular fate (*sukud*) which God alone has predetermined. In this regard, fate, too, has a promissory nature. At birth, God enters into a promissory agreement with each individual in regard to the time, place, and circumstances of his or her death. Death is inevitable and cannot be avoided, for God, in creating the ancestors, made death final. Therefore all that a seer (*ta'u nganda'*), for example, can do is to reveal the time and particular nature of a client's death. Otherwise, when a person's 'time' (*ta'abut umulna*) has come, there is nothing that even the most skilful curer or medium can do to prevent death from taking place. God, however, may be appealed to in the form of a promissory vow. In this way alone, through the direct intervention of God in response to a vow, may life be prolonged beyond its allotted span. Vows are frequently made requesting that the life of someone who appears to be close to death may be prolonged and that he or she be given a temporary reprieve.

The granting of a new life, as well as prolonging an already existing one, is said to be in God's hands alone. Many petitions addressed to God are in the form of a request for children. Childless couples, or those who have lost a child in infancy, are especially likely to make a vow with God. Couples may also seek a child of a particular sex. For example, Sellonga (pseudonym), decided after his wife had given birth to five daughters, that God had willed him to have only daughters. He therefore made a promise with God that if his next child was a son, he would treat it exactly as if it were another daughter. Sellonga's next child was a boy, and in 1979 the youngster, who was then three years old, presented a remarkable figure. Obviously a sturdy boy, the child was dressed by his parents like a girl, in cotton dresses, and wore a gold ear-ring in one ear. When a woman becomes pregnant, it is also customary to make a vow with God, as a precautionary measure to avert danger to herself or to her newly conceived child. Such vows are particularly likely if the woman has never been pregnant before or if her labour is prolonged or difficult.

The most frequent of all vows are made in connection with illness and take the form of a request for a person's recovery. In the case of an especially grave illness, village mediums may advise their patient's family to make a vow, acknowledging that the illness is beyond their powers to treat.

Fate and God's Favour

A vow or pledge to God can be redeemed in a variety of ways. By far the most important is to sponsor a rite of thanksgiving called a *magmaulud* or *magbajanji'*. The *magmaulud* is held only in fulfilment of a pledge to God and never, the villagers maintain, in connection with any other form of vow-taking. Other acts of piety, such as prayers, fasting, or an act of respect towards an elder, are appropriate for minor favours. But all major blessings must be redeemed by the vow-taker by sponsoring a *magmaulud*. The rite is the most frequent of all village ritual observances and, in many respects, its most important, as its performance reflects on the basic promissory nature of relations between God and humankind.

The central element of the *magmaulud* is the *dua'a selamat*, a reading from the religious commentaries (*Kitab* or *Bejanji*). These commentaries are known locally as the *maulud*, hence the name of the rite, and their reading is followed by prayers. The commentaries read on this occasion typically concern the birth (*maulud*) and history of the Prophet Muhammad's life. During the *dua'a selamat*, elderly guests and men of the household, often including one or two invited *imam*, take turns reading from the *Kitab* while seated in a circle on the floor of the sponsor's house. Each reads a few verses and then passes the book to the next man in the circle. Not all the men are able to read, and those who cannot generally sit behind the others. The *magmaulud* is held as an act of thankfulness to God (*magsukul ni Tuhan*) in fulfilment of a pledge for His having granted a member of the house group a special favour. The person who is the object of the favour, who has recovered from illness or safely returned, for example, from a dangerous journey, sits in the centre of the circle. Before the *dua'a* begins, the person who made the original vow announces to the gathering the nature of the favour received and the house group's reason for sponsoring the rite. *Magmaulud* is held in the evening and after the reading, a meal (Plate 32) (or light refreshments) is served to the guests.

In addition to *magmaulud*, a pledge to God may be redeemed by a second rite called *magtimbang*. Frequently, *magmaulud* is followed, at sunrise (*pasod allau*) the next morning, by *magtimbang*, although the two rites may also be held separately. Among the Bajau Laut, *magtimbang* is closely associated with mediumship and its performance is often condemned now by local religious authorities. For this reason, it has diminished markedly in recent years. The rite is performed chiefly in connection with childbirth and illness among new-born infants and small children. Like *magmaulud*, it is essentially a rite of thanksgiving, although it is sometimes also held in anticipation of a favour which has not yet been received. In the latter case, its performance is thought to obligate God to grant the favour being sought.

Magtimbang means literally 'to balance' or 'to weigh in a balance' (*timbangan*). The rite is held in the morning (*subu*), shortly after sunrise, and begins with the bathing of the person to be weighed on the open house platform. Before the weighing takes place, a balance beam is set up over the sponsor's house-platform. The beam is suspended at the centre by a length of rope secured in such a way as to allow the beam to rotate horizontally around its centre. A cradle sling (*dundangan*) made of yellow or green cloth—colours associated with mediumship—is hung from one end of the beam. The person who is the object of the rite, or if it is being performed for an infant, both the mother and her child, are made to sit in the sling. They are dressed in the costume of the mediums: a white shirt and loose green trousers for males; a green blouse and yellow sarong for females. On the opposite end of the beam are suspended the following items:

1. One bunch of bananas;
2. Two bundles of coconuts, one hung each side of the beam;
3. One bundle of firewood;
4. Lemongrass (*sallai/sai*);
5. Salt (*asin*);
6. Chillies (*lara*);
7. A bottle of water (*dakassa' bohé'*);
8. One or two pots of uncooked husked rice (*daleppo' buas*);
9. A handkerchief (*saputangan*); and
10. Gold jewellery (*bulawan* or *dublun*).

The gold jewellery is usually hung from the centre of the beam. Fine sarongs may be hung across the top at either side to adjust the balance. The weight of the person, or persons, sitting in the sling should be perfectly counter-balanced by the weight of the objects suspended from the opposite end (Plate 33). The quantity of these objects is varied to compensate for persons of different weights. On the platform floor, immediately beneath the central pivot of the beam, a mat (*tépo*) is spread. Here plates of rice cakes and incense are set out by members of the sponsoring house group (Plate 34).

As family and guests gather around the beam, the person to be weighed is asked to sit in the sling while the beam is held steady by the *imam* and others assisting him. The objects are then loaded in place at the opposite end, with adjustments by the *imam* until the two are in balance. The person sitting in the sling is asked to raise his or her feet off the platform floor.

The *imam* then blesses the person being 'weighed', while he or she is gently swung up and down. He then turns the beam slowly around three complete counter-clockwise pivots on its centre. Pausing briefly, the *imam* then circles with the beam three times in the reverse direction, restoring it to its original position, with himself and the person sitting on the sling facing eastward (*kaluwa'an*). When the beam has come to rest, the individual on the sling is kissed by each member of the house group in turn and then helped down from the sling while the beam is held steady. He or she is then welcomed by the others with embraces and congratulations. While the objects at the opposite end of the beam are unloaded, the *imam* and other elders sit on the *tépo*, facing the person who has just been weighed, and the *imam* leads the group in prayers.

Afterwards, the coconuts, bananas, and firewood are divided, and distributed partly to the *imam* who performed the rite as a merit-gaining gift (*sarakkah*), and partly to the kin and neighbours who attended the weighing as guests.

Weighing is performed as an act of thanksgiving in fulfilment of a promise. The case of Tia, mentioned earlier in connection with ritual reconciliation (*kiparat*), affords an example, as well as illustrating the importance of promissory agreements more generally.

Tia's husband, Laiti, married later than most village men, and at the time of his marriage, he was already a young man of substantial means. Earlier, Laiti's mother, Akbaraini, had begun to set aside part of his wages for his future marriage. Laiti's eldest brother had married a Sitangkai woman and lived for a number of years with her family in the Philippines. Laiti met Tia on a visit to Sitangkai and made up his mind after their first meeting to marry her. Laiti's parents were opposed. Although he claims to have given them no encouragement, they had by then started negotiations with the family of a girl in Bangau-Bangau. Also, Tia's sister had earlier married, as a polygynous union, the Tausug mayor of Sitangkai, a man greatly feared locally, and Laiti's parents wished to avoid any involvement with the mayor and his relatives. They therefore refused to grant their consent to the marriage. Laiti then went ahead and arranged for the marriage on his own. However, Laiti's parents refused to return the money that he had entrusted to his mother's keeping and because of their refusal to participate in the wedding, Tia's father asked for an unusually large bride-wealth (*dalaham*).

At this point, a fortuitous event occurred: Laiti received RM13,000 in payment for shares in a native timber company. With this, he readily financed his own wedding. When he returned with Tia from Sitangkai, his mother refused to meet her. Laiti and Tia therefore lived separately from Laiti's parents. When I visited Bangau-Bangau in 1974, two years after their marriage, Tia and Laiti's mother, although still enemies (*bantah*), were very close to reconciliation. Not long afterwards, Tia conceived. In order to preclude the possibility of their enmity causing a difficult delivery, the two women, as described in Chapter 6, underwent ritual reconciliation, and the couple afterwards joined Laiti's parental house group.

However, the health of Tia, who had begun to suffer periodic illness shortly after conception, grew worse. Toward the end of her pregnancy, she became extremely ill. Shortly before the time of her delivery, she complained to Akbaraini that she had difficulty seeing properly. Moments later, as she was still talking to her mother-in-law, she fell unconscious, and as she collapsed, she bit her tongue, causing her mouth to fill with blood. Fearing for her life, the family at once called for Laiti. As soon as he arrived, she briefly regained consciousness. Shortly afterwards, she fell unconscious again, and remained in a coma until the next morning. In the meantime, a spirit-medium was called and diagnosed the cause of her illness to be a promise that Laiti had made to Tia's father to bring the young woman back to her natal home in Sitangkai for the delivery of her first child. Such a promise is not uncommon when a woman leaves her natal village in marriage. Her condition was attributed to *busung*, or ill-luck, caused by her husband's failure to fulfil this promise to her father. In this case, the medium advised that the father be summoned from Sitangkai, as Tia was in no condition to travel. Shortly before daybreak, Laiti dispatched a party to bring Tia's father to Bangau-Bangau and they returned the following night. By then, Tia was already feeling better. The medium had only said that Laiti should bring his father-in-law to be with his daughter, but, on his own, Laiti additionally pledged to God that should she recover, he would also hold a *magtimbang* rite.

As soon as Tia was well enough, the rite was performed, attended by the close relatives of the family. Unfortunately, Tia fell ill again shortly afterwards, and for the last two days before delivery suffered periodic spells of unconsciousness. The child was delivered stillborn, and as the placenta could not be expelled, Tia had to be taken to the hospital for emergency surgery. The surgery—although it almost certainly saved her life—is said to have left Tia unable to bear children.

Through her long sickness and recovery, Tia was attended by Laiti's mother, Akbaraini, who, during this time acquired, many villagers say, the skills of an expert midwife (*panguling*). Despite their previous enmity, the two women became extremely close. Later, after Tia was informed by the district medical officer that she could no longer bear children, she and Laiti adopted a daughter, whom they named Asia.

As in this case, *magtimbang* is frequently held for an expectant mother, particularly if it is felt that her life might be in danger. This is done as a way of involving God in a compact, or pledge, meant to ensure her safe delivery. Later, additional weighings may be promised if the child she bears should fall ill. *Magtimbang* is also performed to fulfil a promise made in connection with a near drowning or an escape from being lost or of facing grave danger at sea.

Misfortune, Spiritual Punishment, and Curing

Most villagers believe that, in an ultimate sense, all events are predetermined by an omnipotent God. At the same time, they recognize a host of intermediate effects and causal agencies which influence, in a more direct way, the outcome of events, including moral choice and personal volition.

If an affliction is beyond human power to cope with, an appeal may be addressed directly to God in the form of a vow or promise. However, this is usually a last resort, and initially at least, concern tends to focus on more immediate levels of treatment.

Sickness and other forms of affliction are attributed to a variety of possible causes. Many of these can be described as 'natural'. The villagers recognize, for example, that headaches and mild fevers may result from too much time spent in the sun, or that painful wounds may be received from contact with 'fire coral' (*batu api*) or scorpionfish (*kappo*). In these cases, the symptoms of the affliction are treated as such, without reference to any other than purely 'natural' agencies. In addition, however, the action of human and spirit causes are also recognized; other sources of affliction include soul loss, attack by spirits, sorcery, poisoning, and spiritual punishment for wrongdoing. Sometimes, several causes are thought to work simultaneously.

All sickness, regardless of its cause, is thought to reflect upon the condition of an individual's life-soul (*sumangat*) and upon states of feeling associated with the body.

Life-souls and Transcendental-souls

Interpretations regarding the nature of the soul differ somewhat from person to person but, in general, most individuals distinguish between what I call, following Kiefer (1972b: 129–30), a 'life-soul' (*sumangat*) and a 'transcendental-soul' (*ruah*). Kiefer uses these terms to discuss Tausug soul concepts, which appear to be very similar to those of the Bajau Laut. The transcendental-soul is believed to be created by God and once created, it is said to exist forever. Some describe it as existing separately, and say that it enters the body only when an individual is at prayer. The transcendental-soul is associated primarily with an individual's moral constitution. A person's good and evil deeds are registered in the fate of his or her *ruah*. After death, the soul eventually goes to heaven (*sulga'*), following, for most persons, a period of tribulation and punishment in hell (*nalka*). Except for the very pious, who lead lives without sin, everyone's soul must undergo atonement for the evil deeds he or she has committed in this world. Once it reaches heaven, the transcendental-soul, having passed through hell, is said to be re-embodied and enjoys an existence of unending pleasure. Here, the Bajau Laut say, one 'returns to God'.

The life-soul, on the other hand, is a principal constituent of every living person.[1] After conception, the life-soul is believed to attach itself inside the infant's body. At first, its attachment is weak. The soul may easily enter and leave the body through the anterior fontanelle (*bessok*). As a result, the life of a new-born child is thought to be precarious. Hence, throughout infancy, the hair growing over the fontanelle is left uncut. Later, when the fontanelle closes, the soul's attachment is said to be more secure. Unlike the Tausug, the Bajau Laut do not distinguish as a separate entity what Kiefer (1972b: 130) calls a 'spirit-soul'. Instead, its attributes, including its identification with a person's shadow (*mahung*), are associated with the life-soul.

Life is said to depend upon the conjunction within the body (*baran*) of both the life-soul and breath (*napas*). Death is described as the cessation of breath (*abakkat napas*). While the soul is said to animate the body, it is, nevertheless, a separable entity. Thus, a person's life-soul may detach itself from the body. This commonly happens in sleep. Dreams (*nguppi*) are thought to be the experiences of the life-soul during its disembodied wanderings. Experiences of the soul, revealed through dreams, may be prophetic and are sometimes said to prefigure subsequent events in the waking world. Dreams may also be dangerous. The life-soul, unprotected by its bodily envelope, may be set upon by spirits; or it may become disoriented and lose its way. If the latter occurs, the dreamer may suffer a state of sleeping terror called *eddop*. Deprived of his or her soul, which is unable to finds its way back to the body, the sleeper has difficulty breathing.

Tandoh, a house group leader, described the experience in this way: 'It feels as if someone is choking you. It is difficult to wake up. And if you try to cry out for help, your voice is feeble and choked. So no one can hear you.' Death occurs unless the sleeper is awakened by someone who is aware of his distress. A person who is startled, or experiences a severe shock, is thought to be similarly in danger of soul loss and it is believed may sicken as a consequence.

The prolonged absence of the life-soul from the body causes a loss of vitality, unconsciousness, and finally cessation of breathing and death. In a converse way, inability to breathe, as in drowning, causes the life-soul to desert the body. Similarly, a bodily injury is believed to impair both breathing and the condition of the life-soul. The functioning of each element comprising the living person—body, life-soul, and breath—is thought to be interdependent, with the state of one affecting that of the others. At death, this conjunction is broken. The soul takes permanent leave of the body, breathing ceases, and, unanimated by soul and breath, the body decomposes. After death, the life-soul is said to linger for a time in places that its owner frequented in life. In the final death rites, the life-soul must therefore be exorcized.

The Body, Emotions, and Restraint

The Bajau Laut maintain a strongly embodied sense of person. Even in death, a replica of the body is placed over the grave in the form of the *senduk*, which serves as a representation of the ancestor's body to the extent that it may be 'fed' and even 'bathed', and in attaining heaven, each individual's transcendental-soul is said to be re-embodied, thereafter enjoying an existence of bodily pleasure.

For the Bajau Laut, the body is, above all, the centre of feeling, cognition, intellect, and emotion. For the villagers, the heart/liver (*atai*) is the primary seat of volition and feelings. Emotional states, such as anger (*peddi' atai*) and grief (*asusa' atai*), are identified with the *atai*. The Bajau Laut attach great importance to the genuineness of inter-subjective feelings. A successful marriage calls for both love (*lasa*) and physical passion (*makahandul atai*) and in relations between kin and affines, less stress is placed on formal obligations than on feelings and their authenticity. One should come to the aid of kin, not out of duty alone but because of affection, respect, love, compassion, or pity. To be 'open-hearted' (*pabuka'na atai*) is especially valued and indicates that an individual not only shows his true feelings, but that he is caring and sensitive to the feelings of others. Its opposite, *maglom-lom atai*, describes a person who secretly harbours hatred or bitter feelings while maintaining an outward façade of goodwill and affection. To have a 'bad heart' (*ala'at ataina*) is to be deceiving, false, and dishonest. Emotions should not be held back. This is true not only of love and compassion, but even of hatred, sadness, and anger. During the first days of mourning, surviving kin should vent their grief openly, as a way of coming to terms with their loss. Similarly, anger should be shown and not held back. As Panglima Tiring told me on a number of occasions, disagreements should be dealt with in the open. It is always better to quarrel with others openly than to hold feelings inside and not show them. Verbal quarrels and public shouting matches are a regular feature of daily life in Bangau-Bangau, even between kin and village housemates. This, the headman said, is a good thing. If anger is kept hidden, it does not go away, becoming, instead, a source of possible harm, both to the angry person and to others.

Yet unrestrained feelings may also be dangerous. Intense grief, for example, or the feelings of loneliness (*telingus-lingus*) that a person experiences when separated from family and loved ones, are both thought to weaken the individual, impair the vitality of his or her life-soul, and so reduce its resistance to spiritual attack. Hence, the importance of reconciliation, of coming to terms with anger and grief, and of maintaining equity in interpersonal relations. Feeling states are also projected into the spirit world, the prime source of danger to human enterprise. The spirits are described as impulsive and governed by emotions. They are said to be envious, greedy, quick to anger, irascible, and highly sensitive to slights. Local spirits, in particular, are thought to resent the appearance of newcomers, are irked by their curiosity, and so are said to afflict them with minor illness (*binahu*), simply out of cantankerousness and ill-will. When I returned to Bangau-Bangau with my family in 1979, my wife and daughter, who had never been to the village before, were both almost constantly ill. Garani, a village spirit-medium and friend from my first fieldwork, concerned, told me that the local spirits were momentarily resentful and out of temper. While I was familiar to them, they were irritated by the appearance of strangers, in this case, the newcomers I had brought with me. In particular, their permission (*puhun*) had not been solicited beforehand, leaving them especially cross. Yet, he reassured me, the sickness my wife and daughter suffered was not dangerous. The spirits were merely out of sorts.

While being 'open-hearted' is a virtue, it is not good to be, like the spirits, wholly ruled by feelings. Ideally, emotions should be subject to the exercise of moral discrimination and judgement. While emotions have their source in the *atai*, intelligence, moral judgement, and restraint, while also associated with the body, have their seat in the head (*kok*). Hence, the special importance attributed to the head by the Bajau Laut. The head is also associated with the elders and ancestors, particularly in the headside orientation of boats, houses, and graves. Like the head, the ancestors are a source of moral restraint. As elders, the role played by living leaders, who, in respectful terms, are also addressed as ancestors (*mbo'*), is similarly associated with that of the head. The function of a leader, as Salbangan observed, is to think for (*pikilan*) his followers. Indeed, house group leaders are frequently called *kok luma'* literally, 'house head', and the role they play in village affairs requires that they often rein in the emotions of their followers, reminding them, when feelings run high, of the need for restraint.

Spirit Malevolency and Sorcery

The spirits (*saitan*) are primordial agents of evil that, like God, were present in the universe before the creation of humankind.[2] Although generally unseen, the spirits are thought to populate the visible world, especially the land with its shorelines, ancient rocks, forests, and trees. While there are *saitan* that live in the sea, those on land are vastly more numerous and menacing. Virtually all *saitan* harbour ill intent toward humankind. Embodying unrestrained emotion, they strike out of anger, hatred, envy, or greed, bringing illness, misery, and suffering to human-kind. In the visible world, the places of habitation of the spirits define a geography of unseen powers within which the Bajau Laut must find for themselves an uneasy accommodation.

As agents of illness and death, the spirits are believed to act primarily upon the human life-soul. They either capture the soul or inflict injuries, similar, although unseen, to the injuries caused to the body by wounds. The task of coping with the spirits, treating wounds to the soul, and recovering life-souls captured by the spirits falls chiefly to the spirit-mediums (*jin*). Their task is a never-ending one, for the *saitan* already existed when the first ancestors were created, some as wanderers, others as abiding local spirits.

Spirits, however, are not the sole agents of evil at work in the universe. Human beings may also commit acts of evil, primarily through sorcery and poisoning. The Bajau Laut recognize several different kinds of sorcery, though sorcery itself is not a matter of great concern to most villagers. Its practice is usually attributed to outsiders. Some persons, however, are believed to be able, through the use of spells, to cause objects, such as eggs, nails, or scissors, to be lodged invisibly inside the body of a victim. Here they are thought to swell, or to tear away at the victim's internal organs, causing intense pain, internal bleeding, and possibly death. Harm may also be caused by destroying or burying an effigy made to represent the victim's body. This latter form of sorcery is called *maghinang mundusia*.

In the Semporna district, sorcery by effigy is associated by the villagers especially with the Idahan people (*a'a Ida'an*), who live near Segama in the Lahad Datu district north of Semporna. Culturally, the Idahan appear to be an autochthonous people of eastern Sabah. They are also well known locally for their use of curses (*panukna'*). During the timber boom of the late 1960s, it was the practice of district sawmill operators, or their agents, to make cash advances to illegal loggers in return for the delivery of logs. One villager accepted an advance of RM2,500 from an Idahan contractor, but then sold his logs through another agent. A short time later, the logger died suddenly of internal bleeding. His death was generally attributed to a curse. The villagers believe that a curse can be effective only if the victim is guilty of wrong-doing, or has committed a breach of promise, as had the logger in this case. If the intended victim is blameless, God, it is said, turns back the curse upon the person who pronounced it. Poisoning (*alasun*), because of the element of stealth involved, is considered to be a particularly nefarious crime. I know of no accusations of poisoning, or of deaths attributed to it in Bangau-Bangau. However, several villagers claim that they are able to detect poisons, and counteract their effects, should others try to introduce them into their food. In general, however, the lack of serious concern with sorcery and poisoning very likely reflects the fact that the Bajau Laut tend to give open expression to hostility.

Busung, *Misfortune, and Fate*

One of the most frequent single causes of affliction is a condition that the Bajau Laut describe as *kabusungan*, referring to a state or condition of *busung* (calamity or ill-fatedness), interpreted most often as a form of spiritual punishment. Even illness or injury that is thought to have a natural origin, or be caused by spirit attack, may be attributed, in a final sense, to *busung*. The villagers say that the most symptomatic form of *busung* is a swollen stomach, but many kinds of illness are associated with the condition: paralysis, inability to speak, sterility, high fever, severe headaches, lassitude, and loss of appetite. Any form of chronic, or long-term illness is likely to be attributed to *busung*. In addition, other forms of misfortune may also be interpreted as evidence of a state of *busung*, including accidents, physical injuries, lack of success in fishing, or loss of nets and other gear at sea, particularly if such ill-luck is experienced repeatedly, or cannot be readily explained by other causes.

To the Bajau Laut, the notion of *busung* is closely related to the idea of personal luck (*sukud*). Just as one's fate in the hereafter—in heaven or hell—is associated with the transcendental-soul, so one's fate in this life is associated with the life-soul. A person's fate is thought to be predetermined by God in terms of a compact, or promise, concluded at the time of birth. The Bajau Laut talk frequently of fate. In general, the notion is advanced to explain events that appear to be beyond ordinary comprehension. These events may include sickness and other forms of misfortune. As an expression of one's *sukud*, such events are thought to be beyond an individual's volition or purposeful control. The villagers may explain—by reference to fate—why one family prospers while another, just as hard-working, remains poor; or why one youngster is stricken by illness while others are spared. When used in this sense, *sukud* has nothing to do with an individual's actions, or his personal intentions. However, the villagers believe that wrongful actions may spoil an individual's store of good luck and so create a generalized state of ill-fatedness. If serious enough, this condition may extend to a person's family, house group, or even to the whole community.

Many forms of wrongful action are believed to produce a state of *busung*, causing one to 'become *binusung*'. Some of these have already been mentioned: failure to fulfil a vow; the false swearing of an oath; enmity or quarrelsomeness; refusal to submit to mediation; or accept the verdict of a village hearing. Still other actions include disrespect towards parents and other elders; impiety, including carelessness with food which is considered to be a gift of God; and violation of ritual proscriptions. While it is believed that *binusung* is usually brought on by the sufferer's own actions, there are also people, particularly elders, who are thought to have the power to inflict *busung* on others. This they do in retaliation for personal slights or acts of discourtesy. It is also believed that deceased ancestors, if neglected or shamed by the conduct of their descendants, may cause the latter to suffer *busung*. For example, Kobol (pseudonym), whose parents are both dead, consulted a seer regarding a recurring headache for which he had been unable to find a remedy, and was told that he was suffering *busung* caused by his parents, who felt that he had 'forgotten' them. Kobol denied that this was so, saying that he continued to remember his parents, and thought of them often. The seer, however, recommended that Kobol make his remembrance (*magentoman-entoman*) known in an overt way. He therefore advised that Kobol be bathed on his father's grave. The bathing was performed by Kobol's father's brother, and was followed by a brief meal (*labot*) served in Kobol's house to those who had witnessed the bathing. Any ritual act performed in expiation of wrongdoing, for the purpose of lifting a state of *busung*, is called *magbusung*. In general, *busung* operates within the community as a powerful form of sanction, upholding relations of respect, particularly between parents and children, leaders and their followers, elders and juniors, safeguarding pledges and contractual relationships, and compelling the peaceful resolution of disputes.

Ta'u Anambal *and* Ta'u Anawal

In dealing with illness, the Bajau Laut distinguish between two major forms of curing. The first is called *anambal*, literally 'to heal by the use of medicines' (*tambal*). These medicines are chiefly herbal, made from the roots, bark, leaves, or other parts of plants, and may be taken internally, or applied externally as poultices and dressings.[3] Heat and massage may also be used. *Anambal* is most often employed in treatment of ailments believed to have natural causes (Plate 35). Most elders have some knowledge of herbal medicines, but there are also persons recognized and consulted as expert herbalists. Such persons are known as *penanambal* or *ta'u anambal*.

The second form of curing is called *anawal*, literally 'to heal by the use of spells' (*tawal* or *nawal*). Again, most village elders have some knowledge of curative spells, and often treat the members of their house group without compensation. But there are also persons who are consulted as experts in the use of spells, called *penanawal* or *ta'u anawal*. The spell is generally recited either over the affected part of the body, or at the top of the head, at the site of the *bessok*, which represents the bodily passageway of the life-soul. Recitation of the spell is accompanied by 'blowing' (*nitiup*). *Anawal* is frequently employed in treatment of afflictions of the soul and is sometimes combined with the use of herbal medicines.

Those who are expert curers often have a knowledge of both spells and herbal medicines, and are able to diagnose as well as treat complaints. Curers are paid a small fee for their services. Curing is generally a private matter, rather than a public observance, and techniques of treatment vary considerably from one curer to another. Some insist that there are traditional payments required for different forms of treatment; these are invariable and the efficacy of the cure may be nullified if the patient fails to pay them. Others leave the amount to be paid to the patient. Curative spells, unlike most types of spiritual formulae, are not ordinarily taught within the family circle. The Bajau Laut believe that knowledge of *tawal* must be carefully guarded, and, if it is transmitted to others, it must be paid for. Otherwise, it will shorten the life (*apu'ut umulna*) of the person who teaches it. Generally, to learn *tawal* a person apprentices himself to an expert, working for his master as long as he is being taught. It is possible that the apprentice may work for his master, or contribute to the support of his household, for several weeks or even longer, without being taught a thing, while the master attempts to assay his character and make certain that the prospective student is serious and can be trusted with the power he acquires through the spells he is taught. Sometimes, masters are sought in other villages, or even from other ethnic groups. In eastern Sabah, the Idahan, in particular, are famous for their *tawal* as well as for other forms of magic, and a number of villagers have travelled to Lahad Datu to study with Idahan masters.

Ta'u Nganda' *or Seers*

More generally, some persons are described as 'seers', *ta'u nganda'*, literally, 'those who can see (*anda'*)'. Such persons are thought to be clairvoyant. They are said to be able to see into the future, speak with the souls of the dead, discern the whereabouts of missing objects, and read the hidden causes of events. *Ta'u nganda'* are consulted to predict future happenings, foretell one's personal fate, locate lost property, give advice regarding the well-being and whereabouts of loved ones from whom one is separated, or to set auspicious dates for weddings and other gatherings. They may also be asked to determine the cause of illness or other misfortune, and are also frequently curers and possibly spirit-mediums.

There are other powers which, it is believed, an individual may possess through training, or acquire as a special gift. Some men are thought to be invulnerable (*kobolan*). Because he had to transport a very large bride-wealth to Sitangkai, Laiti hired a man believed to possess *kobolan* to guard the boat that carried the *dalaham* and other gifts to Tia's parents. Another power is *sihil*. A person who has knowledge of *sihil* is believed to be able to prevent events occurring; to cause storms or winds to subside, for example; or to make himself invisible, or miraculously transport himself from one place to another in order to escape danger. Like curative spells, a knowledge of *sihil* is acquired through apprenticeship. Before the Second World War, Bajau Laut men from Sitangkai travelled to Tawitawi to live with agricultural Sama in order to study with *sihil* masters. While being trained, they harvested rice and performed other farm work. When they returned, they trained others, so that today there are many Bajau Laut masters, and most elders have at least some knowledge of *sihil*. Most also have some knowledge of protective, or prophylactic spells (*guna-guna*), which are carefully passed on in secret within the family. Also inherited in the family are charms, particularly amulets (*hajjimat*) worn most often around the waist to ward off danger. These charms are highly valued and their effectiveness is often believed to depend upon the wearer's observing special conditions that apply to their use.

As noted in Chapter 2, doctors and other practitioners trained in Western medicine are now available locally through the district hospital and private clinics. In 1979, about one woman in ten had visited the district paranatal clinic at least once, in connection with pregnancy or infant health, and most villagers suffering serious illness are taken to the district hospital for treatment. The villagers see little conflict between Western medicine and local curing. They generally acknowledge the superiority of Western medicine in dealing with afflictions such as malaria, dysentery, or major wounds, while at the same time they consult village curers for complaints believed to have causes relating to spirits, *busung*, or the soul. In addition, most curers have effective means for treating common complaints, such as stingray wounds, skin rashes, broken bones, or bleeding, so that they continue to constitute the first line of treatment for virtually all villagers.

Spirit-mediumship

The most important category of villager curers are the spirit-mediums or *jin*. Most mediums are also medicinal curers and experts in the use of spells, but not all expert curers, either *ta'u anambal* or *ta'u anawal*, are spirit-mediums.

The mediums comprise a separate group of curers. Indeed, the Bajau Laut see the *jin* as comprising a separate category of beings, distinct from ordinary *mundusia*, as standing half-way between humankind and the spirits. They form, within the village, an organized body of practitioners, with their own spokesman, the *nakura' jin*; special clothing; a ritual language and paraphernalia of their own; and responsibility for a complex body of public and private rituals. Above all, the mediums are thought to possess a unique ability that allows them to penetrate the supernatural world, and there make contact with its inhabitants, and so act as brokers or emissaries between ordinary human beings, the spirits, and souls. Through this contact, mediums attain clairvoyance, and so may be counted also as 'seers'.

The source of the medium's gift is said to derive from a personal relationship with the supernatural. Each medium is aided by a personal spirit-helper. Collectively, these helpers are known as *saitan jin*, or simply, like the mediums, as *jin*. The Bajau Laut believe that a medium is chosen by his or her familiar. During apprenticeship, the *jin* gradually learns to master this helper through the use of ritual techniques, thus becoming a true medium. Until this mastery is achieved, the novice typically experiences long periods of severe illness. The Bajau Laut describe this period of apprenticeship, when the novice is undergoing instruction, as *pasakaian*, from the root word *pasakai*, meaning to be a 'guest', someone temporarily affiliated with a group, but not yet a full member.[4] The apprentice, while ill, is both treated and instructed by an expert medium, who usually accepts only one such student at a time.

During this period of instruction, mediums say that the spirit who has chosen the novice comes and goes. Only gradually does the apprentice acquire the power to summon his spirit-helper at will. When the spirit arrives, it speaks and acts through the medium's body, coming, the *jin* say, into the head. During his training, the novice is also taught curative spells, how to prepare herbal medicines, and the techniques used for determining the causes of illness and other misfortunes. All mediums claim to have been reluctant to assume the calling at first, and most say that they relented only out of fear of death or, most often, madness (*binélau*). A few are released by the familiar who singled them out, regain their health, and so resume a normal life without becoming mediums. Throughout 1965, Musa Pailan, who was seriously ill for much of the year, received instruction from her husband, Garani, a practising *jin*, and at the time I left the village, most people regarded her as being on the threshold of becoming a *jin*. However, shortly after I left the village, she experienced a sudden recovery, and her training was abandoned. She did, however, acquire considerable skill as a curer. Some said that it is likely she will undergo the full training later on, should the spirit, as often happens, resume its attentions. Her release, many felt, was probably only temporary.

Earlier, near the middle of my fieldwork, Musa Pailan had a dream in which the spirit appeared to inform her that it was considering transferring its attentions to the anthropologist because of the interest he had shown in mediumship in conversations with her husband. In discussing her dream, Musa Pailan's husband, Garani, explained to me that it was dangerous to study mediumship unless one was prepared to become a medium. Knowledge by itself is insufficient, possibly dangerous. If a medium lacks the power to control his familiar, which is often thought to be impulsive, or potentially violent, or is himself morally deficient, he may die, go mad, or become a sorcerer, and so use his power to injure others. Or he may become the victim of his spirit, or the instrument by which it attacks others. As a result, a master *jin* must impress on his student the seriousness of his calling.

Once a novice is deemed to have gained mastery over his spirit-helper, he or she undergoes a ritual initiation, at which time the new medium dons the clothing of his or her calling: for a man, a white shirt (*baju poté'*) and loose green trousers (*saluar gadum*), and, for a woman, a green blouse (*baju gadum*) and yellow sarong (*siag bianing*). The newly initiated shaman is also outfitted with a medicine box (*duaan*) for use in storing his curing paraphernalia, and an ornamented hanging beam (*hanayan*). The *hanayan* is thought to curse (*lotok*) anyone who shows it disrespect, as, for example, children who play around it, or visitors to the medium's house who carelessly lean against it. It may also curse the *jin* who owns it if he fails to keep it in good repair, or replace it from time to time with a new one. Similarly, the medium's medicine box is believed to have the power to curse anyone who disturbs or tampers with it other than its owner.

Once initiated, the *jin* becomes, like the Melanau *a-bayoh* described by Morris (1967: 198–9), both a medium and, in a limited sense, a shaman. Through training, the *jin* learns to summon his or her familiar at will, and so becomes 'a master of spirits'. While in trance, he or she acts and speaks as a vehicle of the spirits and ancestors, thereby assuming the role of an intermediary between the human and spirit worlds. However, unlike a classical shaman, the Bajau Laut *jin* does not undertake spiritual journeys while in trance nor send out his or her soul on healing missions into the cosmos (Eliade, 1964: 259). For this reason, the *jin* is more appropriately described as a 'spirit-medium' rather than a 'shaman' (Firth, 1964: 689).

A Bajau Laut medium may be either a man or a woman. Despite the spiritual dangers believed to be inherent in the calling, a relatively large number of Bajau Laut undergo training and so become practising mediums during the middle and later years of their lives. In the village of Bangau-Bangau, there were sixteen active mediums in 1965, eleven men and five women, out of a total adult population, twenty years of age or older, of 168 people. Thus nearly one in ten adults was a medium; the percentage being higher among men than women. Socially, the status of the medium is not notably anomalous, except that, through their contact with spirits, all are regarded as potentially dangerous, and so are treated with some degree of care by others. The only apparent characteristic which all mediums have in common is a personal history of prolonged physical illness, often accompanied by emotional disturbance, regarded by the Bajau Laut as a period of semi-madness or irrationality, before being initiated as a practising medium. In some cases, this history of illness begins in adolescence, but none of the mediums now active in Bangau-Bangau was initiated before he or she had reached maturity. Indeed, many were already elderly when, by their own account, they first became *jin*.

Mediums are mostly called on to treat individual clients, usually when they have an illness that has not responded to simpler remedies, and possibly to treatment by other curers. From a diagnosis of the patient's symptoms (*nanam* or *tinanam*), the medium decides upon a suitable course of treatment. Diagnosis may involve reading the pulse (*anasad*), which may be done at the wrists, ankles, upper arm, or temples; and feeling the body for heat, cold, or swelling. A medium may also read his patient's palms. The villagers believe that should the lines of the palm (*laan kulis*) bode ill, and be diagnosed responsible for the patient's illness, a *jin* possesses the power to alter them. In addition, a variety of other diagnostic techniques are employed. The former *nakura' jin* of Bangau-Bangau, Saligantun, frequently used two pieces of white cloth covered with written symbols, including human figures, stars, and sun, which he consulted while in trance (*patika'*).

If the patient's complaint is not serious, the medium may treat it with spells or medicines. In general, however, a medium is normally consulted only in cases in which the trouble is thought to be more serious, requiring the use of the medium's powers to penetrate the unseen world. If its cause is thought to be sorcery, the medium may determine that the source of the patient's ailment is an object, such as an egg, needle, or length of thread, lodged in his or her body. This is removed by sucking (*idut-dutan*). For a curse, the medium typically sends his spirit-familiar to attack the person responsible in order to force him to withdraw the curse. For spiritual punishments inflicted by an ancestor, for example, the remedy is ordinarily to have the patient perform an act of atonement, as in the case of Kobol. For spirit attacks, the medium generally identifies the spirit responsible and the reasons for its attack, usually with the aid of his familiar and, depending on these reasons, prescribes a suitable offering to mollify the spirit. Frequently these offerings are made by the medium himself on behalf of his patient.

Occasionally, a medium may chant a special form of *kata-kata*, a long narrative epic, generally known as *suli-suli jin*, over an ill patient in the presence of other family or house group members. While chanting the *kata-kata*, the *jin* normally lies beside the patient on mats on the floor. Chanting is performed over one, or possibly two or three consecutive nights. When a *jin* falls ill, other *jin* frequently come together as a group to chant over him until he begins to show signs of recovery. *Suli-suli jin* are also chanted during apprenticeship, when novice mediums display signs of psychic or physical disorder. The epic chants are said to be especially sacred to the ancestors and are believed to invite their direct intercession. The ancestors are said to like to hear them sung, as do most elderly villagers, and some say that they act as *sihil*, the words themselves having the magical potency to cure or to alter future events. Their performance is one of the few occasions of true sanctity in the village, when those who have gathered to listen must remain silent, or speak only in whispers, so as not to spoil the pleasure of the ancestors.

Magpai Baha'u: Celebrating the New Rice

In addition to treating individual patients, the spirit-mediums, as a group, undertake a number of public ceremonies intended to maintain or repair relations of goodwill between the village, or a major segment of it such as a house group or cluster, and the ancestors and spirit world as a whole. The timing and organization of these events are planned in each local community by its mediums. The most important of these public ceremonies is called *magpai baha'u*, an annual three-day new rice ritual, which is by far the most impressive of all village ritual undertakings.[5] Another *is magigal jin* (trance-dancing).

The time of *magpai baha'u* is fixed, according to village *jin*, by the appearance of a constellation of stars above the north-eastern horizon of the sky, corresponding to the source of the north-east winds (*utalla' lo'ok*), called the *pupu* (Pleiades?), shortly after sunset (*palawa' allau*).[6] Once these stars appear in position, a group of mediums is sent inland to buy newly harvested rice (*pai baha'u*, literally 'new [unhusked] rice') from local agricultural communities. Not cultivating rice themselves, the timing of the rite is thus determined by the harvest season of their neighbours. In Semporna in the 1960s, the mediums generally travelled to Lihak-Lihak, although at times new rice was also obtained from mediums in Sitangkai, who are said to have made an annual pilgrimage to Tawitawi to purchase newly harvested rice from Sama farmers on the island. The Bangau-Bangau mediums look to the Sitangkai celebration as the principal *magpai baha'u* ceremony in the region. The rice obtained is shared out between the village mediums and is husked, using a wooden mortar and pestle, by the female members of each medium's household.

On the morning of the second day of *magpai baha'u*, eight plates of cooked rice are set out on the floor of the *nakura' jin*'s house, as a food offering to the souls of the village ancestors (*amakan sumangat kembo'-mbo'an*) (Plate 36). The offerings also include drinking water and incense. The ancestors are then invoked by the mediums and invited to eat and drink the meal prepared for them. At the same time, they are asked not to punish their descendants, who are honouring their memory, but, instead, preserve them from calamity. The ancestors are said to be visible to the mediums at this time, and converse freely with them. As soon as the mediums indicate that the ancestors have finished eating, the *nakura' jin* bids the guests who have gathered to take their places, and all eat from the same plates. The mediums then join them.

During the night that follows, a great conclave of ancestors and spirits is said to be assembled by the mediums, and the spiritual guests are entertained with dancing and music played on gongs and drums.[7] First, a special dance platform is prepared on one of the larger village landing-stages and is decorated with coloured flags and sprinkled (*alaksian*) with perfume by the mediums' assistants. Every medium is aided by a lay assistant called a *lembagan*, usually a female member of the medium's house group. As their assistants sprinkle the platform with perfume, the mediums call on the assembled spirits to take with them all sickness and misfortune when they leave the village and return home. Then the *lembagan* dance. When they are finished, the mediums take the floor. The mediums are believed to dance in a state of spirit-possession, their movements controlled by their spirit-helper who has entered their head. The villagers say that the personality of each medium's familiar is revealed by the characteristic mood of his or her dance, whether slow, quick, agitated, or deliberate. The female mediums dance first, followed by the male mediums. Each medium dances singly, and after he or she is finished, the other *jin* gather around to help the dancer recover from possession.

If a medium is unable to participate in the dancing (*igal*), he must present beforehand the ingredients for betel chewing: *sireh* leaves, betel-nut, lime, tobacco, and gambier, to the *nakura' jin*. Otherwise, he is said to arouse the ire of the spirits.

During *magpai baha'u*, the new rice is stored in a bark bin made especially for this purpose, called the *kulit mbo'*, literally, 'the skin of the ancestors'. The bin is roughly 75–90 centimetres high, and is made from the bark of the *balunu'* tree (*Buchanania sessilifolia*). When filled with rice, the bin is placed on mats at the 'headside' of the house, so that during the night, family members sleep with their heads towards it. Following the purchase of rice, preparing this bin is the first act of *magpai baha'u*. The bin is typically fashioned on the morning of the first day of the rite and filled with rice at midday. On the morning following the dancing of the *jin*, the rice is removed from the bin and some of it is pounded into flour. This is used to make special cakes which the mediums call *sanjata*. The remainder is cooked to make both white and turmeric rice. These preparations are called *maghinang magbottong*. Four tall cones of rice, layered white on the bottom, turmeric on the top, are placed on a large tray. These cones are said to represent 'mountains' (*bud*). The top of each cone is drawn to a point by squeezing the rice in coconut oil. Over its sides are placed the *sanjata*. The whole offering is called the *bottong*.

After the *bottong* is prepared, the climactic observance of the *magpai baha'u* celebration takes place. The village mediums assemble at midday, usually at the house of the *nakura' jin*, and are seated along the floor, screened from the view of the spectators by white cloth. An *imam* opens the ritual by chanting in Arabic (*jikil*). While the *imam* chants, the mediums go into trance (*patika*). As one medium, Garani, described it to me later, 'The spirit-helpers come into each medium's head. If a spirit is dissatisfied with the *imam*'s chanting, it will scream and if it is displeased with the offerings, it will cause the mediums to knock down the cones of rice, so that they will have to be formed again properly.' While in trance, each medium is believed to be the vehicle of his or her spirit-helper, through whom the spirit communicates. The mediums enter into a dialogue with the spirits and ancestors conducted in spirit language (*ling saitan*). Each medium generally asks why there is so much sickness in the village, or why so many children have died during the year, and the spirits respond by listing grievances, and by making requests for special favours. At this juncture, the mediums invite questions from the spectators who have gathered. The mediums, as Garani expressed it, act in this exchange like interpreters or 'intermediaries' (*paganti'*), passing questions and answers back and forth between this world and the spirit world. The villagers typically ask advice regarding important decisions they must make, request news of the dead, seek remedies for illness, or advice on problems affecting themselves or other members of their house group. The mediums translate the questions into the language of the spirits; the spirits then speak through the mediums, and the mediums translate the spirits' answers or advice back into ordinary language. The questioning generally lasts for some time, as a great many villagers typically gather to put questions to the spirits and ancestral souls. Finally, the spirits announce through the mediums their intention to take leave, and one by one the mediums return from trance. Later, the rice and cakes used to make the *bottong* are divided by the *nakura' jin* between the mediums and the *imam* who performed the opening chant.

The final morning of the *magpai baha'u* is marked by a ritual bathing (*magtulak bala'*), similar to that performed during *bulan sappal*, conducted by the mediums and one, or possibly several, *imam*. Its purpose is similarly to drive away sickness and other misfortune. In Sitangkai, *magtulak bala'* is followed by a final celebration, called *magkanduri*, held on nearby Sikulan Island. After the bathing, all who took part go directly to the island where an ancient fig tree (*nunuk*) grows, believed to be a gathering place of local spirits. Large fig trees (*Ficus* spp., especially *F. microcarpa*) are thought to be a favoured spirit habitation and in the Semporna district, are often important *tampat* sites. I have never witnessed this gathering, but according to Garani, it is a festive occasion. Offerings are made to the spirits and there is music and further dancing. Also according to Garani, this final celebration, which seems to have much the nature of a picnic, is an ancient rite performed by the *jin* from early times. There is no *nunuk* tree growing near Bangau-Bangau, so that ritual bathing concludes *magpai baha'u*. However, at Labuan Haji there is a *nunuk* tree, located near the edge of the village inlet (*lo'ok*). The site is sacred, and the Labuan Haji people tell how a troop of monkeys once disturbed the offerings placed nearby and were miraculously killed. It is a frequent practice to schedule *magpai baha'u* one day earlier in Bangau-Bangau, so that the mediums from the village can join those of Labuan Haji in dancing at the site of this tree following *magtulak bala'*.

In addition to *magpai baha'u*, the mediums perform further public dances during the year, called *magigal jin*, meant to entertain the village ancestors and the numerous spirits believed to inhabit the surrounding region, and so preserve their continued goodwill. Such dancing is also thought to have a therapeutic virtue, as the spirit guests are said to bear off with them when they disperse the various afflictions and woes suffered by village members. Tandoh insists that there is a marked improvement in village health following *magigal jin*. Garani maintains that, by tradition, such dancing should be performed every lunar month, on the fourteenth or fifteenth night, during the full phase of the moon. This is also the time in which *magpai baha'u* is performed. In practice, the dancing is held less regularly, or at least it was in 1964–5. Its time and planning are fixed by a meeting of mediums called by the *nakura' jin*. During the time that I was in the village, dancing was set one day earlier in Bangau-Bangau, as in the case of *magpai baha'u*, so that the village mediums could take part the following night in the dancing held at Labuan Haji. Similarly, *jin* from Labuan Haji could join in the dancing at Bangau-Bangau. Dances were held twice during the thirteen months that I lived in the village, and as I was preparing to leave Semporna near the end of August 1979, they were again being planned. The dancing itself is similar to that performed during *magpai baha'u*, and involves both the *jin* and their *lembagan*. According to Garani, if the *jin* fail to dance, they go mad and the whole community becomes *binusung*.

Magpai baha'u and *magigal jin* both correspond to, and mark, major periodicities in Bajau Laut life. In particular, they are linked to the cyclic phases of the moon. As already noted, the moon is used by the villagers to arrange meetings at sea and to fix the time of future events. It serves as a major calendar. In Bajau Laut origin myths, the passage from one moon to another also symbolizes a cyclic mode of being which is contrasted with that chosen by the ancestors. The moon 'dies' (*amatai*) again and again, only to be reborn in the never-ending cycle. Human beings, in contrast, die once, never to be reborn. In addition, each nightly moon is separated from the next by an interval of daylight (*allau*). Just as one nightly moon gives way to the next, so similarly at sunset, one day ends and the next begins. This diurnal cycle commences with night (*sangom*) and ends, following the passage of a day, with sunset (*palawa' allau*). Night is generally a time of rest and diminished social activity. The exception is the 'bright moon' period and, above all, nights of full moon. On such nights, people at sea fish, and in the village they gather out of doors, on the house platforms or catwalks, to talk, play the xylophone (*gabbang*), and sing. Such nights are favoured for marriage feasts, recalling the ancestors, and, above all, are the time when the *jin* dance.

Sunrise is the time appropriate to rites of infancy, weighing, and reconciliation, and for ritual bathing. Morning bathing initiates marriage, circumcision, and rites of weighing, and concludes childbirth and *magpai baha'u*. Major rites of transformation incorporate stages that cross the entire diurnal cycle. Marriage begins with morning bathing, climaxes at midday with *magbatal*, and concludes with a feast and a night of dancing. Similarly, *magpai baha'u*, marking the return of the ancestors, opens with the fashioning of the *kulit mbo'*. At midday, the bin is filled with new rice. Next comes the nightly dancing of the *jin*, followed in the morning by the preparation of the new rice, climaxing with the midday feasting of the ancestors. Finally, the rite concludes with early morning bathing. Rites of death and burial take place, by contrast, in the afternoon, while the memorial rites that follow are held in the morning and evening.

Mediumship and the Spirit World

Whenever the village is visited by an epidemic, the mediums are generally called on to construct a spirit-boat (*pamatulakan*) in order 'to carry away' (*tulak*) the sickness-causing spirits. Such epidemics are taken as a sign that the community no longer enjoys the relative goodwill of the spirits and has ceased to represent a sanctuary in which village members are comparatively safe from spirit attack. The loss of sanctuary status is said to be due, most often, to the temporary intrusion of bands of wandering spirits coming from outside the region. Such invasions are thought to disturb the delicate balance that ideally exists between the community and the inhabitants of the spirit world, including, most importantly its local spirit-patrons and protectors.

When I first arrived in Bangau-Bangau, in October 1964, a general breakdown in relations with the spirit world was believed to have occurred several months earlier. Within a short time, several deaths had occurred in the village, and someone in nearly every house group was then sick. Panglima Tiring went from house to house, making a collection of materials and small gifts of money. The spirit-boat was built and equipped by the mediums with materials supplied in this way by each village house group. It was nearly 1.75 metres long, with a rudder, a double set of outriggers, and white sails. Its design was totally different from that of the ordinary fishing boat (*lepa*) used by the villagers. It was provisioned with packets of food (*ketumpat*), firewood, drinking water, and a small cooking hearth. As soon as the boat was constructed, the mediums went from house to house, calling on the spirits to enter special cloths which they carried. Once the *jin* had made a complete circuit of the village, the spirits were persuaded to leave the cloths and enter small human effigy-figures placed on board the boat. The spirits, addressed in spirit language, were then called on to accept the provisions, leave the community, and continue their wanderings elsewhere. The boat was taken to the deep water beyond the mouth of the bay and 'sent on its way' (*amu'un pinalaan*) by the mediums.

Apart from these bands of wanderers, the spirits otherwise tend to be highly localized, their habitations producing a geography through which the villagers must find their way with care. Some of these habitations are well known, while others are unfamiliar. In the course of treating patients, the mediums continually discover new spirit habitations where unwary victims have met with attack. In general, it is best to keep one's distance from places where the spirits are known to live, or if it is necessary to pass close by, first to ask leave, make special greetings, or present the spirit residents with small banners and offerings. Being strongly localized, the spirits tend to resent human visitors. Local spirits are said to find especially annoying the habit that strangers have of asking questions out of curiosity (*kasagan*). As a consequence, persons who visit unfamiliar places frequently suffer a mild form of illness called *binahu*. Its symptoms are stomach and body pain. If the visitor accidentally intrudes into the spirit's home, the result is likely to be more serious. Reflecting these dangers, mediums frequently question patients regarding their recent travels.

The medium, in consequence of his unique relationship with the spirits, is seen essentially as a mediator between his fellow villagers and the inhabitants of the spirit world. If the spirits are offended, he is able to determine the reasons and, with the aid of his familiar, propose an effective solution. The medium is said to have an expert knowledge of the personality of the leading spirits who inhabit this unseen world and of the particular *addat*, or rules of behaviour, that apply there. Through this knowledge, he is able to advise his fellow villagers on the manner in which they can avert conflicts with the spirits, or, if conflicts arise, he is able to counsel them on how the damage can be repaired, reconciliation brought about, and mutual relations of accommodation restored.

What is notable is that the Bajau Laut tend to view the spirits in much the same terms as they look upon the land-based peoples who live surrounding them. The spirits possess a different speech and *addat*. They are identified especially with the shoreline and interior. Geographically, they are beings of the *kaléa*, the landward zone relative to the world inhabited by the Bajau Laut. They tend to be arrogant, are easily offended, and quick to violence. Whereas the Bajau Laut see themselves as a people who talk out their differences, the spirits, like their land-based neighbours, resort unhesitatingly to physical retaliation given the slightest provocation. Like the surrounding shore people, they pose a constant threat. They form an inescapable part of the world in which the Bajau Laut live, but live their lives by an alien *addat* order. The Bajau Laut perceive their community to be not only part of a larger social universe made up of peoples differing in speech and customs, but also part of a larger spiritual universe, populated by diverse groups of unseen beings similarly differing in speech and customs. In either case, ignorance of the ways of outsiders is dangerous. In order to minimize such danger, the existence of outsiders—both human and spirit—must be reckoned with and relations that provide a framework for coping with potential conflicts must be established.

In part, relations with the spirits tend to focus on propitiation of well-known local spirits identified with nearby sacred sites (*tampat*). Spirits such as Si Bangai-Bangai, described presently, act as the spiritual counterparts of land-based patrons, preserving the relative security of the village and its human inhabitants from outside interference. The danger such spirits pose is kept within manageable limits through offerings and an outward show of respect, and so they act as a counterpoise to the much greater danger represented by outsiders who are relative strangers. Consequently, the villagers feel relatively safe from spirit attack within the village perimeters. The greatest danger arises when one leaves this relative security and enters areas in which lesser known, or wholly unfamiliar, spirits hold sway. Also of special danger are the wandering bands of foreign spirits who, from time to time, disturb the relative sanctity of the community, intruding and breaking down the boundaries that separate it from the threatening world beyond.

The mediums are of special importance in maintaining relatively predictable relations between their human clients and the spirit world. They are chiefly responsible for propitiating the spirits of local *tampat* sites on their clients' behalf. In addition, each medium maintains a personal tie with the spirits through his or her spirit-helper. Such helpers are addressed by the mediums as 'friend' (*bagai*), using the same term as used between trading partners in former relations of barter exchange. Like trading partners, the familiar accords its chosen medium protection whenever the latter must approach the alien world of the spirits and souls, and so smooths relations, and advises its partner as to how to deal safely with its unseen inhabitants.

By cultivating this relationship, the medium is able to penetrate the spirit world and gain a first-hand understanding of what takes place there, the personality of its principal inhabitants, and the rules of *addat* that regulate their conduct. By using this knowledge, the medium is able, the villagers believe, to act as an effective mediator, warning his fellow villagers of the potential dangers involved in their dealings with the spirits and, when these dangers are realized, advise them of the measures they need to take to alleviate conflict and restore relations, for their own individual benefit, or for the collective welfare of the community as a whole.

Tampat

The term *tampat* describes any place believed to be endowed with the power to bestow blessings upon those who visit it in order to make or fulfil vows. Physically, a *tampat* may be a tree, a large rock, or a grave, particularly that of a holy man. Rocks regarded as *tampat* are sometimes associated with legends of miraculous petrification.

In the Semporna district, there are two particularly well-known *tampat* sites. One, called Tampat Sing-Sing, consists of a small hillock surrounded by mangrove swamps in the Sing-Sing river estuary. The hillock is believed to be the grave of a *salip*, a holy man descended from the Prophet Muhammad, and is just sufficiently high that it is never inundated when the surrounding tidal swamp is flooded during high tides. Growing from the hillock is a grove of bamboo and *hambulawang* trees (unidentified). Wood of the *hambulawang* tree is commonly used to fashion oars, while bamboo is used for mast spars. The bamboo and *hambulawang* trees are thus associated with the mast and oars of a 'living boat'. The site is said to be guarded by four giant monitor lizards. Though it is rarely visited by the Bajau Laut, many other Bajau from the Semporna district come to the site to seek favours, or to make offerings in fulfilment of a vow. The second *tampat*, Tampat Batu Dua, has the form of two tiny coral islets, which in size and shape roughly resemble two small boats of a type which the Bajau call *sapit*, one 100 metres or so behind the other. The islets or 'rocks' (*batu*) are said to be the petrified boats of two *salip* who were enemies. While pursuing one another, both magically cursed (*lingisan*) the other at exactly the same moment, turning the other *salip* and his boat into a barren coral-rock. Once, while accompanying Panglima Tiring and his family on a fishing voyage north of Bangau-Bangau, I was able to visit the *tampat* and found that the islets did bear an uncanny resemblance to the sharp-prowed *sapit*, each with the irregular outline of a holy man standing on its deck frozen in the act of cursing his enemy. Except for small clumps of grass and the rookeries of sea birds, both islets are totally barren. The Panglima told me that people occasionally visit them to seek blessings.

A few particularly religious people apply the term *tampat* only to sites such as Tampat Sing-Sing and Batu Dua, associated with Islamic holy men. But for most, the term *tampat* describes a much larger variety of sacred places. These especially include the graves of ancestors and places associated with resident spirits, particularly large trees, springs, and isolated rocks. Most important are the graves of former elders who are believed to have possessed magical knowledge while they were alive. After their death, they are thought to continue to apply their knowledge in the service of those of their descendants who continue to honour their memory. In addition, the souls of ancestors may request food offerings or gifts of tobacco, or betel-nut, through communication with the mediums or by appealing directly to their descendants in dreams. Offerings are usually placed by their graveside. Those who neglect such requests, fail to respect the sanctuary of ancestral graves, or dishonour their ancestors by their actions may be visited with affliction.

Many *tampat* are believed to be the dwelling place of spirits. For the Bajau Laut, spirits take a myriad of forms and are known by a variety of names, including some who are addressed, like familiar human beings, by personal names. Spirits may be present anywhere, but are especially associated with rock barriers along the beach, coralline islets, large trees, and the forest behind the shoreline; in general, areas usually away from the village or from frequently travelled sea lanes. Spirits are generally malevolent beings and cause a variety of human woes, including sickness and accidents. Unless making offerings, *tampat* where spirits are believed to dwell are carefully avoided, in order not to disturb or give offence to the spirit inhabitants of these sites. Many elderly men are believed to know special greetings (*salam*) which they recite when passing a *tampat*. These greetings are said to placate the spirits and are included among the carefully guarded *guna-guna* that elders pass on to their children and grandchildren before their death. Some sites require special attention from those who pass close by in boats or from travellers ashore, such as a thrown coin, or a piece of firewood. Ancient *nunuk* trees are a favourite haunt of *saitan*. Once, while visiting blacksmiths on Bumbum Island, Panglima Tiring pointed out to me a large *nunuk* tree growing at the water's edge near Sisipan village. Here one night, some years before the founding of Bangau-Bangau, his elder brother Lapit moored his boat to a pole while fishing the surrounding reefs. During the night, with the coming flood tide, the pole came loose and Lapit's boat drifted against the roots of the tree. When the family awoke in the morning, Lapit was suffering from a stomach ailment. The family returned to Semporna, where Lapit eventually died. Tiny coralline islets are also thought to be a common habitation of spirits. When village fleets arrive in the Ligitan reefs, the head of each family crew customarily plants a small flag (*panji*) of white or coloured cloth at a *tampat* site on a small islet near by before they begin to fish, as a precaution against possible spirit attack. As noted in Chapter 4, during fish drives (*magambit*) this is usually done by the *nakura'* or principal drive leader on behalf of others. Flags are also placed at a *tampat* in repayment for recovery from illness or other misfortune.

Most villages are closely associated with at least one local *tampat* site, representing the principal point of connection between the village community and the spirit world. A large part of the villagers' concern with spirits is directed toward propitiating and keeping at bay those representatives of the spirit world who characteristically live in such *tampat* at the edge of the village's boundaries. One such *tampat* is located near the inshore edge of the bay, close to the foot of the former walkway to Bangau-Bangau. The site consists of a large coral rock which is thought to be the home of a spirit known to the villagers as Si Bangai-Bangai (Plate 37). The present walkway is located about 70 metres further east, so the *tampat* is now much more secluded than it was in 1964–5. Nevertheless, children continue to be warned to stay clear of the site and it is regularly visited by villagers and mediums, who come to plant small flags on the rock, or to make offerings of turmeric rice or rice cakes. Si Bangai-Bangai is the subject of endless lore. During the day, he is said to be invisible. At night, however, when the spirits manifest themselves, many villagers claim to have seen him, during dark or moonless nights, at dusk, or just after sunset, usually as a giant man with a glowing red torso, arms, and head. He is thought to wander the rim of the bay after sunset or, in the form of a sea turtle, he is said to swim beneath the houses of the village or to come alongside moored boats in which families are sleeping. During these nightly travels, he may cause visitors or unwary villagers to fall ill.

One day, I learned that the medium Mirialani (pseudonym) had placed offerings and a white banner for a sick neighbour on the rock where Si Bangai-Bangai made his home. As the tide was especially low, I decided to wade to the rock with my camera and photograph the offerings. Because of the tide, many families were away fishing and so, foolishly, I went unaccompanied. I was not feeling well and in wading back to the headman's house, I became more and more feverish. Fortunately, several young men who were present were able to help me to the government clinic in Semporna, as by this time I found it difficult to walk. The dresser contacted the residency hospital in Tawau, and a military helicopter was sent to evacuate me. At the hospital, I was found to have dengue fever. After my recovery, I returned to Semporna by the next available boat. Back in the village, my friend Garani told me that as I had returned and clearly intended to stay in the village, it was necessary that I attempt to placate, and so gain the acceptance of, Si Bangai-Bangai; otherwise, I could expect to fall ill again. Acting as an intermediary on my behalf, he then made offerings to the spirit. In payment, I purchased a new roof (*sapau*) for the *lepa* in which he and his family lived at the time.

To an extent, Si Bangai-Bangai may be seen as a tangible symbol of the danger and unfamiliarity which the Bajau Laut associate with the land. While he is believed to have caused many in the village, including myself, to suffer illness, his presence none the less makes concrete, and so amenable to control, the dangers which the Bajau Laut associate, more vaguely, with the landward boundaries of their community. By making offerings and showing respect, the villagers are able to maintain an uneasy relationship with this powerful representative of an otherwise unfamiliar and largely antagonistic spirit world.

The Ancestors (*Kembo'-mbo'an*)

The villagers believe that all that occurs in this world is in a final sense pre-ordained by God. God grants to each person a singular fate and an allotted span of years. The spirits and other sources of affliction operate only within this circumscribed sphere of causal agency. Similarly, the mediums and other village curers frequently acknowledge this omnipotency by stressing the limitations of their own powers to effect cures. Each person, it is believed, must ultimately come to terms with his *sukud*, submit himself to God, and give thanks for such favours as he receives.

Like the surrounding shore people, the spirits are accepted as an inescapable part of this fate and of the living world in which each person must live out his or her life. Both are looked upon as a source of trial and suffering. At the same time, the village is also a moral community, bound together in its adherence to *addat*. God is believed to endow each person with a transcendental-soul, representing the moral component of his or her individual being. The transcendental-soul has an existence independent of each individual's worldly fate and continues to exist after one's death. While some say that the soul eventually returns to God, most believe that the ancestors—those kin and villagers who have already died—do not entirely depart, but remain a powerful and enduring force within the living world, but existing unseen, like the spirits. However, in contrast to the *saitan*, the ancestors represent a force for good, protecting their fellow villagers from harm and reminding them of the moral obligations they bear. These obligations have to do, above all, with notions of *tabang* and with acts of giving and sharing prompted by feelings of love, pity, mutual concern, and compassion.

God is said to have created the first ancestors. Following their creation, *Tuhan* informed the *mbo'* that they must die, each in his or her own time. The original ancestors chose to die, not like the moon, but like a banana plant. Hence, human death is final and non-cyclical. In death, mundane existence ceases forever and the individual leaves the earthly world never to return as a living human being. But the image of the banana plant is also one of propagation. Before it dies, each plant sends out new shoots. Life thus continues through one's progeny. In dying, the ancestors survive through their offspring, provided that the latter remember and honour them. At the same time, death is also transformative. In death, each person is transformed into an *mbo'*. Leaving the living world, the deceased becomes a transcendental personality, escaping forever the contingent time of earthly life and death, and so returns to the original ancestors, including the first ancestors created by *Tuhan*. The ancestors thus remain ever present, both in and apart from the everyday world, near and accessible, yet unseen and imperceptible. Through their connection with the first creation, the *mbo'* also return to God, becoming the primary intermediaries between *Tuhan* and subsequent generations of living descendants. Hence, when the *mbo'* grant blessings, these are said by the villagers to come from God through their intercession.

Each individual is thought to have a direct, personal link with the souls of the ancestors (*kembo'-mbo'an*). Like the founders of house groups and clusters, the *mbo'* are looked upon as protectors who care for their followers. In contrast to the spirits, who stand outside the human

community, and act in ways which are essentially antithetical, the ancestors represent an unseen presence within, who intercede and
influence events out of their concern for the well-being of the living, particularly, though not exclusively, their own descendants. However, the
ancestors are invisible, and for this reason, the villagers say, it is often
necessary to employ a medium or seer in order to determine their wishes,
to ensure that they are contented, and to enlist their aid in times of
special need. On occasions, however, the *mbo'* approach the living directly,
chiefly through dreams, or with overt signs of favour or chastisement.

At death, the Bajau Laut believe that an individual's personality is not
entirely extinguished, but lives on through the continued existence of
his or her transcendental-soul and continuing presence as an ancestor.
In addition, some persons are said to give rise to a shade or ghost
(*panggua'*), which lingers for a brief time after death. In some respects,
the shade is the antithesis of the transcendental-soul. It is thought of as a
shadowy manifestation of the corporal body and is sometimes described
as bearing about it an odour of decay and corruption. Indeed, the
panggua' is said to appear at times as a rotting corpse. Sometimes at
night, a sudden wind may blow through the village, bringing with it a
peculiar odour of decay. Some villagers attribute this to the passage of a
company of *panggua'*. Dark nights, when the moon is late in rising, are
associated, in particular, with the visits of travelling ghosts. While I was
living in Bangau-Bangau, several persons claimed to have seen shades,
describing them as blurred, indistinct white figures that disappear and
reappear at will. Sometimes they make themselves known only by their
touch, which is cold, or by smell or sound. A few persons living in the
village are said to possess a knowledge of prayers (*dua'a panggua'*)
which permit them to transform themselves into ghosts, so that their
body becomes insubstantial and they are able to transport themselves
miraculously from place to place. Persons with such powers are called
panggua' allum, 'living shades'.[8] Some villagers insist that only those who
are morally deficient, who died violent or ill-fated deaths, or left this
world with outstanding grievances, give rise to shades. In particular,
those who were quarrelsome or violent in life, are thought to remain
troublesome in death, returning briefly as *panggua'* in order to frighten
the living, disturb their property, or simply to wander familiar places,
lamenting their fate. Mild, kindly persons have little reason to return and
only rarely become shades, it is said. In addition, a dead person may
become a ghost because his body was incorrectly bathed before burial.[9]
If troubling visits by a shade persists, improper bathing is likely to be
suspected and a family may repeat the 'bathing' of the corpse by washing the deceased's grave marker. While disturbing, visits by the *panggua'*
are not regarded as serious and many villagers say that they have never
seen ghosts.

The souls of the ancestral dead, on the other hand, are of far greater
importance. They are fundamentally upholders of the moral order and
are believed to visit their descendants with mild punishment in the event
of wrongdoing. They are also a source of favours second only to God,

and are conceived of in much the same way. The more pious villagers sometimes complain that their neighbours attribute to the ancestors powers that rightly belong to God. As one villager said, 'When a person is in need of help, he thinks first of his ancestors. For us Sea People, ancestors are just below God.' The villagers make frequent petitions to their ancestors. Such petitions may take the form of a simple request for aid, or special favours, or may have the nature of a formal vow, including a promise of repayment, and may be addressed either to the ancestors generally or to a specific ancestor, such as a deceased parent or grand-parent. The notion of 'ancestor' is not necessarily a genealogical one. Individuals may make vows to those who were in life respected leaders, powerful seers, or devout *imam*. Generally, such persons are also deceased kin, but not necessarily so. Personality may be as important as genealogy, and, as a rule, those remembered (*entom*) are nearly always persons who were loved in life, and who are said to have shown generosity and compassion towards others. House groups tend to have a particular *mbo'* whom they honour, much as they have a particular *imam* whom the house elders regularly consult. These are the ancestors that housemates most often remember, feed, and address in prayers. In general, the ancestors are believed to be more approachable than God, and are more direct in their assistance. The ancestors may at times appear in dreams. Sometimes this is only to bring about remembrance, to claim a place in their descendants' thoughts. At other times, they may come to reproach the living for their neglect or forgetfulness, or they may come with a request, asking for something to satisfy a need. In this regard, the ancestors are thought to have needs analogous to those of the living, particularly for food and drink, remembrance, and signs of love and continuing concern. The ancestors frequently visit their descendants to ask for gifts of food, cigarettes, and other favours. Such dream visita-tions, in which the ancestors come to the living with requests, are called *sinu' mangat* or *anu' mangat*. Alternatively, these requests may be con-veyed through a medium acting as an intermediary.[10]

The villagers honour the ancestors in a number of ways. Shortly before the beginning of fasting month, a house group may hold a special feast for the ancestral dead, called *aruah*, to which the house leader invites his village kin and neighbours. Like other house group-sponsored rites, the feast consists of prayers (*dua'a*), led by the *imam* and other elders, followed by a meal of rice and side dishes. The guests are given cakes and packets of turmeric rice to take home with them. The purpose of the *aruah* is to feed and comfort the ancestors and reassure them of their continued remembrance.[11] Before the feast begins, the house leader invokes the souls and invites them to partake in the meal. The souls are believed to gather in great numbers inside the house and join with their living descendants in the feasting. The *aruah* thus constitutes a communion between ancestors and descendants.

Throughout the remainder of the year, similar feasts may be held. Although these may also be called *aruah*, the more common name is *amakan sumangat* ('feeding the souls'), or *maghinang ni kembo'-mbo'an* (literally, 'doings for the ancestors'). The ancestors expect to be remembered and may visit their descendants with minor illnesses, such as headaches or mild fevers, to remind them of their duty. *Maghinang ni kembo'-mbo'an* demonstrates this remembrance. In 'feeding the souls', a brief prayer formula is often recited; for example: *Na amangan na ka'a bo' ka da'ana anumangat pabalik* (Now eat what you are given so that you need not come back asking for more). Here the ancestor is asked to be satisfied with what it is given and not to continue its visitations. As reflected here, the ancestor's requests are thought at times to be burdensome. While the needs of the ancestors must be respected, they, too, should show restraint. The ancestors may also afflict their descendants with mild *busung* in punishment for wrongdoing. This, the villagers say, is to remind them of their moral responsibilities, and so preserve the goodwill of their fellow villagers and their favour with God, whose primary concern is with their transcendental-souls. Feasts may also be held in connection with illness and other misfortunes, in atonement for wrongdoing, or in fulfilment of a vow made to the ancestors. Smaller offerings may also be made at the graveside; placed inside the house (at its headside); or on the house platform. Again, these may be accompanied by a request that the ancestor moderates or ceases its demands.

In addition, the community's ancestors are collectively invoked, fed, and entertained during *magpai baha'u*. At other times, as a subsidiary element in nearly every rite observed by village house groups, prayers are directed to the ancestors and their blessings are sought in furthering the particular purposes of the gathering. For most villagers, the abiding presence of the ancestors is a strongly felt reality.

As seen in earlier chapters, ancestry and ties of descent have little structural significance in Bajau Laut society, yet senior kin, as individuals, tend to enjoy the respect of their descendants and in their person embody village moral authority, as custodians of community *addat* and arbiters of rightful conduct. In an honorific sense, they are addressed by their followers as *mbo'*. Among house group and cluster leaders, however, it is generally those of the same age—that is, the most active cohort of villagers—who exercise the greatest economic and political power in the community. Among village housemates and fishing partners, stress tends to be placed on collateral ties rather than on those of ancestry. But in terms of *addat* and a wider sense of moral community, the ancestors, in transcending death and contingent historical time, become a continuing source of love and support, ideals transported in death to a new level of being. In death, the ancestors remain, transformed and forever accessible, as long as they are remembered, an important force for good, part of a larger unseen society enveloping the world of the living. As long as they are properly remembered, the ancestors serve to remind the living of their duties, to protect and look after them by defending their rights against wrongdoers, and to intercede with God on their behalf in times of need.

1. To complicate matters, most villagers insist that an individual has only one soul. This they refer to, in most contexts, as *sumangat*. The notion of *ruah* is evoked chiefly in connection with death, moral rewards and punishment, and the ancestors. Perhaps, the two terms might best be thought of as signifying different aspects or components of personality—the one, *sumangat*, associated with life and with illness and other threats to life—and the other, *ruah*, with transcendance and immortality. In this latter regard, the notion of *ruah* tends to merge with that of 'ancestor' (*mbo'*).

2. See Chapter 1.

3. The Bajau Laut, as once a sea-nomadic people, make remarkably frequent use of a herbal pharmacology. One frequently used curing technique is to rub the body with leaves (*kiapatapa*). For example, the leaves of the *bangkuru*, a common shrub that grows in the strand zone, are used to 'warm' the body. In addition to childbirth, rubbing the body with fresh *bangkuru* leaves is done on other occasions when the normal temperature of the body has been disturbed, such as after a person has experienced near drowning (*alimbo'*).

4. See Chapter 5 for a discussion of the distinction between visitors (*pasakai*), and house group members. In Sama, *pasakai* sometimes has the connotation of unwelcome visitor or 'parasite'.

5. The performance of a 'new rice' (*pai baha'u*) ceremony by a boat-nomadic fishing people poses a considerable ethnographic paradox. Here, however, three points might be made. First, as Sama speakers, the Bajau Laut are familiar with rice cultivation among their linguistically related neighbours, even if they do not cultivate rice themselves. Secondly, rice is essentially a ritual food. Cassava is the staple, everyday fare, but, by contrast, is devoid of ritual association. Rice was obtained in the past from shore-dwelling groups and in symbolic terms, relations between the human and spirit worlds closely parallel those that exist on the human plane between sea and land people. It might be argued that rice similarly mediates both relationships—representing, at once, an instrument of dependence and, in terms of the spirit world, a means of propitiation. Finally, it is worth noting that rice, in a parallel way, is also a ritual food among the sea-nomadic Moken who grow for themselves the rice they use in rituals, while obtaining from land people rice used for everyday consumption (Ivanoff, 1990; see also Chapter 11).

6. See Chapter 3.

7. According to Bajau Laut time reckoning, as indicated in Chapter 9, each new day begins at sunset. Therefore, this celebration (*magigal jin*) marks the commencement of the third day of *magpai baha'u*.

8. In 1979, a Sama Kubang man from Kampung Hampalan who came to live in Bangau-Bangau was said by others in the village to be a 'living shade' (*panggua' allum*). At the time, he made his living as a professional thief. He was said to be able to enter shops unseen and to take whatever his customers arranged for him to steal for them by prior agreement (an arrangement very similar to that traditionally entered into with boat-builders and other artisans, see Chapter 4). In this way, he is believed, on one occasion, to have stolen all the gold jewellery from a Semporna pawnshop. Occasionally, he makes trips to Tawau and Sandakan on behalf of his customers. He does not trouble his neighbours, as the villagers say that he was instructed in a dream never to steal from fellow Muslims.

9. In Tawitawi, in southern Sulu, Nimmo (1990: 18) reports a similar connection between ghosts and the improper preparation of the corpse for burial. In Bangau-Bangau, the villagers take a number of measures to protect their homes from *panggua'*: one is the placing of a spider conch shell (*kohanga*) over the door.

10. Nagatsu (1995: 8) reports that a fish drive (*magambit*), which he briefly describes, was held at Sitangkai in 1994 under the direction of a spirit-medium acting as its *nakura'* in response to a request from the medium's *mbo'* conveyed through his spirit familiar (*saitan jin*). In this case, the spirit conveyed the message when the medium was reporting to the *mbo'* that he had launched a spirit-boat (*pamatulakan*) in order to remove illness from the community. Through the spirit, the *mbo'* informed the medium that the cause of illness was that he had not, for a very long time, performed *magambit* and that this had made his *mbo'* become angry. The medium promptly organized a *magambit*, not so much for economic reasons, it appears, but to please his *mbo'*.

11. With comings and goings such a regular feature of Bajau Laut life, expressions of remembrance (*magentom-entoman*) are highly valued and are seen as giving meaning, in emotional terms, to the recurrent experiences of departure and reunion. Often, personal objects, as tokens of remembrance (*pagentoman*) are requested, or exchanged between loved ones, as reminders of their feelings towards one another. In relation to the ancestors, the villagers say that death is only a temporary parting. The living must continue 'to remember' the dead (*entom ma siga'*), as a sign of their enduring love, until they are both reunited as *mbo'*.

11
Conclusion

Pakaita, tinimanta; Embal pakaita, tagu'ta—labu.

When we use it, we throw it away; when we don't use it, we take it out—anchor. (Traditional Bajau Laut riddle)

IN this book, my main concern has been with a single maritime fishing community, examining the way of life of its members against a background of history and ongoing adaptation. As 'sea people', interpersonal relations among the Bajau Laut are shaped not only by their dependence on the sea, but also by the relationships they maintain with surrounding shore- and land-based peoples. In examining these relations, I have sought to connect features of this way of life with a distinctive sense of fate, ancestry, and with perceptions of uniqueness shared by the Bajau Laut, as a 'sea people', at once separate, yet inextricably part of a larger, ethnically diverse coastal society.

Sea Nomads in South-East Asia

As a once nomadic boat people, the Bajau Laut comprise one of a number of widely scattered communities of present and former 'sea nomads' (Sopher, 1965) or *populations aquatiques* (Pelras, 1972) found, until a century ago, over large areas of maritime South-East Asia. Today, like the Semporna Bajau Laut, very few of these people remain nomadic.

It is sometimes assumed that all of the South-East Asian sea nomads, including the Bajau Laut, comprise a single ethnolinguistic population (see LeBar, 1964; Sopher, 1965). Recent research, however, particularly by linguists, indicates that this is not so, and that the sea nomads consist of at least three major ethnolinguistic groups, each culturally and linguistically distinct. These three groups are: (a) the Moken and related Moklen of the Mergui Archipelago of Burma, with extensions southward into the islands of south-western Thailand (Court, 1971; Hogan, 1972; Ivanoff, 1985, 1986, 1987, 1989); (b) the Orang Laut, literally the 'sea people', a diverse congeries of variously named groups inhabiting, or once inhabiting, the Riau-Lingga Archipelago, Batam, and the coastal waters of eastern Sumatra and southern Johore (Logan, 1847a, 1847b; Carey, 1970; Andaya, 1975; Sandbukt, 1982; Wee, 1985); and (c) the

Bajau Laut, the largest and most widely dispersed of these groups, living in the Sulu Archipelago of the Philippines, eastern Borneo, Sulawesi, and the islands of eastern Indonesia. Except for a slight overlap in the case of the Moken and Orang Laut, these three groups inhabit notably separate geographical areas (Sandbukt, 1982: 16–18) (Map 11.1). In addition, two of them, the Orang Laut and Bajau Laut, represent specialized maritime communities present within a larger ambit of culturally and linguistically related land- and island-based populations, Malay speaking in the former case, Sama-Bajau speaking in the latter.

In order to place the Bajau Laut within this wider adaptive context, it is useful to compare them briefly with the other sea-nomadic groups.

Moken

The Moken are a northern outlier of Austronesian-speaking peoples, very likely the product of an early migration of Austronesian mariners northward along the western coast of the Malay Peninsula. Today, the Moken live largely surrounded by Burman- and Thai-speaking peoples. The Moken language, including the related Moklen dialect, forms a separate Austronesian language without close links to others (Hogan, 1972: 205; 1989: 2–4). Hogan (1989: 3) calculates the percentage of shared cognates between Moken–Moklen and Malay, the language spoken by most Orang Laut living further south, to be only 44.51–45.60 per cent, indicating that these two groups have no particularly close linguistic affinity.[1] Ross (1994: 77) believes that Moken probably belongs to the Aceh–Chamic group of Austronesian.

Following the British annexation of Tenasserim in 1824, a number of reports were written on the Moken; these were later brought together in a classic monograph *The Selungs of the Mergui Archipelago* (G. Anderson, 1890).[2] This work, together with a number of others (Carrapiett, 1909; White, 1922) give us a more complete picture of the Moken during the late nineteenth and early twentieth centuries than we possess for any other sea-nomadic group at the time, including the Bajau Laut.

At the beginning of the twentieth century, the Moken were primarily boat-dwellers, living in 4.5–9.0 metre vessels constructed of a dug-out base with built-up bulwarks made of split bamboo caulked with resin (G. Anderson, 1890: 19). Boats were decked with bamboo laths and propelled by a single sail made of pandanus leaves stitched with rattan fibre. Movement and economic activities followed a bi-seasonal regime. During the north-east monsoon, from November through April, a period of dry weather in Mergui, the nomads moved westward to the outlying islets of the archipelago. Here they harpooned giant rays, collected molluscs, gathered 'tripang', and, more irregularly, dived for pearl shell. The flesh of the giant ray was cut into strips and dried in the sun. Along with sun-dried molluscs and 'tripang', it was traded to Chinese merchants for export. During the remainder of the year, dominated by the rainy south-west monsoon, the Moken sheltered on the landward side of the larger islands close to the mainland. Here they frequently established

322

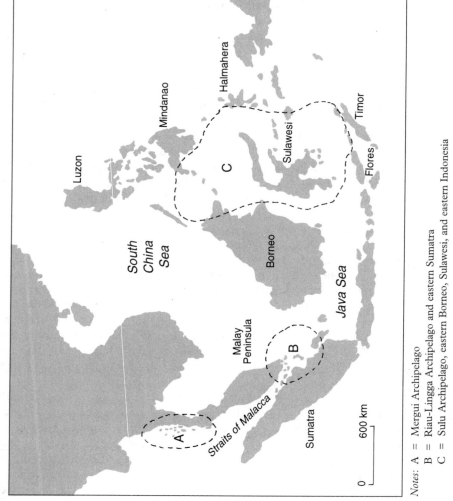

MAP 11.1
Distribution of Sea Nomads in South-East Asia

Notes: A = Mergui Archipelago

B = Riau-Lingga Archipelago and eastern Sumatra

C = Sulu Archipelago, eastern Borneo, Sulawesi, and eastern Indonesia

encampments ashore, where they collected strand resources such as oysters and burrowing marine worms (G. Anderson, 1890: 22). They also made extensive use of the island forests. From March to May, they collected honey and wax, particularly in the northern parts of the archipelago. They mainly bartered these items. They also collected forest resins and eagle-wood toward the end of the north-east monsoon, when tide conditions made it impossible to collect 'tripang'. Eagle-wood was sold through Malay traders. During the rainy season, pigs were also hunted using dogs, several of which were kept aboard each boat (G. Anderson, 1890: 27). Fruits and wild roots were also collected. Of great importance during this season was the collection and curing of pandanus (screw-palm) leaves. For women, the sedentary routine of the wet season was dominated by the making of pandanus mats. These served for both household use and barter, functioning at times as a medium of exchange.

From the earliest reports, it is clear that the Moken, like the Bajau Laut, were heavily involved in external trade. This involvement was mediated primarily by Chinese traders and, to a lesser degree, by Malays. Chinese traders established stable patron–client relationships with groups of boat-dwellers; in ethnographic accounts of the turn of the century, the trader's boat is often described as providing the focus of such groups. Traders accompanied their boat-clients around fishing and gathering grounds, bartering their goods for Moken produce. These goods consisted chiefly of cloth and cooking utensils, but rice was the most important item, constituting the staple food of the Moken. As with the Bajau Laut (Sather, 1975b; 1995a), rice also held and continues to hold a special ritual significance (Ivanoff, 1989; 1990). Traders appear to have reinforced their clients' dependence by supplying them with opium and alcohol to which European observers of the time universally report the Moken to have been much addicted.

By comparison with other sea nomads, the Moken practised a much more generalized subsistence regime, exploiting a notably diverse resource base that encompassed not only sea and strand environments, but also the interior forests of the sparsely inhabited islands they frequented during their annual migrations. Some groups in addition planted shoreline gardens to which they returned from time to time to harvest. More recently, Ivanoff (1990) reports that among the crops cultivated in these swidden gardens is rice, specifically the rice used to meet their ritual needs, while rice for everyday consumption is acquired through trade. Other groups visited brackish estuaries and mangrove swamps, exploiting these areas, not in the specialized manner of some Orang Laut groups, but as one of a number of generalized foraging habitats visited in the course of their seasonal migrations.

Distinguishing the Moken even more sharply from other sea-nomadic groups was the fact that they alone appear to have never been systematically incorporated in a pre-colonial state. The reason is very likely, as Sandbukt (1982: 34) suggests, because pre-colonial states of the region were essentially land- rather than maritime-based and that the Mergui

Archipelago, by comparison with the island areas inhabited by the Sama Bajau and Orang Laut, was a backwater at least in terms of maritime trade. The Moken, although dependent on an external economy, were much less subject to the political domination of surrounding land-based groups than were other South-East Asian sea nomads.

While historically existing independently of nearby land-based polities, Ivanoff (1989) reports that the Moken employ an archaic form of Malay as a ritual language, suggesting a possible past connection, like that of the Orang Laut, with the greater Malay-speaking world to the south. Later, following their northward movement and increasing isolation in Mergui, it is possible that connecting Moken-speaking groups may have adopted the Malay language and been absorbed, like the Orang Laut, in an expanding Malay political and commercial ambit leaving those in the north isolated.[3]

The Moken are described as subdivided into distinct dialect groups, distributed through the Mergui Archipelago along a north–south axis. According to Ivanoff (1985: 173–5), the Moken are divided between five such groups, each identified with the island or island group in which they shelter during the rainy season. These are named, from north to south, as: the Dung (Ross islands), Jait (Owen), Lebi (Sullivan and Lampi), Niawi (St James), and Chadiak (St Matthew) (see also White, 1922: 157). Each group tends towards endogamy, and even neighbouring groups are said to maintain little contact with one another. This appears to be related to the nature of Moken nomadism in which groups seasonally move along parallel seaward–landward routes, from west to east and back, rather than from north to south. Each territorial group comprises about forty boats; in the past its members rendezvoused at least once a year at the end of the sea hunting season for a period of feasting. During other times they dispersed within what are described as recognized 'fishing and gathering territories' in small flotillas of only a few families under the leadership of a headman (potao) (Ivanoff, 1985: 174).

While the Mergui Archipelago is the principal centre of Moken distribution, Moken and Moklen groups also extend into Thailand, and in recent years several Thai groups have been studied by linguists (Court, 1971; Hogan, 1972; 1989) and anthropologists (Ivanoff, 1985; 1987; 1989). Ivanoff reports that, in addition to nomadic communities, there are sedentary Moken living along the south-west coast of Thailand, mainly on the island of Phra Thong, in Phang Nga Province. These people are called the Korat. Ivanoff (1985: 174) estimates the total Moken and Korat population at about 5,000. The closely allied Moklen inhabit the southern margins of the Moken range. While the Moken are chiefly sea nomads, the Moklen live in settled seaside villages where they cultivate rice fields and coconut gardens (Hogan, 1972: 206). Their population is estimated by Hogan (1972: 212) at around 1,000.

Many Moken groups, especially in Thailand, are now faced with environmental loss due to the clearing of mangrove and coastal forests for farming, charcoal production, plantations, and other types of coastal development (Engelhardt, 1987: 11–13). Nomadism is rapidly declining, as many former nomads are being forced into increasing reliance on inshore fishing where they face competition, and, increasingly, assimilation by established coastal populations.

Orang Laut

As with other sea nomads, the Orang Laut are not always readily identifiable in the ethnographic literature because they tend to be known by an array of local names. Confusion extends even to the term 'Orang Laut', which, in Malay, may be applied, not only to sea nomads and former nomads, but also to Malay-speaking people who dwell on the coast in contrast to those who live inland (Sandbukt, 1982: 42–3). Among the sea-nomadic or formerly nomadic Orang Laut, Sandbukt (1982: 72–4) distinguishes between those who speak Malay dialects, the Orang Laut proper, and others, living in small numbers in Johore and eastern Sumatra, who speak a distinct Malayic language, closely related to Malay, but non-intelligible to Malay speakers. These latter groups describe themselves as Duano or Desin Dolak, a Duano translation of 'Orang Laut'. In Johore, they are commonly known to Malay-speaking outsiders as the Orang Kuala. By comparison with most other Orang Laut, they practise an economy more narrowly adapted to life in estuarine or mangrove swamp environments.[4]

The Orang Laut, as we know them from the sixteenth until the end of the nineteenth century, when the great majority abandoned boat nomadism, present a notable contrast to the Moken of the late nineteenth and early twentieth centuries. The Straits of Malacca, along the southern approaches of which the Orang Laut are very largely concentrated, were, and still are a major crossroads of maritime commerce (see Map 11.1). The area is also the primary arena of Malay political history. Historians like Wolters (1967; 1979) on Srivijaya and Andaya (1974; 1975) on the Kingdom of Johore have stressed the important role they see the Malay-speaking Orang Laut as playing in providing the naval power and communicative links on which the hegemony of successive Malay states was based in this critically important maritime zone of otherwise comparatively sparse population. Here, much as in the case of the Bajau Laut, sea nomads appear to have emerged locally, together with related Malay-speaking coastal and strand groups, out of a common cultural and linguistic matrix, being, essentially, part of the same cultural and socio-political ambit.

With the Orang Laut, in contrast to the Moken, boat nomadism is embedded in a complex political order. In the seventeenth and eighteenth centuries, for example, various named groups of Orang Laut were incorporated in the Kingdom of Johore by their formalized ties to the ruler (Andaya, 1974). These ties were articulated in terms of the specific corvée duties assigned to each group ('*suku*'). With corvée duties ('*kerahan*') were associated degrees of status. Andaya (1974: 7), referring to the seventeenth century, outlines the relationships in these terms.

The more powerful and prestigious Orang Laut groups were associated with the larger islands or those islands which were favourably situated on major sea trading lanes.... The duties of the Orang Laut were to gather sea products for the China trade, perform certain special services for the ruler at weddings, funerals, or on a hunt, serve as transport for envoys and royal missives, man the ships and serve as a fighting force on the ruler's fleet, and patrol the waters of the kingdom. Except in times of actual warfare when their services were needed for the fleet, the Orang Laut were usually on patrol providing protection for Johor's traders or to those wanting to trade in Johor while harassing all other shipping.

Groups such as the Orang Suku Galang, who comprised the upper stratum of Orang Laut society, were those whose duty was to provide the naval fighting force for the realm. By contrast, the corvée duty assigned to the Orang Mantang, who formed one of the lowest status '*suku*', was to care for the ruler's hunting dogs. Later, with the breakdown of central hegemony, fighting groups like the Orang Galang appear to have transferred their allegiance to local Malay chieftains who engaged them as pirate crews. As a result, one of the consequences of the suppression of piracy in the mid-nineteenth century was a rapid sedentarization of a number of these groups (Sopher, 1965; Sandbukt, 1984: 7). Former high status communities have now generally embraced Islam and become assimilated into the general Malay population, while marginal low status groups have generally continued, like the Semporna Bajau Laut, to maintain a separate ethnicity, even while becoming sedentary.

The identity and way of life of specific groups of Orang Laut were powerfully shaped by their interaction with surrounding settled populations in a larger, hierarchically constituted field of political and economic relations. '*Suku*' organization appears to have constituted the principal framework by which a number of regional polities, including the Kingdom of Johore, marshalled island and coastal people—including sea nomads—under their rule, and welded them into a tributary and defensive network. Rulers recognized '*suku*' headmen and ascribed their followers '*kerahan*' duties, while '*suku*' were accorded differential status on the basis of the particular duties their members were called upon to perform. The Orang Laut were thus divided, through their relationship to the ruler, into named status groups, each differentially situated to perform specific corvée tasks, these tasks in turn associated with positions in an almost caste-like status hierarchy. To the extent that the Orang Laut functioned as marine foragers, they were clearly 'professional' foragers, whose very existence presupposed political hierarchy and tributary duties to an external ruler.

By the nineteenth century, '*suku*' organization was in rapid disintegration as the power of indigenous rulers was supplanted by that of British and Dutch colonial authorities. A few surviving '*suku*' were mobilized for piratical activity, but many more disappeared. Among the latter were the Orang Kallang, boat-dwellers who, at the beginning of the nineteenth century, occupied the Kallang River in what is now the heart of urban Singapore. Immediately following Singapore's founding, the Orang Kallang developed for a time a highly successful adaptation as 'sampan-men', carrying passengers between vessels at anchor and the port. Eventually, however, they were displaced to Pulau Brani where, in the early decades of this century, they were gradually assimilated (Sandbukt, 1982: 70–2).

The vessels used by the Orang Laut until the first half of the twentieth century appear to have been notably uniform (Gibson-Hill, 1952).[5] They were characteristically built of a dug-out base, with one or more planks to increase the freeboard, and carried a decked aft section made of split bamboo. At the stern of the boat was located the family hearth and cooking area. Boats were light and easily manoeuvrable and were typically crewed, like the Bajau Laut *lepa*, by a single family. In contrast to the neighbouring Malays, Orang Laut fishing was done mainly with spears and harpoons, rather than with specialized nets and large traps, resulting in what Wee (1985) has described as a comparatively 'low-yield subsistence pattern'.

As a distinct Orang Laut subgroup, the Duano of East Sumatra (Sandbukt, 1982; 1984: 10) evolved a highly specialized foraging adaptation that focused on the extremely narrow resource base of brackish mudflats and mangrove swamps. Such specialization did not permit self-sufficiency, and in return for littoral produce the Duano obtained virtually all other necessities from trade with riverine Malay horticulturalists, including cultivated foodstuffs and even their dwelling-boats.

A northern subgroup of Orang Laut, the Urak Lawoi' (dialect form of 'Orang Laut'), inhabit the islands off the western coast of Thailand from Phuket to the Adang island group, along the southern edge of the Moken–Moklen range (Hogan, 1988: 1–2). The Urak Lawoi' population numbers approximately 3,000. Sea nomads in the previous century, they are now settled in seaside villages, living as strand-dwellers in houses near the beach. Here they cultivate crops of rice and coconuts (Hogan, 1972: 206). Although cultivators, some Urak Lawoi' are said to spend several days at a time away from their home villages on boat-dwelling excursions while gathering '*tripang*' and other littoral produce. There is a small amount of intermarriage between the Moken and Urak Lawoi', and some Urak Lawoi' villages contain small complements of visiting or semi-settled Moken (Hogan, 1972: 210).

Ecological Adaptation, Trade, and Traditional States

South-East Asia is a region of long-established maritime traditions. Coastlines are extensive and frame a vast maritime zone of islands and littoral, characterized, in human terms, by notable economic and ethnic diversity, including small communities of maritime foragers. The presence of sea nomadism in South-East Asia appears to be related to the extent of these coastal and island waters and to their notable richness of food resources (Sather, 1995a). Maritime South-East Asia is the primary world centre of marine faunal diversity. Dunn and Dunn (1984: 252) made this observation.

The tropics are far richer in numbers of animals and plant species than are the
temperate ... regions of the world.... [While] this generalization holds true for the
seas at least as much as for the terrestrial realm ... [and o]f the tropical seas ...
those surrounding the mainland and islands of presentday Southeast Asia are
known to contain the greatest wealth of marine life.... The centre of this richness
is Sundaic Southeast Asia, and Ekman's (1953: 18) oft-quoted statement on this
matter bears repeating here: 'The further one moves away from this centre in
any direction, the more the fauna appears as ... progressively impoverished.... '

Much of this richness is due to the existence of two ecosystems unique
to the tropics and particularly well developed in South-East Asia:
(a) coral reefs and (b) littoral mangrove formations (Dunn and Dunn,
1984: 252–3). Significantly, both are fundamentally important habitats
to the sea nomads.

Other littoral environments, such as sandy or rocky shores, are essentially the same as in other parts of the world. Each of these environments
has, of course, a distinctive biota, and, as Dunn and Dunn (1984: 254)
note:

Two or more such biotypes may occur together or within a small area. For
example, a coral reef may fringe any type of shore, and rocks may occur in the
midst of sand beaches. Such areas have a greater variety of species than has each
biotype alone, and for that reason it is likely that mixed environments would be
preferred as subsistence zones by peoples who exploit marine resources.

Indeed, many nomadic communities exploit an extended range of habitats, including such areas of special diversity (Sather, 1985: 183–90).
But from the contemporary ethnographic record, it is also clear that
most sea nomads in the South-East Asian region have developed fairly
narrow modes of adaptation. It is here that the significance of coral reefs
and mangrove habitats is particularly apparent, as these two represent
the major alternative zones of sea-nomadic specialization. Some communities have come to focus on mangrove formations; others on areas of
coral. The Duano live entirely in brackish swamps, centring their economic life wholly around the exploitation of the exceedingly restricted
but rich resource base offered by this particular ecosystem. By contrast,
the Semporna Bajau Laut direct their fishing activity almost exclusively
to coral reefs and to the closely associated coral-sand beaches and shallows. Except to cut firewood, they make no use of mangrove forests and
in fishing, they avoid completely areas of muddy or turbid water.

Each of these three principal sea-nomadic groups is associated with an
archipelagic environment that is both extensive and rich in food resources. Within these environments, a wealth of opportunities exist for
strand foraging and for the exploitation of inshore waters, using nets,
spears, and other gear. But also accessible are shoreline and coastal
forests which hold still further exploitable resources, including wild plant
foods capable of supplementing a protein-rich marine diet (Sandbukt,
1982: 47). What is suggested is therefore a range of possible adaptive
modes, among them more generalized adaptations resembling more closely
hunter-gathering in that they involve the use of a diverse, broader-based
array of food resources. Among the existing sea nomads, the Moken

come closest to realizing this possibility. By contrast, the Orang Laut and Bajau Laut are both more narrowly specialized. The difference appears to be related less to the natural environment than to differences in the social and political settings in which each of these groups is enveloped. Both the Orang Laut and Bajau Laut have historically existed within an economy of exchange-based specialization, in which land and sea adaptations are not only mutually differentiated, but are linked to community identity and hierarchically structured differences of power and status.

Variations in sea-nomadic adaptation therefore relate not only to a group's interaction with its natural environment, but also of equal importance, to its interrelationships with other communities within an encompassing socio-economic and political order. In the case of the Bajau Laut, sea-nomadic communities appear to have emerged out of a larger matrix of ecologically diverse but culturally and linguistically related groups, many connected by trade and trade-related economic interdependence. While it is likely that, within this matrix, sea-nomadic communities originally took the form of more generalized foragers, they very likely became increasingly specialized as exchange networks grew in importance, a growth to which they themselves almost certainly contributed (Sather, 1995a: 259). In the sixteenth century, the Sama-speaking sea nomads of the Sulu–Sabah–eastern Indonesian region already existed within maritime trading states, their status and economic role shaped by their wider political and commercial relations with other peoples. As boat nomads, they in no sense functioned as independent foragers, and in this regard, Bellwood (1985: 136) is almost certainly right to regard them as a comparatively recent historical development. Their origins, however, are another matter.

The Prehistory and Historical Demise of Sea Nomadism

Little is known of the prehistory of the South-East Asian sea nomads. However, all are Austronesian speakers and this fact has prompted some debate among prehistorians concerning the possible role of maritime groups in the early spread of Austronesian-speaking peoples (Sather, 1995a). The most comprehensive theory of Austronesian expansion (Bellwood, 1985) links their spread to cereal cultivation, notably rice horticulture, but linguistic evidence suggests that the proto-Austronesians also possessed well-developed maritime skills (Blust, 1976: 36). It seems likely that these skills contributed in some way to the spread of Austronesian speakers into South-East Asia, but the precise nature of this contribution remains uncertain.

Urry (1981) makes a powerful argument that, because of its role in communications, the sea constitutes the dominant factor in the prehistory of South-East Asia, and that the spread and eventual dominance of Austronesian-speaking peoples in the Indo-Malaysian Archipelago was directly due to their ability to control the sea and hence command seagoing trade. Urry argues that before the development of effective navigational skills, the sea constituted a barrier to wider integration. As a result, a mosaic of cultures developed in maritime South-East Asia before the appearance of skilled mariners, and it was this rich variety of different environments and human cultures that provided the basis on which later trade developed (Urry, 1981: 7). It also, he suggests, contributed to the formation of political hierarchy. Thus, 'the group or groups who gained some mastery of the seas and who could thus transform the barrier into a bridge, could exploit this cultural variety for their own ends. Indeed, if it were done carefully, they had the potential to dominate the whole archipelago.'

Urry (1981: 9) suggests that the early Austronesians, even before they left eastern Asia and began their southward spread into the Philippines, were probably already adapted to coastal conditions and to inter-island trade. As a consequence, trade may itself have been a motive for Austronesian expansion. Groups may have set out seeking not only new land to farm, but exchange goods and new communities to trade with (Urry, 1981: 9). As the Austronesians entered the Indo-Malaysian Archipelago, the geography of the region would have given a further stimulus to trade and to the development of maritime technology. Geography, Urry argues, provided the 'basic outline upon which ... the prehistory of the region [was later] played out'.

The pattern of islands and inland seas provided the stimulus for maritime innovation and the production of goods from the ecological and cultural diversity of the islands supplied the impetus for trade and exchange. Utilizing sea routes the whole pattern of trade and exchange and the strategies for developing producers and consumers was expanded within and beyond the archipelago (Urry, 1981: 23).

Ultimately, this expansion drew the Austronesians westward, throughout insular South-East Asia, to the mainland and beyond. Once the Austronesians began to penetrate insular South-East Asia, the subsequent spread of Austronesian languages is likely to have been linked to trade itself, not necessitating a massive movement of people, but with Austronesian languages replacing the earlier languages of the area through their role as the dominant languages of trade.

Solheim (1975; 1984) has similarly proposed that maritime peoples played a significant role in Austronesian expansion, but sees these people as directly ancestral to the historic sea nomads. As an alternative to the model of southward migration proposed by Bellwood and others, Solheim (1984: 86) has argued that the proto-Austronesians first emerged within insular South-East Asia itself. In this thesis, he proposes that Austric, a possible language grouping encompassing both Austroasiatic and Austronesian, was spoken throughout the whole of South-East Asia, including Sundaland during the late Pleistocene (Solheim, 1975: 152). Later, with rising sea levels, Sundaland became a zone of islands, isolating Austric speakers in the east from those of the west and north, and so produced a split between what he calls 'pre-Austroasiatic' speakers on Sumatra and the South-East Asian mainland and 'pre-Austronesian' speakers in eastern Indonesia and the southern Philippines (Solheim,

1975: 156). Following this split, proto-Austronesian languages developed in insular South-East Asia and from there were carried northward to Taiwan and southern China by maritime voyagers whom he calls 'Nusantao' (Solheim, 1975: 156–8).

In a more recent version of this hypothesis, Solheim (1984: 81) proposes that proto-Austronesian developed initially as a 'barter language' among 'Nusantao' mariners, who came eventually, following this hypothetical northward migration, to occupy the coasts of northern Luzon, southern Taiwan, and southern China. Later, Taiwan became isolated, while elsewhere along the western shores of the South China Sea, the now developing Austronesian languages remained in contact as a result of 'Nusantao' voyaging and so diverged from one another much more slowly. Following the isolation of Taiwan, the resulting 'proto-Malayo-Polynesian' languages were then carried southward, back through the Philippines to Borneo and from there south, east and westward, by groups of bartering 'Nusantao' mariners (Solheim, 1975: 153; 1984: 84–5).

While many elements of Solheim's hypothesis appear to be highly improbable, particularly his account of the emergence of proto-Austronesian and its subsequent dispersion by 'Nusantao' voyaging, his arguments, like those of Urry, have the merit of highlighting the possible role of sea-going peoples and maritime trade in early Austronesian prehistory. Solheim sees the historical sea nomads as representing 'the most direct descendants' of his 'Nusantao', although, as he observes, 'During the last few hundred years their status has deteriorated, bringing them to the bottom of the local pecking order instead of being, as they were around 2,000 years ago, economically prosperous and the masters of their homes and livelihood, the southern and eastern seas, from Madagascar to Japan to Easter Island' (Solheim, 1984: 86). Here Solheim perilously telescopes a vast sweep of South-East Asian and Pacific prehistory; he also ignores the diverse origins of the sea nomads and the existence among them of close cultural and linguistic affinities with related shore- and island-peoples, all suggesting, as I have indicated, less migration than a long and complex history of local interaction and evolution.

Whatever the case, it seems probable that maritime peoples played some part in Austronesian expansion, although the question of whether boat-nomadic groups were involved or not remains a matter of conjecture. More probably, as Bellwood suggests, maritime specializations, including nomadic foraging, developed out of the process of expansion itself. As Urry argues, the geography of the Indo-Malaysian Archipelago would have been a powerful stimulus to such a development. What is known is that by the time of European entry into maritime South-East Asia, boat-nomadic foragers were already widely dispersed, and by then an integral part of the cultural diversity of the region.

It seems probable that sea nomadism developed out of a more generalized pattern of coastal foraging, some elements of which very likely predate Austronesian expansion. Ethnographically, the best evidence for this comes from the Moken. Recently, however, archaeological evidence has come to light from Bukit Tengkorak in the Semporna district of Sabah indicating such a pattern of early coastal adaptation (Bellwood, 1989; Bellwood and Koon, 1989). Here, only a few miles inland from the Bajau Laut community described in this book, archaeological materials reveal the presence of a population living during the first millennium BC in what was then a coastal setting, heavily exploiting the area's marine resources and engaging in long-distance voyaging, while at the same time utilizing the nearby streams and coastal forests. Perhaps the most intriguing feature of this site is the presence of portable earthenware hearths. These hearths, carried on board boats, have historically been the cultural hallmark of the Bajau Laut. The site thus suggests a possible link to the precursors of the historical sea nomads of the region.

While the origin of the sea nomads remains uncertain, their contribution to the subsequent development of maritime trading states and to the networks of communication and long-distance commerce on which these states were based is now reasonably well documented (Wolters, 1967). We know that in the western Malay world, by the end of the first millennium AD petty chiefdoms became progressively 'nested' within one another to form small-scale states (Wolters, 1967, 1982; Benjamin, 1985, 1986). In the process, boat-dwelling mariners not only generated trading wealth and secured and defended the sea lanes essential to this development; they also acted as 'integrating information-carriers', linking together subsidiary chiefs and a developing peasantry (Benjamin, 1986: 16), making possible the larger-scale integration of increasingly centralized polities. In this book, I have traced a similar, though later, process in the Sulu Archipelago.

Today, boat nomadism is everywhere disappearing from maritime South-East Asia. For those who built the first pile-houses at Bangau-Bangau in the late 1950s, the process of sedentarization is now all but complete, and in this book I have tried to capture something of this transformation, as the Bajau Laut in Semporna moved between the past and, to borrow Clifford's apt phrase, a rapidly changing 'present-becoming-future' (Clifford, 1988: 247).

Boat-living families continue to be part of the larger Bangau-Bangau community. But these people are now chiefly Sama Dilaut 'refugees' from the Sibutu and Tawitawi island groups of the southern Philippines who, like their predecessors, have filtered southward, seeking security and a new life in Sabah. Most have returned to their boats, or abandoned their former moorages, in order to escape the late twentieth-century phenomena of civil wars, sectarian and secessionist violence, economic decline, and population pressure (Johnston, 1993). While for the Semporna Bajau Laut change has been largely a matter of positive choice actively embraced by the villagers, many of these newcomers have not been so fortunate. Besides war and armed violence, also contributing to their exodus has been the recent introduction of *agar-agar* cultivation in the southern and south-central islands of Sulu, resulting in the colonization in many areas of local reefs and inshore shallows by land-based groups, including the Tausug (Nimmo, 1986). The destruction of coral, declining fish stocks, and the construction of cultivation platforms has meant the loss by the Sama Dilaut of their traditional fishing grounds and anchorage sites, forcing many to retreat once again to their boats and to migration. For the time being, for these newcomers to Bangau-Bangau—'refugees' and the dispossessed of Sulu—boat nomadism, whatever its past significance, has taken on a new lease on life and new meaning in the present.

1. However, Ivanoff (1989) reports that the Moken make use of Malay as a ritual language. This suggests the possibility that the Moken, like the Orang Laut, may have similarly been part of a larger Malay-dominated cultural and political ambit at some point in the past, later becoming disengaged, or very largely so. Through the nineteenth century, sea nomadic groups in Mergui and south-western Thailand maintained occasional ties with Malay maritime traders.

2. 'Selung' is the Burmese term for the Mergui sea people.

3. I am grateful to Christian Pelras for drawing my attention to these possible connections.

4. In this connection, Sandbukt (1982) draws a sharp distinction in modes of sea-nomadic adaptation between what he calls the 'estuarine'-adapted Duano and other sea-nomadic groups whom he characterizes as 'littoral'-adapted. While potentially useful, the distinction is overdrawn. Many local Orang Laut communities also developed in the past notably specialized adaptations to the mangrove estuaries, for example, the Orang Seletar (Logan, 1847b), while the Duano move in the course of fishing, like other Orang Laut, into the littoral zone, as indicated by the title of Sandbukt's dissertation, 'Duano littoral fishing' (1982). In a strict sense, estuarine environments exist within the littoral, so the two terms are not wholly comparable. Finally, while Sandbukt (1982: 74) stresses the potential of the littoral zone for more generalized modes of adaptation, it must also be noted that some 'littoral' adaptations—Bajau Laut reef-fishing, for example—are as narrowly specialized in their own right as is the 'estuarine' adaptation of the Duano.

5. This is in marked contrast to the Sama–Bajau, who, in the Sulu Archipelago and south-eastern Sabah, employ, from region to region, a great variety of vessels (Spoehr, 1971; Kurais, 1974; Martenot, 1981).

Glossary

a'a	people
a'a déa	land or shore people
a'a dilaut	sea people; see also Sama Dilaut
a'a saddi	other people, non-kin
a'a Sama	Sama–Bajau people
abakkat napas	to cease breathing; death
abettong	pregnant
addat	social norms; customary law
agot	maximum low tide; also called *atoho*
ala'at	bad
ala'at ataina	to be deceiving, false, or dishonest
alalom	open sea; see also *sellang*
allau	day, daylight
amahilala'	putting in order; reconciliation between an estranged couple
amahilala' a'a amatai	preparing the corpse for burial
amakan	feast; ritual meals; also called *labot*
amakan sumangat	offerings to the soul of the dead
ambit	communal netting in which fish are driven into a net enclosure or surround; to move in co-ordination; also called *magambit*
amiss	handline fishing; root word *pissi*
amokot	inlet- or cove-netting
amuhun	ask leave or seek permission; root word *puhun*
anak	child, biological offspring; see also *ondé*
anak i'ipat	adopted child
anak ilu	foster children
anak kabungsuan	youngest child, last-born
anakop	small scale drift-net fishing
anak siaka	eldest child, first-born
anak sumbang	children of brothers
anak tili'	stepchild
anambal	curing by the use of medicines
anawal	curing by the use of spells
anda'	to see
anebba	inshore fishing and gathering
angagap	premarital courting
angan	outer reef-face, reef rim
anua'	to lead, precede
anua' tebba	lead boat in a co-operative fish drive

anuna'	initial proposal of marriage
anunggu' tunang	to provide for one's fiancée during engagement
aruah	feast for the souls of the dead
arung	eldest daughter or eldest sister; see also *oto'*
asusa' atai	grief
ata	slave
atai	liver/heart; considered the bodily centre of feeling, emotion, intellect, and volition
ayuwan	son/daughter-in-law
ayuwan menempuan	spouse of grandson/granddaughter
ba'anan	cluster; house group cluster, localized kindred; a neighbourhood group made up of allied house groups; see also *tumpuk*
babu'	aunt
bagai	friend; trading partner
bagai hap	close friend, intimate
bahangi	commemorative rite for the dead
bai pinaduru'	nursed from the same breasts
balanja'	expenses; expenses incurred in connection with a wedding paid by the groom and his kin
baliu	wind; inside the body; a cause of illness
baliu timul	east wind
baliu uttala'	north wind
balosok	maximum high tide
bangkai	corpse
bangkau	mangrove
bangun	blood-money
bantah	enemy
bapa'	uncle
baran	body
basingan	part of the bride-wealth (*dalaham*) consisting of gold jewellery and cloth; a dower gift made to the bride
bat	sea cucumber, *Holothuria*
batal	recited marriage formula
batu	rock, stone, coral
bessok	anterior fontanelle; the bodily passageway of the life-soul
bilas	reciprocal term used between persons married to siblings; co-sibling-in-law
binangunan	to pay *bangun*
binélau	madness, insanity
binuanan	food sharing; to give or share with others
binuanan daing	sharing of fish for household consumption
binusung	to become *busung*
bituanan	divorced man or woman
bitu'un	star
boggo'	dug-out canoe
bohé'	fresh water, fluid; well, spring; semen
bohé' siam	blessed water
bokko'	marine turtle
buahan	infant cradle, cloth sling; also called *dundangan* or *rundangan*

buas	cooked rice
buas banning/bianing	turmeric rice
bud	mountain
bujang	young unmarried woman
bulan	moon; lunar month
bulan puasa	fasting month, Ramadan
bulan sappal	the month of Safar or 'misfortune' (*bala'*); also called *bulan bala'*
buli'	stern of a boat; back, rear; see also *munda'*
busung	calamity, ill-fortune, ill-fatedness
butas	divorce; also called *magbutas*
dabalutu	a boat crew; also called *dalepa*
dabohé'	siblings of the same semen
daing	fish
daing toho'	dried fish
dalaham	bride-wealth; its payment signals the transfer of jural rights over the wife; composed of *basingan* and *mahalna*
daluma'	housemates, members of one house group
dampo'onan/dampalanakan	an individual's close cognatic kin
danglai	nickname
déa	inland, ashore
denakan	sibling, brother or sister
denakan tili'	step sibling
denda	woman, female
depa'	a fathom length, the distance across outstretched arms, from fingertip to fingertip
diat	indemnification for a minor injury, paid as a token of solicitude
dilaut	of the sea
diniatan	to pay *diat*
dua'a	voluntary prayer, address to God for a variety of special purposes
dua'a selamat	a reading from the Islamic commentaries (*Kitab* or *Bejanji*)
dua'a tulkin	prayer for the dead
dublun	gold brooch, coin, or other item of jewellery, used in traditional payments marking a transfer of jural rights, such as in marriage or adoption; also called *bulawan*
duru'	breast
dusa	sin
empu	grandchild
enggo'	mother; also called *ina'*
entom	to remember
gabbang	xylophone, with bamboo or wooden keys
ginuntingan	haircut ceremony for an infant
gunting	scissors
hailaya puasa	feast marking the end of fasting month; held on the first day of the month of Shawwal; *hari raya puasa* (Malay)
hajjimat	protective charm, amulet

hakka	traditional measure of length for nets (from tip of the thumb to the tip of the index finger)
hali bulan	nightly moon phases
halo	intermediate tidal zone, where the sea appears green
hanayan	ornamented hanging beam used by mediums
handa	wife
hella	husband
hinang	work, action
idut-dutan	treatment by sucking to remove objects from inside the body causing illness
igal	dance; also called *magigal*
imam	spiritual leader, religious leader of a mosque or village prayer-house congregation
imam daerah (Malay)	district *imam*
ipal	brother/sister-in-law
iya'	shame, embarrassment; also called *maka'iya'*
jakat pitla'	alms
jalmin	legal sponsor of an alien
jalminan	alien sponsored by a *jalmin*
janji'	promise, pledge, vow; also called *najal*
jin	spirit-medium
kabusungan	a general state of ill-fatedness; state of jeopardy
kaki	cousin; foot; measure of length approximately 22 centimetres
kaki mendua	second cousin
kaki mentedda'	first cousin
kalangan	row, paddle
kalangan tebba	traditional songs sung usually to the accompaniment of a pounded beat or while rowing
kaléa	landward; see also *kaut*
kaluwa'an	eastward, in direction of the rising sun; see also *kasoddopan*
kamanakan	nephew/niece
kamanakan kaki	child of cousin
kampung	cognatic kin of recognition; all of an individual's acknowledged or presumed kin
kampung (Malay)	village
kasoddopan	westward, in direction of the setting sun; see also *kaluwa'an*
kata-kata	epic narrative tale
kaut	seaward; see also *kaléa*
kawin	marriage; wedding
kawin maglahi	marriage by elopement
kawin magpahanda	marriage by formal negotiation
kawin magpolé	marriage initiated by a public declaration of intent to marry
kembo'-mbo'an	ancestors; see also *mbo'*
ketua kampung (Malay)	village headman
kibut	water-storage jar
kinamatan	ritual first feeding of an infant
kobol	invulnerability

kok	head
kokan	the headside, the lateral orienting point of a boat or house
kuba	cowries; net weights
kubu'	fortification
kubu' batu	artificial coral mound
kubu'-kubu'	a temporary stilt-house shelter
kubul	cemetery, burial place
kulit mbo'	bark bin used to hold 'new rice' (*pai baha'u*) during the *magpai baha'u* ceremony
kusina	cooking shelter, kitchen
laha'	blood
lahat	home area, country, place of origin, village
lahi	run
lamak	a sail
lappohan	earthenware hearth used for cooking
lasa	love, affection, honour, respect, gratitude; also called *kalasa* or *magkalasa*
lato'	edible sea-grapes (algae)
laut	sea, ocean
lella	man, male
lembagan	spirit-medium's lay assistant
lendom	dark
lendoman/bulan lendoman	'dark' phase of the waning moon
lepa	fishing boat
leppo'	cooking pot
ling saitan	spirit language
ling Sama	Bajau speech/language
linggi'	larger drift-net
lo'ok	cove, bay, inlet
luma'	house; house group
luma'ang	low tide
luma'-luma'	roofed enclosure over a grave
ma'asé'/magasé'	concern, pity, sympathy, compassion
magamak	'warming' of a new mother following delivery
magba'an-ba'an	grouping, clustering (of things or persons)
magbantah	formal enmity; root word *bantah*
magbilas	to be related as *bilas*
magbuddi	voluntary, unsolicited aid, affection, or support given from an inner sense of kindness, love, pity, or obligation
magbusung	a ritual act performed in expiation of wrong-doing for the purpose of lifting a state of *busung*
magdangin	reciprocal exchange of labour
magentoman-entoman	remembrance
maghanda	take a wife, formal conclusion of a negotiated marriage
maghinang	ritual occasion; 'doing'
maghinang ni kembo'-mbo'	feasting the ancestors, rite of remembrance for the dead
maghukum	adjudication, public hearing

magigal jin	ritual trance-dancing performed by spirit-mediums (*jin*)
magislam	circumcision
magkaat	worn out; in disrepair; all property destroyed upon its owner's death
magkiparat	rite of reconciliation performed to end a state of formal enmity (*magbantah*); also called *kiparat*
maglahi	elopement
maglindu	lamentation for the dead; also called *magdohong*
magmaulud	rite of thanksgiving performed in fulfilment of a vow; also called *magbajanji'*; see also *magtimbang*
magpassal	stain with henna (performed at the time of marriage)
magsalassai	informal mediation; also called *sinalassai*
magsambi	barter, exchange
magsapah	swear a public oath; also called *anapah*
magsinaggau	abduction as a means of forcing a marriage; also called *magsaggau*
magsukul	thanksgiving
magsulut	state of reconciliation; mutual accord
magtilau	proposal; ask the hand of a woman in marriage
magtimbang	a second rite of thanksgiving frequently performed after *magmaulud*; see also *magmaulud*
magtulak bala'	expel or drive away misfortune; ritual bathing in the sea
magtumbuk sengkol	consecutive marriages between two related families
magutang	incurring and discharging debts; root word *utang*
mahalna	monetary component of the bride-wealth (*dalaham*)
mahung	shadow
makahandul atai	arouse feelings, stir desires, move physical passions, longing
mandelaut	from the sea
mandi sappal	ritual bathing in the sea during the month of Safar (*bulan sappal*)
manpo'on	source, cause of, origin; root word *po'on*
maru	co-wives
maskid	mosque; village prayer-house
mata	eye; mesh opening of a net
mataan	married couple; married couple plus their children; primary kin
mato'a	parents-in-law
matto'a	elders
mbo'	grandparents; ancestors; honorific term for senior leaders
mma'	father
mudin	specialist who performs circumcision
munda'	fore-section of a boat; numerical classifier for boats; see also *buli'*

mundusia	humankind
musim	season, major division of the year
musim baliu	a season of prevailing winds
musim habagat	season of prevailing north north-west winds in January; generally period of strongest winds
musim satan	season of prevailing south winds, from late May to the end of September
musim timul	season of prevailing east winds, in March and April
musim uttala'	season of prevailing north winds, in February and March
nakura'	group leader
nakura' jin	leader of the village spirit-mediums
nakura' luma'	house group leader
nalka	hell
nanam	to diagnose, determine the cause of illness; see also *tinanam*
napas	breath, life
nawal	curative spells
nguppi	dream
nunuk	fig tree, particularly parasitic or strangling fig (*Ficus* spp.), favoured dwelling-place of spirits
on	name; personal name
ondé	a term for children generally; see also *anak*
oto'	eldest son or eldest brother; see also *arung*
pabuka'na atai	open-hearted, generous
pagbuan-buan	small gifts, especially those made by a young man during engagement
pagentoman	a token by which to remember another person
pagmunda'	alliance group consisting of boat-dwelling families that sail and/or moor their boats together
pai	unhusked rice, rice
pai baha'u	newly harvested rice
pala'an	secession from an existing *luma'* in order to found a new house group
palawa' allau	sunset
paliama	constellation or group of stars
pamatulakan	spirit-boat used to carry away (*tulak*) illness and misfortune
pamikitan	affinity; to be related by marriage; also called *magpikit-pikitan*
pamunda'	penis (figurative); see also *munda'*
pana'	spear gun
pandan	pandanus
pandoga	navigational location-finding by the use of landmark alignments
panggi kayu	cassava (*Manihot* spp.); the main dietary staple
panggua'	ghost
panggua' allum	'living shade', a person believed to have the power to make him/herself invisible
Panglima	Sulu title originally bestowed by the sultan on influential regional leaders; later bestowed by the British North Borneo Chartered Company

	on trusted village headmen
panguling	midwife
pannyam	rice cake prepared for ceremonial or ritual occasions
pantan	open house platform or landing-stage
panukna'	curse
pasakai	visitor, guest, a person temporarily affiliated with a group but not a full member
pasakaian	apprenticeship of a novice spirit-medium (*jin*)
pasod allau	sunrise
pasu'	heat; state of spiritual imperilment
patai sabil	death in childbirth; bad death
patika'	trance state
paukum	to join one's affines; to marry into a husband's or wife's house group
peddi' atai	anger
pegawai daerah (Malay)	district officer
pelarian	refugee; alien without Malaysian citizenship
pikit	to stick, join together, adhere
pikit-mamikit	affine; in-laws; those related by marriage
pinalisig	sororate marriage; marriage to a deceased wife's sister
pogol	fish-spear with 2–4 barbed tines
po'on	tree; stem; origin
pu'	island
puasa	fasting
pugai	love spell
puhung	present gifts, out of self-interest, in order to gain support or secure favours from others; the opposite of *magbuddi*; also called *amuhung*
pu'-pu'	islets, a group of islands
pusaka'	property, tangible or intangible, transmitted by inheritance
ruah	transcendental-soul
sa'am	cross-beams that separate the bow and stern sections from the living area of the *lepa*, both fore and aft
sabil	to go berserk; commit suicide; attack others or oneself out of grief or shame; also called *mag-sabil*
saitan	spirit
saitan jin	medium's spirit-helper
saksi'	witness
Sama	Sama–Bajau
Sama Dilaut	Bajau Laut
Sama Mandelaut	Bajau Laut
Sama to'ongan	'the real Sama', Sama Dilaut
sambahayang	obligatory prayers
sambahayang lima waktu	five daily prayers
sangom	night
sapah	to swear
sapau	mat roofing made of '*kajang*' covering the living quarters of a boat

sarakkah	a charitable gift that confers religious merit on the giver
séhé'	companion, ally; fishing partner
selambat	calm water
selibut	smaller drift-net
selikit	smaller fish-spear with 5–12 tines
sellang	deep water, open sea; see also *alalom*
senduk	grave marker
sengkol	cross-member within the hull of the *lepa* supporting the decking planks
siaka	elder sibling
siali	younger sibling
sihil	a form of knowledge or magical power that allows those who have such power to stop events from occurring, of making themselves invisible, or of transporting themselves from place to place
si'it	parents' siblings
sinaggau	to catch
soan	moorage post
soang	river, stream; underwater channel
sokat	marriage gift paid to the bride's kin to secure their goodwill
sollog	sea current
song	current, tide
song luma'ang	ebb current
song umanso'	flood current
subu	morning
subul	young unmarried man; bachelor
sukai	commission, tax
suku'	go-between commissioned to arrange marriage terms
sukud	luck, individual fate
sulga'	heaven
sumangat	life-soul
sumbang	incest
tabang	aid, favour, support; also called *mabang*
tabang-manabang	reciprocal aid
tabla'	equality, in balance
tahik	sea, sea water
tahik selambat	slack water
tai'anakan	close relatives, primary kin
tai' baliu	clouds
talinga	ear; free cord at each end of the headline of a net, used to tie individual nets together; also the two ends of a semi-circle of boats assembled for a fish surround or drive
talun	forest
tambal	medicines
tampat	sacred site; place where people come to seek blessings
tampé	tidemark

tamuni	afterbirth
ta'u anambal	herbalist curer; also called *penanambal*
ta'u anawal	expert in the use of spells; also called *penanawal*
ta'u nganda'	seer; oracle
tawal	curative spell; also called *nawal*
tayum	sea urchin
tebba	a double zone of inshore waters, including both beach shallows and reef rim; a principal netting zone
teddo'	calm, without wind
tellak	bright, light
tellak bulan	'bright' phase of the waxing moon immediately preceding full moon
tendog	follower, dependant
tépo	pandanus sleeping mat; formerly also used to enclose the shrouded body for burial
tilau	to ask
tinanam	diagnosis
tong	headland, cape
to'ongan	true, real, genuine
Tuhan	God
tulak	carry away
tumpuk	cluster; house group cluster
tunang	engagement, betrothal
tunju'	traditional measure of length for nets (from the tip of the raised thumb to the tip of the first finger)
turunan	descent line, a genealogical line of traceable ancestry
tu'ul	wooden piles on which a house is erected
ugama	religion; Islam
utang	debt
wajib	obligatory religious acts: five daily prayers, fasting, and alms-giving
wakil	guardian who gives a woman in marriage; also called *waris*
wakil ketua kampung (Malay)	assistant village headman

Bibliography

Adriani, N. (1900), 'De talen der Togian-eilenden', *Tijdschrift voor Indische Taal-, Land- en Volkenkunde*, 42: 460–90, 539–66.

Allison, Joe E. (1979), 'The Phonology of Sibutu Sama: A Language of the Southern Philippines', *Studies in Philippine Linguistics*, 3(2): 63–104.

Andaya, Leonard (1974), 'The Structure of Power in Seventeenth Century Johor', in Anthony Reid and Lance Castles (eds.), *Pre-colonial State Systems in Southeast Asia: The Malay Peninsula, Sumatra, Bali-Lombok, South Celebes*, Monographs of the Malaysian Branch of the Royal Asiatic Society, No. 6, Kuala Lumpur: Malaysian Branch of the Royal Asiatic Society, pp. 1–11.

_____ (1975), *The Kingdom of Johor, 1641–1728*, Kuala Lumpur: Oxford University Press.

_____ (1993), *The World of Maluku: Eastern Indonesia in the Early Modern Period*, Honolulu: University of Hawaii Press.

Anderson, G. (1890), *The Selungs of the Mergui Archipelago*, London: Truber.

Anderson, Raoul and Wadel, Cato (1972), 'Comparative Problems in Fishing Adaptations', in R. Anderson and C. Wadel (eds.), *North Atlantic Fishermen: Anthropological Essays on Modern Fishing*, Newfoundland Social and Economic Papers, No. 5, Institute of Social and Economic Research, Memorial University of Newfoundland, Toronto: University of Toronto Press.

Anon. (1902a), 'Pulo Gaia and Trusan Treacher', *British North Borneo Herald*, 20: 125.

_____ (1902b), 'Visit to Lahad Datu and Simporna', *British North Borneo Herald*, 20: 110.

_____ (1919), 'Lahad Dato', *British North Borneo Herald*, 38: 210.

Appell, G. N. (1965), 'The Nature of Social Groupings Among the Rungus Dusun of Sabah, Malaysia', Ph.D. thesis, Australian National University.

_____ (1976), 'Introduction. The Direction of Research in Borneo: Its Past Contributions to Anthropological Theory and Its Relevance for the Future', in G. N. Appell (ed.), *The Societies of Borneo*, Special Publication No. 6, Washington, DC: American Anthropological Association, pp. 1–15.

Arong, Jose R. (1962), 'The Badjaw of Sulu', *Philippine Sociological Review*, 10: 134–46.

Asmah Haji Omar (1980), 'The Bajau Darat Language', *Brunei Museum Journal*, 4(4): 11–29.

Banker, Elizabeth F. (1984), 'The West Coast Bajau Language', in Julie King and John Wayne King (eds.), *Languages of Sabah: A Survey Report*, Pacific Linguistics, Series C, No. 78, Canberra: Australian National University, pp. 101–12.

Barbosa, Artemio (1995), 'The Abaknun of Capul Island, Samar, Philippines',

Paper presented at the International Conference on Bajau/Sama Community, Kota Kinabalu, Sabah, June.

Barnes, J. A. (1949), 'Measures of Divorce Frequency in Simple Societies', *Journal of the Royal Anthropological Institute*, 79: 37–62.

_____ (1968), 'Networks and Political Processes', in M. J. Swartz (ed.), *Local-level Politics*, Chicago: Aldine, pp. 107–30.

Barnes, R. H. (1974), *Kédang: A Study of the Collective Thought of an Eastern Indonesian People*, Oxford: Clarendon Press.

Barth, Fredrik (1969), 'Introduction', in Fredrik Barth (ed.), *Ethnic Groups and Boundaries*, Boston: Little, Brown, pp. 9–38.

Bellwood, Peter (1985), *Prehistory of the Indo-Malaysian Archipelago*, Sydney: Academic Press.

_____ (1988), *Archaeological Research in South-eastern Sabah*, Monograph No. 2, Kota Kinabalu: Sabah Museum.

_____ (1989), 'Archaeological Investigations at Bukit Tengkorak and Segurong, Southeastern Sabah', *Bulletin of the Indo-Pacific Prehistory Association*, 9: 122–62.

Bellwood, Peter and Koon, Peter (1989), '"Lapita Colonists Leave Boats Unburned!" The Question of Lapita Links with Island Southeast Asia', *Antiquity*, 63: 613–22.

Bender, Donald R. (1967), 'A Refinement of the Concept of Households, Families, Co-residence, and Domestic Functions', *American Anthropologist*, 69: 493–504.

Benjamin, Geoffrey (1985), 'In the Long Term: Three Themes in Malayan Cultural Ecology', in Karl L. Hutterer, A. Terry Rambo, and George Lovelace (eds.), *Cultural Values and Human Ecology in Southeast Asia*, Michigan Papers on South and Southeast Asia, No. 27, Ann Arbor: Center for South and Southeast Asian Studies, University of Michigan, pp. 219–78.

_____ (1986), 'Between Isthmus and Islands: Reflections on Malayan Palaeo-Sociology', Working Paper, No. 71, Singapore: Department of Sociology, National University of Singapore.

Bentley, G. Carter (1981), 'Migration, Ethnic Identity, and State Building in the Philippines: The Sulu Case', in Charles Keyes (ed.), *Ethnic Change*, Seattle: University of Washington Press, pp. 118–53.

Birch, Ernest W. (1903), 'His Excellency the Governor's Visit to the East Coast', *British North Borneo Herald*, 21: 272.

Black, Ian (1971), 'Native Administration by the British North Borneo Chartered Company, 1878–1915', Ph.D. thesis, Australian National University.

_____ (1976), 'Interethnic Relations and Culture Change under Colonial Rule: A Study of Sabah', in George N. Appell (ed.), *Studies in Borneo Societies*, Special Report No. 12, DeKalb: Center for Southeast Asian Studies, Northern Illinois University, pp. 27–50.

_____ (1983), *A Gambling Style of Government: The Establishment of Chartered Company's Rule in Sabah, 1878–1915*, Kuala Lumpur: Oxford University Press.

Blust, Robert (1976), 'Austronesian Culture History: Some Linguistic Inferences and Their Relations to the Archaeological Record', *World Archaeology*, 8: 19–43.

Bottignolo, Bruno (1995), *Celebrations with the Sun: An Overview of Religious Phenomena among the Badjaos*, Quezon City: Ateneo de Manila University Press.

Burningham, Nick (1992), 'Bajau *Lepa* and *Sope*: "A Seven-part Canoe" Building Tradition in Indonesia', *The Beagle, Records of the Northern Territory Museum of Arts and Sciences*, 10(1): 193–222.

Callaghan, F. G. (1887), 'Darvel Bay, Silam, 2nd October, 1887', *British North Borneo Herald*, 5: 263.

Carey, I. (1970), 'Some Notes on the Sea Nomads of Johore', *Federation Museums Journal*, 15: 181–4.

Carrapiett, W. J. S. (1909), *The Salons*, India, Ethnographic Survey, Burma, no. 2, Rangoon: Office of the Superintendent, Government Printing.

Casiño, Eric (1967), 'Folk Islam in the Life Cycle of the Jama Mapun', *Philippine Sociological Review*, 15: 34–47.

_____ (1976), *The Jama Mapun*, Quezon City: Ateneo de Manila University Press.

Cense, Anton and Uhlenbeck, E. M. (1958), *Critical Survey of Studies on the Languages of Borneo*, The Hague: M. Nijhoff.

Chau, Ju-Kua (1911), *Chau Ju-Kua: His Work on the Chinese and Arab Trade in the Twelfth and Thirteenth Centuries, Entitled Chu-fan-chi*, translated and annotated by Friedrich Hirth and W. W. Rockhill, St. Petersburg: Imperial Academy of Sciences.

Clifford, James (1988), *The Predicament of Culture: Twentieth Century Literature, Ethnography, and Art*, Cambridge: Harvard University Press.

Cohn, Bernard S. (1981), 'Anthropology and History in the 1980s', *Journal of Interdisciplinary History*, 12(2): 227–52.

Collins, James T. (1995), 'Preliminary Notes on the Language of the Bajo Sangkuang Community of Bacan, East Indonesia', Paper presented at the International Conference on Bajau/Sama Community, Kota Kinabalu, Sabah, June.

Combés, Francisco (1904), 'The Natives of the Southern Islands', in Emma H. Blair and James A. Robertson (eds.), *The Philippine Islands, 1493–1898*, Cleveland: Arthur H. Clark, Vol. 40, pp. 99–182.

Conklin, Harold (1955), 'Preliminary Linguistic Survey of Mindanao', Mimeographed, Chicago: Philippine Studies Program.

Cook, Oscar (1924), *Borneo: The Stealer of Hearts*, New York: Houghton Mifflin.

Court, Christopher (1971), 'A Fleeting Encounter with the Moken (the Sea Gypsies) in Southern Thailand: Some Linguistic and General Notes', *Journal of the Siam Society*, 59(1): 83–95.

Crawfurd, John (1856), *A Descriptive Dictionary of the Indian Islands and Adjacent Counties*, London: Bradbury and Evans.

Crocker, W. M. (1887), 'Governor's Trip to Simporna', *British North Borneo Herald*, 5: 162.

Dalrymple, Alexander (1770), 'Account of Some Natural Curiosities at Sooloo', in Alexander Dalrymple, *An Historical Collection of the Several Voyages and Discoveries in the South Pacific Ocean*, London: printed for the author, pp. 1–21.

_____ (1808), *Oriental Repertory*, 2 vols., London: G. Bigg.

Daly, D. D. (1883), 'Government Notification, No. 89', *British North Borneo Herald*, 1: 12–13.

Darmansjah, Abdul Djebar Hapip and Noor, Basran (1979), *Bahasa Bajau*, Jakarta: Pusat Pembinaan dan Pengembangan, Departemen Pendidikan dan Kebudayaan.

Dewall, H. von (1885), 'Aanteekeningen Omtrent de Noordoostkust van Borneo', *Tijdschrift voor Indische Taal-, Land- en Volkenkunde*, 4: 423–58.

Diment, Eunice (1994), 'Bāngingi Sama', in Darrell T. Tyron (ed.), *Comparative Austronesian Dictionary: An Introduction to Austronesian Studies*, Part I: Fascicle 1, Berlin: Mouton de Gruyter, pp. 375–80.

Donop, L. B. von (1887), 'A Visit to Simporna, Sulu, Tawi Tawi, and Silam', *British North Borneo Herald*, 5: 186–8.

Dunn, F. L. and Dunn, D. F. (1984), 'Maritime Adaptations and Exploitation of Marine Resources in Sundaic Southeast Asian Prehistory', in Pieter van de Velde (ed.), *Prehistoric Indonesia: A Reader*, Dordrecht: Floris Publications, pp. 244–71.

Ekman, Sven Petrus (1953), *Zoogeography of the Sea*, London: Sidgwick and Jackson.

Eliade, Mircea (1964), *Shamanism: Archaic Techniques of Ecstasy*, Princeton, New Jersey: Princeton University Press.

Engelhardt, Richard (1987), 'Forest-gatherers and Strand-loopers: Econiche Specialization in Thailand', Unpublished paper, Siam Society Symposium on Enduring Auchthonous Adaptations.

Evans, I. H. N. (1952), 'Notes on the Bajaus and Other Coastal Tribes of North Borneo', *Journal of the Malayan Branch of the Royal Asiatic Society*, 25: 48–55.

_____ (1953), *The Religion of the Tempasuk Dusuns of North Borneo*, Cambridge: Cambridge University Press.

Fallers, Lloyd and Levy, Marion (1959), 'The Family: Some Comparative Considerations', *American Anthropologist*, 61: 647–51.

Firth, Raymond (1957), 'A Note on Descent Groups in Polynesia', *Man*, 57: 4–8.

_____ (1963), *Bilateral Descent Groups: An Operational Viewpoint*, Occasional Paper No. 16, London: Royal Anthropological Institute.

_____ (1964), 'Spirit Mediumship', in J. Gould and W. L. Kolb (eds.), *A Dictionary of the Social Sciences*, London: Tavistock, p. 689.

Follett, Helen (1945), *Men of the Sulu Sea*, New York: Charles Scribner.

Forrest, Thomas (1780), *A Voyage to New Guinea and the Moluccas from Balambangan*, 2nd edn., London: G. Scott.

Fox, James J. (1971), 'Sister's Child as Plant: Metaphors in an Idiom of Consanguinity', in Rodney Needham (ed.), *Rethinking Kinship and Marriage*, London: Tavistock, pp. 219–52.

_____ (1977), 'Notes on the Southern Voyages and Settlements of the Sama-Bajau', *Bijdragen tot de Taal-, Land- en Volkenkunde*, 133: 459–65.

_____ (1984), 'Bajau (Indonesia)', in Richard V. Weekes (ed.), *Muslim Peoples: A World Ethnographic Survey*, 2nd edn., London: Aldwych Press, Vol. 1, pp. 80–1.

Frake, Charles O. (1960), 'The Eastern Subanun of Mindanao', in G. P. Murdock (ed.), *Social Structure in Southeast Asia*, Chicago: Quadrangle Books, pp. 51–64.

_____ (1969), 'Struck by Speech: The Yakan Concept of Litigation', in Laura Nader (ed.), *Law in Culture and Society*, New York: Aldine, pp. 147–67.

_____ (1980), 'The Genesis of Kinds of People in the Sulu Archipelgo', in Charles O. Frake, *Language and Cultural Description: Essays*, Stanford: Stanford University Press, pp. 311–32.

Freeman, Derek (1956), 'Utrolateral and Utrolocal', *Man*, 56: 87–8.

_____ (1958), 'The Family System of the Iban of Borneo', in Jack Goody (ed.), *The Developmental Cycle in Domestic Groups*, Cambridge: Cambridge University Press, pp. 15–52.

_____ (1970), *Report on the Iban*, London: Athlone.

Geoghegan, William H. (1984), 'Sama', in Richard V. Weekes (ed.), *Muslim Peoples: A World Ethnographic Survey*, 2nd edn., London: Aldwych Press, Vol. 2, pp. 654–9.

Gibson-Hill, C. A. (1952), 'The Orang Laut of Singapore River and the Sampan Panjang', *Journal of the Malayan Branch of the Royal Asiatic Society*, 25(1): 161–74.

Goh, Siang Keng (1964), 'Report on Fishing Matters of Semporna District and

Assistance to Fishermen', Unpublished report, Jesselton, Sabah: Fisheries Department.

Gulliver, P. H. (1971), *Neighbours and Networks: The Idiom of Kinship among the Ndendeuli of Tanzania*, Berkeley: University of California Press.

Harrisson, Tom (1973–4), 'The Bajaus: Their Origins and Wider Importance', *Sabah Society Journal*, 6: 38–41.

Harrisson, Tom and Harrisson, Barbara (1971), *The Prehistory of Sabah*, Kota Kinabalu: Sabah Society.

Hogan, David (1972), 'Men of the Sea: Coastal Tribes of South Thailand's West Coast', *Journal of the Siam Society*, 60: 205–35.

_____ (1989), *Urak Lawoi': Basic Structures and a Dictionary*, Pacific Linguistics, Series C, No. 109, Canberra: Australian National University.

Hooker, M. B. (1972), *Adat Law in Modern Malaysia*, Kuala Lumpur: Oxford University Press.

Hunt, J. (1967), 'Some Particulars Relating to Sulo, in the Archipelago Felicia', in J. H. Moor (ed.), *Notices of the Indian Archipelago and Adjacent Countries*, London: Cass; first published Singapore, 1837, Appendix, pp. 31–60.

Ivanoff, Jacques (1985), 'L'épopée de Gaman: Conséquences des rapports entre Moken/Malais et Moken/Birmans', *ASEMI*, 16: 173–94.

_____ (1986), 'Mobilité et flexibilité chez le nomades, l'exemple des Moken: Pour survivre vivons flexibles', in A. Bourgeot and H. Guillaume (eds.), *Nomadisme: Mobilite et Flexibilite?* *Equipe les Sociétés Nomades dans l'Etat*, Departement H, Bulletin de Liaison No. 8, Paris: ORSTOM, pp. 25–39.

_____ (1987), 'Le concept de société "à maison" confronté aux contradictions des cultures Moken et Moklen', in Charles Macdonald (ed.), *De l'hutte au palais: Sociétés "à maison" en Asie du sud-est insulaire*, Paris: Editions du CNRS, pp. 109–31.

_____ (1989), 'Moken: Les naufrages de l'histoire; Une société de nomades marins de L'Archipel de Mergui', Ph.D. thesis, Ecole des Hautes Etudes en Sciences Sociales.

_____ (1990), 'Des ignames au riz: La dialectique du nomade et du sédentaire chez les Moken', *ER*, 120: 71–88.

Jones, L. W. (1962), *North Borneo: Report on the Census of Population Taken on 10th August, 1960*, Kuching: Government Printing Office.

Johnstone, Ralph (1993), 'The Sea Gypsies, Hard Times for a Vanishing Philippine Tribe', *Asiaweek*, 21 April, pp. 46–55.

Kennedy, Raymond (1953), *Field Notes on Indonesia: South Celebes, 1949–50*, New Haven: HRAF.

Kerns, R. A. (1939), *Catalogus van de Boegineesche, tot den I La Galigo-cyclus behoorende handschriften der Leidensche Universiteitsbibliotheek*, Leiden: Universiteitsbibliotheek.

Kiefer, Thomas M. (1969), *Tausug Armed Conflict: The Social Organization of Military Activity in a Philippine Moslem Society*, Philippine Studies Program Research Series, No. 7, Chicago: University of Chicago.

_____ (1971), 'The Sultanate of Sulu: Problems in the Analysis of a Segmentary State', *Borneo Research Bulletin*, 3(2): 46–51.

_____ (1972a), 'The Tausug Polity and the Sultanate of Sulu: A Segmentary State in the Southern Philippines', *Sulu Studies*, 1: 19–64.

_____ (1972b), *The Tausug: Violence and Law in a Philippine Moslem Society*, New York: Holt, Rinehart and Winston.

Kiefer, Thomas M. and Sather, Clifford (1970), 'Gravemarkers and the Repression of Sexual Symbolism: The Case of Two Philippine–Borneo Moslem Societies', *Bijdragen Tot de Taal-, Land- en Volkenkunde*, 126: 75–90.

Kirk, H. J. K. (1962), *The Geology and Mineral Resources of the Semporna Peninsula, North Borneo*, Geological Survey Department, Memoir 14, Kuching: Government Printing Office.

Klug, Linda Marie (1972), 'Kinship and Alliance on Lahat Ano', Ph.D. thesis, University of Pittsburgh.

Kurais, Muhammad (1975), 'Boatbuilding of the Sama', *Mindanao Journal*, 1(4): 67–125.

Leap, William L. (1977), 'Maritime Subsistence in Anthropological Perspective: A Statement of Priorities', in M. Estellie Smith (ed.), *Those Who Live From the Sea: A Study in Maritime Anthropology*, American Ethnological Society Monograph, 62, New York: West, pp. 251–63.

LeBar, Frank et al. (1964), 'Mowken', in Frank LeBar et al. (eds.), *Ethnic Groups of Mainland Southeast Asia*, New Haven: HRAF Press, pp. 263–6.

Logan, J. R. (1847a), 'The Orang Seletar of the Rivers and Creeks of the Old Strait and Estuary of Johore', *Journal of the Indian Archipelago and Eastern Asia*, 1: 295–8.

_____ (1847b), 'The Orang Seletar', *Journal of the Indian Archipelago and Eastern Asia*, 1: 302–4.

Low, Sir Hugh (1880), 'List of Mahomedan Sovereigns of Bruni, or Borneo Proper', *Journal of the Straits Branch of the Royal Asiatic Society*, 5: 24–31.

McFarland, Curtis D. (1980), *A Linguistic Atlas of the Philippines*, Tokyo: Tokyo University of Foreign Studies.

Mair, Lucy (1971), *Marriage*, Harmondsworth: Penguin.

Majul, Cesar Adib (1966a), 'Chinese Relationships with the Sultanate of Sulu', in Alfonso Felix Jr. (ed.), *The Chinese in the Philippines, 1570–1770*, Manila: Solidaridad Publishing House, pp. 143–60.

_____ (1966b), 'Political and Historical Notes on the Old Sulu Sultanate', *Journal of the Malaysian Branch of the Royal Asiatic Society*, 38: 23–42.

_____ (1969), 'The Sulu Sultanate and its Acquisition of Sabah', in *Symposium on Sabah*, Manila: National Historical Commission, pp. 28–39.

_____ (1971), *Muslims in the Philippines: Past, Present and Future Prospects*, Manila: Convislam.

_____ (1981), 'An Analysis of the "Genealogy of Sulu"', *Archipel*, 22: 167–82.

Malaysia, Department of Statistics (1972), *Laporan Am Banci Penduduk 1970* [General Report of the Population Census], Kuala Lumpur.

_____ (1993), *Siaran Perangkaan Bulanan, Sabah* [Monthly Statistical Report, Sabah], Kota Kinabalu: Jabatan Perangkaan Malaysia, Cawangan Sabah.

_____ (1995), *Laporan Am Banci Penduduk 1991* [General Report of the Population Census 1991], 2 vols., Kuala Lumpur: Jabatan Perangkaan Malaysia.

Martenot, Alain (1981), 'Bateau *Sama* de Sitangkai', *Archipel*, 22: 183–207.

Matthes, B. F. (1872), 'Ednige opmerkingen omtrent en naar anleiding van dat gedeelte van Dr. J. J. de Hollander's Handleiding bij de Beoefening der Land- en Volkenkunde van Nederlandsch Oost-Indie', *Bijdragen tot de Taal-, Land- en Volkenkunde van Nederlandsch-Indie*, 19: 1–91.

Molyneux, J. H. (1902), 'The Simporna Expedition', *British North Borneo Herald*, 20: 32–3, 219–21.

Moody, David C. (1984), 'Conclusion', in Julie King and John Wayne King (eds.), *Languages of Sabah: A Survey Report*, Pacific Linguistics, Series C, No. 78, Canberra: Australian National University, pp. 325–37.

Morris, H. S. (1967), 'Shamanism among the Oya Melanau', in Maurice Freedman (ed.), *Social Organization: Essays Presented to Raymond Firth*, London: Frank Cass, pp. 189–216.

Morris, P. G. (1978), 'Notes on the Distribution, Geology and Invertebrate

350 BIBLIOGRAPHY

Faunas of Some Coral Reefs in Darvel Bay, Sabah, Malaysia', *Sarawak Museum Journal*, 26: 211–33.

Murdock, G. P. (1949), *Social Structure*, New York: Macmillan.

_____ (1960), 'Cognatic Forms of Social Organization', in G. P. Murdock (ed.), *Social Structure in Southeast Asia*, Chicago: Quadrangle Books, pp. 1–14.

Nagatsu, Kazufumi (1995), '*Magambit*: Sama's Traditional Fishing Technique and its Change', *SAMA: Bajau Studies Newsletter*, 1: 7–8.

Nimmo, H. Arlo (1965), 'Social Organization of the Tawi-Tawi Badjaw', *Ethnology*, 4: 421–39.

_____ (1972), *The Sea People of Sulu*, San Francisco: Chandler.

_____ (1986), 'Recent Population Movements in the Sulu Archipelago: Implications to Sama Cultural History', *Archipel*, 32: 25–38.

_____ (1990), 'Religious Beliefs of the Tawi-Tawi Bajau', *Philippine Studies*, 38: 3–27.

Noorduyn, J. (1991), *A Critical Survey of Studies on the Languages of Sulawesia*, Leiden: KITLV Press.

North Borneo (1929), *North Borneo Annual Report, 1929*, Jesselton: Government Printing Department.

Pallesen, A. Kemp (1972), 'Reciprocity in Samal Marriage', *Sulu Studies*, 1: 123–42.

_____ (1979), 'The Pepet in Sama-Bajaw', in Nguyen Dang Liem (ed.), *South-East Asian Linguistic Studies*, Vol. 3, Pacific Linguistics, Series C, No. 45, Canberra: Australian National University, pp. 115–41.

_____ (1985), *Culture Contact and Language Convergence*, Linguistic Society of the Philippines, Monograph Series, No. 24, Manila: Linguistic Society of the Philippines.

Pallesen, A. Kemp and Pallesen, Anne (1965), 'Samal Phonemics', Unpublished manuscript.

Paton, T. R. (1963), *A Reconnaissance Soil Survey of the Semporna Peninsula, North Borneo*, Colonial Research Studies, No. 36, London: HMSO.

Pelras, Christian (1972), 'Notes sur quelques populations aquatiques de l'Archipel Nusantarien', *Archipel*, 3: 133–68.

_____ (forthcoming), *The Bugis*, Oxford: Blackwell.

Peranio, Roger (1961), 'Descent, Descent Line, and Descent Group in Cognatic Social Systems', in V. Garfield (ed.), *Proceedings of the 1961 Annual Spring Meetings of the American Ethnological Society*, Seattle: University of Washington, pp. 93–113.

Pigafetta, Antonio (1906), *Magellan's Voyage Around the World*, translated by J. A. Robertson, 3 vols., Cleveland: Arthur H. Clark.

Pires, Tomé (1944), *The Suma Oriental of Tomé Pires: An Account of the East, From the Red Sea to Japan, Written in Malacca and India in 1512–1515*, translated by Armando Cortesao, 2 vols., London: Hakluyt Society.

Pryer, W. B. (1883), 'Notes on Northeastern Borneo and the Sulu Islands', *Royal Geographical Society Proceedings*, 5: 91.

_____ (1887), 'On the Natives of British North Borneo', *Journal of the Royal Anthropological Institute*, 16: 229–36.

Radcliffe-Brown, A. R. (1950), 'Introduction', in A. R. Radcliffe-Brown and Daryll Forde (eds.), *African Systems of Kinship and Marriage*, London: Oxford University Press, pp. 1–85.

Reid, Anthony (1983), 'The Rise of Makassar', *Review of Indonesian and Malaysian Affairs*, 17: 117–60.

Ross, Malcolm D. (1994), 'Some Current Issues in Austronesian Linguistics', in Darrell T. Tyron (ed.), *Comparative Austronesian Dictionary: An Introduction to Austronesian Studies*, Part I: Fascicle 1, Berlin: Mouton de Gruyter, pp. 45–120.

Rutter, Owen (1922), *British North Borneo: An Account of Its History, Resources and Native Tribes*, London: Constable.

Sahlins, Marshall (1963), 'Remarks on Social Structure in Southeast Asia', *Polynesian Society Journal*, 72: 39–50.

St John, Spenser (1863), *Life in the Forests of the Far East*, 2 vols., London: Smith Elder.

Saleeby, Najeeb (1905), *Studies in Moro History, Law and Religion*, Manila: Bureau of Printing.

_____ (1908), *The History of Sulu*, Division of Ethnography Publications, Vol. 4, Part 2, Manila: Philippine Bureau of Sciences.

Sandbukt, Oyvind (1982), 'Duano Littoral Fishing: Adaptive Strategies Within a Market Economy', Ph.D. thesis, Cambridge University.

_____ (1984), 'The Sea Nomads of Southeast Asia: New Perspectives on Ancient Traditions', *Annual Newsletter of the Scandinavian Institute of Asian Studies*, 17: 3–13.

Sather, Clifford (1971a), 'Sulu's Political Jurisdiction over the Bajau Laut', *Borneo Research Bulletin*, 3(2): 58–62.

_____ (1971b), 'Kinship and Domestic Relations Among the Bajau Laut of Northern Borneo', Ph.D. thesis, Harvard University.

_____ (1975a), 'Bajau Laut', in Frank M. LeBar (ed.), *Ethnic Groups of Insular Southeast Asia*, New Haven: HRAF Press, Vol. 2, pp. 9–12.

_____ (1975b), 'There was a Boy: A Bajau Laut Prose Narrative Tale from Sabah', *Sarawak Museum Journal*, 23: 197–206.

_____ (1976), 'Kinship and Contiguity: Variation in Social Alignments Among the Semporna Bajau Laut', in George N. Appell (ed.), *The Societies of Borneo*, Special Publications, No. 6, Washington: American Anthropological Association, pp. 40–65.

_____ (1978), 'The Bajau Laut', in V. T. King (ed.), *Essays on Borneo Societies*, Hull Monographs on South-East Asia, No. 7, Oxford: Oxford University Press, pp. 172–92.

_____ (1984), 'Sea and Shore People: Ethnicity and Ethnic Interaction in Southeastern Sabah', *Contributions to Southeast Asian Ethnography*, 3: 3–27.

_____ (1985), 'Boat Crews and Fishing Fleets: The Social Organization of Maritime Labour Among the Bajau Laut of Southeastern Sabah', *Contributions to Southeast Asian Ethnography*, 4: 165–214.

_____ (1993a), 'Bajau', in David Levinson (ed.), *Encyclopedia of World Cultures*, Vol. 5: *East and Southeast Asia*, Boston: G. K. Hall, pp. 30–5.

_____ (1993b), 'Samal', in David Levinson (ed.), *Encyclopedia of World Cultures*, Vol. 5: *East and Southeast Asia*, Boston: G. K. Hall, pp. 217–21.

_____ (1993c), 'Tausug', in David Levinson (ed.), *Encyclopedia of World Cultures*, Vol. 5: *East and Southeast Asia*, Boston: G. K. Hall, pp. 261–5.

_____ (1993d), 'Ethnicity and Political History: The Bajau Laut Community of Semporna, Southeastern Sabah', Paper presented at the International Seminar on Bajau Communities, Indonesian Institute of Sciences (LIPI), Jakarta, November.

_____ (1995a), 'Sea Nomads and Rainforest Hunter-gatherers: Foraging Adaptations in the Indo-Malaysian Archipelago', in Peter Bellwood, James J. Fox, and Darrell Tryon (eds.), *The Austronesians: Historical and Comparative Perspectives*, Department of Anthropology, Research School of Pacific and Asian Studies Publication, Canberra: Australian National University, pp. 229–68.

_____ (1995b), 'The Ideology and Politics of Settling Down: The Bajau Laut

of Semporna', Paper presented at the International Conference on Bajau/
Sama Community, Kota Kinabalu, June.

Scheffler, Harold (1966), 'Ancestor Worship in Anthropology, or Observations
on Descent Groups', *Current Anthropology*, 7: 541–8.

Sellato, Bernard (1989), *Nomades et Sédentarisation a Bornéo: Histoire Économique
et Sociale*, Paris: Ed. de l'Ecole des Hautes Etudes en Sciences Sociales.

Sharer, Hans (1963), *Ngaju Religion: The Conception of God Among a South
Borneo People*, translated by Rodney Needham, The Hague: Martinus Nijhoff.

Skeat, W. W. and Ridley, H. N. (1900), 'The Orang Laut of Singapore', *Journal
of the Straits Branch of the Royal Asiatic Society*, 33: 247–50.

Smith, Kenneth D. (1984), 'The Languages of Sabah: A Tentative Lexicostatistical
Classification', in Julie K. King and John Wayne King (eds.), *Languages of
Sabah: A Survey Report*, Pacific Linguistics, Series C, No. 78, Canberra:
Australian National University, pp. 1–49.

Solheim, Wilhelm II (1975), 'Reflections on the New Data of Southeast Asian Prehistory: Austronesian Origin and Consequence', *Asian Perspectives*, 18(2): 146–60.

_____ (1984), 'The Nusantao Hypothesis: The Origin and Spread of Austronesian Speakers', *Asian Perspectives*, 26(1): 77–88.

Sopher, David (1965), *The Sea Nomads: A Study Based on the Literature of the
Maritime Boat People of Southeast Asia*, Memoir of the National Museum,
No. 5, Singapore.

Southall, Aidan (n.d.), *Alur Society*, Cambridge: W. Heffer.

Spoehr, Alexander (1971), *The Double Outrigger Canoe of Zamboanga and the
Sulu Archipelago, Southern Philippines*, Occasional Papers of Bernice P. Bishop
Museum, 24, 7, Honolulu.

_____ (1973), *Zamboanga and Sulu: An Archaeological Approach to Ethnic
Diversity*, Ethnology Monograph, No. 1, Pittsburgh: University of Pittsburgh.

Spreeuwenberg, A. F. van (1846), 'Een blik op de Minahasa', *Tijdschft voor
Nederlandsch Indie*, 8(1): 23–49.

Stirrat, R. L. (1975), 'The Social Organization of Fishing in a Sinhalese Village',
Modern Ceylon Studies, 6(2): 140–62.

Sweeney, P. L. Amin (1968), 'Silsilah Raja-raja Berunai', *Journal of the
Malaysian Branch of the Royal Asiatic Society*, 41(2): 1–82.

Taylor, Carl N. (1930), 'The Bajaos: Children of the Sea', *The Philippine
Magazine*, 27: 158–9, 176.

_____ (1931), 'The Sea Gypsies of Sulu', *Asia*, 31: 477–83, 534–5.

Ter Haar, B. (1948), *Adat Law in Indonesia*, New York: Institute of Pacific
Relations.

Treacher, W. H. (1890), 'British Borneo: Sketches of Brunai, Sarawak, Labuan
and North Borneo', *Journal of the Straits Branch of the Royal Asiatic Society*,
21: 19–121.

Tregonning, K. G. (1960), *North Borneo*, London: HMSO.

Turner, Victor (1967), *The Forest of Symbols: Aspects of Ndembu Ritual*, Ithaca:
Cornell University Press.

Urry, James (1981), 'A View from the West: Inland, Lowland and Islands in
Indonesian Prehistory', Paper presented at the 51st ANZAAS Congress,
Brisbane.

Valera, J. (1962), 'The Old Forts of Semporna', *Journal of the Sabah Society*, 2:
40–1.

Verheijen, Jils A. J. (1986), *The Sama/Bajau Language in the Lesser Sundas
Islands*, Pacific Linguistics, Series D, No. 70, Canberra: Australian National
University.

Verschuer, F. H. van (1883), 'De Badjo's', *Tijdschrift van het Koninklijke Aardrijkskundig Genootschap*, 7: 1–7.

Vosmaer, J. N. (1839), 'Korte beschrijving van het Zuid-Oostelijk Schiereiland van Celebes', *Verhandelingen van het Bataviaasch Genootschap van Kunsten en Wetenschappen*, 17: 63–184.

Walton, Janice and Moody, David C. (1984), 'The East Coast Bajau Languages', in Julie King and John Wayne King (eds.), *Languages of Sabah: A Survey Report*, Pacific Linguistics, Series C, No. 78, Canberra: Australian National University, pp. 113–23.

Warren, Carol (1983), *Ideology, Identity and Change: The Experience of the Bajau Laut of East Malaysia, 1969–1975*, South East Asia Monograph Series, No. 14, Townsville: James Cook University.

Warren, James F. (1971), *The North Borneo Chartered Company's Administration of the Bajau, 1878–1909*, Center for International Studies, Southeast Asia Series, No. 22, Athens: Ohio University Press.

_____ (1978), 'Who Were the Balangingi Samal? Slave Raiding and Ethnogenesis in Nineteenth-century Sulu', *Journal of Asian Studies*, 37: 477–90.

_____ (1979), 'The Sulu Zone: Commerce and the Evolution of a Multi-ethnic Polity, 1768–1898', *Archipel*, 18: 133–68.

_____ (1981), *The Sulu Zone, 1768–1898*, Singapore: Singapore University Press.

Waterson, Roxana (1990), *The Living House: An Anthropology of Architecture in South-East Asia*, Singapore: Oxford University Press.

Wee, Vivienne (1985), 'Melayu: Hierarchies of Being in Riau', Ph.D. thesis, Australian National University.

White, Walter (1922), *Sea Gypsies of Malaya*, London: Seeley, Service.

Wolhoff, G. J. and Abdurrahim (1960), *Sejarah Goa*, Makassar: Jajasan Kebudayaan Sulawesi Selatan dan Tenggara.

Wolters, O. W. (1967), *Early Indonesian Commerce: A Study of the Origins of Srivijaya*, Ithaca: Cornell University Press.

_____ (1979), 'Studying Srivijaya', *Journal of the Malaysian Branch of the Royal Asiatic Society*, 52(2): 1–32.

_____ (1982), *History, Culture, and Region in Southeast Asian Perspective*, Singapore: Institute of Southeast Asian Studies.

Wood, Elizabeth (1979), *Ecological Study of Coral Reefs in Sabah*, World Wildlife Fund, Project Malaysia, 15, London.

Wulff, Inger (1964), 'Features of Yakan Culture', *Folk*, 6: 53–72.

_____ (1971), 'The Yakan of Basilan', *Silliman Journal*, 18: 436–40.

_____ (1974–5), '*Bulan Sapal*—a Month of Misfortune: Concepts and Rituals Among the Yakan of Basilan, Southern Philippines', *Folk*, 16/17: 381–400.

_____ (1984), 'Yakan', in Richard V. Weekes (ed.), *Muslim Peoples: A World Ethnographic Survey*, 2nd edn., London: Aldwych Press, Vol. 2, pp. 863–6.

Yanagisako, Sylvia (1979), 'Family and Household: The Analysis of Domestic Groups', *Annual Review of Anthropology*, 8: 161–205.

Yap, Beng Liang (1978), *Sistem Kepercayaan Orang Bajau Omadal, Sabah*, Jabatan Pengajian Melayu, Kertas Data, No. 21, Kuala Lumpur: Universiti Malaya.

Zacot, Francois (1978), 'The Voice of the Bajo People', in *Proceedings: Second International Conference on Austronesian Linguistics*, Vol. 1: *Western Austronesian*, *Pacific Linguistics*, Series C, No. 61, Canberra: Australian National University, pp. 665–78.

_____ (1986), 'Mobilité et flexibilité: Le Cas des Badjos, Nomades de la Mer',

in A. Bourgeot and H. Guillaume (eds.), *Nomadisme: Mobilité et Flexibilité?*
Equipe Les Sociétés Nomades dan L'Etate, Departement H, Bulletin de Liaison
No. 8, Paris: ORSTOM, pp. 41–55.

Index